Certification Study Guide, 6th edition

Preparing for the Certification in Infection Prevention and Control (CIC®) Exam

Sixth edition, June 2015
Sixth printing, November 2022

Revised for digital edition with updated Errata, March 2018
Current Errata may be viewed at:
http://www.apic.org/store in the listings for the print and digital versions of this book

ISBN: 978-1-933013-63-3

Disclaimer:

The Association for Professionals in Infection Control and Epidemiology, its affiliates, directors, officers, and/or agents (collectively, "APIC") provides this *Certification Study Guide*, 6th edition ["study guide"] solely for the purpose of providing information to APIC members and the general public. The material presented in this study guide has been prepared in good faith with the goal of providing accurate and authoritative information regarding the subject matter covered. However, APIC makes no representation or warranty of any kind regarding any information, apparatus, product, or process discussed in this study guide and any linked or referenced materials contained therein, and APIC assumes no liability therefore. This study guide was developed to assist individuals preparing for the Certification in Infection Prevention and Control® (CIC®) examination administered by the Certification Board of Infection Control (CBIC®). APIC does not guarantee that using this guide will result in passing the CIC® exam.

WITHOUT LIMITING THE GENERALITY OF THE FOREGOING, THE INFORMATION AND MATERIALS PROVIDED IN THIS *CERTIFICATION STUDY GUIDE*, 6TH EDITION ARE PROVIDED ON AN "AS-IS" BASIS AND MAY INCLUDE ERRORS, OMISSIONS, OR OTHER INACCURACIES. THE USER ASSUMES THE SOLE RISK OF MAKING USE AND/OR RELYING ON THE INFORMATION AND MATERIALS PROVIDED IN THIS STUDY GUIDE. APIC MAKES NO REPRESENTATIONS OR WARRANTIES ABOUT THE SUITABILITY, COMPLETENESS, TIMELINESS, RELIABILITY, LEGALITY, UTILITY, OR ACCURACY OF THE INFORMATION AND MATERIALS PROVIDED IN THIS STUDY GUIDE OR ANY PRODUCTS, SERVICES, AND TECHNIQUES DESCRIBED IN THIS STUDY GUIDE. ALL SUCH INFORMATION AND MATERIALS ARE PROVIDED WITHOUT WARRANTY OF ANY KIND, INCLUDING, WITHOUT LIMITATION, ALL IMPLIED WARRANTIES AND CONDITIONS OF MERCHANTABILITY, FITNESS FOR A PARTICULAR PURPOSE, TITLE, AND NON-INFRINGEMENT.

IN NO EVENT SHALL APIC BE LIABLE FOR ANY INDIRECT, PUNITIVE, INCIDENTAL, SPECIAL, OR CONSEQUENTIAL DAMAGES ARISING OUT OF OR IN ANY WAY CONNECTED WITH THE USE OF THIS STUDY GUIDE OR FOR THE USE OF ANY PRODUCTS, SERVICES, OR TECHNIQUES DESCRIBED IN THIS STUDY GUIDE, WHETHER BASED IN CONTRACT, TORT, STRICT LIABILITY, OR OTHERWISE.

All inquiries about this book or other APIC products and services may be directed to:

APIC
1400 Crystal Drive, Suite 900
Arlington, VA 22202

Phone: 202-789-1890
Toll-free: 1-800-650-9570
Fax: 202-789-1899

Email: info@apic.org

Web: www.apic.org

TABLE OF CONTENTS

ACKNOWLEDGEMENTS

The Association for Professionals in Infection Control and Epidemiology gratefully acknowledges the valuable contributions from each of the following individuals:

LEAD AUTHOR

Carol McLay, DrPH, BSN, RN, CIC
CEO
Infection Control International
Lexington, KY

CONTRIBUTING AUTHORS, 6th ed.

Lisa Caffery, MS, BSN, RN-BC, CIC
Infection Prevention Coordinator
Genesis Medical Center
Davenport, IA

Cindy Prins, PhD, MPH, CIC, CPH
Clinical Assistant Professor and PhD
Program Director, Department of Epidemiology, College of Public Health & Health Professions and College of Medicine
University of Florida
Gainesville, FL

CONTRIBUTING AUTHORS, 5th ed.

Cindy Prins, PhD, MPH, CIC, CPH
Clinical Assistant Professor and PhD
Program Director, Department of Epidemiology, College of Public Health & Health Professions and College of Medicine
University of Florida
Gainesville, FL

Lisa Caffery, MS, BSN, RN-BC, CIC
Infection Prevention Coordinator
Genesis Medical Center
Davenport, IA

Frances M. Feltovich, MBA, RN, CIC, CPHQ
Director, Business Practices/ Regulatory Compliance
Houston Methodist Hospital
Texas Medical Center
Houston, TX

Maryann Gierloff, PhD, RN, CIC
Associate Professor
North Park University
Chicago, IL

Marilyn Hanchett, RN, MA, CPHQ, CIC
Association for Professionals in Infection Control and Epidemiology
Washington, DC

Marie Kassai, RN, BSN, MPH, CIC
Infection Prevention Consultant
MRK Consulting, LLC
West Paterson, NJ

Laura S. Netardus, RN, MN, CIC
Supervisor, Infection Control
North Florida Regional Medical Center
Gainesville, FL

Miranda Williams, MPH, RN, CIC
Infection Control Specialist
North Florida Regional Medical Center
Gainesville, FL

REVIEWERS, 6th ed.

Frances M. Feltovich, MBA, RN, CIC, CPHQ
Director, Business Practices/ Regulatory Compliance
Houston Methodist Hospital
Texas Medical Center
Houston, TX

Irena L. Kenneley, PhD, APHRN-BC, CIC
Associate Professor
Faculty Development Director
Case Western Reserve University
Frances Payne Bolton School of Nursing
Cleveland, OH

Laura S. Netardus, RN, MN, CIC
Supervisor, Infection Control
North Florida Regional Medical Center
Gainesville, FL

Barbara Smith, RN, BSN, MPA, CIC
Mt. Sinai Health System-St. Luke's and Roosevelt Hospitals
New York, NY

Miranda Williams, MPH, RN, CIC
Infection Control Specialist
North Florida Regional Medical Center
Gainesville, FL

PRODUCTION TEAM

Susan F. Sandler
Associate Director, Practice Resources
Association for Professionals in Infection Control and Epidemiology

Caroline H. Fuchs, CAE
Vice President, Marketing and Practice Resources
Association for Professionals in Infection Control and Epidemiology

Christina James, MPA
Editorial Assistant
Association for Professionals in Infection Control and Epidemiology

Sarah Vickers
Art Director (cover art)
Association for Professionals in Infection Control and Epidemiology

DESIGN AND LAYOUT

Project Design Company
Washington, DC

PRINTING

King Printing
Lowell, MA

DECLARATIONS OF CONFLICTS OF INTEREST

Carol McLay, DrPH, BSN, RN, CIC is a volunteer member of the Society for Healthcare Epidemiology of America's External Affairs Committee.

Lisa Caffery, MS, BSN, RN-BC, CIC serves on the Board of Directors and Chair of the Resolutions Committee for the Iowa Nurses Association.

Cindy Prins, PhD, MPH, CIC, CPH has nothing to disclose.

PREFACE

Congratulations on your decision to sit for the Certification in Infection Prevention and Control (CIC®) examination! The CIC® credential identifies healthcare professionals who have demonstrated mastery of knowledge needed to practice infection prevention and control. Achievement of the CIC® qualification is a significant milestone in the Infection Prevention Competency Model by representing the career transition point from novice to proficient and clearly shows your employer and colleagues that you are dedicated to your professional growth.

This *Certification Study Guide*, 6th edition, was created to help you prepare to take the certification exam. It provides study tips as well as specific guidance for reviewing primary and secondary resources used by the Certification Board of Infection Control to write the exam. The questions in this guide were written by a team of experts in the field of infection prevention to assist you in assessing your knowledge and preparedness for the exam. Questions have been reviewed by a panel of infection preventionists for accuracy. Every question includes a rationale of the correct answer and at least one reference where you can find additional information on the topic.

Changes and additions found in the 6th edition reflect the eight domains of the examination content outline that came into use in July 2015. We hope that this new edition will continue to support your path to earning the CIC® as effectively as all prior editions.

Whether you are just beginning the journey to certification or you are preparing to recertify, remember: success begins with a positive mindset. Positive thinking helps with stress management and can even improve your health. Positive thinking can produce a positive attitude, and a positive attitude leads to positive results. You can succeed!

Warm regards,

Carol McLay, DrPH, BSN, RN, CIC

INTRODUCTION: HOW TO USE THIS GUIDE

APIC's *Certification Study Guide*, 6th edition, was written to reflect current infection prevention practices as assessed by the Certification Board of Infection Control (CBIC) practice analysis.

Key Features

- This study guide contains more than 650 practice questions spanning eight review chapters and three practice exams. Questions are formatted similar to those on the actual Certification in Infection Prevention and Control (CIC®) exam.
- Questions have been written by a team of experts in the field of infection prevention and control and reviewed by a panel of infection preventionists.
- Most of the questions are written at the higher levels of cognitive domain (application or analysis). Practicing with more difficult questions is one of the keys to success!
- The answer and rationale sections that are included with each question set and practice exam provide immediate feedback and explanations when answering questions. This section is located at the end of each question set to mimic an actual exam and enable you to assess your progress as you study.
- References are provided for each question, and the references used to write for this guide are the same as those used by CBIC to write the CIC® exam.
- The guide was designed to function as a workbook—use the notes area in the outside margins of the review chapters and practice exams to capture your thoughts, note a specific reference, or work through a problem.
- Although this guide is primarily focused on preparing candidates for initial certification via CBIC's Computer Based Test (CBT), it may also be used to review material in preparation for the Self-Achievement Recertification Exam (SARE).

Book Organization

This study guide is divided into three sections:

Section I consists of two chapters and provides background information and orientation to the CIC® examination as well as test-taking strategies and recommendations for international and repeat test-takers.

Section II consists of eight chapters that correspond to the areas of testing defined by the Certification Board of Infection Control (CBIC).

1. Identification of Infectious Disease Processes
2. Surveillance and Epidemiologic Investigation
3. Preventing/Controlling the Transmission of Infectious Agents
4. Employee/Occupational Health
5. Management and Communication
6. Education and Research
7. Environment of Care
8. Cleaning, Sterilization, Disinfection, Asepsis

Each chapter has key concepts and a list of primary and secondary references that are pertinent to the content area—including notable chapters from the *APIC Text*—for preparatory reading, review, and in-depth study. This is followed by a series of practice questions specific to that content area and an answer key with rationales for the correct answers and references for further information. This information will facilitate your review of specific topics in preparation for the CIC® exam.

Section III includes three comprehensive exams reflecting all of the eight core competencies that are measured in the CIC® exam. All three of these exams include 135 questions—the same number of questions that is used to compute your score on the CIC® exam.

How to Use This Study Guide

Candidates planning to take the CIC® examination should read the introductory chapters of this book in order to become familiar with the structure of the exam. It is important to understand what is being tested before creating your study plan. This guide also provides test-taking strategies and helpful tips that can be followed as you prepare for the exam.

Once you have read the introductory chapters, you are ready to develop your study plan. You can start by reviewing pertinent sections of the primary references used by CBIC; these will be your principle study sources (see Chapter 1). Use this study guide to focus your efforts and reinforce the information learned from the primary references. Answer the practice questions at the end of Chapters 3 through 10 and review the rationales for the correct answers. This will provide you with important information that will help you to understand the basis for the correct answer. For more in-depth information, go back to the reference(s) listed for each question. When you are ready, dive into the practice exams. Once you complete an exam, review the answers and rationales for each of the questions. Use the score analysis at the end of each exam to identify content areas that may need further review.

SECTION I. PREPARING FOR THE CERTIFICATION IN INFECTION PREVENTION AND CONTROL (CIC®) EXAMINATION

Chapter 1
THE CIC® EXAM

This chapter provides a summary overview of the Certification in Infection Prevention and Control (CIC®) examination. A detailed description of the exam, eligibility requirements, scoring methods, and more can be found in the *Certification in Infection Prevention and Control Candidate Handbook* provided by the Certification Board of Infection Control and Epidemiology (CBIC®) at www.cbic.org.

DESCRIPTION OF THE CIC® EXAMINATION

The CIC® examination is developed by CBIC. CBIC's responsibilities include determining the exam content outline and specifications, developing and maintaining an item bank of approved exam questions, approving individual exams for administration, and setting the passing score that indicates successful achievement and attainment of the CIC® credential. CBIC also sets the criteria for eligibility for those applying to sit for the exam. Prometric manages the test sites, administers the exam, and scores and conduct statistical analysis of the exam.

The CIC® exam is administered in two forms—the Computer Based Test (CBT) and the Self-Achievement Recertification Examination (SARE). The CBT is intended for initial (first-time) certification and is also an option for recertification. The SARE is for recertification of currently certified professionals only. Once certified, the CIC® credential is valid for a 5-year period from the year it is attained.

COMPUTER BASED TEST

CBIC's CBT is an objective, multiple-choice examination consisting of 150 questions. The candidate's score is based on 135 of those questions. Fifteen of the 150 questions are pretest questions and are not included in the final score.

Testing Time

Candidates have 3 hours to complete the CBT. During the exam, candidates may click on the time box in the lower right portion of the screen or select the time key to monitor testing time.

Content

The examination content for both the CBT and the SARE is based upon results of a practice analysis that CBIC conducts via survey every 5 years. This is in accordance with certification industry best practices and is intended to ensure that the CIC examination focuses on current infection prevention practice.

As of the date of publication of this study guide, the topics identified by the most recent practice analysis and included in the current exam are as follows (the number of questions for each topic on the CBT is in parentheses):

1. Identification of Infectious Disease Processes (22 questions)
2. Surveillance and Epidemiologic Investigation (24 questions)
3. Preventing/Controlling the Transmission of Infectious Agents (25 questions)
4. Employee/Occupational Health (11 questions)
5. Management and Communication (13 questions)
6. Education and Research (11questions)
7. Environment of Care (14 questions)
8. Cleaning, Sterilization, Disinfection, Asepsis (15 questions)

Construction of Test Items

The components of the multiple-choice questions on the CBT are as follows:

- The stem of the question. The stem includes the description of the situation or presents the central problem. It includes a question or an incomplete situation; this is the question that must be answered
- Three incorrect answers called distractors
- The correct answer

Most items have four options: A, B, C, or D. Some items are complex multiple-choice and include a stem followed by four or five choices. For these questions, the answer options are different combinations of the choices listed. The following is an example of this question format:

Question: Your patient has a low absolute neutrophil count. Of the following choices, which is *true* of this patient?

1) They are especially susceptible to infection
2) You can determine the absolute neutrophil count by multiplying the total white blood cell (WBC) count by the percentage of mature and immature neutrophils
3) The patient's WBC count is between 4,000 and 10,000
4) The patient's complement system will only be activated through the alternative pathway

   a. 1, 2, 3
   b. 2, 3, 4
   c. 1, 3, 4
   d. 1, 2, 4

The distractors are written to appear as logical answers to the question. They may be based on information provided in the stem, but they do not actually answer the question, are incorrect, or may not reflect best practice.

All items have only one correct choice. There is no penalty for wrong answers; candidates should guess when they do not know the answer.

Cognitive Levels

Exam items are divided into three cognitive levels.

Level 1: Recall

Level 1 exam questions test the memorization or recall of practice-specific information, such as specific facts, generalizations, concepts, principles, processes, procedures, or theories. This is the lowest level of learning outcomes in the cognitive domain. Questions may use verbs such as *define, list, state, identify, label,* and *name* or inquiry words such as *who, when, where,* or *what*. Twenty-five percent of the questions on the examination will be Level 1.

Level 2: Application

Application questions test simple interpretation or application of limited data. This requires the ability to apply rules, methods, concepts, principles, laws, or theories and to recognize the elements and relationships among data. Questions at this level will ordinarily be structured in an "if/then" or "how can *x* be used to *y*" fashion. Sixty percent of the questions on the exam will be Level 2.

Level 3: Analysis

Analysis questions primarily test the evaluation of data, the analysis of the relationships between parts, or the organizational principles involved. Questions may use verbs such as *differentiate* or *compare/contrast*, or ask "how does *x* relate to *y*?" Fifteen percent of the questions will be Level 3.

THE SELF-ACHIEVEMENT RECERTIFICATION EXAM (SARE)

The SARE is a 150-question, multiple-choice, web-based examination designed to assess the knowledge of professionals in infection prevention and control and epidemiology who are seeking recertification. SARE questions are not identical to any of the questions in the active pool of questions used on the CBT but were developed or redesigned by the CBIC Test Committee specifically for the purposes of the SARE. Like the CBT, SARE questions are based on the most current CBIC practice analysis, and the content outline is identical to the other examinations. The questions developed are held to the same standards and analysis as the other examinations. However, the SARE is geared toward the advanced infection prevention and control recertifier who is, at minimum, a 5-year practitioner. For this reason, some questions may be more difficult than those on the CBT, which is geared toward a 2-year practitioner. The purpose/goal of the SARE is to demonstrate continued knowledge and mastery in the field of infection prevention and control.

The six objectives for the current SARE are as follows:

1. Identify infectious disease processes.
2. Describe the components of an effective surveillance system.
3. Discuss the processes used in preventing/controlling the transmission of infectious agents.
4. Describe the components required for managing an infection control program.
5. Describe the methods used to develop education and research projects.
6. Identify infection control aspects of employee health

Candidates who decide to take the SARE are required to order the exam in the same calendar year that recertification is due. The exam may be ordered no later than December 1 and must be submitted by December 31 of the recertifying year. Candidates are able to log in and out as many times as necessary to complete the exam (within the recertification and submission deadline).

PASSING SCORE

Passing scores are determined based on the responses that are provided for each of the 135 scored questions. The Angoff method is used to set the minimum passing score for both the CBT and SARE. This is a method in which subject matter experts have determined how many correct answers are required for a competent candidate to successfully complete the examination. A candidate's ability to pass the examination depends on the knowledge and skill he or she displays, and not on the performance of other candidates. The actual passing score may change slightly for each version of the examination to account for the slight variation in the difficulty of questions on each version of the examination.

REFERENCES

Nearly all questions in the CBT and SARE are based on chapters in the primary references. However, CBIC also uses the secondary references listed below, and these may be useful to help clarify more detailed issues in specific practice settings or in content areas such as microbiology.

Primary References:

Grota P, ed. *APIC Text of Infection Control and Epidemiology,* 4th edition, Volume I, Volume II, and Volume III. Washington, DC: Association for Professionals in Infection Control and Epidemiology, 2014. Also available online at http://text.apic.org [subscription required].

Brooks K. *Ready Reference for Microbes,* 3rd edition. Washington, DC: Association for Professionals in Infection Control and Epidemiology, 2012.

Heymann D, ed. *Control of Communicable Diseases Manual,* 19th edition. Washington, DC: American Public Health Association, 2008.

Kulich P, Taylor D, eds. *The Infection Preventionist's Guide to the Lab.* Washington, DC: Association for Professionals in Infection Control and Epidemiology, 2012.

Secondary References:

Current Recommendations of the Advisory Committee on Immunization Practices (ACIP).

Current guidelines, standards, and recommendations from CDC, APIC, SHEA, and Public Health Agency of Canada.

Pickering, Larry K, ed. *Red Book*, 29th ed., Elk Grove Village, IL: American Academy of Pediatrics; 2012.

Please note: In the CIC exam, the term "standards precautions" is equivalent to the Canadian term "routine practices."

ELIGIBILITY REQUIREMENTS

Successful certification indicates competence in the actual practice of infection prevention and control and healthcare epidemiology, and is intended for individuals who are actively accountable for the infection prevention and control program within their current position.

In order to qualify to sit for your initial (first-time) certification, or if your certification has lapsed and you wish to renew your certification, you must meet the following CBIC requirements:

You are accountable for the infection prevention and control activities/program in your setting and this is reflected in your current job description.

AND

You have a post-secondary degree (e.g. associates'* or baccalaureate degree).

AND

You have had sufficient experience (recommended: two years) in infection prevention and control, which includes all three (3) of the following:

1. Identification of infectious disease processes
2. Surveillance and epidemiologic investigation
3. Preventing and controlling the transmission of infectious agents

AND

And at least two (2) of the remaining five (5) components:

1. Employee/occupational health
2. Management and communication
3. Education and research
4. Environment of care
5. Cleaning, sterilization, disinfection, and asepsis

**Equivalent to Canadian two- or three-year diploma*

Candidates will be required to submit the following documentation with their application:

- Attestation Statement (completed, signed and dated by supervisor)
- Proof of Degree
- CV/Resume
- Official Job Description

APPLICATION PROCESS

To apply online at CBIC.org, a copy of your license or highest degree, as well as a signed attestation statement from your current supervisor or director, will need to be uploaded in order to successfully complete an online application. Payment by credit card is the only form of payment accepted when applying online.

Within seven business days of a completed application, you will receive an email from CBIC with instructions on how to schedule your exam with Prometric. If your application is not approved, you will receive a notice from the CBIC Executive Office.

Candidates recertifying by SARE must complete the SARE application. The SARE must be ordered in the same calendar year the candidate is due for recertification.

SCHEDULING THE EXAM

The CBT is administered 5 days a week at Prometric test centers throughout the United States and internationally. Testing center locations may be found by visiting www.Prometric.com/cbic.

There are no prescheduled testing dates. Once a candidate's eligibility is confirmed, the testing agency will send a notice that includes instructions on how to schedule an examination appointment.

Candidates can schedule their examination by one of two methods:

- By phone (US toll-free) at 800-278-6222 (times are in Eastern Time): Monday through Friday 8:00 a.m. - 8:00 p.m.
- Online at www.prometric.com/cbic 24 hours a day, 7 days a week

TAKING THE CBT

What to Bring to the Exam

Candidates should arrive at least 30 minutes before the scheduled exam appointment.

Candidates will be required to present one form of valid, government-issued identification (e.g., driver's license, passport, or other federal or military ID) with the candidate's signature and a recognizable photograph. The identification document must be in Latin characters. A candidate who is testing outside of his or her country of citizenship must present a valid passport.

All other personal items, including all watches, must be locked in a locker for test security purposes. Candidates will be screened with a metal detector wand during check-in.

Please note: Only silent, non-programmable calculators without alpha keys or printing capabilities are allowed in the testing room.

If you do not provide correct identification at the time of the exam, it is considered a missed appointment. You will be required to pay a rescheduling fee before choosing another appointment.

Test Center Regulations

Candidates must observe the following regulations when they arrive at the test center:

1. Candidates will be continuously monitored by video, physical walk-throughs, and the observation window during the test. All testing sessions are video and audio recorded.
2. Individuals will be required to present one form of valid, government-issued identification (e.g., driver's license, passport, or other federal or military ID), with the candidate's signature and a recognizable photograph. A candidate who is testing outside of his or her country of citizenship must present a valid passport.
3. Candidates will be scanned with a metal detector wand prior to every entry into the test room.
4. Individuals will be asked to raise slacks/pant legs above the ankles and pull sleeves up (if long sleeves are worn) prior to every entry into the test room.
5. Candidates will be asked to empty and turn pockets inside out prior to every entry into the test room to confirm that they have no prohibited items.

6. Candidates must not bring any personal/unauthorized items into the testing room. Such items include but are not limited to outerwear, hats, food, drinks, purses, briefcases, notebooks, pagers, watches, cellular telephones, recording devices, and photographic equipment. Weapons are not allowed.
7. Candidates are required to sign out each time they leave the test room. They must also sign back in and show their IDs to the Test Center Administrator (TCA) in order to be readmitted to the test room.
8. Candidates are prohibited from communicating, publishing, reproducing, or transmitting any part of the test, in any form or by any means, verbal or written, for any purpose.
9. Candidates must not talk to others in the room or refer to their screens, testing materials, or written notes in the test room.
10. Candidates must not use written notes, published materials, or other testing aids, except those allowed by the test sponsor.
11. Candidates are allowed to bring soft ear plugs (with no wires/cords attached) or center-supplied tissues in the test room.
12. Any clothing or jewelry items allowed to be worn in the test room must remain on the candidate at all times. Removed clothing or jewelry items must be stored in the locker provided upon entry to the testing center.
13. Individuals must return all materials issued to by the TCA at the end of the test.
14. Individuals are not allowed to use any electronic devices or phones during breaks.
15. If a break is taken during the exam, the individual must return to his or her original, assigned seat.
16. Repeated or lengthy departures from the test room for unscheduled breaks will be reported by the TCA.
17. If a candidate needs access to an item stored in the test center during a break, such as food or medicine, he or she must inform the TCA before retrieving the item. Candidates are not allowed to access any prohibited item (as defined by the client practice applicable for the test that is being taken).

18. Candidates must conduct themselves in a civil manner at all times when on the premises of the testing center. Exhibiting abusive behavior towards the TCA, or any other staff member of the test center, may result in criminal prosecution.

19. To protect the privacy of all testers, the TCA can neither confirm nor deny if any particular individual is present or scheduled at the test center.

20. Persons not scheduled to take a test are not permitted to wait in the test center.

Note: Client practice policies applicable to individual exams may supersede any of these regulations.

Testing Accommodations

Prometric makes every effort to provide reasonable testing accommodations that enable all candidates to take examinations on a level playing field. Prometric offers various testing aides to meet most needs, such as special scheduling/timing, location/setting, software, equipment, or the use of personal assistants or interpreters.

The Score Report

A score report is generated immediately upon completion for the both the CBT and the SARE exams. According to CBIC, once candidates receive their score report indicating that they have passed the exam, they may immediately begin using the CIC® credential after their names and in their titles. It takes approximately 4 to 6 weeks to receive the official certificate from the CBIC Executive Office.

PASS/FAIL RATE

In 2013, the passing rate for candidates taking the CBT was approximately 58 percent; however, on average, the pass rate for the CBT in recent years has been approximately 65 percent. The pass rate for the SARE in 2013 was 88 percent.

The number of correct answers needed to pass depends on the difficulty of the examination questions, but the percentage required to pass has been approximately 75 percent correct in recent years.

Chapter 2
TEST-TAKING TIPS AND STRATEGIES

Taking any exam can be a stressful experience. When preparing to take the Certification in Infection Prevention and Control (CIC®) exam, it is just as important to know how to take a test and to use strategies to answer test questions, as it is to know the content.

PREPARATION FOR THE EXAM

Initial Steps

1. Decide what date you can be ready to take the test—first time test-takers may need up to 6 months to prepare; however, actual preparation time needed varies greatly depending on individual experience, education needs, learning style, etc. The Certification Board of Infection Control and Epidemiology (CBIC) makes no specific recommendation regarding time frame for preparation.

2. Make a contract with yourself to take the test on the date you select.

3. Assess the resources available for studying. You should have access to all of the primary references used by CBIC; these will be your principal study sources. Three of the primary resources for the exam are available through the Association for Professionals in Infection Control and Epidemiology (APIC) and may be ordered through APIC's online store (www.apic.org/store). The following additional resource are also available:

   a) Infection Prevention Competency Review course: Available through APIC, this online course provides additional review and assessment of the latest infection prevention and control practices in an interactive online format. The course also offers continuing education credits. Visit www.apic.org for more information.

   b) CBIC Practice Examination: This practice exam is a 70-question computer-based test that approximates the content, cognitive levels, and difficulty of the Computer Based Test (CBT). Visit www.cbic.org to learn more and purchase.

c) EPI Intensive (formerly EPI 101 and 102): APIC offers these face-to-face courses twice a year. The EPI® curriculum provides fundamental training in infection prevention and control. Although not required, these courses can be helpful in preparing you for the CIC® exam. Visit www.apic.org for more information.

d) APIC webinars: APIC has a vast library of on-demand webinars that cover a broad range of topics and are free for APIC members. Visit http://webinars.apic.org to learn more.

e) APIC chapters: Many APIC chapters have formal study groups to help members prepare for the initial exam or for recertifition. APIC membership and chapter membership are required. Visit www.apic.org to learn more about APIC membership and to find a local chapter.

f) IP Talk: IP Talk is an online forum provided by APIC where members can ask questions of others in the APIC community. Connect with others who are preparing for the exam or to get tips and encouragement from those who have attained their certification. APIC membership is required to participate.

4. Read through the Candidate Handbook from the CBIC website. It may be helpful to download and print it for future reference.

5. Have a positive mindset. You can do this! Use positive self-talk and self-reassurance.

Developing Thinking Skills

1. Understand thought processes related to Cognitive Levels 1, 2, and 3 items in the test

2. Build your thinking skills

a) Concentrate on learning the subject well, not just memorizing facts; think quality—not quantity.

b) Develop memory skills that trigger retrieval of needed facts: acronyms (PERRL: Pupils Equal Round and Reactive to Light), acrostics (Every Good Boy Does Fine), ABCs (each letter stands for a term), imaging (visualize picture), rhymes, music, and links.

c) Improve higher-level thinking skills by exercising the analysis of memorized facts; small group reviews are good for this.

Knowing the Content

1. Prepare well for studying—take an organized approach such as developing a formal study schedule.
2. Select the time of day that you are most able to concentrate (Are you a morning, afternoon, or night person?).
3. Create your own study area or space if possible.
4. Schedule a consistent study time and reward yourself daily for consistency and for your accomplishments.
5. Define and organize the content to be studied. Candidates should review the content outline to familiarize themselves with the domains of study. See Table 2-1 for commonly used study methods.
6. Do a content assessment of study materials. Content review may be organized as follows:
    a) No review required
    b) Minimal review will be necessary
    c) Intensive review necessary
    d) Start from the beginning
7. To avoid feeling overwhelmed, break content review into series of smaller, more manageable goals.
8. Review your strengths and weaknesses. The practice questions and tests in this study guide can help to identify areas of strengths and weaknesses. Your goal should be to achieve a correct response rate of at least 80 percent on the practice questions and practice tests.
9. Budget study time wisely.
10. Stay focused on your goal.

Table 2-1. Study Methods

Method	Definition	Approaches	Advantages/ Disadvantages
Memorization	The process of committing something to memory	• Repeating information by rote • Reading and rereading content	Advantages: Can be helpful for recall questions Disadvantages: Passive learning style; may not be helpful for application or analysis questions; knowing content does not necessarily equate to understanding
Communication skills-based	Using reading, writing, and/or active listening to synthesize information	• Taking notes and formulating questions during lectures or when reading • PQRST approach: *Preview:* skim material for the important points *Question:* formulate initial questions to be answered *Read:* read related materials and focus on information that answers the initial questions *Summary:* Summarize the information in your own words (e.g., notes, spider diagrams, flow charts, voice recordings); this helps process the information *Test:* Go back and answer the questions that were first formulated; avoid adding more questions that may distract or change the subject.	Advantages: Develops critical thinking skills; can be particularly useful in study groups; helps individuals process information "in their own words" Disadvantages: Individual may miss important points of information (don't know what you don't know).
Cues	Using signals or hints (e.g., visual, verbal, etc.) to learn and trigger recall of information	• Flash card training	Advantages: puts information in a discreet, separate form allowing the individual to change the order; creates mental triggers to aid memory
Summary	Condensing large amounts of information to shorter notes, key facts, or keywords and definitions	• Outlines that list important facts, keywords, and definitions in a shorter format • Tree diagrams that show relationships between facts • Spider diagrams or mind maps that create a visual summary of how information is interrelated	Advantages: helps the individual process and synthesize information; focuses learning efforts; breaks down large pieces of information; can help contextualize information

Method	Definition	Approaches	Advantages/ Disadvantages
Visual imagery	Creating visual representations of information to help encode and retain it in memory	• Loci: a method of visualizing information that is in a physical location (e.g., location of specific objects in a room) • Diagrams that summarize and reorganize information in a way that is practical and useful; can help with learning and recalling information quickly	Advantages: can be an effective memory aid; can help visual learners understand and retain information
Mnemonics/ acronyms	Using linguistic devices such as formulas or rhymes that can aid in memorizing and recalling information	• Using acronyms (e.g., central line-associated bloodstream infection = CLABSI) • Creating mnemonics (e.g., MY (measles) CHICKEN (chicken pox/ varicella) HEZ (herpes zoster/ shingles) TB (tuberculosis) to help remember the diseases that require Airborne Isolation) • Creating rhymes or songs	Advantages: can be an effective memory aid, particularly for facts, definitions, terms, or other types of foundational knowledge
Exam strategies	Using methods to ensure that every aspect of an exam question is considered before answering.	• Black-red-green: Underlining relevant parts of a question using three colors. *Black* for ***bla****tant* information or instructions (i.e., what must be done), *red* for ***re****ference* points or ***re****quired* input (e.g., definitions, terms, facts, etc. that form the knowledge base needed to answer the question), and *green* for ***gre****mlins* to denote subtle signals that may be easily missed or to highlight hints on how to proceed (i.e. ***gre****en* lights) • Point, evidence, explanation: Identifying the main point, presenting evidence to support the point, and explaining or summarizing the point	Advantages: helps the individual break down a question, identify critical components of what is being asked, and take a thoughtful approach to finding the correct answer
Time management, organization, lifestyle changes	Using specific tactics to structure study practices, establish good study habits, boost motivation, and avoid procrastination	• Creating a study schedule and study goals to create structure and help with time management • Using a "traffic light" system to identify information by level of importance: green for simple topics to be studied first, yellow for important topics that may require more time for study, and red for topics of the lowest priority or are complex but not vital • Changing dietary or exercise habits to increase energy, improve health, boost concentration, etc.	Advantages: can help individuals stay disciplined, motivated, and confident

Preparing for the CBT

Familiarizing yourself with the look and feel of the computer-based testing environment in advance of your exam can alleviate anxiety and minimize pretest mistakes such as getting lost on the way to the testing center or failing to arrive with the correct ID and paperwork. Being better prepared for the test experience will allow you to perform better on the day of your test.

Prometric offers a product called *Test Drive* that provides candidates with a real world, end-to-end practice run before the date of their scheduled test. *Test Drive* takes 30 minutes and gives candidates a complete run-through of the testing experience they will encounter on their actual testing day. During the run-through, the candidate will participate in:

- The scheduling and registration process
- The complete check-in process
- Introduction to test center staff and surroundings
- A live 15-minute sample test demonstrating the testing process

Test Drive scheduling is available online at the Prometric website (www.Prometric.com). Knowing in advance what to expect at the test center may help some candidates to be more confident and comfortable on exam day.

General Study Tips

1. Study in short intervals (e.g., 20 to 30 minutes).
2. Do a quick review of material on exam day.
3. Use your study plan and keep to a schedule.
4. Actively study by taking notes as you study.
5. Use study aids, study guides, and/or review courses. Study in groups if you have friends and APIC chapter members who can get together to test one another. It may be helpful to schedule weekly study group meetings to keep everyone on track.
6. Know when to quit. Take a break or stop for the day when your energy and attention wanes.

7. Allow extra time to study chapters that have complex information. Be sure to account for extra time needed in your study schedule.

8. After you have reviewed the primary resources for a topic in the CBIC content outline, take the practice questions at the end of the respective chapter in this study guide. This will help identify areas that need more review.

9. When reading the practice questions, pay attention to the key words that bring to your attention specific points to be considered before selecting your answer. Examples of key words include:

   - *First*
   - *Initial*
   - *Least*
   - *Most*
   - *Safest*
   - *Next*
   - *Correct*
   - *Effective*
   - *Appropriate*
   - *Avoid*
   - *Incorrect*
   - *Ineffective*
   - *Unlikely*

10. Look for absolute word options such as *must, always, never, every,* and *only*. Eliminating these options can help to answer the question.

11. There are some essential laboratory values that you should know. These include arterial blood gas results, serum tests of renal function, serum chemistry, and complete blood count. Laboratory values used on the CIC® exam will either be within normal range, or significantly abnormal. You should also be able to recognize deviations from the normal values. The ability to correlate certain lab values with various illnesses with help you answer some of the more difficult questions.

Taking the Exam

1. Be prepared on the day of exam: know the site, building, travel route, and travel time.
2. Get plenty of rest the night before the test—don't cram.
3. Gather all of the necessary items that you will need to bring to the exam (see Chapter 1)—it may be helpful to do this the night before.
4. Wear your favorite comfortable clothes to the exam.
5. Eat something before you go. Having a proper meal will help with mental acuity during the exam.
6. Try to relax. Take your time and read directions carefully.
7. Read over each question thoroughly before you look at the answer. Do not skim the information or read too quickly.
8. Look for hints in the wording of the question's stem.
9. Adjectives such as most, first, best, and initial, indicate that you must establish priorities.
10. Identify key words in the test question.
11. Do not focus on irrelevant background information.
12. Thoroughly consider each answer choice; do not choose based on hunches or gut feelings.
13. Do not look for a specific answer before you have considered all of the choices.
14. Eliminate options that are clearly wrong or incorrect.
15. Select the best answer from the choices that you have been given. Do not worry if the answer that you think should be there is not provided.
16. Do not spend time worrying over your answers to test questions once you have made your selection. Usually your first choice is the right one.
17. Answer every question! If you are unsure of the answer, make an educated guess and select an answer. There is no penalty for wrong answers.

18. Pace yourself—don't spend too much time on a single question.

19. Take a break when you need one.

20. Notify the proctors at the testing site if there are any problems.

21. Use the stress-reducing techniques that work best for you. Stretch or take several deep breaths to relax and refocus.

Psych yourself up for taking the exam, and work on stress reduction.

Remember:

1. Maintain a good attitude.

2. Keep your goals in mind.

3. Think positively.

4. Use positive self-talk.

5. Expect success.

6. Feel good about yourself.

7. Know yourself.

8. Realize that failure is possible.

9. Persevere, endure.

TIPS FOR REPEAT TEST-TAKERS

It is devastating to discover that you did not pass the CIC® exam. If you are unsuccessful the first time you take the test, you may be tempted to say, "I am never doing this again!"—but do not give up!

If you do not pass the CBT, you must submit a new application to CBIC, including appropriate documentation and fees. CBIC will then determine your eligibility to retake the CBT. An individual may retake the CBT a maximum of four times per year and no more than once every 90 days. Use this waiting period to focus your review and to learn and apply the test-taking strategies in this book.

It is important that you prepare for the test differently for your next attempt. Many unsuccessful candidates may assume that they did not study hard enough or learn enough content. Although that may be true for some, for others memorizing more facts may not mean more right answers.

The first step is to make the commitment to test again. Decide when you want to schedule your test and allow yourself enough time to prepare accordingly.

Next, determine what factors led to the unsuccessful result. Consider the reasons why you did not pass the exam on the first try:

- Did you know the content?
- Did you have difficulty understanding the questions?
- Did you have the tendency to predict answers?
- Did you have the tendency to answer questions based only upon your personal experiences?
- Did you consider each answer choice?
- Did you have difficulty with the computer-based testing method?
- Did you lose your concentration?
- Were you distracted?
- Were you hungry or thirsty?

Once you understand the reasons that may have led to your unsuccessful attempt, the next step is to establish a plan of action. You are now familiar with the CBT, and you know what to expect. Although you will not receive the same questions, the content of the questions, the style, and the kinds of answer choices will not change.

What you already know has been presented in the score report from the testing supervisor. Your raw score for each major category is indicated. Congratulate yourself for the topics that you have already mastered, and identify your areas of weakness.

Create a study plan for reviewing primary and secondary sources on the areas of weakness that you identified. Use the practice questions and exams in this guide to retest your knowledge. You may also want to look into other education opportunities or resources you did not use previously that may help reinforce content or provide more practice for applying what you have learned. If you have not done

so already, reach out to your local APIC chapter to see if they have a study group or visit the APIC online community on IP Talk for tips and encouragement from other APIC members. You are not alone!

The night before the exam, focus on relaxation strategies and make sure that you get 8 hours of sleep. Keep your goals in mind and think positively!

TIPS FOR INTERNATIONAL TEST-TAKERS

Language and cultural differences may present challenges for international infection preventionists (IPs) taking the CIC® exam; however, this can be overcome through adequate preparation.

The CIC® exam is administered in select international countries. A complete list of locations can be found on the Prometric website (www.Prometric.com/cbic). The test sites follow the same protocols and security measures that are followed in the United States.

At the time of publication of this guide, the CIC® exam is only available in English. If you have difficulty reading and comprehending English, you may consider taking classes in English as a second language (ESL) before sitting for the CIC® exam. It may be helpful to take an English medical terminology course.

The English vocabulary may be challenging for international IPs. Words in English often have more than one meaning. It is important to be able to identify words as they are used in context. Study the words that are used in the practice questions in this guide and in the primary and secondary sources. Make a list of unfamiliar words, and use a dictionary to look them up.

Cultural differences may also exist between the infection prevention processes in the United States and those in other countries. Completing the practice questions in this book and using APIC's educational resources and member networks will help build your knowledge of cultural practices and enable you to accurately identify infection prevention practices in the United States.

Many IPs educated outside of the United States may not be familiar with the multiple-choice question format. Your test-taking experience may have consisted of oral exams or written responses to essay or short-answer questions. Multiple-choice questions are commonly used in the United States because they objectively measure knowledge and they are easy to administer and score.

The practice questions and exams in this study guide will help you become more proficient at taking multiple-choice questions. The more questions you complete, the more skillful you will become at deciphering a question, identifying the key information in a question, and choosing the best answer option. Review the information on the CBIC website and thoroughly read the CBIC *Candidate Handbook* to familiarize yourself with the test and its requirements.

Many international IPs may be unfamiliar with the abbreviations used in the United States. Please refer to the list of abbreviations located in the back of this study guide (p. 477).

Prometric offers testing aides that can benefit international test takers. Test accommodation solutions include extra time to take the test for ESL candidates, word-to-word translation dictionaries, and interpreters who will verbally translate exams from one language to another. A complete list of accommodations can be found at www.Prometric.com.

SECTION II. CBIC CONTENT OUTLINE REVIEW AND PRACTICE QUESTIONS

Chapter 3
IDENTIFICATION OF INFECTIOUS DISEASE PROCESSES

NOTES

The CIC® exam will have a total of twenty-two (22) questions addressing Identification of Infectious Disease Processes. The content will test knowledge of the following:

A. Interpret the relevance of diagnostic and laboratory reports

B. Identify appropriate practices for specimen collection, transportation, handling, and storage

C. Correlate clinical signs and symptoms with infectious disease process

D. Differentiate between colonization infection and contamination

E. Differentiate between prophylactic empiric and therapeutic uses of antimicrobials

KEY CONCEPTS

- The infectious disease process refers to the interaction between the pathogenic microorganism, the environment, and the host.
- Clinical microbiology encompasses the study of pathogens such as bacteria, viruses, fungi, and parasites, which cause disease or infection in humans. The microbiology laboratory plays a critical role in the diagnosis of infectious disease.
- The identification and management of infectious disease requires fundamental knowledge of microorganisms, microbial pathogenesis, host defense mechanisms, and basic laboratory techniques, as well as an understanding of the basic principles behind antimicrobial therapy.

NOTES

RESOURCES FOR STUDY

Nearly all questions on Identification of Infectious Disease Processes are based on chapters in the primary references, but secondary references may be useful to help clarify more detailed issues.

Primary Reference:

1. Grota P, ed. *APIC Text of Infection Control and Epidemiology,* 4th edition. Washington, DC: Association for Professionals in Infection Control and Epidemiology, 2014. Also available online at http://text.apic.org [subscription required].

Notable Chapters:

21 Risk Factors Facilitating Transmission of Infectious Agents

22 Microbial Pathogenicity and Host Response

23 The Immunocompromised Host

24 Microbiology Basics

25 Laboratory Testing and Diagnostics

26 Antimicrobials and Resistance

70 Biofilms

71 *Bordetella pertussis*

72 *Clostridium difficile* Infection and Pseudomembranous Colitis

73 Creutzfeldt-Jakob Disease and other Prion Diseases

74 Central Nervous System Infection

75 Enterobacteriaceae

76 Enterococci

77 Environmental Gram-negative Bacilli

78 Fungi

79 A: Diarrheal Diseases - Viral

79 B: Diarrheal Diseases - Bacterial

79 C: Diarrheal Diseases - Parasitic

80 Herpes Virus

NOTES

81 HIV/AIDS

82 Influenza

83 Foodborne Illnesses

84 *Legionella pneumophila*

85 Lyme Disease (*Borrelia burgdorferi*)

86 Measles, Mumps, Rubella

87 *Neisseria meningitidis*

88 Parvovirus

89 Rabies

90 Respiratory Syncytial Virus

91 Sexually Transmitted Diseases

92 Skin and Soft Tissue Infections

93 Staphylococci

94 Streptococci

95 Tuberculosis and Other Mycobacteria

96 Viral Hemorrhagic Fevers

97 Viral Hepatitis

98 West Nile Virus

99 Parasites

2. Brooks K. *Ready Reference for Microbes,* 3rd edition. Washington, DC: Association for Professionals in Infection Control and Epidemiology, 2012.

3. Heymann D, ed. *Control of Communicable Diseases Manual,* 19th edition. Washington, DC: American Public Health Association, 2008.

4. Kulich P, Taylor D, eds. *The Infection Preventionist's Guide to the Lab.* Washington, DC: Association for Professionals in Infection Control and Epidemiology, 2012.

NOTES

Secondary Reference:

1. Current Recommendations of the Advisory Committee on Immunization Practices (ACIP).
2. Current guidelines, standards, and recommendations from CDC, APIC, SHEA, and Public Health Agency of Canada.
3. Pickering, Larry K, ed. *Red Book*, 29th ed., Elk Grove Village, IL: American Academy of Pediatrics; 2012.

PRACTICE QUESTIONS

NOTES

1. A patient was just admitted to a long-term care facility from the local hospital. The patient is being treated for psoriasis. The psoriasis does not appear to be responding to treatment, and 48 hours later, the infection preventionist (IP) receives a report that a Certified Nursing Assistant has developed an itchy rash. The patient's physician visits and determines that the patient has crusted scabies and not psoriasis. Another name for crusted scabies is:

   a. American scabies

   b. Norwegian scabies

   c. Canadian scabies

   d. English scabies

2. Guidelines for transporting specimens include:

   1) Transport within 2 hours of collecting a specimen

   2) Transport in leakproof specimen containers and sealable leakproof bags

   3) Transport specimen in the syringe used to collect it

   4) Refrigerate all specimens prior to transport

      a. 1, 4

      b. 2, 3

      c. 1, 2

      d. 3, 4

3. Which is *true* about a tuberculin skin test (TST):

   a. Positive TST indicates active tuberculosis (TB) infection

   b. Negative TST rules out active TB infection

   c. Positive TST indicates past exposure to TB

   d. Negative TST indicates past exposure to TB

4. The optimal time to collect a sputum specimen for acid-fast bacilli (AFB) testing to rule out TB would be:

   a. First thing in the morning

   b. After a respiratory treatment

   c. Prior to the patient going to bed

   d. Prior to a respiratory treatment

NOTES

5. A hospital has hired a new manager of the Microbiology section of the Laboratory. During the initial discussion with the manager about the Infection Prevention and Control program, the IP stresses the importance of collaboration between the departments in reducing healthcare-associated infections (HAIs). Of the choices below, which activity will best meet this goal?
   - **a.** The Microbiology staff's compliance with the annual flu vaccination program and tuberculosis skin testing
   - **b.** The Microbiology staff's participation in the periodic infection prevention educational sessions for hospital staff
   - **c.** Microbiology's prompt notification to the Infection Prevention and Control Department of any organism's unusual resistance pattern
   - **d.** The Microbiology manager's attendance at local, state, and/or national infection prevention and control educational conferences

6. The primary immune response after exposure to a communicable disease pathogen or vaccine is production of:
   - **a.** Immunoglobulin G (IgG)
   - **b.** Immunoglobulin M (IgM)
   - **c.** Immunoglobulin A (IgA)
   - **d.** Immunoglobulin C (IgC)

7. When are IgM antibodies to Hepatitis A virus (HAV) detectable in the blood?
   - **a.** Within 24 hours of exposure
   - **b.** Within 3 weeks of exposure
   - **c.** 30 days after exposure
   - **d.** 8 to 12 weeks after exposure

8. The incubation period for pertussis in immunocompetent persons is usually:
   - **a.** 7 to 10 days
   - **b.** 3 to 5 days
   - **c.** 1 to 2 days
   - **d.** 2 to 4 days

NOTES

9. A patient who was hospitalized for 2 days calls 3 days after discharge complaining that he has developed healthcare-associated scabies due to his recent inpatient stay. The IP knows that his scabies infestation is not healthcare-associated because:

- **a.** Scabies is only transmitted through contaminated linens, and the IP confirmed that all linens the patient came into contact with had been properly laundered
- **b.** The incubation period for scabies is longer than 5 days
- **c.** The incubation period for scabies is shorter than 3 days
- **d.** Scabies is only transmitted through direct contact and none of the healthcare personnel who cared for the patient are infested

10. A nurse is concerned that a patient in the neurology ward has a prion disease after receiving a lab report stating that the patient had a positive nucleic acid test for John Cunningham virus (JCV) in the cerebrospinal fluid. What is the best response to give this nurse?

- **a.** The test is positive for Creutzfeldt-Jakob disease, which is a prion disease
- **b.** The test is positive for *Campylobacter jejuni*, which is not a prion disease
- **c.** The test is positive for JCV (a polyomavirus), which is not a prion disease
- **d.** The test is positive for JCV (a polyomavirus), which is a prion disease

11. An IP is conducting an educational session to help the nursing staff understand infectious disease transmission. She explains that the initial element in virulence is the ability of an organism to survive in the external environment during transit between hosts. What is the second element of virulence?

- **a.** Secretion of enzymes that enhance spread through tissues
- **b.** A mechanism for transmission to a new host
- **c.** Invasion and dissemination in the host
- **d.** Avoidance of host resistance

NOTES

12. The management of an infected surgical site includes the following foundational principles:

1) Open and drain the incision
2) Debride fibrous debris and necrotic soft tissue
3) Replace hardware
4) Implement antimicrobial management as needed
5) Manage the open wound

- **a.** 1, 2, 3, 4
- **b.** 2, 3, 4, 5
- **c.** 1, 3, 4, 5
- **d.** 1, 2, 4, 5

13. During annual TST, an employee's test result was read as 10 mm induration. The employee's last TST was negative. This initial result indicates a:

- **a.** Positive test
- **b.** False positive
- **c.** Negative test
- **d.** False negative

14. A microbe that can grow in the absence of oxygen but is also able to utilize oxygen for growth is a/an:

- **a.** Aerobe
- **b.** Obligate anaerobe
- **c.** Facultative anaerobe
- **d.** Microaerophilic aerobe

15. Western blot testing for human immunodeficiency virus (HIV) is used to detect:

- **a.** HIV DNA in a serum sample
- **b.** HIV RNA in a serum sample
- **c.** HIV antibodies in a serum sample
- **d.** HIV proteins in a serum sample

NOTES

16. An infection preventionist (IP) is reviewing the cerebrospinal fluid (CSF) results from a patient admitted the previous night. The CSF is cloudy and has an elevated white blood cell count (WBC), markedly increased neutrophils, low glucose level, and elevated protein concentration. What type of meningitis should she suspect?

a. Bacterial

b. Viral

c. Fungal

d. Aseptic

17. Which of the following statements about influenza is *false*?

a. Influenza is primarily spread between individuals via respiratory secretions (droplets)

b. Viral shedding starts 48 to 72 hours after infection and typically 48 hours before the onset of symptoms

c. Viral shedding normally persists for less than 5 days but can be longer in children and in immunocompromised persons

d. The typical influenza symptomology is not always predictive of influenza in elderly or immunocompromised persons

18. Which of the following statements is *false* regarding influenza viruses?

a. They are divided into three categories: A, B, and C

b. Influenza A strains have been the predominant cause of worldwide epidemics (pandemics)

c. Influenza A and B strains have been named according to the city or state and year of their initial isolation

d. Influenza B strains have not been associated with large epidemics

19. Which factor is commonly associated with *Clostridium difficile* infections (CDIs)?

a. Chemotherapeutic agents

b. ACE inhibitors

c. Prophylactic antibiotics or antibiotic to treat a primary bacterial infection

d. Antiviral medication to treat a primary viral infection

NOTES

20. The IP is reviewing the history of a patient who has been in the facility on a ventilator for 1 week. All of the following are risk factors for colonization and infection with multidrug-resistant pathogens except:

a. Antimicrobial therapy in preceding 90 days

b. Current hospitalization of 5 days or more

c. Immunosuppressive state or therapy

d. Low frequency of antibiotic resistance in the facility

21. The current community-acquired pneumonia (CAP) national quality measures used in the United States include all of the following *except*:

a. Antibiotic timing (within 6 hours of arrival)

b. Antibiotic selection

c. Blood cultures performed in the Emergency Department before antibiotics were administered

d. Ensure that all patients are screened for pneumococcal vaccination

22. Measures that can be practiced for prevention of aspiration include all of the following except:

a. Antibiotic prophylaxis

b. Oropharyngeal cleaning and decontamination with an aseptic agent (e.g., chlorhexidine)

c. Orotracheal intubation, unless contraindicated, rather than nasotracheal intubation

d. The head of the bed elevated at an angle of 30 to 45 degrees

23. All of the following are descriptions of patients with immunocompromised status *except*:

a. HIV with CD4 count <200

b. Leukemia or lymphoma

c. Neutropenia (absolute neutrophils count <500/mm3)

d. 1 year post-bone marrow transplant

24. The paroxysmal stage of pertussis usually lasts:

a. 1 to 6 weeks

b. 11 to 15 weeks

c. 15 to 20 weeks

d. 6 to 21 weeks

25. Which of the following is *not* an effect of malnutrition on the body's immune system?

- **a.** Intestinal bacteria may be altered
- **b.** Tissue integrity is impaired
- **c.** Mucosal secretions are decreased
- **d.** Urine may be colonized with bacteria

26. Lyme disease is commonly found in all of the following regions of the United States *except*:

- **a.** New England
- **b.** Mid-Atlantic
- **c.** Upper Midwest
- **d.** Southeast

27. All of the following organisms can penetrate the intact epithelium of the conjunctiva or cornea *except*:

- **a.** *Staphylococcus aureus*
- **b.** *Streptococcus pneumoniae*
- **c.** *Neisseria meningitidis*
- **d.** *Neisseria gonorrhoeae*

28. A patient is admitted with pruritic lesions on the hands, webs of fingers, wrists, the extensor surfaces of the elbows and knees, and the outer surfaces of the feet, armpits, buttocks, and waist. The most likely diagnosis is:

- **a.** Scarlet fever
- **b.** Herpes zoster
- **c.** Scabies
- **d.** Measles

29. Which of the following is *not* likely to contaminate total parenteral nutrition?

- **a.** *Mycobacterium fortuitum*
- **b.** *Candida albicans*
- **c.** *Pseudomonas aeruginosa*
- **d.** *Staphylococcus epidermidis*

NOTES

NOTES

30. A urine specimen collected from an indwelling urinary catheter was sent to the laboratory for culture and sensitivity testing. Culture results reported a colony count of 50,000 CFU/mL of *Escherichia coli*. Sensitivity testing reported resistance to cephalosporin and sensitivity to ciprofloxacin. This organism is an example of:

a. Methicillin resistance

b. Aminoglycoside resistance

c. Extended-spectrum beta-lactam (ESBL) resistance

d. Quinolone resistance

31. A patient has a nasal swab positive for methicillin-resistant *Staphylococcus aureus* (MRSA) in the absence of symptoms. This is an example of:

a. Normal flora

b. Colonization

c. Asymptomatic infection

d. Symptomatic infection

32. Which of the following is *not* a mechanical barrier to infection?

a. Intact skin

b. Mucous membranes

c. Secretions

d. Cilia

33. Patients with cell-mediated immunity dysfunction are susceptible to infections attributed to pathogenic intracellular bacteria. Examples of these organisms include:

1) *Salmonella typhi*

2) *Bacteroides fragilis*

3) *Listeria monocytogenes*

4) *Staphylococcus aureus*

a. 2, 3

b. 1, 3

c. 1, 2

d. 3, 4

NOTES

34. What is the name for a substance that prevents water-soluble elements such as antibiotics and disinfectants from reaching pathogens?

a. Cell wall

b. Biofilm

c. Sludge

d. Biocarbon

35. A Gram-negative bacterium that is responsible for chronic antral gastritis and is a major factor in peptic ulcer disease is:

a. *Streptococcus pyogenes*

b. *Salmonella typhi*

c. *Clostridium difficile*

d. *Helicobacter pylori*

36. The spirochete *Borrelia burgdorferi* is the agent responsible for:

a. Legionnaires' disease

b. Lyme disease

c. Aseptic meningitis

d. Syphilis

37. Higher morbidity rates in chronic Hepatitis B virus (HBV) carriers are associated with a co-infection of which of the following:

a. Hepatitis A

b. Hepatitis D

c. Hepatitis C

d. Hepatitis E

38. Gram stains classify an organism as Gram-positive or Gram-negative. The determinant factors for Gram stains are cell wall components of:

a. Peptidoglycans

b. Lipids

c. Polysaccharides

d. Mycolic acids

NOTES

39. An example of an obligate intracellular parasitic bacterium would be an organism responsible for:

1) Hepatitis
2) Q fever
3) Malaria
4) Epidemic typhus

a. 2, 3
b. 2, 4
c. 3, 4
d. 1, 2

40. Which one of the following statements is *true* regarding bacterial spores?

a. They are resistant to antibiotics
b. They allow the bacteria to multiply in adverse condition
c. They are usually formed by Gram-negative bacteria
d. They can be identified with Gram stain

41. Which organism found in food poisoning causes the most rapid onset of symptoms?

a. *Salmonella enteritidis*
b. *Shigella sonnei*
c. *Staphylococcus aureus*
d. *Escherichia coli*

42. The IP is teaching nurses how to assess infection risks in patients. Depletion of what cell type provides the best indication of susceptibility to most bacterial infections?

a. Monocyte
b. Eosinophil
c. Neutrophil
d. Lymphocyte

NOTES

43. A 14-year-old boy from rural Maryland was seen in the emergency room with fever, fatigue, chills, headache, and a large annular lesion on his left thigh, which the patient described as burning and itching. What is the most probable vector of this child's illness?

a. Tick

b. Mosquito

c. Flea

d. Louse

44. Which immune marker represents past exposure to disease?

a. IgG

b. IgE

c. IgM

d. IgA

45. The Emergency Department reports three cases of cramping, abdominal pain, and diarrhea within a 24-hour period. All persons are from the same community, and onset of symptoms was within 12 to 36 hours of a picnic they all attended. The IP suspects which of the following foodborne illnesses:

a. *Salmonella*

b. *Hepatitis A*

c. *Staphylococcus aureus*

d. *Clostridium perfringens*

46. When reviewing the Gram stain of a person with a wound infection, the IP sees Gram-positive organisms in clusters. Which organism would this most likely represent?

a. *Streptococcus*

b. *Enterococcus*

c. *Corynebacterium*

d. *Staphylococcus*

NOTES

47. The IP receives a call from a young man who thinks he was exposed to HIV. He has just taken his first test (an enzyme-linked immunosorbent assay [ELISA]), which was negative. Which of the following is the most likely time frame after exposure in which HIV antibodies would be measureable in a blood test?

a. 6 months

b. 1 to 3 months

c. 12 months

d. 7 days

48. The causative organism of Creutzfeldt-Jakob disease is a:

a. Helminth

b. Diphtheroid

c. Spirochete

d. Prion

49. Anaerobic cultures should be used for any of the following sites *except*:

a. Blood

b. Transtracheal aspirate

c. Spinal fluid

d. Sputum

50. Routine microbiologic sampling is indicated for which of the following?

a. Respiratory therapy equipment

b. Dialysis fluid

c. Sterile disposable equipment

d. Operating room surfaces

ANSWERS AND RATIONALES

NOTES

1. **B Norwegian scabies**

Rationale: Crusted scabies is a severe form of scabies that can occur in individuals who may be immunocompromised, elderly, disabled, or debilitated. It is also called Norwegian scabies. In immunodeficient individuals and in senile patients, infestation often appears as a generalized dermatitis more widely distributed than the burrows, with extensive scaling and sometimes vesculation and crusting (Norwegian or crusted scabies); the usual severe itching may be reduced or absent.

References: Scabies. In: Heymann D. *Control of Communicable Diseases Manual*, 19th edition. Washington, DC: American Public Health Association, 2008; *APIC Text*, 4th edition, Chapter 99 - Parasites

2. **C 1, 2**

Rationale: The appropriate selection, collection, and transport of specimens to the diagnostic microbiology laboratory are essential parts in the accurate identification of microorganisms that cause infections that affect patient care and infection prevention. Transportation guidelines include:

- All specimens must be promptly transported to the laboratory, preferably within 2 hours of collection.
  - Delays or exposure to temperature extremes compromises the test results.
- Specimens should be transported in a container designed to ensure survival of suspected agents.
  - Never refrigerate spinal fluid, genital, eye, or internal ear specimens because these samples may contain microorganisms sensitive to temperature extremes.
- Materials for transport must be labeled properly, packaged, and protected during transport.
  - A transport medium can be used to preserve the viability of microorganisms in clinical samples (e.g., Stuart, Amies, and Carey-Blair transport media).
- Use leakproof specimen containers and transport them in sealable, leakproof plastic bags.
- Never transport syringes with needles attached.
- Laboratories must have enforceable criteria for rejection of unsuitable specimens.

Reference: Specimen Collection and Transport. In: Kulich P, Taylor D, eds. *Infection Preventionists' Guide to the Lab*. Washington, DC: Association for Professionals in Infection Control and Epidemiology, 2012.

NOTES

3. **(C) Positive TST indicates past exposure to TB**

Rationale: TST involves injection of purified protein derived from the mycobacterial cell wall. The test relies on the fact that persons who have been infected with TB will have a delayed-type hypersensitivity reaction to this reagent. The TST is a screening tool to detect people with latent TB infection (LTBI); it cannot be used for ruling in or ruling out active TB. This is because a positive TST merely indicates a history of LTBI at some time in the past—it conveys no information regarding the current status of the person's infection (which may even have been cured previously). Likewise, a negative test does not rule out active TB because people with active tuberculosis may well have a negative TST, even in the presence of positive controls. In fact, up to 20 percent of persons with active TB will have negative TST results.

Reference: *APIC Text*, 4th edition, Chapter 95 - Tuberculosis and Other Mycobacteria

4. **(A) First thing in the morning**

Rationale: Because pulmonary disease is the most common form of TB, patients with suspected TB should have a chest radiograph. If the radiograph is abnormal or the patient has respiratory complaints, sputum specimens should be collected for acid-fast bacilli (AFB) staining, culture, or other direct tests. The first sputum may be obtained on admission, but subsequent cultures are usually obtained in the morning on consecutive days. A total of three specimens collected on separate days is generally adequate, and once one specimen is AFB positive, subsequent samples are not needed. Specimens should be delivered promptly to the laboratory for processing.

Reference: *APIC Text*, 4th edition, Chapter 95 - Tuberculosis and Other Mycobacteria

5. **(C) Microbiology's prompt notification to the Infection Prevention and Control Department of any organism's unusual resistance pattern**

Rationale: The clinical microbiology laboratory is an important partner in the practice of infection prevention. The active involvement and cooperation of the microbiology laboratory is critical to the functioning of the infection control program, particularly in surveillance and the use of laboratory services for epidemiologic purposes. Surveillance requires high-quality laboratory data that are timely and easily accessible. The Centers for Disease Control and Prevention (CDC) recommends that all healthcare organizations establish systems to ensure that clinical microbiology laboratories promptly notify infection control staff or a medical director/designee when a novel resistance pattern for the facility is detected.

Reference: Siegel JD, Rhinehart E, Jackson M, et al. *Management of Multidrug-Resistant Organisms In Healthcare Settings, 2006*. CDC website. 2006. Available at: http://www.cdc.gov/hicpac/pdf/MDRO/MDROGuideline2006.pdf.

6. **(B) Immunoglobulin M (IgM)**

Rationale: During the primary immune response that occurs after a communicable disease pathogen or vaccine is encountered, the class of antibody that is produced first is IgM. IgG antibodies develop a few weeks later. IgG antibodies are a good indication of the convalescence period and generally mark the establishment of long-term immunity to the pathogen.

Reference: Microbial Immunology. In: Kulich P, Taylor D, eds. *Infection Preventionists' Guide to the Lab*. Washington, DC: Association for Professionals in Infection Control and Epidemiology, 2012.

NOTES

7. **B 5 to 10 days after exposure**

Rationale: Hepatitis A is an acute liver disease caused by HAV. Clinical features of acute hepatitis are not specific for HAV infection, so serological diagnosis is necessary. IgM antibodies to HAV (IgM anti-HAV), which are used to diagnose acute HAV infection, are detectable within 3 weeks of exposure and are present at the onset of jaundice. Titer declines over 4 to 6 weeks and antibodies are usually not detectable after 6 to 12 months. IgG anti-HAV is also detectable at onset of jaundice and remains positive lifelong, indicating immunity to HAV.

Reference: Hepatitis A. In: Heymann D, ed. *Control of Communicable Diseases Manual,* 19th edition. Washington, DC: American Public Health Association, 2008.

8. **A 7 to 10 days**

Rationale: Pertussis (whooping cough) is a highly communicable, acute, infectious respiratory disease caused by *Bordetella pertussis*. The incubation period of pertussis in immunocompetent patients is usually 7 to 10 days, with a range of 6 to 21 days. In rare cases, the incubation period may be a long as 42 days.

Reference: *APIC Text*, 4th edition, Chapter 71 - *Bordetella pertussis*

9. **B The incubation period for scabies is longer than 5 days**

Rationale: The incubation period for scabies may be as short as 10 days but is typically between 4 and 6 weeks. Therefore, the patient could not have acquired scabies during the hospital stay because, based on the incubation period, he would need to have been exposed at least 5 days before he was admitted.

Reference: *APIC Text*, 4th edition, Chapter 99 - Parasites

10. **C The test is positive for JCV (a polyomavirus), which is not a prion disease**

Rationale: JCV is a polyomavirus that can cause a demyelinating disease called progressive multifocal leukoencephalopathy in immunocompromised individuals. Because of the name and some presenting symptoms, JCV is sometimes confused with Creutzfeldt-Jakob disease (CJD), which is a prion disease.

Reference: Viruses. In: Brooks K. *Ready Reference for Microbes*, 3rd edition. Washington, DC: Association for Professionals in Infection Control and Epidemiology, 2012.

11. **B A mechanism for transmission to a new host**

Rationale: The second element in virulence is a mechanism for transmission to a new host. For example, insect vectors may transmit pathogens by injecting material from salivary glands or defecation into sites of penetration of host skin. Some viruses can survive and be transmitted to hands from environmental surfaces, such as bed rails. Some bacteria possess mechanisms of motility. When a microorganism reaches a favorable site for inducing disease, it must adhere to the structure that it will infect in order to survive.

Reference: *APIC Text*, 4th edition, Chapter 22 - Microbial Pathogenicity and Host Response

NOTES

12. D 1, 2, 4, 5

Rationale: Each infected wound has a unique patient profile, unique characteristics of the operation, and potentially unique bacteriological features. The diversity of variables in the infected surgical site has resulted in a diverse number of options that are employed in management. The foundation principles in the management of the infected surgical site are (1) open and drain the incision, (2) debride fibrinous debris and necrotic soft tissue, (3) remove foreign bodies, (4) implement antimicrobial management as needed, and (5) manage the open wound.

Reference: *APIC Text*, 4th edition, Chapter 37 - Surgical Site Infection

13. A Positive test

Rationale: A positive test is determined by the number of millimeters of induration (not erythema) caused by the reaction to the tuberculin. Different cut points are used depending on the likelihood of the individual having a TB infection and the likelihood that the infection, if present, will progress to active TB. A 10-mm reaction in a healthcare worker is considered a positive test. All healthcare personnel with positive baseline TST results should be referred for medical and diagnostic evaluation; additional skin testing is not needed.

Reference: Jensen PA, Lambert LA, Iademarco MF, et al. Guidelines for Preventing the Transmission of Mycobacterium tuberculosis in Health-Care Settings, 2005. *MMWR* 2005 December 30. 41(RR-17). 1-141. Available at: http://www.cdc.gov/mmwr/preview/mmwrhtml/rr5417a1.htm?s_cid=rr5417a1_e.

14. C Facultative anaerobe

Rationale: Facultative anaerobes will utilize oxygen if it is present but are still able to grow in the absence of oxygen. Microbes that must have oxygen to grow are called aerobes, whereas microbes that only grow in the absence of oxygen are called obligate anaerobes. Microaerophilic bacteria need a small amount of oxygen for growth.

Reference: *APIC Text*, 4th edition, Chapter 24 - Microbiology Basics

15. C HIV antibodies in a serum sample

Rationale: The Western blot is a confirmatory test that is performed on all samples that have tested positive for HIV on enzyme immunoabsorbent assay (EIA). HIV proteins are run through a gel matrix and then transferred to a thin membrane. The membrane is incubated with a serum sample, washed, and then incubated with a secondary antibody. If antibodies to the HIV proteins that were run through the gel matrix are present in the serum sample, they will complex with those proteins and will not be washed away. A secondary antibody with a fluorescent tag will then bind to the HIV antibody-protein complex, and this allows the antibody-protein complexes to be visualized.

Reference: *APIC Text*, 4th edition, Chapter 81 - HIV/AIDS

NOTES

16. Ⓐ **Bacterial**

Rationale: The diagnosis of bacterial meningitis rests on examination of the CSF. The CSF appearance is typically cloudy, depending on the presence of significant concentrations of WBCs, red blood cells (RBCs), bacteria, and/or protein. In untreated bacterial meningitis, the WBC count is elevated. Bacterial meningitis usually leads to a neutrophil predominance in CSF, typically between 80 and 95 percent. The CSF glucose concentration is <40 mg/dL in approximately 50 to 60 percent of patients. The CSF protein concentration is elevated in virtually all patients with bacterial meningitis (see Table 3-1).

Table 3-1. Findings in CSF Analysis for Meningitis

Reference Values					
Component	Adult	Neonate	Bacterial Infection	Viral Infection	Fungal Infection
Color/clarity	Clear/colorless		Cloudy	Clear/hazy	Clear/hazy
Protein (mg/dL)	15-45	115-170	↑	Normal to ↑	Normal to ↑
Glucose (mg/dL)	50-80	60% of plasma value	↓	Normal to ↓	Normal to ↓
WBC count Agglutinating capacity	0-5	0-30	↑	Normal to ↑	↑
WBC Differential					
Lymphocytes	62 ± 34	20 ± 18	↓	Normal to ↑	Normal to ↑
Monocytes	36 ± 20	72 ± 22	↓	Normal to ↑	Normal to ↑
Neutrophils	2 ± 5	3 ± 5	↑	Normal to ↓	Normal to ↓
Eosinophils	Rare	Rare	Rare	Rare	Rare

References: *APIC Text*, 4th edition, Chapter 25 - Laboratory Testing and Diagnostics; Urinalysis, Fluid Analysis, Chemistry, and Hemotology. In: Kulich P, Taylor D, eds. *The Infection Preventionist's Guide to the Lab*. Washington, DC: Association for Professionals in Infection Control and Epidemiology, 2012.

17. Ⓑ **Viral shedding starts 48 to 72 hours after infection and typically 48 hours before the onset of symptoms**

Rationale: Influenza viruses are spread from person to person primarily through large-particle respiratory droplet transmission. Transmission via large-particle droplets requires close contact between source and recipient, because droplets do not remain suspended in the air and generally travel only a short distance (≤1 meter) through the air. Contact with respiratory-droplet contaminated surfaces is another possible source of transmission. The typical incubation period for influenza is 1 to 4 days (average 2 days). Adults shed influenza virus from the day before symptoms begin through 5 to 10 days after illness onset. However, the amount of virus shed, and presumably infectivity, usually decreases rapidly by 3 to 5 days after onset. Young children also might shed virus several days before illness onset, and children can be infectious for 10 or more days after onset of symptoms. Severely immunocompromised persons can shed virus for weeks or months.

Reference: *APIC Text*, 4th edition, Chapter 82 - Influenza

NOTES

18. (D) Influenza B strains have not been associated with large epidemics

Rationale: Influenza viruses are divided into three categories, designated A, B, and C. All three contain negative-sense, segmented, single-strand RNA molecules. Influenza A viruses are the most common clinical isolates, and they are subdivided by differences in two surface proteins: hemagglutinin (H) and neuraminidase (N). Three H and two N antigenic subtypes account for virtually all human infections. The most prevalent influenza A strains in humans in the last 30 years have been H3N2 and H1N1. In recent years, influenza A and B strains also have been named according to the city or state and year of their initial isolation, for example, A/Texas/36/91 (H1N1) or B/Hong Kong/330/2001. Influenza A strains have been the predominant causes of worldwide epidemics (pandemics). Influenza B strains also cause epidemic disease, but the clinical illnesses tend to be milder than illnesses caused by influenza A. Influenza C strains are much less common (<1 percent of influenza infections), and they produce generally mild illness (usually a "common cold"). Influenza C strains have not been associated with large epidemic.

Reference: *APIC Text*, 4th edition, Chapter 82 - Influenza

19. (C) Prophylactic antibiotics or antibiotic to treat a primary bacterial infection

Rationale: *Clostridium difficile* is a spore-forming, Gram-positive anaerobic bacillus that produces two exotoxins: toxin A and toxin B. It is a common cause of antibiotic-associated diarrhea (AAD). It accounts for 15 to 25 percent of all episodes of AAD. The risk for disease increases in patients with:

- Antibiotic exposure
- Proton pump inhibitors
- Gastrointestinal surgery/manipulation
- Long length of stay in healthcare settings
- A serious underlying illness
- Immunocompromising conditions
- Advanced age

Reference: *APIC Text*, 4th edition, Chapter 72 - *Clostridium difficile* Infection and Pseudomembranous Colitis

20. (D) Low frequency of antibiotic resistance in the facility

Rationale: Pneumonia may be caused by a wide variety of pathogens, but multidrug-resistant organisms (MDROs) are becoming more relevant as etiologic agents. Risk factors for colonization and infection with MDROs are as follows:

- Antimicrobial therapy in preceding 90 days
- Current hospitalization of 5 days or more
- High frequency of antibiotic resistance in the community or in the specific hospital unit
- Presence of risk factors for healthcare-associated pneumonia
- Immunosuppressive state or therapy

Reference: *APIC Text*, 4th edition, Chapter 36 - Pneumonia

NOTES

21. D Ensure that all patients are screened for pneumococcal vaccination

Rationale: The core quality measures are a set of standards defined by The Joint Commission (TJC) and the Centers for Medicare & Medicaid Services (CMS) to create core measures for disease management for CAP. The measures create consistent evidence-based practice in facilities caring for CAP patients. The CMS measures hospitals' adherence to the measures and publishes the results. The core measures for CAP include:

- Oxygen assessment within 24 hours before or after arrival at the hospital
- Patients over 65 screened for pneumococcal vaccination and administration before discharge, if necessary
- Blood cultures performed in the Emergency Department before antibiotics were administered
- Antibiotic timing (within 6 hours of arrival)
- Antibiotic selection
- Adult smoking cessation advice and counseling provided
- Influenza vaccination

Reference: *APIC Text*, 4th edition, Chapter 36 - Pneumonia

22. A Antibiotic prophylaxis

Rationale: The following precautions should be practiced for prevention of aspiration:

- Use of noninvasive ventilation, when possible, to reduce the need for and duration of endotracheal intubation. This refers to all modalities that assist ventilation without the use of an endotracheal tube.
- Perform orotracheal intubation unless contraindicated. Nasotracheal intubation has been associated with higher incidence of nosocomial sinusitis, making the patient more prone to development of pneumonia through aspiration of infected secretions.
- The head of the bed should be elevated at an angle of 30 to 45 degrees.
- Oropharyngeal cleaning and decontamination should be performed with an aseptic agent (e.g., chlorhexidine).
- Stress ulcer prophylaxis may be provided with proton-pump inhibitors, histamine-2 receptor antagonist, or sucralfate.

Reference: *APIC Text*, 4th edition, Chapter 36 - Pneumonia

23. D 1 year post-bone marrow transplant

Rationale: Patients with immunocompromised status include those with the following:

- Neutropenia (absolute neutrophils count <500/mm^3)
- Leukemia or lymphoma
- HIV with CD4 count <200
- Splenectomy
- Early post-transplant
- On cytotoxic chemotherapy
- On high-dose steroid therapy: >40 mg prednisone or its equivalents (>160 mg hydrocortisone, >32 mg methylprednisolone, >6 mg dexamethasone, >200 mg cortisone) daily for >2 weeks

Reference: *APIC Text*, 4th edition, Chapter 36 - Pneumonia

NOTES

24. (A) 1 to 6 weeks

Rationale: Pertussis (whooping cough) is a highly communicable, acute, infectious respiratory disease caused by *Bordetella pertussis*. The onset of pertussis, known as the catarrhal stage, begins with coryza (runny nose), sneezing, low-grade fever, and a mild, occasional cough that gradually becomes more severe. The cough that began during the catarrhal stage progresses steadily, becoming paroxysmal (numerous rapid coughs). It is during this second paroxysmal stage that the diagnosis of pertussis is usually suspected. The classic symptoms of pertussis include whoop, vomiting, apnea, and cyanosis immediately after a paroxysm of coughing. Infants younger than 6 months may have an atypical presentation with a short catarrhal stage, gagging and gasping, or apnea as prominent early manifestations. The whoop may be absent. The paroxysmal stage usually lasts 1 to 6 weeks but may persist for as long as 10 weeks.

Reference: *APIC Text*, 4th edition, Chapter 71 - *Bordetella pertussis*

25. (D) Urine may be colonized with bacteria

Rationale: Malnutrition affects the body's immune system by altering the intestinal bacteria, impairing the integrity of the tissue, and decreasing mucosal secretions (see Table 3-2).

Table 3-2. Effects of Protein/Calorie Malnutrition on Immune Function

Barrier functions
• Tissue integrity is impaired: decreased intestinal epithelium/mucosal lining, atrophy of the gut's associated lymphoid tissue (part of the immunologic barrier of the intestine).
• Respiratory tract cilia are decreased.
• Mucosal secretions are reduced.
• Intestinal bacteria may be altered; colonization in the normally sterile upper small bowel may occur.
• Acid secretion may be decreased in the stomach.

Reference: *APIC Text*, 4th edition, Chapter 47 - Nutrition and Immune Function

26. (D) Southeast

Rationale: Lyme disease is caused by the bacterium *Borrelia burgdorferi* and is transmitted to humans through the bite of infected black-legged ticks. Typical symptoms include fever, headache, fatigue, and a characteristic skin rash called erythema migrans. If left untreated, infection can spread to joints, the heart, and the nervous system. In the United States, Lyme disease has been reported in all 50 states but occurs most commonly in three principal areas: New England and the Mid-Atlantic states, the upper Midwest with concentration in the Great Lakes region, and several counties in northern California.

Reference: *APIC Text*, 4th edition, Chapter 85 - Lyme Disease (*Borelli burgdorferi*)

NOTES

27. Ⓐ ***Staphylococcus aureus***

Rationale: Healthcare-related ocular infections are rare but may lead to catastrophic consequences such as compromised vision and/or blindness. Only a few organisms can penetrate the intact epithelium of the conjunctiva or cornea. Among these are *Neisseria gonorrhoeae, Neisseria meningitidis, Streptococcus pneumoniae, Listeria monocytogenes,* and *Corynebacterium diphtheriae*. For all others, a breach in the protective epithelial barrier or mucous membranes must occur.

Reference: *APIC Text*, 4th edition, Chapter 63 - Ophthalmology Services

28. Ⓒ **Scabies**

Rationale: Skin infestations by the mite *Sarcoptes scabiei* var. *hominis* are commonly known as scabies. Humans are the natural reservoir of *S. scabiei* var. *hominis*. Mites are transmitted through direct contact with infested persons; less frequently, transmission may occur through contact with clothing or bedding (fomites). Spread of the mite to a different part of the body can occur by manual transfer or scratching. Approximately two-thirds of cases have burrow-type pruritic lesions on hands, webs of fingers, wrists, extensor surfaces of elbows and knees, as well as outer surfaces of feet, armpits, buttocks, and waist. Spread can also occur to arms, trunk, legs, penis, scrotum, and nipples.

Reference: *APIC Text*, 4th edition, Chapter 99 - Parasites

29. Ⓐ ***Mycobacterium fortuitum***

Rationale: With strict adherence to aseptic compounding technique, contamination of the total parental nutrition (TPN) solution is rarely the cause of sepsis. However, TPN can foster microbial growth. Organisms that have been reported to proliferate in TPN include fungi (*Candida albicans or Malassezia furfur*); Gram-positive bacteria (coagulase-negative *Staphylococcus, Staphylococcus saprophyticus,* or *Staphylococcus epidermidis*); and Gram-negative bacteria (*Escherichia coli* or *Pseudomonas aeruginosa*) bacteria. *Candida* is one of the most frequently reported organisms.

Reference: *APIC Text*, 4th edition, Chapter 47 - Nutrition and Immune Function

30. Ⓒ **Extended-spectrum beta-lactam (ESBL) resistance**

Rationale: ESBLs are β-lactamases found in common Gram-negative bacteria, such as *E. coli* and *Klebsiella pneumoniae*, which confer resistance to all β-lactam drugs except the carbapenems. *Klebsiella* species and *E.coli* are the most common ESBL-producing pathogens. ESBLs are enzymes that mediate resistance to extended-spectrum (third-generation) cephalosporins (e.g., ceftazidime, cefotaxime, and ceftriaxone) and monobactams (e.g., aztreonam) but do not affect cephamycins (e.g., cefoxitin and cefotetan) or carbapenems (e.g., meropenem or imipenem). The presence of an ESBL-producing organism in a clinical infection can result in treatment failure if one of the above classes of drugs is used. ESBLs can be difficult to detect because they have different levels of activity against various cephalosporins.

References: *APIC Text*, 4th edition, Chapter 26 - Antimicrobials and Resistance; Centers for Disease Control and Prevention (CDC). *Laboratory Detection of Extended-Spectrum β-Lactamases (ESBLs)*. CDC website. 2010. Available at: http://www.cdc.gov/hai/settings/lab/lab_esbl.html

NOTES

31. (B) Colonization

Rationale: Colonization is the presence of microorganisms on skin, on mucous membranes, in open wounds, or in excretions or secretions in the absence of adverse clinical signs or symptoms.

Reference: *APIC Text*, 4th edition, Chapter 24 - Microbiology Basics

32. (C) Secretions

Rationale: Mechanical barriers include skin, mucous membranes, and tears. The skin forms a physical barrier that is very impermeable to most infectious agents. Movement due to cilia or peristalsis helps to keep air passages and the gastrointestinal tract free from microorganisms. The trapping effect of mucus that lines the respiratory and gastrointestinal tract helps protect the lungs and digestive systems from infection. Chemical factors include fatty acids in sweat that inhibit the growth of bacteria. Lysozyme and phospholipase found in tears, saliva, and nasal secretions can break down the cell wall of bacteria and destabilize bacterial membranes. The low pH of sweat and gastric secretions prevents growth of bacteria.

Reference: *APIC Text*, 4th edition, Chapter 92 - Skin and Soft Tissue Infections

33. (B) 1, 3

Rationale: As a host becomes progressively more immunocompromised, progressively fewer virulent organisms are able to become pathogenic. Thus, patients with major immune defects are subject to a larger number and greater variety of infectious diseases. The most common opportunistic bacterial infections associated with cell-mediated immunity dysfunction are primarily intracelluar pathogens that include:

- *Listeria monocytogenes*
- *Salmonella spp.*
- *Mycobacterium spp.,* including *M. tuberculosis*
- *Nocardia (N. asteroides,* others)
- *Legionella pneumophila,* other species of *Legionella*
- *Rhodococcus equi*
- *Pseudomonas pseudomallei*

Reference: *APIC Text*, 4th edition, Chapter 23 - The Immunocompromised Host

34. (B) Biofilm

Rationale: A biofilm is any group of microorganisms in which cells stick to each other on a surface. These adherent cells are frequently embedded within a self-produced matrix of extracellular polymeric substance. Biofilm extracellular polymeric substance—which is also referred to as slime—is a polymeric conglomeration generally composed of extracellular DNA, proteins, and polysaccharides. Biofilms may form on living or nonliving surfaces and can be prevalent in natural, industrial, and hospital settings.

Reference: *APIC Text*, 4th edition, Chapter 70 - Biofilms

NOTES

35. **D** ***Helicobacter pylori***

Rationale: *H. pylori* is a Gram-negative bacterium that causes chronic gastritis in humans. This bacterium is also considered to be a common cause of ulcers worldwide: as many as 90 percent of people with ulcers have detectable *H. pylori*. It is also linked to the development of duodenal ulcers and stomach cancer. However, more than 80 percent of individuals infected with the bacterium are asymptomatic, and it has been postulated that it may play an important role in the natural stomach ecology.

Reference: Bacteria. In: Brooks K. *Ready Reference for Microbes,* 3rd edition. Washington, DC: Association for Professionals in Infection Control and Epidemiology, 2012.

36. **B** **Lyme disease**

Rationale: Lyme disease is caused by the bacterium *Borrelia burgdorferi* and is transmitted to humans through the bite of infected black-legged ticks. Typical symptoms include fever, headache, fatigue, and a characteristic skin rash ca lled erythema migrans. If left untreated, infection can spread to joints, the heart, and the nervous system. Lyme disease is diagnosed based on symptoms, physical findings (e.g., rash), and the possibility of exposure to infected ticks; laboratory testing is helpful if used correctly and performed with validated methods. Most cases of Lyme disease can be treated successfully with a few weeks of antibiotics. Steps to prevent Lyme disease include using insect repellent, removing ticks promptly, applying pesticides, and reducing tick habitat.

Reference: *APIC Text*, 4th edition, Chapter 85 - Lyme Disease (*Borrelia burgdorferi*)

37. **B** **Hepatitis D**

Rationale: Hepatitis D, also known as "delta hepatitis," is a serious liver disease caused by infection with the Hepatitis D virus (HDV), which is an RNA virus structurally unrelated to the Hepatitis A, B, or C viruses. Hepatitis D, which can be acute or chronic, is uncommon in the United States. HDV is an incomplete virus that requires the helper function of HBV to replicate and only occurs among people who are infected with HBV. HDV is transmitted through percutaneous or mucosal contact with infectious blood and can be acquired either as a co-infection with HBV or as superinfection in persons with HBV infection. There is no vaccine for Hepatitis D, but it can be prevented by Hepatitis B vaccination in persons who are not already HBV infected.

Reference: *APIC Text*, 4th edition, Chapter 97 - Viral Hepatitis

38. **A** **Peptidoglycans**

Rationale: The Gram stain is the most important and universally used staining technique in the bacteriology laboratory. It is used to distinguish between Gram-positive and Gram-negative bacteria, which have distinct and consistent differences in their cell walls. Gram-positive bacteria have a thick peptidoglycan cell wall that does not allow the crystal violet/iodine complex to be removed during the alcohol wash. Under the microscope, Gram-positive organisms appear dark violet, purple, or blue. Gram-negative bacteria contain a lipopolysaccharide layer as part of their cell wall. The alcohol wash disrupts this layer and the crystal violet/iodine complex is rinsed out of the cell wall. As a result, Gram-negative cells are colorless until counterstained with safranin. Under the microscope, Gram-negative organisms appear pink or red.

Reference: *APIC Text*, 4th edition, Chapter 24 - Microbiology Basics

NOTES

39. (B) 2, 4

Rationale: Intracellular parasites are parasitic microorganisms that are capable of growing and reproducing inside the cells of a host. Obligate intracellular parasites cannot reproduce outside their host cell, meaning that the parasite's reproduction is entirely reliant on intracellular resources. All viruses are obligate intracellular parasites. Obligate intracellular parasitic bacteria include *Chlamydia, Rickettsia, Coxiella*, and certain species of *Mycobacterium*.

Reference: Bacteria. In: Brooks K. *Ready Reference for Microbes*, 3rd edition. Washington, DC: Association for Professionals in Infection Control and Epidemiology, 2012.

40. (A) They are resistant to antibiotics

Rationale: The function of a spore is to permit the cell to survive unfavorable conditions such as extremes of temperature or moisture. Spores become dormant at these times; they do not multiply in adverse conditions. Instead, the spore protects the bacteria until favorable conditions occur, at which time the bacteria can begin to multiply. Spores are usually formed by Gram-positive bacteria.

Reference: *APIC Text*, 4th edition, Chapter 24 - Microbiology Basics

41. (C) *Staphylococcus aureus*

Rationale: Eating foods contaminated with toxins produced by S. aureus causes staphylococcal food poisoning. Food workers who carry *Staphylococcus* and then handle food without washing their hands contaminate foods by direct contact. The bacterium can also be found in unpasteurized milk and cheese products. *Staphylococcus* is salt tolerant and can grow in salty foods like ham. As the bacterium multiplies in food, it produces toxins that can cause food poisoning. Staphylococcal toxins are resistant to heat and cannot be destroyed by cooking. Foods at highest risk of producing toxins from *Staphylococcus aureus* are those that are made by hand and require no cooking. Some examples of foods that have caused staphylococcal food poisoning are sliced meat, puddings, pastries, and sandwiches. Staphylococcal toxins are fast acting, sometimes causing illness in as little as 30 minutes after eating contaminated foods, but symptoms usually develop within 1 to 6 hours. Patients typically experience several of the following: nausea, retching, vomiting, stomach cramps, and diarrhea.

References: Foodborne Intoxications - Stahylococcal. In: Heymann D, ed. *Control of Communicable Diseases Manual,* 19th edition. Washington, DC: American Public Health Association, 2008; *APIC Text*, 4th edition, Chapter 83 - Foodborne Illnesses

42. (C) Neutrophil

Rationale: Neutrophils are the most abundant (40 to 75 percent) type of white blood cell and are formed from stem cells in the bone marrow. They are short-lived and highly motile. Neutrophils may be subdivided into segmented neutrophils (or segs) and banded neutrophils (or bands). They form part of the polymorphonuclear cell family together with basophils and eosinophils. Neutropenia is a granulocyte disorder characterized by an abnormally low number of neutrophils. Neutrophils usually make up 50 to 70 percent of circulating white blood cells and serve as the primary defense against infections.

Reference: *APIC Text*, 4th edition, Chapter 22 - Microbial Pathogenicity and Host Response

NOTES

43. (A) Tick

Rationale: This child's symptoms are consistent with Lyme disease. Typical symptoms include fever, headache, fatigue, and a characteristic skin rash called erythema migrans. If left untreated, infection can spread to joints, the heart, and the nervous system. Lyme disease is diagnosed based on symptoms, physical findings (e.g., rash), and the possibility of exposure to infected ticks; laboratory testing is helpful if used correctly and performed with validated methods. The black-legged tick (*Ixodes scapularis*), commonly known as a deer tick, can transmit the organisms responsible for anaplasmosis, babesiosis, and Lyme disease. This tick is widely distributed in the northeastern United States.

Reference: *APIC Text*, 4th edition, Chapter 85 - Lyme Disease (*Borrelia burgdorferi*)

44. (A) IgG

Rationale: IgG is the major circulating and extravascular (interstitial) antibody. IgG is the late-occurring immunoglobulin in an immune response and is the longest lived. IgG represents past exposure to disease.

Reference: *APIC Text*, 4th edition, Chapter 22 - Microbial Pathogenicity and Host Response

45. (A) *Salmonella*

Rationale: Most persons infected with *Salmonella* develop diarrhea, fever, and abdominal cramps 12 to 72 hours after infection. The illness usually lasts 4 to 7 days, and most persons recover without treatment. However, in some persons, the diarrhea may be so severe that the patient needs to be hospitalized. In these patients, the *Salmonella* infection may spread from the intestines to the bloodstream and to other body sites, possibly resulting in death if the person is not treated promptly with antibiotics. Infants, elderly persons, and those with impaired immune systems are more likely to have a severe illness from *Salmonella*.

Reference: *APIC Text*, 4th edition, Chapter 83 - Foodborne Illnesses

46. (D) *Staphylococcus*

Rationale: *Staphylococcus* is a genus of Gram-positive bacteria. Under the microscope, they appear round (cocci) and form in grape-like clusters. *Staphylococcus* includes at least 40 species. Of these, nine have two subspecies and one has three subspecies. Most are harmless and reside normally on the skin and mucous membranes of humans and other organisms. Found worldwide, they are a small component of soil microbial flora.

Reference: Bacteria. In: Brooks K. *Ready Reference for Microbes*, 3rd edition. Washington, DC: Association for Professionals in Infection Control and Epidemiology, 2012.

47. (B) 1 to 3 months

Rationale: People usually develop measurable levels of HIV antibodies within 30 days of infection, though some may take longer—up to 3 months in some cases. Before this happens, there is a period when antibody levels are too low to reliably be detected. This is called the "window period." It is during this time that an infected person can pass HIV to others but still have a negative result if given an antibody test.

Reference: *APIC Text*, 4th edition, Chapter 81 - HIV/AIDS

NOTES

48. D Prion

Rationale: Prion diseases or transmissible spongiform encephalopathies (TSEs) are a family of rare progressive neurodegenerative disorders that affect both humans and animals. They are distinguished by long incubation periods, characteristic spongiform changes associated with neuronal loss, and a failure to induce inflammatory response. The causative agents of TSEs are believed to be prions. The term "prions" refers to abnormal, pathogenic agents that are transmissible and able to induce abnormal folding of specific normal cellular proteins called prion proteins that are found most abundantly in the brain. The functions of these normal prion proteins are still not completely understood. The abnormal folding of the prion proteins leads to brain damage and the characteristic signs and symptoms of the disease. Prion diseases are usually rapidly progressive and always fatal.

Reference: *APIC Text*, 4th edition, Chapter 73 - Creutzfeldt-Jakob Disease and other Prion Diseases

49. D Sputum

Rationale: An anaerobic bacteria culture is a method used to grow anaerobes from a clinical specimen. Anaerobes are commonly found on mucous membranes and other sites such as the vagina and oral cavity. Therefore, specimens likely to be contaminated with these organisms should not be submitted for culture. Specimens that are not suitable for anaerobic cultures include:

- Sputum
- Rectal swab
- Nasal or throat swab
- Urethral swab
- Voided urine

Reference: *APIC Text*, 4th edition, Chapter 24 - Microbiology Basics

50. B Dialysis fluid

Rationale: Microbiological environmental testing is not generally recommended. Environmental culturing can be costly and may require special laboratory procedures. Additionally, in most cases no standards for comparison exist. Because of the lack of standards, environmental testing may generate inconclusive data that could result in the implementation of unnecessary procedures or treatment. Routine microbiologic sampling for quality assurance purposes should be limited to (1) biologic monitoring of sterilization processes, (2) monthly cultures and endotoxin testing of water and dialysate in hemodialysis units, and (3) short-term evaluation of the impact of infection prevention measures or changes in infection prevention protocols.

Reference: *APIC Text*, 4th edition, Chapter 24 - Microbiology Basics

Chapter 4
SURVEILLANCE AND EPIDEMIOLOGIC INVESTIGATION

NOTES

The CIC® exam will have a total of twenty-four (24) questions addressing Surveillance and Epidemiologic Investigation. The content will test knowledge of the following:

A. Design of Surveillance Systems

1. Conduct a risk assessment on the population served, services provided, and regulatory or other requirements
2. Develop goals and objectives based upon the risk assessment
3. Develop a surveillance plan based on the goals identified from the risk assessment
4. Evaluate periodically the effectiveness of the surveillance plan and modify as necessary
5. Create a notification system based on surveillance plan including epidemiologically significant findings
6. Integrate surveillance activities across health care settings (e.g., ambulatory, home health, long term care, acute care)
7. Establish mechanisms for identifying individuals with communicable diseases requiring follow-up and/or transmission based precautions

B. Collection and Compilation of Surveillance Data

1. Use a systematic approach to record surveillance data
2. Organize and manage data in preparation for analysis
3. Calculate the incidence or prevalence of infections
4. Calculate specific infection rates/ratios (e.g., provider-specific, unit-specific, device-specific, procedure-specific, Standardized Infection Ratio)
5. Use of standardized definitions

NOTES

C. Interpretation of Surveillance Data

1. Generate, and validate surveillance data
2. Use basic statistical techniques to describe data (e.g., mean, standard deviation, rates, ratios, proportions)
3. Monitor and interpret the relevance of antimicrobial susceptibility patterns
4. Compare surveillance results to published data and/or other relevant benchmarks
5. Analyze and interpret data using appropriate methods
6. Prepare and present findings in an appropriate format that is relevant to the audience/stakeholders (e.g., graph, tables, charts)
7. Develop and facilitate corrective action plans based on surveillance findings
8. When to implement an epidemiological study to investigate a problem (e.g., case control, cohort studies

D. Outbreak Investigation

1. Verify existence of outbreak
2. Collaborate with appropriate persons to establish the case definition, period of investigation, and case-finding methods
3. Define the problem using time, place, person, and risk factors
4. Formulate hypothesis on source and mode of transmission
5. Implement and evaluate control measures, including ongoing surveillance
6. Prepare and disseminate reports

KEY CONCEPTS

- Surveillance is an essential component of an effective infection prevention program.
- Surveillance activities should support a system that can identify risk factors for infection and other adverse advents, implement risk-reduction measures, and monitor the effectiveness of interventions.

NOTES

- Surveillance plays a critical role in identifying outbreaks, emerging infectious diseases, antibiotic-resistant organisms, and bioterrorist events so that infection prevention measures can be instituted.
- Epidemiology, the study of the frequency, distribution, cause, and control of disease in populations, forms the basis of all health-related studies. It provides the background for interventions to reduce transmission of infecting organisms, reduce the number of healthcare-associated infections, and protect healthcare providers from infection. Understanding the relationships of host, environment, and organism will aid the infection preventionist in designing studies to determine the cause of healthcare-associated infections and design interventions.

RESOURCES FOR STUDY

Nearly all questions on Surveillance and Epidemiologic Investigation are based on chapters in the primary references, but secondary references may be useful to help clarify more detailed issues.

Primary Reference:

1. Grota P, ed. *APIC Text of Infection Control and Epidemiology*, 4th edition. Washington, DC: Association for Professionals in Infection Control and Epidemiology, 2014. Also available online at http://text.apic.org [subscription required].

Notable Chapters:

1 Infection Prevention and Control Programs

6 Healthcare Informatics and Information Technology

10 General Principles of Epidemiology

11 Surveillance

12 Outbreak Investigations

13 Use of Statistics in Infection Prevention

14 Process Control Charts

15 Risk-adjusted Comparisons

16 Quality Concepts

17 Performance Measures

NOTES

18	Patient Safety
19	Qualitative Research Methods
20	Research Study Design
33	Urinary Tract Infection
34	Intravascular Device Infections
35	Infections in Indwelling Medical Devices
36	Pneumonia
37	Surgical Site Infection
72	*Clostridium difficile* Infection and Pseudomembranous Colitis
75	Enterobacteriaceae
76	Entercocci
77	Environmental Gram-Negative Bacilli
93	Staphlococci

2. Brooks K. *Ready Reference for Microbes*, 3rd edition. Washington, DC: Association for Professionals in Infection Control and Epidemiology, 2012.
3. Heymann D, ed. *Control of Communicable Diseases Manual*, 19th edition. Washington, DC: American Public Health Association, 2008.
4. Kulich P, Taylor D, eds. *The Infection Preventionist's Guide to the Lab*. Washington, DC: Association for Professionals in Infection Control and Epidemiology, 2012.

Secondary Reference:

1. Current Recommendations of the Advisory Committee on Immunization Practices (ACIP).
2. Current guidelines, standards, and recommendations from CDC, APIC, SHEA, and Public Health Agency of Canada.
3. Pickering, Larry K, ed. *Red Book*, 29th ed., Elk Grove Village, IL: American Academy of Pediatrics; 2012.

NOTES

PRACTICE QUESTIONS

1. Identify the median in the following list of numbers: 6, 2, 9, 7, 1, 4

a. 9

b. 7

c. 5

d. 4

2. In a study of whether Operating room A (OR A) is associated with a higher number of surgical site infections (SSIs) than Operating room B (OR B), the infection preventionist (IP) is testing whether:

H_o: OR A SSI rate = OR B SSI rate
H_a: OR A SSI rate ≠ OR B SSI rate

The IP concludes that the SSI rate in OR A is not equal to the SSI rate in OR B, but in reality the two rates are equal. What type of statistical error has she committed?

a. No error has been committed

b. She committed a Type I error

c. She committed a Type II error

d. She committed an error equal to β

3. For which of the following procedure(s) is the surveillance period for deep incisional or organ/space SSI 90 days?

1) Cesarean section

2) Craniotomy

3) Coronary artery bypass graft

4) Laminectomy

a. 1, 2

b. 2, 3

c. 3, 4

d. 1, 4

NOTES

4. An appropriate indicator to monitor process compliance would be:

a. Class 1 SSI rate

b. Appropriate antibiotic dosage

c. Central line–associated bloodstream infections (CLABSIs) in the Neonatal Intensive Care Unit (NICU)

d. Infections caused by multidrug-resistant organisms

5. What key infection control activity is defined as the systematic, ongoing collection, management, analysis, and interpretation of data followed by the dissemination of these data to public health programs to stimulate public health action?

a. Research

b. Surveillance

c. Benchmarking

d. Accreditation

6. An IP is reading a journal article that states that the data the authors collected are normally distributed. What does this mean?

a. When the data are plotted on a curve, it is skewed

b. The mean is less than the median

c. The skewness value is equal to 1

d. The mean, median, and mode of the data are equal

7. Which of the following is indicative of a superficial SSI?

a. Pain at the incision site 10 days after a breast reduction procedure; drainage is culture-positive for methicillin-susceptible *Staphylococcus aureus* (MSSA)

b. Stitch abscess that is cultured 14 days after surgery and is positive for *Enterococcus faecalis*

c. Purulent drainage from an episiotomy that occurs within 5 days of delivery

d. Burn wound that cultures positive for *Acinetobacter baumannii* 10 days after debridement procedure

NOTES

8. An IP is preparing the quarterly report for the Infection Control Committee. What information will be needed to calculate a CLABSI rate for the ICU?

1) The total number of patients in the unit for the time period
2) The total number of central line catheters for the time period
3) The number of patients who had bloodstream infections identified
4) The number of device days for the time period

a. 2, 3
b. 1, 3
c. 1, 2
d. 3, 4

9. What type of rate would the IP want to calculate to give feedback to the surgeons at her facility?

a. Procedure-specific
b. Provider-specific
c. Unit-specific
d. Device-specific

10. The IP has been benchmarking her data to other facilities performing similar activities for a period of time. The IP should analyze the entire process to ensure that which of the following conditions are met?

1) Standardized definitions are used consistently
2) Overall rates are used to accurately track trends over time
3) Adequate training of personnel to collect, store, manage, and analyze data
4) Data are calculated using the same methodology as a nationally validated system

a. 1, 2, 3
b. 2, 3, 4
c. 1, 3, 4
d. 1, 2, 4

NOTES

11. The chi-square test can be used:

1) To evaluate the effect of a variable on outcomes
2) To analyze continuous data
3) To calculate an odds ratio or relative risk
4) If each cell of the table is greater than 5

a. 1, 2, 3
b. 1, 2, 4
c. 2, 3, 4
d. 1, 3, 4

12. The measure of central tendency *most* affected by outliers is:

a. Mean
b. Median
c. Mode
d. Range

13. The *p* value in statistical test results indicates:

a. Causation
b. The probability of having committed a Type I error
c. The probability of having committed a Type II error
d. The probability of data being accurate and valid

14. On a normally distributed data set, what percentage of values lies within three standard deviations from the mean?

a. 68.2
b. 95.5
c. 92.4
d. 99.7

15. Which statistical test is used when the data are small in numbers?

a. Fisher's exact
b. *t* test
c. Chi-square
d. *z* test

NOTES

16. Statistical process control (SPC) charts are used for all of the following purposes *except*:

a. Monitor the process of care

b. Facilitate the determination of variation

c. Eliminate natural variation

d. Monitor outcomes

17. Seventy-five patients were admitted to the Medical-Surgical ICU. Forty were on the surgical service and 35 were on the medical service. Fifteen patients developed a healthcare-associated infection with methicillin-resistant *Staphylococcus aureus* (MRSA). Nine of the patients with MRSA infection were on the surgical service. There were 230 patient days in the ICU for the surgical patients in January, and 325 patient days for medical patients. What was the incidence density of MRSA attack infection for patients on the surgical service?

a. 29 infections per 1,000 patient days

b. 26 infections per 1,000 patient days

c. 19 infections per 100 patient days

d. 39 infections per 1,000 patient days

18. Plague is endemic in parts of the Southwest United States. The word "endemic" means:

a. Natives are immune to plague

b. An expected number of cases occurs each year in a given geographical area

c. Plague has become resistant to all forms of treatment for this population

d. The disease is seen in a seasonal pattern each year for this area

19. A pandemic differs from an epidemic in that:

a. Only one disease is involved

b. It is usually vectorborne

c. There is a higher mortality rate

d. Several countries or continents are involved

NOTES

20. Specificity of a test for infection or disease is calculated as:

a. The number of true negatives divided by the number of positives found, times 100

b. The number of true negatives divided by the total number of persons with disease, times 100

c. The number of true positives divided by the total number of persons with disease, times 100

d. The number of true negatives divided by the total number of persons without disease, times 100

21. A measure of dispersion that reflects the variability in values around the mean is called the:

a. Variance

b. Standard deviation

c. Range

d. Bell curve

22. In any normal distribution, the proportion of observations that are within two standard deviations of the mean is closest to:

a. 0.50

b. 0.68

c. 0.95

d. 0.98

23. The most important feature of nonparametric tests is that they:

a. Make no assumption about variance in the populations

b. Can only be used with ordinal levels of measurements

c. Require a normal distribution

d. Require equal population variances

24. Which of the following indicates a strong positive correlation?

a. $r = 0$

b. $r = -0.993$

c. $r = 0.603$

d. $r = 0.45$

NOTES

25. The Employee Health Service has notified the IP that seven employees have *P. aeruginosa* folliculitis. Initial investigation reveals that six of the seven cases belong to the same health club. Working on the hypothesis that the whirlpool at the health club is associated with the infections, the IP decides to conduct a case-control study using two controls for each case. Which of the following groups is the most appropriate control?

a. Non-ill family members of the ill employees

b. Non-ill hospital employees matched for age and sex

c. Hospitalized patients with *P. aeruginosa* folliculitis matched for age and sex

d. Non-ill members of the health club matched for age and sex

26. Which of the following steps are *not* included in hypothesis testing?

a. State the null and alternative hypotheses

b. Set the significance level

c. Eliminate outliers

d. Compare the probability value to the significance level

27. The range of the correlation coefficient is:

a. -1 to 0

b. 0 to 1

c. -1 to 1

d. None of the above

28. If the index of kurtosis is -1.99, then the curve is:

a. Relatively flat

b. Negatively skewed

c. More peaked

d. A typical bell-shaped curve or normal distribution

29. The IP monitors all patients who have coronary artery bypass graft surgery for infections and pneumonia. The probability or likelihood of an event occurring is the:

a. Risk

b. Attack rate

c. Host factor

d. Incidence

NOTES

30. When a study is completed, a report should be written to give the results and evaluation of the study. A good way to display data is by charts or tables. A table is used to illustrate data:

a. Using only one coordinate

b. Arranged in rows and columns

c. Using a system of coordinates

d. Showing multiple complex factors at one time

31. Calculate the mode for the following set of numbers:
2, 11, 5, 21, 3, 11, 8, 26

a. 24

b. 10.8

c. 11

d. 9.5

32. As the sample size increases, how is the power of the study affected?

a. Power is independent of sample size

b. Power is increased

c. Power is decreased

d. Power approaches 0

33. The term for an extraneous variable that systematically varies with the independent variable and influences the dependent variable is a:

a. Predictor variable

b. Moderating variable

c. Experimental variable

d. Confounding variable

NOTES

34. When a normal distribution is graphed, which of the following are *true*?

1) There is a continuous, symmetrical distribution in which both tails extend to infinity
2) The mean, median, and mode are identical
3) 68.3 percent of the area lies between the mean and 32 standard deviations
4) The shape of the curve is determined by the mean and standard deviation

   a. 1, 2, 3
   b. 2, 3, 4
   c. 1, 3, 4
   d. 1, 2, 4

35. Which of the following is *not* considered one of the criteria for causality:

a. The incidence of disease is higher in those who are exposed to the factor
b. Evidence that the independent and dependent variables are related
c. The association has been observed in numerous studies
d. The onset of disease must precede exposure to the causal factor

36. Which of the following are *true* about a frequency polygon:

1) Is useful for showing two sets of data on a single graph
2) Uses bars on the *x* axis
3) Uses connecting lines and data points
4) Depicts the percentage of the total that each data point represents

   a. 1, 3
   b. 1, 4
   c. 3, 4
   d. 2, 4

NOTES

37. Targeted surveillance focuses on:

- **a.** Tracking high-risk, high-volume procedures and potentially preventable healthcare-associated infections (HAIs)
- **b.** Providing whole-house infection rates
- **c.** Tracking infections that are publicly reported
- **d.** Using the electronic surveillance systems to identify infections

38. The new IP for a long-term care facility is assessing adherence to the facility's hand hygiene policies. Which of the following should he include when reporting his findings?

- **a.** The number of hand hygiene episodes performed by personnel divided by the volume of soap used in the facility
- **b.** The number of hand hygiene episodes performed by personnel divided by the number of patient days times 1,000
- **c.** The number of hand hygiene episodes performed by personnel divided by the volume of alcohol-based hand rub
- **d.** The number of hand hygiene episodes performed by personnel divided by the number of hand hygiene opportunities by ward or service

39. Which of the following viruses is the causative agent in Kaposi's sarcoma?

- **a.** Herpes zoster virus
- **b.** Human herpesvirus 8
- **c.** Epstein-Barr virus
- **d.** Human papillomavirus (HPV)

40. The IP receives a call from the ER about a 38-year-old male with a 4-week history of cough and fever. He has just returned from an extended trip to the southwestern United States. Coccidioidomycosis is on the list of possible diagnoses. Which of the following is true regarding the epidemiology of coccidioidomycosis?

- **a.** *Coccidioides* spp. are usually found at high elevations
- **b.** *Coccidioides* spp. are usually found in wet climates
- **c.** Up to 50 percent of people in endemic areas have been exposed to *Coccidioides* spores
- **d.** *Coccidioides* spp. are found on the surface of the soil

NOTES

41. The IP wishes to know the proportion of a disease that could be prevented by eliminating the exposure in the entire study population. In order to determine this information, the IP will need to calculate the:

a. Attributable fraction

b. Attributable risk

c. Population attributable risk percent

d. Negative predictive value

42. The precision of an estimate of a relative risk depends on which of the following:

a. Generalisability

b. Size of the study

c. Validity of the study

d. Presence of bias

43. The most common reservoir for highly pathogenic avian influenza H5N1 virus is:

a. Migratory birds

b. Pigeons and doves

c. Water fowl

d. Domestic poultry

44. Indirect and direct causes of disease may form a complex network of events that determines the level of disease in a community. Which of the following is the term for this interrelation of events?

a. Applied epidemiology

b. Iceberg phenomenon

c. Causal web

d. Dendrogram

45. Which of the following statements is true when the prevalence of a disease is very low?

a. The sensitivity of a diagnostic test is greatly increased

b. The specificity of a diagnostic test is much greater

c. The negative predictive value of a diagnostic test is very low

d. The positive predictive value of a diagnostic test is lowered

NOTES

46. On July 7, a 30-year-old male is admitted to the medical ICU with a 2-day history of acute gastroenteritis symptoms. The IP suspects the patient is infected with norovirus. Which of the following statements regarding the epidemiology of norovirus infection supports this?

a. Most norovirus outbreaks are caused by genotype GII.2

b. Severe cases of norovirus are most common in adults aged 25 to 45

c. Noroviruses are the most common cause of epidemic gastroenteritis worldwide

d. Norovirus outbreaks occur most commonly in the summer months

47. What is the attributable risk between the exposed and unexposed population in the following table?

	Unexposed	Exposed
Disease	9	17
No Disease	7	5

a. 0.21

b. 0.56

c. 0.30

d. 0.77

48. A 40-year-old female is admitted with a 3-day history of diarrhea and fever. She is placed in Contact Isolation for a suspected *Clostridium difficile* infection (CDI). The patient also reports that she has had increasing abdominal pain for the past year, and inflammatory bowel disease (IBD) is in the list of potential diagnoses. Which of the following statements is most accurate regarding the relationship between IBD and CDI?

a. IBD is associated with increased morbidity and mortality associated with CDI

b. Most patients with IBD acquire CDI in inpatient settings

c. CDI generally develops more slowly after hospital admission among patients with IBD compared with patients without IBD

d. IBD does not affect the risk of CDI from antibiotic exposure

NOTES

49. Which of the following statements about TB and airborne diseases among homeless individuals is most accurate?

a. Most TB infections among homeless individuals are reactivations of established disease

b. Sputum testing detects more than 90 percent of patients with TB

c. Screening for TB with chest X-ray may be the most cost- effective approach

d. Directly observed therapy in the acute hospital setting is associated with the highest completion rates

50. In a case-control study, the association between obesity and *Clostridium difficile* was examined. The table below provides the results. Which of the following odds ratios is correct?

Body Mass Index (BMI)	Cases	Controls
BMI 30 or higher	55	30
BMI less than 25	45	70

a. 0.35

b. 2.85

c. 1.83

d. 0.55

NOTES

ANSWERS AND RATIONALES

1. **C 5**

Rationale: The median of a data set is the number that 50 percent of values fall below and 50 percent of values fall above. The data here are not presented in numerical order so first they must be ordered from lowest to highest: 1, 2, 4, 6, 7, 9.

There is an even number of values in this set so to find the median one must identify the two central numbers and then average them. The two central numbers are 4 and 6; 4 + 6 = 10 and 10/2 = 5.

Reference: *APIC Text*, 4th edition, Chapter 13 – Use of Statistics in Infection Prevention

2. **B She has committed a Type I error**

Rationale: If the IP concluded that the SSI rate in OR A is not equal to the SSI rate in OR B, then she rejects the null hypothesis. However, in this case the null hypothesis was true; therefore she has committed a Type I error. This value is equal to α.

Reference: *APIC Text*, 4th edition, Chapter 13 – Use of Statistics in Infection Prevention

3. **B 2, 3**

Rationale: According to the Centers for Disease Control and Prevention (CDC) SSI surveillance definitions, postoperative surveillance for deep incisional or organ/space SSIs should be conducted for 90 days on craniotomy and coronary artery bypass procedures. Superficial incisional SSIs are only followed for a 30-day period for all procedure types.

Reference: *APIC Text*, 4th edition, Chapter 11 – Surveillance

4. **B Appropriate antibiotic dosage**

Rationale: A surveillance program should monitor a variety of outcomes, processes, and events, and some indicators should focus on personnel.

A process measure focuses on a process or the steps in a process that lead to a specific outcome. Process measures are commonly used to evaluate compliance with desired care or support practices or to monitor variation in these practices. Examples of process indicators include medication errors; influenza vaccination rates in personnel, residents, or patients; hepatitis B immunity rates in personnel; and personnel compliance with infection prevention protocols, such as Standard Precautions, Isolation Precautions, tuberculin skin testing, hand hygiene, instrument processing, sterilization quality assurance testing, environmental cleaning, communicable disease reporting, antimicrobial prescribing and administration, and installing and maintaining barriers during construction and renovation projects.

An outcome measure is a measure that indicates the result of the performance (or nonperformance) of a function(s) or process(es). Examples of outcome indicators that may be monitored include HAIs (e.g., bloodstream, urinary tract, pneumonia, surgical site, conjunctivitis, upper respiratory tract, or local intravenous site), infection or colonization with a specific organism (e.g., *C. difficile*, MRSA, vancomycin-resistant enterococci or other antibiotic-resistant organisms, respiratory syncytial virus, or rotavirus); decubitus ulcers; phlebitis related to peripheral intravascular therapy; pyrogenic reaction or vascular access infection in hemodialysis patients; resident or patient falls; influenza or tuberculin skin test conversions in patients, residents, or healthcare providers; and sharps injuries and blood/body fluid exposures in healthcare providers.

Reference: *APIC Text*, 4th edition, Chapter 11 – Surveillance

NOTES

5. **(B) Surveillance**

Rationale: Surveillance has been defined as the "ongoing collection, collation, and analysis of data and the ongoing dissemination of information to those who need to know so that action can be taken." Surveillance is an essential component of an effective infection prevention and control program. Surveillance includes the collection of data with the ultimate objective of dissemination of that data to support and improve public health activities.

Reference: *APIC Text*, 4th edition, Chapter 11 - Surveillance

6. **(D) The mean, median, and mode of the data are equal**

Rationale: If the data are normally distributed, then the mean, median, and mode are all equal and the curve will have a bell shape, with most observations clustering at the center and then tapering off on either side of the center.

Reference: *APIC Text*, 4th edition, Chapter 13 - Use of Statistics in Infection Prevention

7. **(A) Pain at the incision site 10 days after a breast reduction procedure; drainage is culture positive for methicillin-susceptible *Staphylococcus aureus* (MSSA)**

Rationale: SSI continues to be a major source of morbidity, economic cost, and even death in surgical patients. To meet the criteria for a superficial SSI, the infection must occur within 30 days after the operation and involve only skin or subcutaneous tissue. In addition, one of the following must be met:

- Purulent drainage, with or without laboratory confirmation, from the superficial incision
- Organisms isolated from an aseptically obtained culture of fluid or tissue from the superficial incision
- *And* patient has at least one of the following:
  - Purulent drainage from the superficial incision
  - Organisms isolated from an aseptically obtained culture of fluid or tissue from the superficial incision
  - Superficial incision that is deliberately opened by a surgeon, attending physician, or other designee

    And patient has at least one of the following signs or symptoms: pain or tenderness, localized swelling, redness, or heat. A culture negative finding does not meet this criterion.
  - Diagnosis of superficial incisional SSI by the surgeon or attending physician or other designee

References: Centers for Disease Control and Prevention. *Procedure-associated Module - Surgical Site Infection (SSI) Event*. CDC website. January 2014. Available at: http://www.cdc.gov/nhsn/pdfs/pscmanual/9pscssicurrent.pdf; *APIC Text*, 4th edition, Chapter 37 - Surgical Site Infection

NOTES

8. (D) 3, 4

Rationale: The numerator would be the number of patients who had bloodstream infections identified and who had a central line during the time period.

The denominator would be the number of device days (at the same time every day, count the number of patients with one or more central lines) for the time period.

Basic Formula for All Types of Rates

- Rate = x/y × k

Where:

- x = The numerator, which equals the number of times the event (e.g., infections) has occurred during a specified time interval
- y = The denominator, which equals a population (e.g., number of patients at risk) from which those experiencing the event were derived during the same time interval
- k = A constant used to transform the result of division into a uniform quantity so that it can be compared with other, similar quantities. A whole number (fractions are inconvenient) such as 100, 1,000, 10,000, or 100,000 is usually used (selection of k is usually made so that the smallest rate calculated has at least one digit to the left of the decimal point) or is determined by accepted practice (the magnitude of numerator compared with denominator).

Reference: *APIC Text*, 4th edition, Chapter 13 - Use of Statistics in Infection Prevention

9. (B) Provider-specific

Rationale: Providing feedback of appropriate SSI surveillance data to surgeons has been shown to be important to reducing SSI risk. Furthermore, providing active rather than passive feedback of surveillance results to surgeons has the greatest effect in reducing SSI rates. When surgical teams are engaged in examining their SSI rates and in appraising clinical processes, there is greater probability of success in reducing infection rates.

Reference: *APIC Text*, 4th edition, Chapter 17 - Performance Measures

10. (C) 1, 3, 4

Rationale: To accurately trend surveillance data over time within a facility or compare rates between facilities, surveillance criteria (i.e., case definitions) must be consistently used to determine the presence of an HAI, occurrence of an event, or compliance with a process. Rates, rather than raw numbers, must be used to accurately track trends over time. Personnel who are responsible for collecting and managing surveillance data must have adequate training in reviewing medical records, interpreting clinical notes, applying standardized criteria for identifying cases, using appropriate statistical and risk adjustment methods, and using computer tools and technology (especially electronic records, spreadsheets, and databases) to collect, store, manage, and analyze data. Whenever possible, data should be expressed as rates or ratios that are calculated using the same methodology as a nationally validated surveillance system. This allows an organization to compare its rates with another organization or a recognized benchmark.

Reference: *APIC Text*, 4th edition, Chapter 11 - Surveillance

NOTES

11. (D) 1, 3, 4

Rationale: Chi-square tests (χ^2) can be used to test the association between two classifications of a set of counts or frequencies (discrete data). This data are commonly displayed as a contingency table or 2 x 2 table where rows represent one variable and columns represent the other. The null hypothesis is that there is no association between the two variables. Row and column totals (marginal totals) are used to predict what count would be expected for each cell if the null hypothesis were true. A test statistic is calculated from the observed and expected frequencies. The larger the test statistic (for given degrees of freedom) the more likely there is to be a statistically significant association between the two variables. Chi-square tests are used for medium to large samples (see Figure 4-1). The Fisher's exact test is used in place of the χ^2 when the sample size number is less than 20 or any one cell in the table is less than 5.

Figure 4-1. Formula for chi-square

$$\chi^2 = \frac{(0-E)^2}{E}$$

Where:

O = observed frequency

E = expected frequency

Reference: *APIC Text*, 4th edition, Chapter 13 - Use of Statistics in Infection Prevention

12. (A) Mean

Rationale: Measures of central tendency describe how observations cluster around a middle value and locate only the center of a distribution measure. The methods include mean, median, and mode. The most commonly used parameter is the arithmetic mean (average). The mean of a data set is inaccurate if there are extreme values (outliers) in a data set. Most statistical tests use the mean because it is more amenable to mathematical manipulation than the median or the mode. However, because the mean includes the value of each observation, it is the measurement most affected by outliers (unusually high or low values), especially when the number of observations is small. As the sample size gets very large, outliers are less important.

Reference: *APIC Text*, 4th edition, Chapter 13 - Use of Statistics in Infection Prevention

13. (B) The probability of having committed a Type I error

Rationale: A Type I error occurs when one rejects the null hypothesis (H_0) when it is true. This is also called a false-positive result (as we incorrectly conclude that the research hypothesis is true when in fact it is not). The *p* value or calculated probability is the estimated probability of rejecting the null hypothesis of a study question when that hypothesis is true.

Reference: *APIC Text*, 4th edition, Chapter 13 - Use of Statistics in Infection Prevention

NOTES

14. (D) 99.7

Rationale: Standard deviation is a measure of dispersion of the raw scores that reflects the variability in values around the mean. It employs the squared deviations from the mean (variance), which therefore gives added emphasis to larger deviations. The standard deviation indicates how small the variability is (i.e., the spread) among observations. If the variability is small, all the values are close to the mean. If it is large, the values are not close to the mean.

The significance of the standard deviation is that with normal (bell-shaped) distributions, the following empirical rules for the normal curve apply:

- The interval from one standard deviation below the mean to one standard deviation above the mean contains approximately 68 percent of the measurements.
- The interval from two standard deviations below the mean to two standard deviations above the mean contains approximately 95 percent of the measurements.
- The interval from three standard deviations below the mean to three standard deviations above the mean contains approximately 99.7 percent (or approximately all) of the measurements. (see Figure 4-2)

Figure 4-2. Normal Distribution

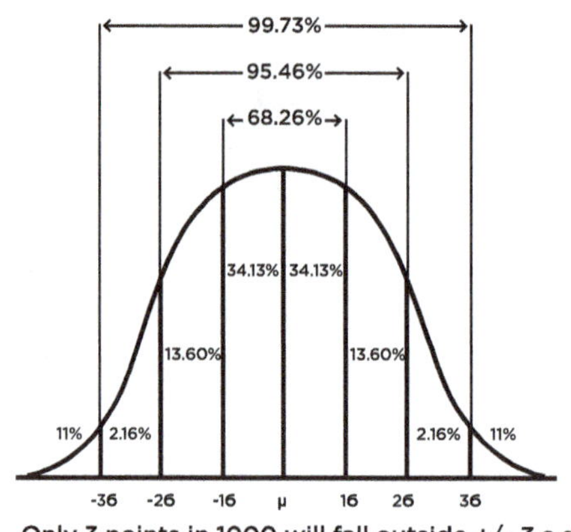

Only 3 points in 1000 will fall outside +/- 3 s.d.

Source: Potts A. Use of Statistics in Infection Prevention. In: Grota P, ed. *APIC Text of Infection Control and Epidemiology*, 4th edition. Washington, DC: Association for Professionals in Infection Control and Epidemiology, 2014.

Reference: *APIC Text*, 4th edition, Chapter 13 - Use of Statistics in Infection Prevention

15. (A) Fisher's exact

Rationale: Fisher's exact test is a statistical significance test used in the analysis of contingency tables. Although in practice it is employed when sample sizes are small, it is valid for all sample sizes.

Reference: *APIC Text*, 4th edition, Chapter 13 - Use of Statistics in Infection Prevention

16. (C) Eliminate natural variation

Rationale: SPC is a method of quality control that uses statistical methods and is an essential component of quality assurance and performance improvement. The principles of statistical process control are used to monitor both processes and outcomes in a systematic and statistically valid manner. Control charts can assist in determining special-cause or common-cause variations, which may be helpful for early detection of abnormal events.

Reference: *APIC Text*, 4th edition, Chapter 14 - Process Control Charts

NOTES

17. **(D) 39 infections per 1,000 patient days**

Rationale: The incidence rate is the number of new cases per population at risk in a given time period. When the denominator is the sum of the person-time of the at-risk population, it is also known as the incidence density rate or person-time incidence rate.

The incidence-density rate for this scenario is 9 (new cases of MRSA) ÷ 230 (total number of patient days) x 1,000 = 39.13 (round to 39) infections per 1,000 patient days.

Reference: *APIC Text*, 4th edition, Chapter 13 - Use of Statistics in Infection Prevention

18. **(B) An expected number of cases occurs each year in a given geographical area**

Rationale: The term "endemic" refers to the usual incidence of a given disease within a geographical area during a specified time period.

Reference: *APIC Text*, 4th edition, Chapter 10 - General Principles of Epidemiology

19. **(D) Several countries or continents are involved**

Rationale: The term "pandemic" refers to an epidemic of disease spread over a wide geographical area across countries or continents.

Reference: *APIC Text*, 4th edition, Chapter 10 - General Principles of Epidemiology

20. **(D) The number of true negatives divided by the total number of persons without disease, times 100**

Rationale: Sensitivity (also called the true positive rate) measures the proportion of actual positives that are correctly identified as such (e.g., the percentage of sick people who are correctly identified as having the condition). Specificity (sometimes called the true negative rate) measures the proportion of negatives that are correctly identified as such (e.g., the percentage of healthy people who are correctly identified as not having the condition).

Specificity = True negatives ÷ True negatives + False positives

Reference: *APIC Text*, 4th edition, Chapter 13 - Use of Statistics in Infection Prevention

21. **(B) Standard deviation**

Rationale: Measures of dispersion describe the degree of variation or dispersion of values in a population or in a sample. Measures of dispersion are a type of descriptive statistic. Measures of dispersion include the range, deviation, standard deviation, and variance. Standard deviation is a measure of dispersion of the raw scores that reflects the variability in values around the mean. The standard deviation indicates how small the variability is (i.e., the spread) among observations. If the variability is small, all the values are close to the mean. If it is large, the values are not close to the mean.

Reference: *APIC Text*, 4th edition, Chapter 13 - Use of Statistics in Infection Prevention

NOTES

22. (C) 0.95

Rationale: Standard deviation is a measure of dispersion of the raw scores that reflects the variability in values around the mean. The significance of the standard deviation is that with normal (bell-shaped) distributions, the following empirical rules for the normal curve apply (see Figure 4-2):

- The interval from one standard deviation below the mean to one standard deviation above the mean contains approximately 68 percent of the measurements.
- The interval from two standard deviations below the mean to two standard deviations above the mean contains approximately 95 percent of the measurements.
- The interval from three standard deviations below the mean to three standard deviations above the mean contains approximately 99.7 percent (or approximately all) of the measurements.

Reference: *APIC Text*, 4th edition, Chapter 13 - Use of Statistics in Infection Prevention

23. (A) Make no assumption about variance in the populations

Rationale: Nonparametric data make no assumption about the distribution of the population values and can be used with discrete data (e.g., infection, no infection), nominal and ordinal data, and interval data. The main advantage of nonparametric methods is that the assumptions of normality are not required.

Reference: *APIC Text*, 4th edition, Chapter 13 - Use of Statistics in Infection Prevention

24. (C) r = 0.603

Rationale: Correlation is a statistical technique that shows whether pairs of variables are related. Correlation calculates a value, *r*, that measures the degree (strength) of the relationship. The calculated values can range between +1 and -1. The closer r is to 31, the stronger the relationship. A positive correlation exists when one variable increases and causes the other to increase as well (e.g., the longer a urinary catheter is in place, the greater the risk of developing a urinary tract infection). A negative correlation occurs when one variable increases and causes the other to decrease (e.g., increased hand washing results in fewer infections). The association between two variables decreases as *r* approaches 0 (with a value of 0, there is no correlation).

Reference: *APIC Text*, 4th edition, Chapter 13 - Use of Statistics in Infection Prevention

25. (D) Non-ill members of the health club matched for age and sex

Rationale: Case-control studies begin with the identification of persons who have the outcome of interest. Then a control group of individuals without the outcome is selected for comparison. The selection of an appropriate control group is critical in that control patients must not only have the outcome of interest but also should be similar to the cases in the potential for exposure during the period of risk being evaluated. Controls are matched to cases on one or more attributes (i.e. age, gender, smoking status, etc.). Each case/control pair then has identical values on the matching factors. Therefore, the most appropriate controls would be non-ill members of the health club.

Reference: *APIC Text*, 4th edition, Chapter 20 - Research Study Design

NOTES

26. (C) Eliminate outliers

Rationale: A common use of statistics is hypothesis testing. It is a statement of expected results. Hypothesis testing uses the distribution of a known area in the normal curve. It estimates the likelihood (probability) that a result did not occur by chance.

Steps to hypothesis testing include:

- State the research question
- Specify the null and alternative hypotheses
- Calculate test statistic
- Compute probability of test statistic or rejection region
- State conclusions

Outliers are observations that deviate from all others significantly. They may occur by accident or they may be results of measurement errors. Analysis and dealing with outliers is an important component of statistical analysis. Sometimes careful analysis of outliers, their removal, or weighting down can change the conclusions considerably. Outliers should be investigated to determine the optimal method of analysis.

Reference: *APIC Text*, 4th edition, Chapter 13 - Use of Statistics in Infection Prevention

27. (C) -1 to 1

Rationale: Correlation is used to calculate the direction and magnitude of a relationship between two variables. Correlation calculates a value, *r*, that measures the degree of the relationship. The calculated values can range between +1 and -1. The closer *r* is to ±1, the stronger the relationship. A positive correlation exists when one variable increases and causes the other to increase as well (e.g., the longer a urinary catheter is in place, the greater the risk of developing a urinary tract infection). A negative correlation occurs when one variable increases and causes the other to decrease (e.g., increased hand washing results in fewer infections). The association between two variables decreases as *r* approaches 0 (with a value of 0, there is no correlation).

Reference: *APIC Text*, 4th edition, Chapter 13 - Use of Statistics in Infection Prevention

28. (A) Relatively flat

Rationale: Two terms are used to describe the shape of a frequency distribution: "skewness" and "kurtosis."

Kurtosis refers to how flat or peaked a curve is (see Figure 4-3):

- Mesokurtic is a typical bell-shaped curve or normal distribution.
- Leptokurtic is the more peaked curve.
- Platykurtic is the flatter curve.

Statistical packages calculate kurtosis. A value of 0 indicates mesokurtosis, positive numbers indicate leptokurtosis, and negative numbers indicate platykurtosis.

NOTES

Figure 4-3. General forms of kurtosis

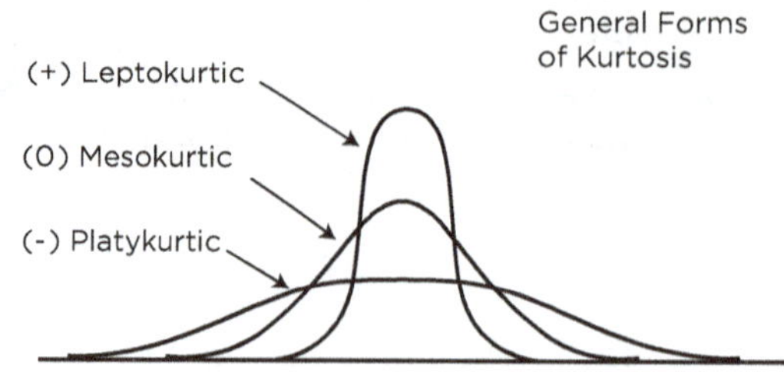

Source: Potts A. Use of Statistics in Infection Prevention. In: Grota P, ed. *APIC Text of Infection Control and Epidemiology*, 4th edition. Washington, DC: Association for Professionals in Infection Control and Epidemiology, 2014.

Reference: *APIC Text*, 4th edition, Chapter 13 - Use of Statistics in Infection Prevention

29. **A Risk**

Rationale: In epidemiology, risk is defined as the probability that an event will occur (e.g., that an individual will become ill or die within a stated period of time or age).

Reference: *APIC Text*, 4th edition, Chapter 13 - Use of Statistics in Infection Prevention

30. **B Arranged in rows and columns**

Rationale: A table is an organized set of data elements (values) that uses a model of vertical columns (which are identified by their name) and horizontal rows. The cell is the unit where a row and column intersect. A table has a specified number of columns, but can have any number of rows. Each row is identified by the values appearing in a particular column subset that has been identified as a unique key index.

Reference: *APIC Text*, 4th edition, Chapter 13 - Use of Statistics in Infection Prevention

31. **C 11**

Rationale: The mode represents the observation(s) that occur(s) most frequently in a data set and determines the height and shape of a curve. Data sets may have more than one mode and can be bimodal or multimodal. Small data sets may be nonmodal (e.g., there are no repeated values). The mode is most useful for describing qualitative data and is used for nominal data and bimodal distributions. It is the least stable of the three measures of central tendency. The mode for this set of numbers is 11, as it occurs most frequently.

Reference: *APIC Text*, 4th edition, Chapter 13 - Use of Statistics in Infection Prevention

NOTES

32. (B) Power is increased

Rationale: The power of a test is its ability to detect a specified difference (e.g., the probability of rejecting the null hypothesis when it is false). The power of a hypothesis test is affected by three factors:

1. Sample size (n). In general, the greater the sample size, the greater the power of the test.
2. Significance level (α). The higher the significance level, the higher the power of the test.
3. The "true" value of the parameter being tested. The greater the difference between the "true" value of a parameter and the value specified in the null hypothesis, the greater the power of the test. That is, the greater the effect size, the greater the power of the test.

Reference: *APIC Text*, 4th edition, Chapter 13 - Use of Statistics in Infection Prevention

33. (D) Confounding variable

Rationale: A confounding variable is a variable that has an important confounding effect on the result but is not among the variables being studied. It can suggest a false relationship between variables, or it can hide a relationship that exists.

Reference: *APIC Text*, 4th edition, Chapter 13 - Use of Statistics in Infection Prevention

34. (D) 1, 2, 4

Rationale: If the distribution (spread) of the values is even on both sides of the mean (both halves are equal), it is a normal distribution (see Figure 6-2). Properties of a normal distribution include:

- Forms a symmetric bell-shaped curve
- 50 percent of the scores lie above and 50 percent below the midpoint of the distribution
- The population clusters around a central point and then trails off symmetrically in both directions with fewer and fewer large and small individuals at the upper and lower ends, respectively
- Mean, median, and mode are located at the midpoint of the x axis

Reference: *APIC Text*, 4th edition, Chapter 13 - Use of Statistics in Infection Prevention

NOTES

35. (D) The onset of disease must precede exposure to the causal factor

Rationale: The criteria for causality are known as Hill's criteria and use epidemiological methods to determine whether a factor is causal for a given disease. Hill's criteria for causation are as follows:

1. *Strength of association:* The incidence of disease should be higher in those who are exposed to the factor under consideration than in those who are not exposed; that is, the stronger the association between an exposure and a disease, the more likely the exposure is to be causal. For example, lung cancer is common in those who smoke.
2. *Consistency:* This means that the association should be observed in numerous studies, preferably by different researchers using different research methodologies.
3. *Specificity:* Refers to an association between one factor and one disease, and this association is more likely to be causal. This criterion also refers to the extent to which the occurrence of one factor can be used to predict the occurrence of another (disease). In reality, such a one-to-one relationship is rare due to the multifactorial causes of most diseases and because, sometimes, the same factor(s) can cause more than one disease.
4. *Temporality:* This must also be addressed when determining cause of disease. Essentially, exposure to the hypothesized causal factor must precede the onset of disease.
5. *Biological gradient:* The biological gradient is a dose-response relationship between increased exposure to a factor and increased likelihood of disease. For example, the longer one smokes, the more likely one is to develop lung cancer. If the association demonstrates a biological gradient between the factor (exposure) and effect (disease), the relationship is more likely to be causal.
6. *Plausibility:* The association in question should also be biologically plausible in light of current knowledge. This criterion may be the most elusive and variable of the nine. Because biological knowledge is ever expanding, lack of biological plausibility does not necessarily disprove a theoretical association.
7. *Coherence:* There should be coherence between known information about the biological spectrum of the disease and the associated factor, that is, the association should be in accordance with other facts known about the natural history of the disease.
8. *Analogy:* Associations derived from experiments add considerable weight to evidence supporting causal associations. These experiments can be animal model studies or clinical trials; however, although animal models may be helpful, many diseases do not manifest the same way in animals and humans.
9. Finally, if similar associations have been shown to be causal, by analogy the association is more likely to be causal. Determining causality may also help to determine at which points the natural history of a disease may be interrupted, so that prevention and control efforts are effective. It can also add information on the natural history of a disease.

Reference: *APIC Text*, 4th edition, Chapter 10 - General Principles of Epidemiology

NOTES

36. (A) 1, 3

Rationale: Graphic or pictorial statistics present the numerical data that have been collected in graphs or charts, creating a picture of the data. A frequency polygon (see Figure 4-4) is a graph of a frequency distribution with values of the variable on the x axis and the number of observations on the y axis; data points are plotted at the midpoints of the intervals and are connected with a straight line.

Figure 4-4. Frequency Polygon

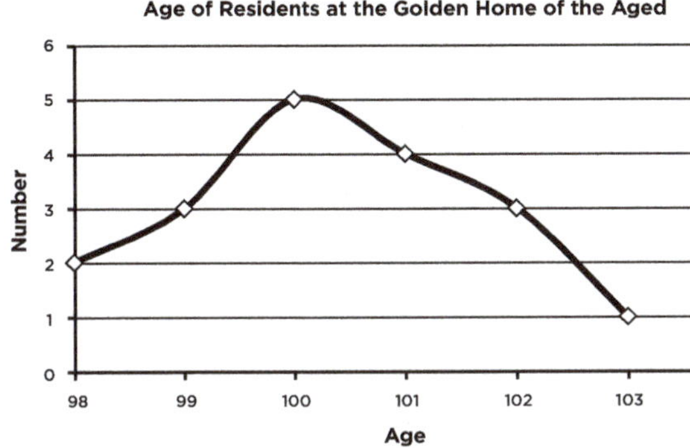

Source: Potts A. Use of Statistics in Infection Prevention. In: Grota P, ed. *APIC Text of Infection Control and Epidemiology*, 4th edition. Washington, DC: Association for Professionals in Infection Control and Epidemiology, 2014.

Reference: *APIC Text*, 4th edition, Chapter 10 - General Principles of Epidemiology

37. (A) Tracking high-risk, high-volume procedures and potentially preventable healthcare-associated infections (HAIs)

Rationale: Targeted surveillance is one method used for HAI surveillance. Targeted surveillance focuses on particular units, invasive procedures, infections related to medical devices, and organisms of epidemiological significance.

Reference: *APIC Text*, 4th edition, Chapter 11 - Surveillance

38. (D) The number of hand hygiene episodes performed by personnel divided by the number of hand hygiene opportunities by ward or service

Rationale: The CDC guideline and the Joint Commission require that healthcare personnel adherence to recommended hand hygiene policies be monitored and that healthcare personnel be provided with information about their performance. Acceptable methods for measuring hand hygiene adherence include:

- Periodically conduct an observational study to determine the rate of adherence (number of hand hygiene episodes performed/number of hand hygiene opportunities) by ward or service. In addition to monitoring the rate of adherence, facilities may also assess the quality of hand hygiene adherence (time spent per hand hygiene episode, whether soap was used, etc.)
- Monitor the volume of specific hand hygiene products (e.g., soap, hand rub, hand lotion) used per 1000 patient days
- Monitor adherence to artificial fingernail policies

Reference: Boyce JM, Pittet D. Guideline for hand hygiene in health-care settings. *Morbid Mortal Weekly Rev.* 2002 October 25; 51(RR1):1-44. Available at: http://www.cdc.gov/mmwr/PDF/rr/rr5116.pdf.

NOTES

39. (B) Human herpesvirus 8

Rationale: Kaposi's sarcoma is a tumor caused by human herpesvirus 8 (HHV8, also known as Kaposi's sarcoma-associated herpesvirus or KSHV). Kaposi's sarcoma (KS) is a systemic disease that can present with cutaneous lesions with or without internal involvement. KS lesions are nodules or blotches that may be red, purple, brown, or black and are usually papular. They are typically found on the skin, but spread elsewhere is common, especially the mouth, gastrointestinal tract and respiratory tract. Growth can range from very slow to explosively fast and is associated with significant mortality and morbidit.

References: *APIC Text*, 4th edition, Chapter 80 - Herpes Virus; Kaposi Sarcoma. In: Heymann D, ed. *Control of Communicable Diseases Manual*, 19th edition. Washington, DC: American Public Health Association, 2008.

40. (C) Up to 50 percent of people in endemic areas have been exposed to *Coccidioides* spores

Rationale: Coccidioidomycosis is a reemerging infectious disease caused by inhalation of airborne spores of the soil fungus *Coccidioides immitis* or *C. posadasii. Coccidioides* spp. are native to arid and desert areas in North America (California, Arizona, Texas, Utah, Nevada, New Mexico, and northern parts of Mexico), Central America, and South America. *Coccidioides* spp. are found in lower elevation areas that receive less than 20 inches of rain per year and have warm, sandy soil. They are usually found 4 to 12 inches below the surface. Among persons living in coccidioidomycosis-endemic areas, approximately 10 to 50 percent have been exposed to *Coccidioides* spp.

References: *APIC Text*, 4th edition, Chapter 78 - Fungi; Coccidioidomycosis. In: Heymann D, ed. *Control of Communicable Diseases Manual*, 19th edition. Washington, DC: American Public Health Association, 2008.

41. (C) Population attributable risk percent

Rationale: Attributable risk percent (ARP) is a calculation that can be derived from the attributable risk, which is the difference in rate of a condition between an exposed population and an unexposed population. ARP gives the proportion of cases attributable (and avoidable) to this exposure in relation to all cases.

It can be calculated as: (relative risk - 1) ÷ relative risk

Reference: *APIC Text*, 4th edition, Chapter 13 - Use of Statistics in Infection Prevention

42. (B) Size of the study

Rationale: The precision of the relative risk is related to the power of a study. Statistical power is affected chiefly by the size of the effect and the size of the sample used to detect it.

Reference: *APIC Text*, 4th edition, Chapter 13 - Use of Statistics in Infection Prevention

43. (D) Domestic poultry

Rationale: Highly pathogenic avian influenza A (H5N1) virus—referred to as HPAI H5N1 and sometimes shortened to H5N1—is a virus that occurs mainly in birds, especially domestic poultry. H5N1 is highly contagious among birds and can be deadly to them. Though relatively rare, sporadic human infections with this virus have occurred and have caused serious illness and death.

References: *APIC Text*, 4th edition, Chapter 82 - Influenza; Influenza. In: Heymann D, ed. *Control of Communicable Diseases Manual*, 19th edition. Washington, DC: American Public Health Association, 2008.

NOTES

44. C Causal web

Rationale: Causation is an essential concept in epidemiology. The web of causation refers to the interrelationship of multiple factors that contribute to the occurrence of a disease.

Reference: *APIC Text*, 4th edition, Chapter 10 - General Principles of Epidemiology

45. D The positive predictive value of a diagnostic test is lowered

Rationale: The measures of sensitivity and specificity describe how well the proposed screening test performs against a "gold standard" test. Sensitivity and specificity are independent of prevalence of disease. The positive predictive value (PPV) describes the probability of having the disease given a positive screening test result in the screened population. The negative predictive value (NPV) describes the probability of not having the disease given a negative screening test result in the screened population. PPV and NPV are disease prevalence dependent. Generally a higher prevalence will increase the PPV and decrease the NPV.

Reference: *APIC Text*, 4th edition, Chapter 13 - Use of Statistics in Infection Prevention

46. C Noroviruses are the most common cause of epidemic gastroenteritis worldwide

Rationale: Noroviruses (NoVs) are the most common cause of epidemic gastroenteritis worldwide and the leading cause of foodborne outbreaks in the United States. Severe disease associated with NoV occurs most frequently among older adults, young children, and immunocompromised patients. NoV outbreaks occur year round, but activity increases in the United States during the winter months; 80 percent of reported outbreaks occur during November-April. Most NoV outbreaks are attributed to genotype GII.4, which evolves rapidly over time.

References: *APIC Text*, 4th edition, Chapter 79A - Diarrheal Diseases: Viral; Gastroenteritis, Acute Viral. In: Heymann D, ed. *Control of Communicable Diseases Manual*, 19th edition. Washington, DC: American Public Health Association, 2008.

47. A 0.21

Rationale: Attributable risk (AR) is the difference in rate of a condition between an exposed population and an unexposed population. The formula for attributable risk is as follows: IE - IU = AR, where IE = incidence in exposed and IU = incidence in unexposed.

IE is calculated by dividing the number of exposed people who get the disease by the total number who are exposed. Similarly, the IU is calculated by dividing the number of unexposed people who get the disease by the total number who are not expose.

In this table, AR = 0.77 - 0.56 = 0.21

Reference: *APIC Text*, 4th edition, Chapter 13 - Use of Statistics in Infection Prevention

NOTES

48. (A) IBD is associated with increased morbidity and mortality associated with CDI

Rationale: As CDI has become more common, CDI in individuals with IBD has become a focus of increased attention. IBD has been identified as an independent risk factor for *C. difficile* colonization and disease; patients with IBD have increased severity of illness and higher death rates from CDI.

References: *APIC Text*, 4th edition, Chapter 72 - *Clostridium difficile* Infection and Pseudomembranous Colitis; Diarrhea, Acute. In: Heymann D, ed. *Control of Communicable Diseases Manual*, 19th edition. Washington, DC: American Public Health Association, 2008.

49. (C) Screening for TB with chest X-ray may be the most cost-effective approach

Rationale: TB incidence is higher in homeless populations than in the general population. Molecular epidemiology studies indicate that most TB cases occurring in the homeless are primary infections. The spread of TB among the homeless is related to recent person-to-person transmission, which produces outbreaks with large clusters in which more than 50 percent of persons are infected. Homeless shelters are major sites of transmission. Screening by chest radiography either periodically in all residents or specifically in symptomatic persons (e.g., chronic coughers) appears to be the most cost-effective approach for TB detection and diagnosis in this population.

Reference: *APIC Text*, 4th edition, Chapter 95 - Tuberculosis and Other Mycobacteria

50. (B) 2.85

Rationale: The odds ratio is the probability of having a particular risk factor if a condition or disease is present divided by the probability of having the risk factor if the disease or condition is not present. It is used for all types of studies with nominal data, but it is used mostly for retrospective and cross-sectional studies. The odds ratio is sometimes called the cross-product ratio or relative odds.

In a 2 x 2 table, the odds ration is calculated as = ad ÷ bc.

Body Mass Index (BMI)	Controls	Cases
BMI 30 or higher	A	B
BMI less than 25	C	D

In this scenario, the odds ration is calculated as (55 x 70) ÷ (30 x 45) = 2.85

Reference: *APIC Text*, 4th edition, Chapter 13 - Use of Statistics in Infection Prevention

Chapter 5
PREVENTING/CONTROLLING THE TRANSMISSION OF INFECTIOUS AGENTS

The CIC® exam will have a total of twenty-five (25) questions on Preventing/Controlling the Transmission of Infectious Agents. The content will test knowledge of the following:

A. Develop evidence-based/informed infection prevention and control policies and procedures

B. Collaborate with relevant groups and agencies in planning community/facility responses to biologic threats and disasters (e.g., public health, anthrax, influenza)

C. Identify and implement infection prevention and control strategies related to:

1. Hand hygiene
2. Cleaning, disinfection, and sterilization
3. Wherever healthcare is provided (e.g., patient care units, operating room, ambulatory care center, home health, pre-hospital care)
4. Infection risks associated with therapeutic and diagnostic procedures and devices (e.g., dialysis, angiography, bronchoscopy, endoscopy, intravascular devices, urinary drainage catheter)
5. Recall of potentially contaminated equipment, food, medications, and supplies
6. Transmission-based Precautions
7. Appropriate selection, use, and disposal of Personal Protective Equipment
8. Patient placement, transfer, and discharge
9. Environmental pathogens (e.g., Legionella, Aspergillus)
10. Use of patient care products and medical equipment
11. Immunization programs for patients

NOTES

NOTES

12. The influx of patients with known/suspected communicable diseases (e.g., bioterrorism, emerging infectious diseases, syndromic surveillance)
13. Principles of safe injection practices (e.g., parenteral medication administration, single use of syringes and needles, appropriate use of single and multi-dose vials)
14. Identifying, implementing and evaluating elements of Standard Precautions/Routine Practices (e.g., respiratory hygiene/cough etiquette)
15. Antimicrobial stewardship

KEY CONCEPTS

- Understanding the modes of transmission of infectious organisms and the appropriate application of basic principles of infection prevention and control is vital to the success of an infection control program.
- Healthcare-associated infections (HAIs) are an important measure of quality, and infection preventionists (IPs) play a critical role by leading initiatives to prevent them. There is growing consensus that our ultimate goal should be the elimination of HAIs.
- Evidence-based recommendations provide a framework for healthcare institutions to prioritize and implement strategies to reduce infection risk.
- Compliance with currently recommended evidence-based practices can result in a dramatic reduction in infection rates.
- Eliminating HAIs requires clear goals, committed leadership, access to resources, effective personnel management, and ongoing vigilance.

RESOURCES FOR STUDY

Nearly all questions on Preventing/Controlling the Transmission of Infectious Agents are based on chapters in the primary references, but secondary references may be useful to help clarify more detailed issues.

NOTES

Primary Reference:

1. Grota P, ed. *APIC Text of Infection Control and Epidemiology*, 4th edition. Washington, DC: Association for Professionals in Infection Control and Epidemiology, 2014. Also available online at http://text.apic.org [subscription required].

Notable Chapters:

1	Infection Prevention and Control Programs
4	Accrediting and Regulatory Agencies
5	Infection Prevention and Behavioral Interventions
7	Product Evaluation
26	Antimicrobials and Resistance
27	Hand Hygiene
28	Standard Precautions
29	Isolation Precautions (Transmission-based Precautions)
30	Aseptic Technique
31	Cleaning, Disinfection, and Sterilization
32	Reprocessing Single-use Devices
33	Urinary Tract Infection
34	Intravascular Device Infections
35	Infections in Indwelling Medical Devices
36	Pneumonia
37	Surgical Site Infection
38	Burns
39	Dialysis
40	Geriatrics
41	Neonates
42	Pediatrics
43	Perinatal Care

NOTES

44 Infection Prevention in Oncology and other Immunocompromised Patients

45 Solid Organ Transplantation

46 Hematopoietic Stem Cell Transplantation

47 Nutrition and Immune Function

48 Ambulatory Care

49 Behavioral Health

50 Cardiac Catheterization and Electrophysiology

51 Correctional Facilities

52 Child Care Services

53 Dental Services

54 Emergency and Other Pre-Hospital Medical Services

55 Endoscopy

56 Home Care

57 Hospice and Palliative Care

58 Imaging Services and Radiation Oncology

59 Intensive Care

60 Interventional Radiology

61 Long-term Care

62 Long-term Acute Care

63 Ophthalmology Services

64 Ambulatory Surgery Centers

65 Postmortem Care

66 Rehabilitation Services

67 Respiratory Care Services

68 Surgical Services

69 Xenotransplantation

NOTES

78 Fungi

84 Legionella pneumophila

114 Heating, Ventilation, and Air Conditioning

115 Water Systems Issues and Prevention of Waterborne Infectious Diseases in Healthcare Facilities

106 Sterile Processing

116 Construction and Renovation

117 Public Health

119 Emergency Management

120 Infectious Disease Disasters: Bioterrorism, Emerging Infections, and Pandemics

122 Animals Visiting in Healthcare Facilities

123 Body Piercing, Tattoos, and Electrolysis

2. Brooks K. *Ready Reference for Microbes*, 3rd edition. Washington, DC: Association for Professionals in Infection Control and Epidemiology, 2012.

3. Heymann D, ed. *Control of Communicable Diseases Manual*, 19th edition. Washington, DC: American Public Health Association, 2008.

4. Kulich P, Taylor D, eds. *The Infection Preventionist's Guide to the Lab*. Washington, DC: Association for Professionals in Infection Control and Epidemiology, 2012.

Secondary Reference:

1. Current Recommendations of the Advisory Committee on Immunization Practices (ACIP).

2. Current guidelines, standards, and recommendations from CDC, APIC, SHEA, and Public Health Agency of Canada.

3. Pickering, Larry K, ed. *Red Book*, 29th ed., Elk Grove Village, IL: American Academy of Pediatrics; 2012.

NOTES

PRACTICE QUESTIONS

1. A woman in active labor with confirmed influenza has been admitted to an acute care facility. Recommendations for preventing influenza transmission between hospitalized infected mothers and their infants include:

1) Keep the isolette at least 3 feet away from the mother when she is not interacting with the baby
2) Temporarily separate the mother from her baby following delivery during the hospital stay
3) All feedings should be provided by a healthy caregiver if possible
4) The baby should receive formula during the 5-day period following the mother's symptom onset

a. 1, 2

b. 2, 3

c. 3, 4

d. 1, 4

2. Most healthcare-associated pathogens are transmitted from patient to patient via:

a. Improper isolation practices

b. Inadequate sterilization of medical instruments

c. Hands of healthcare personnel

d. Ineffective disinfection of medical devices

3. A patient is admitted with pruritic lesions on the hands, webs of fingers, wrists, extensor surfaces of elbows and knees, and the outer surfaces of the feet, armpits, buttocks, and waist. What type of isolation does this person require?

a. Contact

b. Droplet

c. Airborne

d. No isolation required

NOTES

4. An autopsy is ordered on a patient who was diagnosed with tuberculosis (TB). Which of the following statements is correct regarding postmortem care of a deceased TB patient?

- **a.** Autopsy rooms should be at positive pressure with respect to adjacent areas, and room air must be exhausted directly outside
- **b.** An oscillating autopsy saw should be used to reduce the infectious aerosols
- **c.** An approved mask is necessary for respiratory protection
- **d.** Standard Precautions are sufficient because *Mycobacterium tuberculosis* needs a living host to survive

5. Which of the following patients is not at high risk for a healthcare-associated fungal infection?

- **a.** Burn patient
- **b.** Premature baby in the Neonatal Intensive Care Unit
- **c.** Bone marrow transplant patient
- **d.** Patient who underwent joint replacement surgery

6. The infection preventionist (IP) receives a call from a nurse who is scheduling a patient for surgery at her ambulatory surgery center. The nurse tells the IP that the patient is colonized with methicillin-resistant *Staphylococcus aureus* (MRSA). Which of the following best describes colonization?

- **a.** The presentation of clinical signs of illness or inflammation
- **b.** An acute bacterial disease caused by an obligate anaerobic, non-spore-forming rod
- **c.** The permanent presence of bacteria that is part of the normal flora
- **d.** The presence of microorganisms without the signs/ symptoms of an infection

7. What type of respiratory protection (mask) is recommended for immune and nonimmune healthcare personnel when caring for a patient with smallpox?

- **a.** Surgical mask
- **b.** Exam mask
- **c.** N95 or higher level respirator
- **d.** Procedure mask

NOTES

8. An outbreak of aspergillosis is suspected after several oncology patients are identified with positive cultures. The IP suspects a heating, ventilation, and air conditioning (HVAC) malfunction and begins an outbreak investigation. The IP has been asked to make recommendations for environmental cultures. All of the following needs to be considered *except*:

- **a.** Identifying the purpose of culturing and appropriate methods beforehand
- **b.** Meeting with the facility legal staff to discuss notification of the patients
- **c.** Anticipating decisions and planned actions to results of culturing before undertaking the process
- **d.** Determining whether there are existing standards to interpret results

9. The U.S. Phamacopoeia (USP) recommends that multidose vials be disposed of:

- **a.** 14 days after opening
- **b.** 30 days after opening
- **c.** 28 days after opening
- **d.** When all the medication has been used

10. The policy for therapy animals in healthcare facilities should include all of the following *except*:

- **a.** Hand hygiene must be performed after contact with the animal
- **b.** Animal must be bathed within 24 hours prior to visiting the healthcare facility
- **c.** Animals must be healthy and current with immunizations
- **d.** Small animals are never allowed to sit on a patient's bed

NOTES

11. An IP has been asked to provide infection prevention consultation to a long-term care facility (LTCF). As a part of this consultation, she checks to make sure which of the following program components are in place:

1) Decolonizing residents with MRSA
2) Establishing an antimicrobial stewardship program
3) Implementing an annual influenza vaccination program
4) Collecting environmental cultures of high-touch areas

a. 1, 2
b. 2, 3
c. 3, 4
d. 1, 4

12. A hospital is beginning a major construction project. The IP has been asked to join the planning team to assist with the development of the Infection Control Risk Assessment (IRCA) for the project. What is the purpose of the ICRA?

a. Develop and oversee the construction project schedule
b. Minimize infectious hazards for patients and healthcare personnel
c. Provide direction for level three and four projects only
d. Coordinate systems start-ups

13. An "antibiotic time out" occurs:

a. Daily
b. Weekly
c. Within 24 to 48 hours of culture results being available
d. Within 96 hours of culture results being available

14. Of the following methods of disinfection and sterilization, which will kill all organisms, including all bacterial spores?

1) Pasteurization
2) Ortho-phthalaldehyde
3) Steam sterilization
4) Ethylene oxide

a. 1, 2
b. 2, 3
c. 1, 3
d. 3, 4

NOTES

15. Hydrogen peroxide vapor (HPV) has been shown to be effective for decontamination of patient rooms and is known to kill spores and other microbes. Despite its benefits, there are some drawbacks to using HPV. Which of the following could be a major drawback to using HPV to clean patient rooms?

a. It is effective in decontaminating surfaces but not equipment

b. It leaves a residue that, over time, can damage equipment in the room

c. It lengthens room turnover because it takes a prolonged period of time to complete room treatment

d. It is most effective for areas closer to the unit and less effective around the edges of the room

16. While making rounds in one of the Intensive Care Units, the IP observes a patient who has just been intubated and is on a ventilator. He notes that the patient is in a supine position. Which of the following positions should he recommend to the nurse in order to be compliant with a pneumonia prevention bundle?

a. The patient should be turned to his side to facilitate drainage of secretions

b. The patient should be placed in reverse Trendelenburg position

c. The patient's head of the bed should be elevated to an angle of 30 to 45 degrees

d. The patient should sit upright at a 60 to 75 degree angle

17. A patient with bacterial meningitis due to *Neisseria meningitidis* requires what type of Transmission-based Precautions?

a. Contact Precautions

b. Standard Precautions

c. Droplet Precautions

d. Airborne Precautions

NOTES

18. Which federal agencies in the United States have published regulations pertaining to infection and medical or regulated waste?

1) U.S. Environmental Protection Agency (EPA)
2) U.S. Occupational Safety and Health Administration (OSHA)
3) U.S. Food and Drug Administration (FDA)
4) U.S. Department of Transportation (DOT)

a. 1, 2, 3
b. 2, 3, 4
c. 1, 2, 4
d. 1, 3, 4

19. Exposure to contaminated healthcare waste does not necessarily result in infection. The following factors must be present for contaminated waste to be capable of causing infection:

1) Dose and host susceptibility
2) Portal of entry
3) Portal of exit
4) Presence and virulence of a pathogen

a. 1, 3, 4
b. 1, 2, 4
c. 2, 3, 4
d. 1, 2, 3

20. Which of the following statements is *true* regarding the storage of sterilized items in the Sterile Processing Department?

1) Sterilized items should be stored on a shelf with a solid bottom
2) Sterilized items should be stored in high traffic areas for easy access
3) Sterilized items should be stored in a room with positive air pressure
4) Sterilized items should be stored 8 to 10 inches from the floor

a. 1, 2, 3
b. 1, 3, 4
c. 2, 3, 4
d. 1, 2, 4

NOTES

21. Which of the following situations present the greatest risk for the transmission of pathogens via healthcare personnel hands?

1) Unit secretary with artificial nails
2) Environmental services worker with unchipped nail polish
3) Nurse practitioner with artificial nails
4) Registered nurse (RN) with chipped nail polish

a. 1, 2
b. 2, 3
c. 3, 4
d. 1, 4

22. Which of the following does *not* meet the requirements for an airborne isolation room?

a. Negative airflow isolation room (negative air pressure relative to the corridor)
b. At least 15 to 20 air exchanges per hour
c. Direct exhaust to the outside
d. Daily monitoring of the air pressure with visual indicators

23. According to the Centers for Disease Control and Prevention (CDC), central venous catheters (CVCs) should be replaced:

a. Every 72 to 96 hours
b. Every 7 days
c. After 1 month
d. If malfunctioning

24. The IP has been asked to join the Antimicrobial Stewardship Team at his facility. The IP reviews current recommendations and understands that effective strategies to curb antimicrobial resistance include all of the following *except*:

a. Formulary restriction
b. Administer antibiotics with overlapping activity
c. Automatic stop orders
d. Antimicrobial cycling

NOTES

25. When coordinating an active surveillance culture (ASC) plan, the IP should incorporate all of the following recommendations from the CDC *except*:

a. Provide additional personnel to obtain cultures and additional laboratory personnel to process the cultures

b. Monitor adherence to Standard Precautions

c. Provide a mechanism for communicating results to healthcare providers

d. Measure outcome to evaluate the effectiveness of the ASC program and Contact Precautions

26. Numerous outbreaks of infections have been attributed to unsafe injection practices. The IP designs an educational program to review safe injection practices with all nursing staff. These practices include:

1) Use single-dose vials whenever possible and avoid using multidose vials

2) Discard saline bags used for intravenous (IV) flushes for multiple patients after 1 hour

3) Enter medication vials with a new needle and syringe, even on the same patient

4) Use needles and syringes for only one patient

a. 1, 2, 3

b. 1, 3, 4

c. 1, 2, 4

d. 2, 3, 4

27. Respiratory hygiene/cough etiquette includes all but the following:

a. Covering the mouth and nose with the hands when coughing and sneezing

b. Offering a surgical mask to a coughing patient

c. Discarding used masks and tissues appropriately and performing hand hygiene

d. Posting signs in public areas in languages appropriate to the population served and educating healthcare staff, patients, and visitors

NOTES

28. Which type of isolation always requires a private room?

- **a.** Contact Precautions
- **b.** Standard Precautions
- **c.** Airborne Precautions
- **d.** Droplet Precautions

29. Which of the following is recommended for use when inserting a central venous catheter or a peripherally inserted catheter?

- **a.** A cap
- **b.** A clean gown
- **c.** Nonsterile gloves
- **d.** Small drapes

30. During an influenza outbreak in an acute care setting, all of the following measures should be implemented *except*:

- **a.** Perform rapid influenza virus testing of patients and personnel with recent onset of symptoms suggestive of influenza
- **b.** Implement Airborne Precautions for all patients with suspected or confirmed influenza
- **c.** Restrict staff movement from areas of the facility having outbreaks
- **d.** Restrict or limit elective medical and surgical admissions

31. Which of the following veins, when used for catheter insertion, has been associated with a lower incidence of central line-associated bloodstream infection (CLABSI)?

- **a.** Brachial
- **b.** Femoral
- **c.** Internal jugular
- **d.** Subclavian

32. All of the following methods for measuring hand hygiene adherence are acceptable *except*:

- **a.** Using electronic systems that allow continuous monitoring over time and automatic data download and analysis
- **b.** Monitoring the volume of gloves used per 1,000 patient days
- **c.** Monitoring adherence to artificial fingernail policies
- **d.** Periodically conducting an observational study to determine the rate of adherence (number of hand hygiene episodes

performed/number of hand hygiene opportunities) by ward or service

NOTES

33. Which of the following does *not* describe indirect contact transmission?

a. Mites from a scabies-infested patient

b. Equipment that is not cleaned, disinfected, or sterilized adequately between patients

c. Food and water supplies that are not prepared and maintained according to sanitation standards

d. Inadequate hand hygiene performed by a care provider

34. The CDC recommendations for decreasing CLABSI include all of the following *except*:

a. Educational programs

b. Routine replacement of catheters

c. The use of chlorhexidine for skin antisepsis

d. The use of maximal sterile barrier precautions

35. An RN is caring for a patient who presented to the Emergency Department with symptoms consistent with influenza. When caring for this patient, she should use which of the following types of precautions?

a. Standard Precautions

b. Standard and Droplet Precautions

c. Airborne Precautions

d. Droplet Precautions if influenza is confirmed

36. Coughing, sneezing, and talking are best associated with which form of disease transmission?

a. Airborne transmission

b. Direct contact transmission

c. Droplet transmission

d. Indirect contact transmission

NOTES

37. All of the following are true and should be communicated to patients before administering influenza vaccination *except*:

a. The vaccine is formulated annually to protect against influenza strains likely to circulate in the United States in the upcoming winter

b. Inactivated influenza vaccine contains noninfectious viral components and cannot cause influenza

c. Patients who received specific antivirals (i.e., acyclovir, famciclovir, or valacyclovir) within the preceding 24 hours should not receive influenza vaccination

d. Fever, malaise, myalgia, and other systemic symptoms can occur after vaccination

38. Elements of a ventilator-associated pneumonia (VAP) prevention bundle that have been suggested by the Institute for Healthcare Improvement (IHI) include all of the following practices *except*:

a. Elevation of the head of the bed

b. Weekly "sedation vacations" and assessment of readiness to extubate

c. Peptic ulcer disease prophylaxis

d. Deep venous thrombosis prophylaxis

39. Which of the following statements is *true* regarding CVCs?

a. Anticoagulant therapy can reduce the risk of catheter-related infection

b. Positioning at the insertion site minimizes catheter tip malposition

c. The CVC should be sutured in place

d. Stopcocks can increase the contamination rate

40. The CDC and WHO guidelines for hand hygiene recommend the use of an alcohol-based hand rub in all of the following situations *except*:

a. After direct patient contact

b. Before donning sterile glove

c. When hands are visibly soiled

d. When moving from a contaminated body site to a clean body site during patient care

NOTES

41. What percentage of Creutzfeldt-Jakob disease (CJD) cases are sporadic (vs. familial)?

- **a.** 65 percent
- **b.** 85 percent
- **c.** 15 percent
- **d.** 1 percent

42. Which of the following is *not* part of the bundle practices to reduce VAP?

- **a.** Keeping the head of the bed raised to 30 to 45 degrees elevation unless medically contraindicated
- **b.** Performing regular oral care on a ventilated patient
- **c.** Taking sedation "vacations" to assess patients' ability to breathe on their own
- **d.** Changing ventilator circuits every 48 hours

43. Which of the following bioterrorism agents has the highest fatality rate?

- **a.** Q fever
- **b.** Ricin
- **c.** Smallpox
- **d.** Severe acute respiratory syndrome (SARS)

44. The epidemiological triangle includes a model of dynamic interaction, where a change in any component alters the existing equilibrium. This model is particularly useful in the study of infectious disease. How can IPs use the epidemiological triangle during outbreak investigations?

- **a.** Examination of host factors such as increasing antimicrobial resistance as a result of antibiotic pressure
- **b.** Examination of host factors such as changes in immunity or diagnostic/therapeutic procedures within populations served
- **c.** Consideration of agent factors such as improving influenza vaccination rates for healthcare workers
- **d.** Consideration of agent factors such as a change in cleaning agents used in the hospital environment

NOTES

45. The IP should recommend all of the following prevention measures for a pregnant influenza-infected patient during delivery *except*:

a. During labor and delivery, the patient should wear a mask

b. The patient should be placed on Droplet Precautions

c. After the infant is born, the mother should wear a surgical mask and then practice hand hygiene before handling the baby

d. All persons who come within 3 feet of the mother should wear a surgical mask and practice hand hygiene before and after contact with the mother

46. An urban community is experiencing an outbreak of *Bordetella pertussis*. Several employees have contacted the IP at their healthcare facility for information on the tetanus, diphtheria, and pertussis (Tdap) vaccine. They question the need for the vaccine because they received it as a child. The IP should inform them that the Advisory Committee for Immunization Practices (ACIP) recommends that:

a. All adults aged 19 and older should receive at least one dose of Tdap

b. If the employee is pregnant, she should not receive the vaccine

c. All individuals must receive the vaccine every 10 years

d. Individuals who have had the disease do not need to receive the vaccine

47. Antimicrobial stewardship promotes the judicious use of antimicrobials to:

a. Increase antimicrobial selective pressure

b. Ensure that the right therapy is given to the right patient with the right dose and duration

c. Support the development of new antimicrobials

d. Contain healthcare costs

NOTES

48. What is not considered a risk factor for young girls to develop a urinary tract infection?

a. Bubble baths and prolonged soaking in the bathtub

b. Direction of wiping with toilet paper (from back to front)

c. Excessive holding of urine

d. Delayed bladder emptying

49. All of the following maternal infections would require withholding breast milk from the newborn *except*:

a. Breast abscess

b. Human immunodeficiency virus (HIV)

c. Untreated, active TB

d. Hepatitis C

50. While the IP performs environmental rounds in the Pharmacy, she observes a pharmacy technician using poor technique while working under the laminar airflow hood. She reviews the Pharmacy's policy for the frequency of training on aseptic technique for employees preparing sterile solutions. Which of the following is the best recommended frequency of infection prevention and control training for unlicensed employees who prepare sterile solutions?

a. Monthly until the employee can demonstrate proficiency by return demonstration

b. Every 6 months for 1 year after the date of hire

c. Annually on employee's anniversary date of hire with other training programs

d. Annually and whenever unacceptable technique is observed

NOTES

ANSWERS AND RATIONALES

1. **(B) 2, 3**

Rationale: Pregnant women and infants are at increased risk of hospitalization from influenza complications. Although it is well-recognized that the ideal setting for care of a healthy-term newborn while in the hospital is within the mother's room, newborns that become infected with influenza are at increased risk for severe complications. To reduce the risk of influenza in the newborn, CDC recommends that facilities consider temporarily separating the mother who is ill with suspected or confirmed influenza from her baby following delivery during the hospital stay. Throughout the course of temporary separation, all feedings should be provided by a healthy caregiver if possible. Mothers who intend to breastfeed should be encouraged to express their milk.

Reference: *APIC Text*, 4th edition, Chapter 82 - Influenza

Centers for Disease Control. Guidance for the Prevention and Control of Influenza in the Peri- and Postpartum Settings. Available at: https://www.cdc.gov/flu/professionals/infectioncontrol/peri-post-settings.htm. Accessed January 10, 2018.

2. **(C) Hands of healthcare personnel**

Rationale: According to literature, most healthcare-associated pathogens are transmitted from patient to patient via the hands of healthcare personnel. Hand hygiene, therefore, is the simplest and most effective, proven method to reduce the incidence of HAIs.

Reference: *APIC Text*, 4th edition, Chapter 8 - Legal Issues

3. **(A) Contact**

Rationale: Skin infestation by the mite *Sarcoptes scabiei* var. *hominis* is commonly known as scabies. Mites are transmitted through direct contact with infested persons; less frequently, transmission may occur through contact with clothing or bedding (fomites). Spread of the mite to a different part of the body can occur by manual transfer or scratching. Because of the high risk of transmission, the diagnosis of scabies should be considered in any patient with a pruritic cutaneous eruption, especially those involving the hands, wrist, and elbows. Patients in a hospital or other healthcare facility should be placed in Contact Precautions until 24 hours after treatment.

Reference: *APIC Text*, 4th edition, Chapter 99 - Parasites

4. **(C) An approved mask is necessary for respiratory protection**

Rationale: OSHA classifies performance of an autopsy on a known or suspected case of TB to be a high-hazard procedure requiring personnel to use approved respiratory protection. In areas where TB is prevalent and the health history is unknown, respiratory protection is prudent, especially for medical examiner's cases.

Reference: *APIC Text*, 4th edition, Chapter 65 - Postmortem Care

5. **(D) Patient who underwent joint replacement surgery**

Rationale: Fungi are increasingly being identified as healthcare-associated pathogens. Patients at high risk for healthcare-associated fungal infections include patients with leukemia, patients with solid tumors and leukopenia, bone marrow transplant patients, injection drug users, patients who have undergone intra-abdominal or cardiothoracic surgery, burn victims, and premature or low birth weight infants.

NOTES

Reference: *APIC Text*, 4th edition, Chapter 78 - Fungi

6. **(D) The presence of microorganisms without the signs/symptoms of an infection**

Rationale: The term colonization generally denotes the presence of a microorganism in the absence of symptoms or deep tissue invasion. Colonizing organisms (e.g., *N. gonorrhoeae* colonization of pharynx, *Salmonella* spp. colonization of stool, MRSA colonization of the nares, and yeast in the genital tract) may facilitate transmission to others or may lead to disease in the colonized individual during a disruptive situation (e.g., normal flora out of balance from antimicrobial treatment, invasive device, or wound).

Reference: *APIC Text*, 4th edition, Chapter 24 - Microbiology Basics

7. **(C) N95 or higher level respirator**

Rationale: Smallpox is a disease caused by variola viruses, members of the Orthopoxvirus genus. Smallpox was eradicated in the 1970s as the result of a massive worldwide immunization program. Because smallpox does not have an animal reservoir and has been eradicated from the human population, the only way that smallpox can occur is as a result of intentional exposure from a bioterrorism attack. A single confirmed case of smallpox would be a global health emergency. Routine smallpox vaccination ended in the early 1970s when smallpox was eradicated; thus, approximately 42 percent of the U.S. population has never been vaccinated against it. The length of immunity is unclear; residual immunity varies from person to person, but smallpox immunity is estimated to only last approximately 3 to 5 years for most people (range 1 to 10 years). Revaccinees (those who have been vaccinated in the past and receive a booster) are much more likely to have a sustained immune response than primary vaccinees (those who are receiving the vaccine for the first time). Survivors of the disease achieve lifelong immunity to smallpox. Smallpox may be spread person to person via droplets, aerosol, or even through hand-to-hand contact. Hospitalized patients need to be isolated using Airborne and Contact Precautions. Airborne Precautions require healthcare providers and others to do the following: (1) place patient in a private room with monitored negative pressure in relation to surrounding areas, (2) wear respiratory protection (N95 respirator) when entering the patient room, and (3) limit the transport of the patient from the room, and if movement is absolutely necessary, place a surgical mask on the patient, if possible. In addition to wearing gloves and gown as outlined in Standard Precautions, Contact Precautions also require the following: (1) wear gloves when entering the room, (2) remove gloves before leaving the patient's room, and (3) wash hands immediately with an antimicrobial agent or a waterless antiseptic agent. In addition, wear a gown when entering the room and remove the gown before leaving the patient's environment. Dedicate the use of noncritical patient care equipment to a single patient (or cohort of patients), if possible.

Reference: *APIC Text*, 4th edition, Chapter 29 - Isolation Precautions

NOTES

(Transmission-based Precautions)

8. (B) Meeting with the facility legal staff to discuss notification of the patients

Rationale: When an outbreak is identified or suspected, an environmental source may be present, and confirmatory testing is appropriate. A critical review of the indications for airborne particulate monitoring or cultures must be done in light of basic principles of outbreak investigation (e.g., establishing that an outbreak exists). One may also consider the following guidance:

- Purpose of culturing and appropriate methods should be identified beforehand.
- Decisions and planned actions regarding results of culturing should be anticipated before undertaking the process.
- Determination should be made whether there are existing standards to interpret results.

Reference: *APIC Text*, 4th edition, Chapter 114 - Heating, Ventilation, and Air Conditioning

9. (C) 28 days after opening

Rationale: A multidose vial is a vial of liquid medication intended for parenteral administration (injection or infusion) that contains more than one dose of medication. Multidose vials are labeled as such by the manufacturer and typically contain an antimicrobial preservative to help prevent the growth of bacteria. The preservative has no effect on viruses and does not protect against contamination when healthcare personnel fail to follow safe injection practices. USP Standard <797> requires that a multidose vial be discarded within 28 days after its first opening in accordance with USP Chapter <51> unless specified by the manufacturer. The CDC recommends refrigerating the vials after opening if recommended by the manufacturer, cleaning the rubber diaphragm of the vial with alcohol before inserting a device into the vial, using a sterile device each time a vial is accessed, and avoiding touch contamination of the device before penetrating the rubber diaphragm. The multidose vial should be discarded when empty, when suspected or visible contamination occurs, or when the manufacturer's stated expiration date is reached. Medications packaged as multidose should be assigned to a single patient whenever possible.

Reference: *APIC Text*, 4th edition, Chapter 110 - Pharmacy Services

10. (D) Small animals are never allowed to sit on a patient's bed

Rationale: Healthcare facilities should develop and implement infection prevention guidelines and develop policies to minimize the potential risks associated with having animals in healthcare facilities. These should require that animals be of good temperament, well-groomed, and healthy and that that their handlers be educated on infection prevention practices, including hand hygiene. The following infection prevention and safety guidelines should be in place:

- The healthcare facility develops policies and guidelines for the safety of the patients and animals involved in visitation, animal-assisted activities, and animal-assisted therapy. The healthcare facility should designate a person or persons to implement the policies, coordinate animal-human interactions, and act as a liaison to the animal handlers visiting the facility.
- Participating animals must have a temperament test (behavioral assessment) by an experienced person or recognized group.

NOTES

- Animals are required to be bathed within 24 hours before the visit.
- Animals may wear a shirt, vest, or other protective clothing to control allergies. Wiping the animal with a baby or pet wipe will help control dandruff.
- Animals must have clean ears.
- Animals must have nails that are short with no rough edges. Animals must be trained not to scratch the patient. For additional protection, animals may wear protective foot coverings.
- Animals must be healthy and current with immunizations, including rabies vaccination and others required in the state in which the healthcare facility is located. An annual physical examination by a licensed veterinarian should include dental and dermatological evaluation. Animals should be free of communicable diseases and parasites and be on a flea control program.
- Animals must be free of any skin condition or wounds.
- Handlers must ensure that animals do not lick or come in contact with a patient's open wound or devices.
- If an animal is allowed on a patient's bed, a barrier such as a disposable cloth, towel, or sheet can be placed between the animal's coat and the patient's linen. The barrier is removed and discarded when the animal leaves.
- Animals are kept on a short leash or in a carrier or basket. The use of retractable leashes is discouraged.
- The animal's handler/volunteer must be healthy and free of communicable diseases. The facility is strongly encouraged to consider a recommendation to handlers that they receive annual influenza shots and may be able to offer the vaccine to handlers for free as part of the annual flu vaccination program.

Reference: *APIC Text*, 4th edition, Chapter 122 - Animals Visiting Healthcare Facilities

11. **B 2, 3**

Rationale: Antibiotic resistance continues to pose a significant problem for residents in LTCFs because of the overuse and misuse of antibiotics. Antimicrobial stewardship refers to coordinated interventions designed to improve and measure the appropriate use of antimicrobials by promoting the selection of the optimal antimicrobial drug regimen, dose, duration of therapy, and route of administration. The Infectious Diseases Society of America and the Society for Healthcare Epidemiology of America support broad implementation of antimicrobial stewardship programs across all healthcare settings including LTCFs. In addition, it is recommended that influenza vaccination be provided to all residents of LTCFs. Influenza outbreaks in LTCFs may have severe and even deadly consequences for residents. Because influenza is easily transmitted, it is important that influenza vaccination is offered to all residents to provide both individual protection and "herd immunity" (i.e., group protection) in the LTCF. Research has shown the effectiveness of influenza immunization programs among the geriatric population and long-term care resident.

References: *APIC Text*, 4th edition, Chapter 61 - Long-term Care; Dellit TH, Owens RC, McGowan JE, et al. Infectious Diseases Society of America and the Society for Healthcare Epidemiology of America Guidelines for Developing an Institutional Program to Enhance Antimicrobial Stewardship. *Clin Infect Dis* 2007;44 (2): 159-177.

NOTES

12. (B) Minimize infectious hazards for patients and healthcare personnel

Rationale: An IRCA must guide a strategic, proactive design to mitigate environmental sources of microbes, prevent infectious hazards through architectural design (e.g., hand washing and hand hygiene stations; isolation rooms; materials selection for surfaces and furnishings), and provide control measures that mitigate potential contamination during actual construction or renovation (e.g., dust barriers, pressure differentials, protection of air handlers).

Reference: *APIC Text*, 4th edition, Chapter 116 - Construction and Renovation

13. (C) Within 24 to 48 hours of culture results being available

Rationale: Much of antimicrobial prescribing is unnecessary or inappropriate. The CDC has advocated implementing taking an "antibiotic time out" (ATO) whereby prescribing clinicians formally assess three pieces of essential information during clinical rounds: correct dosing, duration of therapy, and indication for treatment. An ATO should be taken when culture results are available, usually within 24 to 48 hours.

References: Appendix G. In: Brooks K. *Ready Reference for Microbes*, 3rd edition. Washington, DC: Association for Professionals in Infection Control and Epidemiology, 2012; Moody J, Cosgrove S, Olmsted R, et al. Antimicrobial stewardship: a collaborative partnership between infection preventionists and healthcare epidemiologists. *Am J Infect Control* 2012 Mar; 40(2):94-95.

14. (D) 3, 4

Rationale: Both steam sterilization and ethylene oxide gas sterilization will kill bacterial spores and all other microorganisms. Steam sterilization can only be used for items that are tolerant of high temperatures, such as metal surgical tools. Ethylene oxide gas sterilization is a low-heat method for items that are not heat tolerant. Items that are sterilized by ethylene oxide must be allowed time for aeration before use.

Reference: *APIC Text*, 4th edition, Chapter 31 - Cleaning, Disinfection, and Sterilization

15. (C) It lengthens room turnover because it takes a prolonged period of time to complete room treatment

Rationale: The use of HPV has been shown to decrease the incidence of *C. difficile* infection, and it is effective on surfaces and equipment throughout the room. Drawbacks of this method are that it cannot be utilized while the patient is in the room and that the process lasts a prolonged period of time. Because of these issues, it can be challenging to use for daily cleaning, and it may delay room turnover compared to traditional terminal cleaning methods.

Reference: *APIC Text*, 4th edition, Chapter 31 - Cleaning, Disinfection, and Sterilization

16. (C) The patient's head of the bed should be elevated to an angle of 30 to 45 degrees

Rationale: There are five components of care to prevent VAP:

1. Elevation of the head of the bed
2. Daily sedative interruption and assessment of readiness to extubate
3. Peptic ulcer disease prophylaxis
4. Deep vein thrombosis prophylaxis
5. Daily oral care with chlorhexidine

Reference: *APIC Text*, 4th edition, Chapter 36 - Pneumonia

NOTES

17. Ⓒ Droplet Precautions

Rationale: *N. meningitidis* is an aerobic, Gram-negative diplococcus that colonizes the nasopharynx of many healthy individuals. Microbial and host factors combine to allow this organism to invade the bloodstream and enter the central nervous system, causing severe sepsis and meningitis. Hypervirulent strains may be transmitted from person to person through respiratory secretions, causing outbreaks of meningococcal disease. Rapid identification of the pathogen, institution of Droplet Precautions based on suspicion of meningococcal disease, initiation of appropriate antibiotic therapy, and administration of chemoprophylaxis of healthcare personnel who were in direct contact with the patient's nasopharyngeal secretions are the most important interventions.

Reference: *APIC Text*, 4th edition, Chapter 29 - Isolation Precautions (Transmission-based Precautions)

18. Ⓒ 1, 2, 4

Rationale: On the federal level in the United States, several agencies have published regulations pertaining to "infectious," "medical," or "regulated" waste. The U.S. EPA, OSHA, and DOT have such regulations. In addition, both the CDC and EPA have issued guidance documents pertaining to medical waste management. At the request of the U.S. Congress, the Agency for Toxic Substances and Disease Registry prepared and published a comprehensive review of the public health implications of medical waste.

Reference: *APIC Text*, 4th edition, Chapter 113 - Waste Management

19. Ⓑ 1, 2, 4

Rationale: Pathogenic organisms are found in many different day-to-day settings. Household garbage, bed linens, soiled diapers, and unwashed hands are all examples of environments in which pathogens can be found routinely. A number of studies have shown that though hospital wastes can have a greater variety of organisms than residential wastes, those from households are more heavily contaminated. For waste to be capable of causing infection, the following specific factors are necessary: (1) dose, (2) host susceptibility, (3) presence of a pathogen, (4) virulence of a pathogen, and (5) portal of entry. All five of these factors must be present for infection to occur from waste.

Reference: *APIC Text*, Chapter 113 - Waste Management

NOTES

20. (B) 1, 3, 4

Rationale: Physical storage restrictions are recommended to support an environment that is conducive to maintaining the sterility of reprocessed items. Sterilized items should be stored as follows:

- Eighteen inches from the ceiling if there is a sprinkler head or according to the fire code
- Eight to 10 inches from the floor
- At least 2 inches from an outside wall
- Away from sprinklers and air vents
- In areas of limited traffic
- Clean workroom or clean holding area(s): Airflow must be positive pressure with respect to surrounding areas with a minimum of four air exchanges per hour. In an area with controlled temperature and humidity (18°C to 22°C [65°F to 72°F], relative humidity less than 35 to 75 percent, and at least 4 [preferably 10] air exchanges per hour).
- Soiled workroom or soiled holding area(s): Airflow must be negative pressure with respect to surrounding areas with a minimum of 10 air exchanges per hour.
- The first item in is the first item out (first in, first out [FIFO]). Items should be rotated. Place newer items in the back part of the area where they are stored.
- Open-rack storage should have a solid bottom to prevent soiling or contamination from the floor
- Consideration should be given to storage that will minimize the collection of dust on surfaces
- Sterilized items should be arranged in a manner that prevents packages from being crushed, bent, compressed, or punctured. Items should not be stored under sinks or under exposed water or sewer pipes. Windowsills should be avoided. Closed or covered cabinets are preferred. Open shelving may be used if the area has limited access, has monitored ventilation, and is frequently cleaned and disinfected.

Reference: *APIC Text*, 4th edition, Chapter 106 - Sterile Processing

21. (C) 3, 4

Rationale: Freshly applied nail polish does not increase the number of bacteria recovered from periungual skin, but chipped nail polish may support the growth of larger numbers of organisms on fingernails. However, healthcare personnel who wear artificial nails are more likely to harbor Gram-negative pathogens on their fingertips than are those who have natural nails, both before and after hand washing.

Reference: Boyce JM, Pittet D. Guideline for Hand Hygiene in Health-Care Settings: Recommendations of the Healthcare Infection Control Practices Advisory Committee and the HICPAC/SHEA/APIC/IDSA Hand Hygiene Task Force. *MMWR* 2002 October. 51(RR-16): 1-45. Available at: http://www.cdc.gov/mmwr/PDF/rr/rr5116.pdf.

NOTES

22. (B) At least 15 to 20 air exchanges per hour

Rationale: Airborne Precautions are used to prevent transmission of infectious organisms that remain suspended in the air and travel great distances. These diseases include measles, smallpox, chickenpox, pulmonary tuberculosis, avian influenza, and possibly SARS-associated coronavirus. In acute care and long-term care settings, patients should be placed in an airborne infection isolation room (AIIR) with negative air pressure relative to the corridor and at least 6 to 12 air exchanges with direct exhaust of air to the outside. Air pressure should be monitored daily with visual indicators (e.g., smoke tubes, flutter strips). The door should be kept shut.

Reference: *APIC Text*, 4th edition, Chapter 29 - Isolation Precautions (Transmission-based Precautions)

23. (D) If malfunctioning

Rationale: According to the CDC Guidelines for the Prevention of Intravascular Catheter-Related Infections, CVCs, PICCs, hemodialysis catheters, or pulmonary artery catheters should not be routinely removed to prevent catheter-related infections. A guidewire exchange should be used to replace a malfunctioning nontunneled catheter if no evidence of infection is present.

Reference: *APIC Text*, 4th edition, Chapter 34 - Intravascular Device Infections

24. (B) Administer antibiotics with overlapping activity

Rationale: Antimicrobial stewardship refers to coordinated interventions designed to improve and measure the appropriate use of antimicrobials by promoting the selection of the optimal antimicrobial drug regimen, dose, duration of therapy, and route of administration. Antimicrobial stewardship is the best investment for preventing the proliferation of multidrug-resistant pathogens and the adverse events associated with the drugs used to treat such pathogens. Recommended strategies for antimicrobial stewardship include formulary restriction, automatic stop orders, and antimicrobial cycling.

Reference: *APIC Text*, 4th edition, Chapter 26 - Antimicrobials and Resistance

25. (B) Monitor adherence to Standard Precautions

Rationale: The infection prevention program should include the following when planning for active surveillance cultures: providing additional personnel to obtain cultures and additional laboratory personnel to process these cultures, ensuring turnaround time for screening results, monitoring adherence to Contact Precautions, providing a mechanism for communicating results to healthcare providers, and measuring outcomes to evaluate the effectiveness of active surveillance cultures and Contact Precautions.

Reference: *APIC Text*, 4th edition, Chapter 29 - Isolation Precautions (Transmission-based Precautions)

NOTES

26. (B) 1, 3, 4

Rationale: Since 1999, more than 125,000 patients in the United States have been notified of potential exposure to Hepatitis B virus, Hepatitis C virus (HCV), and HIV due to unsafe injection practices. Many of these incidents involved healthcare providers reusing syringes, resulting in contamination of medication vials or containers, which were used then on subsequent patients. Injection safety and other basic infection control practices are central to patient safety. Safe injection practices include:

- Never administer medications from the same syringe to more than one patient, even if the needle is changed
- Do not enter a vial with a used syringe or needle
- Medications packaged as single-use vials must never be used for more than one patient
- Medications packaged as multiuse vials should be assigned to a single patient whenever possible
- Bags or bottles of IV solution must not be used as a common source of supply for more than one patient
- Absolute adherence to proper infection control practices must be maintained during the preparation and administration of injected medications

References: *APIC Text*, 4th edition, Chapter 21 - Risk Factors Facilitating Transmission of Infectious Agents; Centers for Disease Control and Prevention (CDC). The One and Only Campaign. CDC website. Available at: http://www.cdc.gov/injectionsafety/1anOnly.html

27. (A) Covering the mouth and nose with the hands when coughing and sneezing

Rationale: According to the CDC, respiratory hygiene/cough etiquette strategies are used to prevent the transmission of all respiratory infections in healthcare settings. Respiratory hygiene and cough etiquette include covering the mouth and nose with a tissue during coughing and sneezing or offering a surgical mask to the coughing patient, discarding the mask or tissue appropriately and performing hand hygiene, posting signs in public areas in languages appropriate to the population served, and educating healthcare staff, patients, and visitors.

Reference: *APIC Text*, 4th edition, Chapter 29 - Isolation Precautions (Transmission-based Precautions)

28. (C) Airborne Precautions

Rationale: According to the CDC Isolation Guidelines, private rooms are not required for Contact and Droplet Precautions (though they are preferred). Patients on Contact or Droplet isolation with the same disease may share a room if necessary. Patients on Airborne Isolation require a private room.

Reference: *APIC Text*, 4th edition, Chapter 29 - Isolation Precautions (Transmission-based Precautions)

29. (A) A cap

Rationale: According to the CDC Guidelines for the Prevention of Intravascular Catheter-Related Infections, maximal sterile barrier precautions must be used for the insertion of CVCs, PICCs, or guidewire exchanges. This includes the use of a cap, mask, sterile gown, sterile gloves, and a sterile full-body drape for the insertion.

Reference: *APIC Text*, 4th edition, Chapter 34 - Intravascular Device Infections

NOTES

30. (B) Implement Airborne Precautions for all patients with suspected or confirmed influenza

Rationale: During an influenza outbreak in an acute care setting, the following measures should be taken to protect patients and staff and to reduce the risk of healthcare-associated influenza transmission:

- Perform rapid influenza virus testing of patients and personnel with recent onset of symptoms suggestive of influenza.
- Implement Droplet Precautions for all patients with suspected or confirmed influenza.
- Separate suspected or confirmed influenza patients from asymptomatic patients.
- Restrict staff movement from areas of the facility having outbreaks.
- Immunize unvaccinated patients and healthcare personnel with current recommended, available influenza vaccine.
- Administer influenza antiviral chemoprophylaxis and treatment to patients and healthcare personnel according to current recommendations.
- Consider antiviral chemoprophylaxis for all healthcare personnel, regardless of their vaccination status, if the health department determines the outbreak is caused by a variant of influenza virus that is a suboptimal match with the vaccine.
- Limit or stop elective medical and surgical admissions.
- Restrict cardiovascular and pulmonary surgery to emergency cases during influenza outbreaks, especially those characterized by high attack rates and severe illness, in the community or acute care facility.

Reference: *APIC Text*, 4th edition, Chapter 82 - Influenza

31. (D) Subclavian

Rationale: According to the CDC Guidelines for the Prevention of Intravascular Catheter-Related Infections, a subclavian site, rather than a jugular or femoral site, should be used in adult patients to minimize infection risk for nontunneled CVC placement. Use of the femoral vein for central venous access in adult patients should be avoide.

Reference: *APIC Text*, 4th edition, Chapter 34 - Intravascular Device Infections

32. (B) Monitoring the volume of gloves used per 1,000 patient days

Rationale: Hand hygiene is a critical component of patient and employee safety. Evaluation and repeated monitoring of hand hygiene practices, as well as healthcare personnel and senior managers' knowledge and perception of the problem of HAI and the importance of hand hygiene at the healthcare facility, is a vital component of any successful hand hygiene campaign. Unobtrusive direct observation of hand hygiene practices by a trained observer is considered the gold standard for evaluating compliance. Electronic systems for the automatic monitoring of hand hygiene compliance are now available and can significantly facilitate data collection. Consumption of hand hygiene products such as soap and alcohol-based hand rub is another useful indicator. Adherence to artificial fingernail policies may also be monitored. Healthcare personnel should receive feedback about defective practices as well as improvement strategies.

Reference: *APIC Text*, 4th edition, Chapter 27 - Hand Hygiene

NOTES

33. (A) Mites from a scabies-infested patient

Rationale: Contact transmission is the most common mode of transmission and is divided into two subgroups: direct contact and indirect contact. Indirect transmission involves the transfer of an infectious agent through a contaminated intermediate object or person. Hands of healthcare personnel may transmit pathogens after touching an infected or colonized body site on one patient or a contaminated inanimate object. Transmission may occur if hand hygiene is not performed; if equipment is inadequately cleaned, disinfected, or sterilized; or if there is exposure to contaminated food and water that were not prepared and maintained according to sanitation standards. Mites from a scabies-infested patient are an example of direct contact transmission.

Reference: *APIC Text*, 4th edition, Chapter 21 - Risk Factors Facilitating Transmission of Infectious Agents

34. (B) Routine replacement of catheters

Rationale: The CDC Guidelines for the Prevention of Intravascular Catheter-Related Infections do not recommend routinely replacing CVCs, PICCs, hemodialysis catheters, or pulmonary artery catheters to prevent catheter-related infections.

Reference: *APIC Text*, 4th edition, Chapter 34 - Intravascular Device Infections

35. (B) Standard and Droplet Precautions

Rationale: Influenza viruses are spread from person to person primarily through large-particle respiratory droplet transmission. Transmission via large- particle droplets requires close contact between source and recipient persons, because droplets do not remain suspended in the air and generally travel only a short distance (1 meter or less) through the air. Droplet Precautions are intended to prevent transmission of pathogens spread through close respiratory or mucous membrane contact with respiratory secretions. Standard precautions apply to all patients, regardless of suspected or confirmed infection status.

Reference: *APIC Text*, 4th edition, Chapter 82 - Influenza

36. (C) Droplet transmission

Rationale: Respiratory droplets carrying infectious pathogens transmit infection when they travel directly from the respiratory tract of the infectious individual to susceptible mucosal surfaces of the recipient. Transmission occurs when large droplets (greater than 5 μm) containing the infectious agent are propelled a short distance through the air (e.g., by coughing, sneezing, or talking) and come into direct contact with conjunctivae or mucous membranes. When droplets land or infectious secretions are deposited on surfaces close to the patient, pathogens can be acquired indirectly by healthcare personnel.

Reference: *APIC Text*, 4th edition, Chapter 21 - Risk Factors Facilitating Transmission of Infectious Agents

NOTES

37. **(C) Patients who received specific antivirals (i.e., acyclovir, famciclovir, or valacyclovir) within the preceding 24 hours should not receive influenza vaccination**

Rationale: There is no contraindication for patients receiving the influenza vaccine if they received specific antivirals within the preceding 24 hours. Precautions must be taken when administering the zoster vaccine to patients who have received antivirals (i.e., acyclovir, famciclovir, or valacyclovir) 24 hours before vaccination; use of these antiviral drugs should be avoided for 14 days after zoster vaccination.

Before administering the influenza vaccine, patients should be informed of the following:

1. The vaccine is formulated annually to protect against influenza strains likely to circulate in the United States in the upcoming winter.
2. Inactivated influenza vaccine contains noninfectious viral components and cannot cause influenza. LAIV can cause nasal congestion, sore throat, and headache for a few days.
3. Respiratory diseases unrelated to influenza vaccination can occur after vaccination.
4. Fever, malaise, myalgia, and other systemic symptoms can occur after vaccination, especially in persons with no prior exposure to influenza vaccine (e.g., young children). However, in placebo-controlled studies, rates were similar between vaccine and placebo recipients.
5. Influenza vaccine should not be administered to persons known to have anaphylactic hypersensitivity to eggs or other components of the vaccine without first consulting a physician.

Reference: *APIC Text*, 4th edition, Chapter 82 - Influenza

38. **(B) Weekly "sedation vacations" and assessment of readiness to extubate**

Rationale: VAP in a critically ill patient significantly increases risk of mortality and, at a minimum, increases ventilator time, length of stay, and cost of care. The IHI Ventilator Bundle is a grouping of best practices that, when applied together, may result in substantially greater improvement. The key components of the IHI Ventilator Bundle are:

- Elevation of the head of the bed
- Daily "sedation vacations" and assessment of readiness to extubate
- Peptic ulcer disease prophylaxis
- Deep venous thrombosis prophylaxis
- Daily oral care with chlorhexidine

Reference: *APIC Text*, 4th edition, Chapter 36 - Pneumonia

39. **(D) Stopcocks can increase the contamination rate**

Rationale: According to the CDC Guidelines for the Prevention of Intravascular Catheter-Related Infections, a CVC with the minimum number of ports or lumens essential for the management of the patient should be used. Stopcocks used for injection of medications, administration of IV infusions, and collection of blood samples represent a potential portal of entry for microorganisms into vascular access catheters and IV fluids. Stopcocks should be capped when not being used. In general, closed catheter access systems are associated with fewer catheter-related infections than open systems and should be used preferentially.

Reference: *APIC Text*, 4th edition, Chapter 34 - Intravascular Device Infections

NOTES

40. (C) When hands are visibly soiled

Rationale: Hand hygiene is a critical component of patient and employee safety. Use of alcohol-based hand rubs has increased adherence of healthcare personnel to recommended hand hygiene policies and have been associated with reduced HAI rate. However, when hands are heavily soiled or greasy, hand sanitizers may not work well. Hand washing with soap and water is recommended in such circumstances.

References: *APIC Text*, 4th edition, Chapter 27 - Hand Hygiene; Boyce JM, Pittet D. Guideline for hand hygiene in health-care settings. *Morbid Mortal Weekly* Rev. 2002 Oct25;51(RR1):1-44; World Health Organization (WHO). *WHO Guidelines on Hand Hygiene in Health Care*. WHO website. 2009. Available at: http://whqlibdoc.who.int/publications/2009/9789241597906_eng.pdf?ua=1

41. (B) 85 percent

Rationale: CJD occurs naturally in either of two forms: the sporadic type (occurring at a rate of 1 case per 1 million population) and the familial type due to a genetic mutation that can be passed from generation to generation and has been documented in geographical clusters in various parts of the world. The percentage of sporadic CJD is 85 percent. Sporadic CJD has no gender restrictions and occurs at a mean onset of 50 to 70 years of age.

Reference: *APIC Text*, 4th edition, Chapter 73 - Creutzfeldt-Jakob Disease and Other Prion Diseases

42. (D) Changing ventilator circuits every 48 hours

Rationale: The following best practices, often included in a ventilator bundle, can help prevent VAP:

- Keep the head of the patient's bed raised between 30 and 45 degrees unless other medical conditions do not allow this to occur.
- Check the patient's ability to breathe on his or her own every day so that the patient can be taken off of the ventilator as soon as possible.
- Clean the patient's hands with soap and water or an alcohol-based hand rub before and after touching the patient or the ventilator.
- Clean the inside of the patient's mouth on a regular basis.
- Clean or replace equipment between uses on different patients.

Reference: *APIC Text*, 4th edition, Chapter 36 - Pneumonia

43. (C) Smallpox

Rationale: Smallpox is an acute, contagious, and sometimes fatal disease caused by the variola virus (an orthopoxvirus), and marked by fever and a distinctive progressive skin rash. The majority of patients with smallpox recover, but death may occur in up to 30% of cases. Bioterrorism agents can be separated into three categories, depending on how easily they can be spread and the severity of illness or death they cause. Category A agents, which includes smallpox, are considered the highest risk to national security because they:

- Can be easily disseminated or transmitted from person to person
- Result in high mortality rates and have the potential for major public health impact
- Might cause public panic and social disruption
- Require special action for public health preparedness

Reference: *APIC Text*, 4th edition, Chapter 120 - Infectious Disease Disasters: Bioterrorism, Emerging Infections, and Pandemics

NOTES

44. (B) Examination of host factors such as changes in immunity, or diagnostic/therapeutic procedures within populations served

Rationale: The epidemiological triangle consists of three elements: host, agent, and environment. The host is the human, the environment consists of all external factors associated with the host, and the agent may be a bacteria, virus, fungi, etc. Within the model presented, increasing antimicrobial resistance represents a change in the agent (or pathogen), not a change in the host. Improving healthcare personnel influenza vaccination rates would be an environmental factor change for patients by decreasing their exposure to flu. It is also a host factor change for healthcare personnel because vaccination improved their immunity. A change in cleaning agents represents environmental factors. Host factors such as changes in immunity (e.g., increased numbers of immunocompromised patients) or changes in diagnostic/therapeutic procedures (such as new surgical procedures) would be significant findings for outbreak investigations. The IP can use the epidemiological triangle to analyze and communicate how these changes increased the risk of HAIs.

Reference: *APIC Text*, 4th edition, Chapter 10 - General Principles of Epidemiology

45. (A) During labor and delivery, the patient should wear a mask

Rationale: Pregnant women and infants are at increased risk of hospitalization from influenza complications. Pregnant women with influenza in the Labor and Delivery suite should be placed on Droplet Precautions; she does not need to wear a mask during the time of delivery. After the infant is born, the mother should put on a surgical mask and then practice hand hygiene before handling the baby. All persons who come within 3 feet of the mother should wear a surgical mask and practice hand hygiene before and after contact with the mother. All persons in the delivery room should practice hand hygiene before and after handling the baby.

Reference: *APIC Text*, 4th edition, Chapter 82 - Influenza

46. (A) All adults aged 19 and older should receive at least one dose of Tdap

Rationale: Pertussis (whooping cough) is a highly communicable, acute, infectious respiratory disease caused by *Bordetella pertussis*. ACIP recommends a single Tdap dose for persons aged 11 to 18 years who have completed the recommended childhood diphtheria and tetanus toxoids and pertussis/diphtheria and tetanus toxoids and acellular pertussis (DTP/DTaP) vaccination series and for adults aged 19 to 64 years.

Reference: Centers for Disease Control and Prevention. Updated Recommendations for Use of Tetanus Toxoid, Reduced Diphtheria Toxoid and Acellular Pertussis (Tdap) Vaccine from the Advisory Committee on Immunization Practices, 2010. *MMWR* 2011 Jan 14;60(01):13-15.

47. (B) Ensure that the right therapy is given to the right patient with the right dose and duration

Rationale: Antimicrobial stewardship refers to coordinated interventions designed to improve and measure the appropriate use of antimicrobials by promoting the selection of the optimal antimicrobial drug regimen, dose, duration of therapy, and route of administration. Antimicrobial stewards seek to achieve optimal clinical outcomes related to antimicrobial use, minimize toxicity and other adverse events, reduce the costs of health care for infections, and limit the selection for antimicrobial-resistant strains.

Reference: *APIC Text*, 4th edition, Chapter 26 - Antimicrobials and Resistance; Dellit TH, Owens RC, McGowan JE, et al. Infectious Diseases Society of America and the Society for Healthcare Epidemiology of America Guidelines for Developing an Institutional Program to Enhance Antimicrobial Stewardship. *Clin Infect Dis* (2007) 44 (2): 159-177.

NOTES

48. B Direction of wiping with toilet paper (from back to front)

Rationale: Approximately 2.2 percent of girls under the age of 2 develop a urinary tract infection (UTI). Risk factors for young girls include:

- History of maternal UTI
- Family history of vesicoureteral reflux
- History of dysfunctional voiding patterns
- Constipation

Although often reported as a cause, direction of wiping with toilet paper is not a risk factor. Identified risk factors include bubble baths and prolonged soaking in the bathtub, excessive holding of urine, and delayed bladder emptying.

Reference: *APIC Text*, 4th edition, Chapter 33 - Urinary Tract Infection

49. D Hepatitis C

Rationale: The only infections in which breast milk must be withheld from the newborn are: (1) presence of a breast abscess, (2) herpes simplex virus lesion on breast, and (3) infection with HIV, West Nile virus, or human T-cell lymphotropic virus type I or II. If mastitis is present, breast-feeding can continue. If a breast abscess is present, the mother should pump the breast milk and discard it (until 24 to 48 hours after surgical drainage and appropriate antimicrobial therapy). Women with open, active, untreated pulmonary TB cannot breast-feed because they are to have no direct contact with the newborn. However, breast milk can be pumped and given to the newborn, provided that the treatment the woman is receiving is not a contraindication for breast-feeding. Currently, maternal HCV is not considered a contraindication for breast-feeding. The decision to breast-feed in the presence of maternal HCV must be an informed decision made by the woman in consultation with her healthcare provider.

Reference: *APIC Text*, 4th edition, Chapter 43 - Perinatal Care

50. D Annually and whenever unacceptable techniques are observed

Rationale: Quality problems associated with compounded sterile and nonsterile pharmacy preparations have resulted in recalls, patient injury, and death. The American Society of Health System Pharmacists requires that all personnel be properly trained by the following means:

- Prior to commencing any compounding, perform thorough didactic instruction in the theory and practice of sterile preparations, with evaluation of technique annually (for low- and medium-risk level) and semiannually (for high-risk level)
- Compounder evaluations should include a formal written exam and practical evaluation of aseptic technique using growth media (media fills)

Reference: *APIC Text*, 4th edition, Chapter 110 - Pharmacy Services

Chapter 6
EMPLOYEE/OCCUPATIONAL HEALTH

NOTES

The CIC® exam will have a total of eleven (11) questions addressing Employee/Occupational Health. The content will test knowledge of the following:

A. Review and/or develop screening and immunization programs

B. Collaborate regarding counseling, follow up, and work restriction recommendations related to communicable diseases and/or exposures

C. Collaborate with occupational health to evaluate infection prevention-related data and provide recommendations

D. Collaborate with occupational health to recognize healthcare personnel who may represent a transmission risk to patients, coworkers, and communities

E. Assess risk of occupational exposure to infectious diseases (e.g., Mycobacterium tuberculosis, bloodborne pathogens)

KEY CONCEPTS

- Healthcare personnel face a wide range of hazards on the job including needlestick injuries, back injuries, latex allergy, violence, and stress.
- According to the U.S. Centers for Disease Control and Prevention, cases of nonfatal occupational injury and illness in healthcare personnel are among the highest of any industry sector.
- An occupational health program is an essential and corner-stone element in efforts to provide a safe environment for patients and healthcare personnel.
- Elements of an occupational health program include surveillance, education, immunization, and injury prevention and response.

NOTES

RESOURCES FOR STUDY

Nearly all questions on Employee/Occupational Health are based on chapters in the primary references, but secondary references may be useful to help clarify more detailed issues.

Primary Reference:

1. Grota P, ed. *APIC Text of Infection Control and Epidemiology*, 4th edition. Washington, DC: Association for Professionals in Infection Control and Epidemiology, 2014. Also available online at http://text.apic.org [subscription required].

Notable Chapters

71	*Bordetella pertussis*
80	Herpes Virus
81	HIV/AIDS
82	Influenza
86	Measles, Mumps, Rubella
87	*Neisseria meningitidis*
95	Tuberculosis and Other Mycobacteria
97	Viral Hepatitis
100	Occupational Health
101	Occupational Exposure to Bloodborne Pathogens
102	Volunteers, Contract Workers, and Other Nonemployees Who Interact with Patients
103	Immunization of Healthcare Personnel
104	Pregnant Healthcare Personnel
105	Minimizing Exposure to Blood and Body Fluids

2. Brooks K. *Ready Reference for Microbes*, 3rd edition. Washington, DC: Association for Professionals in Infection Control and Epidemiology, 2012.

3. Heymann D, ed. *Control of Communicable Diseases Manual*, 19th edition. Washington, DC: American Public Health Association, 2008.

4. Kulich P, Taylor D, eds. *The Infection Preventionist's Guide to the Lab*. Washington, DC: Association for Professionals in Infection Control and Epidemiology, 2012.

NOTES

Secondary Reference:

1. Current Recommendations of the Advisory Committee on Immunization Practices (ACIP).

2. Current guidelines, standards, and recommendations from CDC, APIC, SHEA, and Public Health Agency of Canada.

3. Pickering, Larry K, ed. *Red Book*, 29th ed., Elk Grove Village, IL: American Academy of Pediatrics; 2012.

NOTES

PRACTICE QUESTIONS

1. The infection preventionist (IP) is assisting Employee Health with personnel tuberculosis (TB) skin testing. Which of the following represents a known tuberculin skin test (TST) conversion in a healthcare worker?
   - **a.** Prior tuberculin test results are not available, but the current result is 16 mm after 48 hours
   - **b.** Tuberculin reaction 1 year ago was 9 mm, and the current results are 13 mm
   - **c.** A prior tuberculin reaction was not measured, but the employee states it was dime-sized. The current result is 11 mm
   - **d.** Tuberculin reaction 1 year ago was 3 mm, and the current result is 18 mm

2. A food service worker is diagnosed with Hepatitis A. How long should this employee be on work restrictions?
   - **a.** Until 14 days after symptoms resolve
   - **b.** Until 7 days after onset of jaundice
   - **c.** Until 14 days after onset of jaundice
   - **d.** Until 10 days after symptoms resolve

3. Because there is no vaccine for Hepatitis C, there have been national recommendations for prevention and control of Hepatitis C virus (HCV) infections. These include all but which recommendation?
   - **a.** Screening and testing of blood donors
   - **b.** Risk-reduction counseling and screening of persons at risk for Hepatitis C infection
   - **c.** A national registry for all healthcare personnel known to be Hepatitis C antibody positive
   - **d.** Adherence to Standard Precautions and safe work practices in healthcare settings

NOTES

4. The U.S. Public Health Service's Advisory Committee on Immunization Practices (ACIP) recommends all of the following immunizations be provided to healthcare personnel *except*:

a. Hepatitis A and B vaccines

b. Influenza vaccine

c. Measles, mumps, and rubella (MMR) and varicella-zoster vaccines (if not immune)

d. Bacillus Calmette-Guérin (BCG)

5. Which of the following statements is *true* regarding storage of vaccines?

a. Vaccines should be taken out of the original packaging

b. Vaccines should be stored in a labeled container/bin on the middle shelf a few inches from the wall

c. Vaccines should be packed tightly into the fridge

d. Vaccines should be stored in the top of the refrigerator

6. An employee is exposed to a patient known to have chronic Hepatitis B. The employee is a known responder to the Hepatitis B vaccine, which was given to him as a student 5 years ago. What is the recommended postexposure treatment for the employee?

a. Test the employee and all close personal contacts for Hepatitis B

b. Start the Hepatitis B series on the employee because of the length of time since vaccination

c. No treatment is recommended for a known responder

d. Recommend giving the employee the Hepatitis A vaccine

7. An employee who is not immune to varicella-zoster was exposed to a patient with active chickenpox. How long must the employee remain on work restrictions?

a. Until evaluated by a physician

b. From day 10 after exposure to day 21 after exposure

c. No work restriction is necessary if no signs and symptoms are present

d. At the discretion of the hospital infectious disease physician

NOTES

8. Which of the following are acceptable methods for follow-up testing among healthcare personnel with unprotected exposure to TB?

1) QuantiFERON-TB Gold testing (QFT-G) of sputum at the time of exposure and 12 weeks after exposure
2) QFT-G testing of blood at the time of exposure and 12 weeks after exposure
3) TST via tine tests at the time of exposure and 12 weeks after exposure
4) TST via the intradermal method at the time of exposure and 12 weeks after exposure
5) Chest radiograph for personnel with prior positive TST or QFT-G results
6) Chest radiograph for symptomatic personnel with positive TST or QFT-G results

a. 1, 3, 6
b. 2, 3, 5
c. 1, 4, 6
d. 2, 4, 6

9. What is the appropriate temperature for vaccines that require refrigeration?

a. 46°F to 55°F (8°C to 13°C)
b. 25°F to 35°F (-4°C to 2°C)
c. 25°F to 45°F (-4°C to 7°C)
d. 35°F to 46°F (2°C to 8°C)

10. The IP is reviewing the immunization records of healthcare personnel at their facility and discovers that employees born before 1957 do not have any record of receiving MMR vaccine. What should she recommend to the Human Resources Director regarding employees born before 1957?

a. They are considered immune and do not require follow-up
b. They should receive two doses of the vaccine 4 weeks apart
c. They are only required to provide proof of immunity to measles
d. They are required to provide proof of immunity to measles, mumps, and rubella

NOTES

11. Staff assisting with bronchoscopy of a patient with suspected TB must wear which type of respiratory protection?

a. Surgical/procedure mask

b. Face shield

c. Protection is not required

d. A fit-tested respirator or powered air purifying respirator (PAPR)

12. An employee has sustained a needlestick injury from a blood-contaminated needle. The source patient was Hepatitis B virus (HBV) positive, and the employee had completed one of the three vaccinations in the Hepatitis B series. Which of the following is the correct postexposure prophylaxis (PEP) for this patient?

a. Complete the Hepatitis B vaccine series

b. Complete the Hepatitis B vaccine series and provide Hepatitis B immunoglobulin

c. Provide Hepatitis B immunoglobulin and begin interferon therapy

d. No PEP is needed

13. The IP is developing a seasonal influenza immunization promotion program and decides to survey some healthcare personnel to determine their knowledge and attitude about influenza vaccines. Several healthcare personnel state that they do not want to be immunized because they believe that the vaccine can give them the flu. What is the best response the IP can give to alleviate this fear?

a. The symptoms of the flu from the vaccine are much milder than actually getting the flu, so they are better off being immunized

b. There are no known reactions or side effects to the flu vaccine

c. Any symptoms they experience are due to allergies to components of the vaccine, so they will not get the flu from the vaccine

d. They might experience symptoms that are due to the immune response to the vaccine, but they cannot get the flu from the vaccine

NOTES

14. Dialysis staff are most at risk for exposure to bloodborne pathogens during:

1) Initiation and termination of dialysis
2) Reprocessing, cleaning, and disinfection procedures
3) Medication administration
4) Vascular access hemorrhage

a. 1, 2
b. 2, 3
c. 2, 4
d. 1, 3

15. According to the Centers for Disease Control and Prevention (CDC), which type of thermometer should be used in a vaccine storage unit?

a. Fluid-filled biosafe liquid thermometer
b. Infrared thermometer
c. Chart recorder
d. Probe in a glycol-filled bottle with an external monitoring device

16. A patient in the Emergency Room is diagnosed with bacterial meningitis due to *Neisseria meningitidis*. The patient was not properly isolated, and a number of employees entered her room without wearing a mask. Which employee should receive PEP?

a. The phlebotomist who drew blood on the patient
b. The respiratory therapist who intubated the patient
c. The radiology technician that performed the chest radiograph
d. The employee from admissions that registered the patient

17. U.S. Occupational Safety & Health Administration (OSHA) mandates that which of the following vaccines be provided at no cost to healthcare providers and others at risk for blood and body fluid exposure?

a. Hepatitis A
b. Hepatitis B
c. BCG
d. Meningococcal

NOTES

18. Which of the following is *not* proof of measles immunity for healthcare personnel?

- **a.** Documentation of vaccination with two doses of live measles virus-containing vaccine
- **b.** Laboratory evidence of immunity
- **c.** Born after 1957
- **d.** Laboratory confirmation of disease

19. There has been a local bioterrorism event and three healthcare personnel were exposed to inhalation anthrax. They have been decontaminated and are taking PEP, and they would like to return to work. The incubation period of inhalation anthrax is usually about 7 days but can be as long as 2 months. What should the IP's recommendation be regarding work restrictions for these employees?

- **a.** They will not be allow to return to work for the duration of the 2-month incubation period
- **b.** They will not be allowed to return to work for the duration of prophylactic treatment
- **c.** They may return to work but must wear respiratory protection while in the facility
- **d.** They may return to work with no restrictions

20. The occupational health nurse has requested the IP's assistance in reporting the nursing needlestick rate annually. Which formula should be used?

- **a.** Total number of needlesticks reported by nursing divided by the average daily census
- **b.** Total number of needlesticks reported by nursing divided by the needle devices used by nursing
- **c.** Total number of needlesticks reported by nursing divided by the number of full-time nurses employed during the year
- **d.** Total number of needlesticks reported by nursing divided by the number of injections given by nurses

NOTES

21. The IP is asked to recommend the length of time a staff member who has developed influenza should be excluded (furloughed) from work duties. The staff member was diagnosed with influenza on March 15. She consults the CDC infection Control Guidance for the Prevention and Control of Influenza in Acute Care Facilities and recommends that the employee should:

a. Remain off work until March 20

b. Remain off work for the duration of the illness

c. Remain off work until March 21

d. Remain off work for 5 days (March 20) or until symptoms have resolved, whichever is longer

22. An employee is exposed to a known HIV-positive patient's blood via needlestick after giving an intramuscular injection. The patient has a known high viral load. After the employee has thoroughly washed the exposed area with soap and water, what is the next step that should be taken following this exposure?

a. The employee needs to be counseled about using safer sex practices and to avoid pregnancy, breast-feeding, and blood and organ donation for 3 months after exposure

b. The employee should be treated as soon as possible with expanded multidrug PEP

c. The employee should have baseline testing for HIV, Hepatitis B antigen, and Hepatitis B antibody

d. The employee should be counseled by a clinician knowledgeable about HIV transmission risks

23. An IP is participating on a multidisciplinary team formed to decrease sharps injuries in an Ambulatory Surgical Center. Of the following possible activities, which would be most likely to assist the team?

a. A quarterly review of sharps injury data stratified by surgical team

b. An analysis of employee participation in the Hepatitis B vaccination program

c. Root cause analyses after exposure incidents

d. A review of surgery duration in cases in which sharp injuries were reported

24. A new employee who needs to be tested for TB infection before starting work has a history of BCG vaccination. Which method of TB testing would be the best choice in this situation?

a. The TST would be the best method to use because it is the most cost-effective testing method

b. A TST would be the best method to use because it distinguishes latent from active TB infection

c. An interferon-gamma release assay (IGRA) blood test would be the best method to use because prior BCG immunization does not cause a false positive with this test

d. An IGRA blood test would be the best method to use because it is a rapid test and provides results within 30 minutes

25. Which of the following is *not* evidence of varicella immunity in healthcare personnel?

a. Evidence of two doses of the varicella vaccine

b. Laboratory evidence of immunity

c. Laboratory confirmation of disease

d. Born before 1980

NOTES

NOTES

ANSWERS AND RATIONALES

1. **D Tuberculin reaction 1 year ago was 3 mm, and the current result is 18 mm**

Rationale: Interpretation of the TST depends on measured TST induration in millimeters, the person's risk for being infected with M. tuberculosis, and risk for progression to active TB if infected. The TST test should be interpreted according to the CDC guidelines. A healthcare worker without known exposure who demonstrates an increase of ≥10 mm is considered a positive result. (See Table 6-1)

Table 6-1. Interpretations of TST and QFT Results According to the Purpose of Testing for *M. tuberculosis* Infection in Healthcare Setting

Purpose of Testing	TST	QFT
Baseline	≥10 mm is considered a positive result (either first or second step)	Positive (only one-step)
Serial testing without known exposure	Increase of ≥10 mm is considered a positive result (TST conversion)	Change from negative to positive (QFT conversion)
Known exposure (close contact)	≥5 mm is considered a positive result in persons who have a baseline TST result of 0 mm; an increase of ≥10 mm is considered a positive result in persons with a negative baseline TST result or previous follow-up screening TST result of ≥0 mm	Change to positive

Source: Jensen PA, Lambert LA, Iademarco MF, et al. Guidelines for preventing the transmission of Mycobacterium tuberculosis in health-care settings, 2005. *MMWR Recomm Rep* 2005 Dec 30;54(RR-17):47.

References: *APIC Text*, 4th edition, Chapter 95 - Tuberculosis and Other Mycobacteria; *APIC Text*, 4th edition, Chapter 100 - Occupational Health; Jensen PA, Lambert LA, Iademarco MF, et al. Guidelines for preventing the transmission of Mycobacterium tuberculosis in health-care settings, 2005. *MMWR Recomm Rep* 2005 Dec 30;54(RR-17):1-141

2. **B Until 7 days after onset of jaundice**

Rationale: According to the ACIP, food service workers who are diagnosed with Hepatitis A must be restricted from food handling until 7 days after the onset of jaundice.

References: *APIC Text*, 4th edition, Chapter 100 - Occupational Health; Advisory Committee on Immunization Practices (ACIP). ACIP Recommendations. ACIP Website. Available at: http://www.cdc.gov/vaccines/acip/recs/index.html

NOTES

3. **C A national registry for all healthcare personnel known to be Hepatitis C antibody positive**

Rationale: No vaccine against HCV infection exists. National recommendations for prevention and control of HCV infection, issued in 1998, emphasize primary prevention activities to reduce the risk for HCV transmission. These activities include screening and testing of blood donors, viral inactivation of plasma-derived products, risk-reduction counseling and screening of persons at risk for HCV infection, and adherence to Standard Precautions and safe work practices in healthcare settings.

Reference: *APIC Text*, 4th edition, Chapter 101 - Occupational Exposure to Bloodborne Pathogens

4. **D Bacillus Calmette-Guérin (BCG)**

Rationale: Immunization programs provide protection from vaccine-preventable diseases for both the workers and those under their care. The infectious diseases for which vaccines are available for pre-exposure intervention include Hepatitis A and B, influenza, measles, mumps, rubella, tetanus, pertussis, and varicella-zoster (chickenpox).

References: *APIC Text*, 4th edition, Chapter 100 - Occupational Health; Advisory Committee on Immunization Practices (ACIP). ACIP Recommendations. ACIP Website. Available at: http://www.cdc.gov/vaccines/acip/recs/index.html

5. **B Vaccines should be stored in a labeled container/bin on the middle shelf a few inches from the wall**

Rationale: Vaccine storage and handling errors can reduce vaccine potency and result in inadequate immune responses and protection against disease. The CDC recommends the following regarding vaccine storage:

- Vaccines need to be placed in the central area of the unit, away from walls, vents, and coils
- Avoid placing vaccines on the top shelf
- There must be enough room to store the year's largest inventory without crowding
- A calibrated thermometer should be placed inside each storage unit
- The storage unit must be dedicated to the storage of vaccines

Reference: Centers for Disease Control and Prevention (CDC). *Vaccine Storage and Handling Toolkit*. CDC website. 2012. Available at: https://www.cdc.gov/vaccines/hcp/admin/storage/toolkit/storage-handling-toolkit.pdf

NOTES

6. **Ⓒ No treatment is recommended for a known responder**

Rationale: According to the CDC guidelines, when the employee is known to have responded (converted) to positive Hepatitis B antibody following immunization series, no treatment is recommended.

Table 6-2. Recommended Postexposure Prophylaxis for Exposure to Hepatitis B Virus

Vaccination and Antibody Response Status of Exposed Healthcare Personnel*	Source HBsAg† Positive	Source HBsAg† Negative	Source Unknown or Not Available for Testing
Unvaccinated	HBIG§ × 1 and initiate Hepatitis B vaccine series¶	Initiate Hepatitis B vaccine series	Initiate Hepatitis B vaccine series
Previously vaccinated			
Known responder**	No treatment	No treatment	No treatment
Known nonresponder††	HBIG × 1 and initiate revaccination or HBIG × 2§§	No treatment	If known high-risk source, treat as if source were HBsAg positive.
Antibody response unknown	Test exposed person for anti-HBs¶¶ 1. If adequate,** no treatment is necessary. 2. If inadequate,†† HBIG × 1 and vaccine booster.	No treatment	Test exposed person for anti-HBs: 1. If adequate,¶ no treatment is necessary. 2. If inadequate,¶ administer vaccine booster and recheck titer in 1 to 2 months.

** Persons who have previously been infected with HBV are immune to reinfection and do not require postexposure prophylaxis.*

† Hepatitis B surface antigen.

§ Hepatitis B immune globulin; dose is 0.06 mL/kg intramuscularly.

¶ Hepatitis B vaccine.

*** A responder is a person with adequate levels of serum antibody to HBsAg (i.e., anti-HBs >10 mIU/mL).*

†† A nonresponder is a person with inadequate response to vaccination (i.e., serum anti-HBs <10 mIU/mL).

§§ The option of giving one dose of HBIG and reinitiating the vaccine series is preferred for nonresponders who have not completed a second 3-dose vaccine series. For persons who previously completed a second vaccine series but failed to respond, two doses of HBIG are preferred.

¶¶ Antibody to HBsAg.

Source: Centers for Disease Control and Prevention. Updated U.S. Public Health Service guidelines for the management of occupational exposures to HBV, HCV, and HIV and recommendations for postexposure prophylaxis. *MMWR Recomm Rep* 2001 June 29; 50(RR11):22.

References: *APIC Text*, 4th edition, Chapter 101 - Occupational Exposure to Bloodborne Pathogens; Centers for Disease Control and Prevention. Updated U.S. Public Health Service Guidelines for the Management of Occupational Exposures to HBV, HCV, and HIV and Recommendations for Postexposure Prophylaxis. *MMWR Recomm Rep* 2001 June 29; 50(RR11):1-42

NOTES

7. **B From day 10 after exposure to day 21 after exposure**

Rationale: According to the ACIP guidelines, a nonimmune healthcare worker who has direct contact with a patient with varicella zoster should be excluded from work duty from the 10th day after the first day of exposure through the 21st days after the last exposure.

Reference: *APIC Text*, 4th edition, Chapter 100 - Occupational Health

8. **D 2, 4, 6**

Rationale: QFT-G is a blood assay. Intradermal rather than tine testing methods should be used for TST. Testing should be administered at the time of exposure and repeated at 12 week postexposure to look for possible converters. Chest radiographs are performed only on those with prior positive screening results who are currently symptomatic.

Reference: *APIC Text*, 4th edition, Chapter 100 - Occupational Health

9. **D 35°F to 46°F (2°C to 8°C)**

Rationale: Most routinely recommended vaccines should be stored in a refrigerator between 35°F and 46°F (2°C and 8°C), with a desired average temperature of 40°F (5°C). Exposure to temperatures outside this range may result in reduced vaccine potency and increased risk of vaccine-preventable diseases.

Reference: Centers for Disease Control and Prevention (CDC). *Vaccine Storage and Handling Toolkit*. CDC website. 2012. Available at: https://www.cdc.gov/vaccines/hcp/admin/storage/toolkit/storage-handling-toolkit.pdf

10. **D They are required to provide proof of immunity to measles, mumps, and rubella**

Rationale: All persons working in healthcare facilities should be immune to measles, mumps, and rubella. It is reasonable to require proof of immunization. Proof of immunity consists of documented vaccination with one or more doses of live vaccine on or after the first birthday, laboratory evidence of immunity to these diseases, or history of these diseases based on a healthcare worker diagnosis. Although birth before 1957 is considered acceptable evidence of measles, rubella, and mumps immunity, ACIP recommends that healthcare facilities consider vaccinating unvaccinated personnel born before 1957 who do not have laboratory evidence of measles, rubella, and mumps immunity; laboratory confirmation of disease; or vaccination with two appropriately spaced doses of MMR vaccine for measles and mumps and one dose of MMR vaccine for rubella.

References: *APIC Text*, 4th edition, Chapter 103 - Immunization of Healthcare Personnel; McLean HQ, Fiebelkorn AP, Temte JL, et al. Prevention of Measles, Rubella, Congenital Rubella Syndrome, and Mumps, 2013: Summary Recommendations of the Advisory Committee on Immunization Practices (ACIP). *MMWR Recomm* Rep 2013 Jun 14;62(RR-04):1-34. Available at: http://www.cdc.gov/mmwr/preview/mmwrhtml/rr6204a1.htm#Tab3

11. **D A fit-tested respirator or powered air purifying respirator (PAPR)**

Rationale: Healthcare personnel assisting with bronchoscopy should wear appropriate personal protective equipment including a fit-tested respirator or a PAPR.

Reference: *APIC Text*, 4th edition, Chapter 55 - Endoscopy

NOTES

12. **B Complete the Hepatitis B vaccine series and provide Hepatitis B immunoglobulin**

Rationale: HBV is transmitted by percutaneous or mucosal exposure to infectious blood or body fluids. The risk of HBV seroconversion after a percutaneous injury ranges from 23 to 62 percent depending on the Hepatitis B e antigen (HBeAg) status of the source person. For exposed persons who are in the process of being vaccinated but have not completed the vaccination series, vaccination should be completed as scheduled, and Hepatitis B immune globulin (HBIG) should be added as indicated. Both HBIG and the Hepatitis B vaccine should be administered as soon as possible after exposure (preferably within 24 hours).

Reference: *APIC Text*, 4th edition, Chapter 101 - Occupational Exposure to Bloodborne Pathogens

13. **D They might experience symptoms that are due to the immune response to the vaccine, but they cannot get the flu from the vaccine**

Rationale: Vaccination is the primary method for preventing influenza and its complications. Healthcare personnel compliance with annual influenza vaccination is an expected behavior to protect patients, staff, and families. There are two forms of vaccination available: the inactivated, injectable vaccine and the live/attenuated, intranasal vaccine (LAIV). Inactivated influenza vaccine contains noninfectious viral components and cannot cause influenza. LAIV can cause nasal congestion, sore throat, and headache for a few days. Some mild symptoms such as nasal congestion, sore throat, and headache can occur as a result of the immune response to the vaccine but these are typically minor and short-lived.

Reference: *APIC Text*, 4th edition, Chapter 103 - Immunization of Healthcare Personnel

14. **A 1, 2**

Rationale: Staff members must follow Standard Precautions when exposure to blood or other potentially infectious materials is anticipated or likely. Times during which exposure is most likely to occur include initiation and termination of dialysis and during reprocessing, cleaning, or disinfection procedures.

Reference: *APIC Text*, 4th edition, Chapter 39 - Dialysis

15. **D Probe in a glycol-filled bottle with an external monitoring device**

Rationale: The CDC recommends using a temperature probe in a bottle filled with a thermal buffer, like glycol, that connects to an external monitoring device. This allows for temperatures to be monitored without having to open the unit door. In addition, the CDC recommends the use of digital data loggers. The CDC does not recommend the use of fluid-filled biosafe liquid thermometers, infrared thermometers, or chart recorders.

Reference: Centers for Disease Control and Prevention (CDC). *Vaccine Storage and Handling Toolkit*. CDC website. 2012. Available at: https://www.cdc.gov/vaccines/hcp/admin/storage/toolkit/storage-handling-toolkit.pdf

NOTES

16. (B) The respiratory therapist who intubated the patient

Rationale: PEP is advised for persons who have had intensive, unprotected contact with infected patients. *Unprotected* means without wearing a mask, and intensive contact would be mouth-to-mouth resuscitation, endotracheal intubation, endotracheal tube management, or close examination of the oropharynx. Prophylactic therapy should be administered immediately after the unprotected exposure. Current recommended regimens to eradicate carriage are rifampin 600 mg orally every 12 hours for 2 days; a single dose of ciprofloxacin 500 mg orally; or a single dose of ceftriaxone 250 mg intramuscularly. Rifampin and ciprofloxacin are not recommended for pregnant women.

Reference: *APIC Text*, 4th edition, Chapter 100 - Occupational Health

17. (B) Hepatitis B

Rationale: Exposure to bloodborne pathogens poses a serious risk to healthcare personnel. Avoiding occupational blood exposures through adherence to Standard Precautions and other safe work practices is essential. The most effective means to prevent transmission of bloodborne pathogens in healthcare settings include Hepatitis B vaccination, the use of appropriate barriers to prevent blood and body fluid contact, and preventing percutaneous injuries by eliminating unnecessary needle use, implementing devices with safety features, using safe work practices when handling needles and other sharp devices, and safely disposing of sharps and blood-contaminated materials. OSHA's Bloodborne Pathogen Standard mandates provision of Hepatitis B vaccine at no cost to all healthcare personnel and others at occupational risk for blood exposure.

Reference: *APIC Text*, 4th edition, Chapter 101 - Occupational Exposure to Bloodborne Pathogens

18. (C) Born after 1957

Rationale: According to the ACIP, the following are proof of measles immunity for healthcare providers: (1) documentation of vaccination with two doses of live measles virus-containing vaccine, (2) laboratory evidence of immunity, (3) laboratory confirmation of disease, or (4) born before 1957. The latest recommendations also state that for unvaccinated personnel who were born before 1957 and who lack laboratory evidence of measles, rubella, or mumps immunity or laboratory confirmation of disease, healthcare facilities should consider vaccinating personnel with two doses of MMR vaccine at the appropriate interval (for measles and mumps) and one dose of MMR vaccine (for rubella), respectively.

References: *APIC Text*, 4th edition, Chapter 103 - Immunization of Healthcare Personnel; McLean HQ, Fiebelkorn AP, Temte JL, et al. Prevention of Measles, Rubella, Congenital Rubella Syndrome, and Mumps, 2013: Summary Recommendations of the Advisory Committee on Immunization Practices (ACIP). *MMWR Recomm* Rep 2013 Jun 14;62(RR-04):1-34. Available at: http://www.cdc.gov/mmwr/preview/mmwrhtml/rr6204a1.htm#Tab3

NOTES

19. D They may return to work with no restrictions

Rationale: Although work restrictions in such a scenario would likely be influenced by outside agencies such as the local and state Health Departments and the CDC, inhalation anthrax is not transmissible among humans so these exposed healthcare workers pose no risk to patients or other employees.

References: Brunette GW, ed. *CDC Health Information for International Travel 2014*. New York: Oxford University Press, 2014; *APIC Text*, 4th edition, Chapter 120 - Infectious Disease Disasters: Bioterrorism, Emerging Infections, and Pandemics

20. C Total number of needlesticks reported by nursing divided by the number of full-time nurses employed during the year

Rationale: The rates of needlestick injuries can be identified by occupational category. For example: total number of needlesticks reported by nursing in 1 year divided by number of full-time equivalent nurses employed in that year equals the rate of needlesticks per full-time equivalent nurse per year.

Reference: *APIC Text*, 4th edition, Chapter 100 - Occupational Health

21. D Remain off work for 5 days (March 20) or until symptoms have resolved, whichever is longer

Rationale: Influenza is primarily spread between individuals via respiratory secretions (droplet spread). Viral shedding starts 24 to 48 hours after infection, and typically 24 hours before the onset of symptoms. Shedding normally persists less than 5 days but can be longer in children and in immunocompromised persons. Thus, adults are typically infectious from the day before symptoms begin until approximately 5 days after the onset of illness. Staff members who develop influenza illness should be furloughed for 5 days after diagnosis or the duration of their illness, whichever is longer.

Reference: *APIC Text*, 4th edition, Chapter 82 - Influenza

22. B The employee should be treated as soon as possible with expanded multidrug PEP

Rationale: Because the patient is known to have a high HIV viral load, the exposure should be considered an increased risk for transmission. According to the CDC, most HIV exposures warrant a two-drug regimen using two nucleoside reverse transcriptase inhibitors (NRTIs) or one NRTI and one nucleotide reverse transcriptase inhibitor. The CDC recommends that the addition of a third (or even fourth) drug should be considered for exposures that pose an increased risk for transmission or that involve a source in whom antiretroviral drug resistance is likely.

References: *APIC Text*, 4th edition, Chapter 101 - Occupational Exposure to Bloodborne Pathogens; Kuhar DT, Henderson DK, Struble KA, et al. Updated US Public Health Service guidelines for the management of occupational exposures to human immunodeficiency virus and recommendations for postexposure prophylaxis. Infect Control Hosp Epidemiol. 2013 Sep;34(9):875–892

NOTES

23. (C) Root cause analyses after exposure incidents

Rationale: The root cause analysis process takes a retrospective look at adverse outcomes and determines what happened, why it happened, and what an organization can do to prevent the situation from recurring. When conducting a root cause analysis, a multidisciplinary team discovers basic and contributing causes for what happened. The entire process identifies changes to a particular process or system that improves safety or reduces process error. Performing a root cause analysis is the best approach to take to accomplish the goal of decreasing sharp injuries.

Reference: *APIC Text*, 4th edition, Chapter 16 - Quality Concepts

24. (C) An interferon-gamma release assay (IGRA) blood test would be the best method to use because prior BCG immunization does not cause a false positive with this test

Rationale: An IGRA would be the best choice in this case because it will not be affected by the employee's prior BCG vaccination. Other advantages of IGRAs are that they do not require a follow-up visit to read the test and that the results are available within 24 hours. However, IGRA testing is generally more expensive than TST.

References: *APIC Text*, 4th edition, Chapter 95 - Tuberculosis and Other Mycobacteria; Centers for Disease Control and Prevention (CDC). TB Elimination Interferon-Gamma Release Assays (IGRAs) - Blood Tests for TB Infection. CDC website. 2012. Available at: http://www.cdc.gov/tb/publications/factsheets/testing/igra.htm

25. (D) Born before 1980

Rationale: According to the ACIP, the following are proof of immunity for varicella in a healthcare provider: (1) evidence of two doses of the varicella vaccine, (2) laboratory evidence of immunity to varicella, or (3) laboratory confirmation of disease. Birth before 1980 should not be considered proof of immunity for healthcare providers.

Reference: Marin M, Güris D, Chaves SS, et al. Prevention of Varicella - Recommendations of the Advisory Committee on Immunization Practices (ACIP). *MMWR Rec Rep* 2007 June; 56(RR04);1-40. Available at: http://www.cdc.gov/mmwr/preview/mmwrhtml/rr5604a1.htm#box

Chapter 7
MANAGEMENT AND COMMUNICATION

The CIC® exam will have a total of thirteen (13) questions addressing Management and Communication. The content will test knowledge of the following:

NOTES

A. Planning

1. Develop, evaluate, and revise a mission and vision statement, goals, measurable objectives, and action plans for the Infection Prevention and Control Program
2. Assess needs then recommend specific equipment, personnel, and resources for the Infection Prevention and Control Program
3. Participate in cost benefit assessments, efficacy studies, evaluations, and standardization of products
4. Recommend changes in practice based on current evidence, clinical outcomes, and financial implications
5. Incorporate business modeling to assign value to prevention of and/or presence of healthcare-associated infection (e.g., cost/benefit analysis, return on investment)

B. Communication and Feedback

1. Provide infection prevention and control findings, recommendations, and reports to appropriate stakeholders
2. Facilitate implementation of policies, procedures, and recommendations
3. Communicate effectively with internal and external stakeholders (e.g., transitions of care, reporting of notifiable diseases)
4. Collaborate with internal and external stakeholders in the identification and review of adverse and sentinel events
5. Evaluate and facilitate compliance with accreditation standards/regulatory requirements
6. Perform and create a personalized development plan (e.g., set goals, maintain competence)

NOTES

C. Quality/Performance Improvement and Patient Safety

1. Participate in quality/performance improvement and patient safety activities related to infection prevention and control (e.g., failure mode and effects analysis, plan-do-study-act)
2. Develop, monitor, measure, and evaluate performance indicators to drive quality improvement initiatives
3. Select and apply appropriate quality/performance improvement tools (e.g., "fishbone" diagram, Pareto charts, flow charts, Strengths-Weaknesses-Opportunities-Threats, Gap Analysis)

KEY CONCEPTS

- Successful approaches for preventing and reducing healthcare-associated infections (HAIs) relies on the effective interplay of multiple management systems.
- A comprehensive organizational approach is essential to manage infection risk and improve patient safety. This approach involves managing structures and systems that change organizational culture and individual behaviors and that support sustainable improvements.
- Infection prevention must be fully integrated into the structure, systems, metrics, and culture of the healthcare organization.
- An effective infection prevention program encompasses responsibility, collaboration, consultation, and a broad vision to look at community risks and resources.

RESOURCES FOR STUDY

Nearly all questions on Management and Communication are based on chapters in the primary references, but secondary references may be useful to help clarify more detailed issues.

Primary Reference:

1. Grota P, ed. *APIC Text of Infection Control and Epidemiology*, 4th edition. Washington, DC: Association for Professionals in Infection Control and Epidemiology, 2014. Also available online at http://text.apic.org [subscription required].

NOTES

Notable Chapters

1	Infection Prevention and Control Programs
2	Competency and Certification of the Infection Preventionist
3	Education and Training
4	Accrediting and Regulatory Agencies
5	Infection Prevention and Behavioral Interventions
6	Healthcare Informatics and Information Technology
8	Legal Issues
9	Staffing
16	Quality Concepts
17	Performance Measures
18	Patient Safety

2. Brooks K. *Ready Reference for Microbes*, 3rd edition. Washington, DC: Association for Professionals in Infection Control and Epidemiology, 2012.

3. Heymann D, ed. *Control of Communicable Diseases Manual*, 19th edition. Washington, DC: American Public Health Association, 2008.

4. Kulich P, Taylor D, eds. *The Infection Preventionist's Guide to the Lab*. Washington, DC: Association for Professionals in Infection Control and Epidemiology, 2012.

Secondary Reference:

1. Current Recommendations of the Advisory Committee on Immunization Practices (ACIP).

2. Current guidelines, standards, and recommendations from CDC, APIC, SHEA, and Public Health Agency of Canada.

3. Pickering, Larry K, ed. *Red Book*, 29th ed., Elk Grove Village, IL: American Academy of Pediatrics; 2012.

NOTES

PRACTICE QUESTIONS

1. Which of the following terms refers to patient harm that is the result of treatment by the healthcare system rather than from the health condition of the patient?
   a. Adverse event
   b. Dire consequence
   c. Unanticipated event
   d. Sentinel event

2. The antibiogram is usually prepared by:
   a. Infection Prevention and Control Department
   b. Laboratory
   c. Pharmacy
   d. Information Technology Department

3. The Safe Medical Device Act (SMDA) falls under which U.S. federal program?
   a. Centers for Disease Control and Prevention (CDC)
   b. Food and Drug Administration (FDA)
   c. National Institutes of Health (NIH)
   d. Agency for Healthcare Research and Quality's (AHRQ)

4. The Joint Commission standards for infection prevention and control include all of the following, *except*:
   a. Collaboration of representatives from relevant components and functions within the organization in the implementation of the program
   b. Effective management of the infection prevention and control program
   c. Minimizing the risk for development of an healthcare-associated infection (HAI) through an organization-wide infection prevention program
   d. Specific staffing requirement of one infection preventionist (IP) for every 100 beds in the facility

NOTES

5. Each year in the United States, what percentage of hospitalized patients develop HAIs?

a. Less than 2 percent

b. 4 percent

c. 10 percent

d. 20 percent

6. Human factor limitations that contribute to errors include:

1) Overdependence on multitasking skills

2) Permanent night shifts

3) Limited memory capacity

4) Stress, fatigue, and sensory overload

a. 1, 2, 3

b. 2, 3, 4

c. 1, 3, 4

d. 1, 2, 4

7. The Institute for Healthcare Improvement uses the Model for Improvement—a two-part model designed to accelerate improvement for healthcare processes and outcomes. What are the key component areas of this model?

1) Setting aims, establishing measures, selecting changes

2) Plan-do-study-act

3) Contemplation, action, termination

4) Perceived seriousness and cues to action

a. 1, 2

b. 2, 3

c. 3, 4

d. 1, 4

NOTES

8. Failure mode and effects analysis (FMEA) is used to examine adverse events and identify what went wrong and what might prevent it from happening again. Which statement best describes the mode element of FMEA?

- **a.** The way of operating or using a system or process, or a way or manner in which a thing is done
- **b.** The results or consequences of an action
- **c.** The detailed examination of the elements or structure of something—perhaps a process, substance, or situation
- **d.** Lack of success, nonperformance, nonoccurrence, or breaking down or ceasing to function

9. A number of research studies have examined the relationship between nurse staffing levels and the risk of HAIs in the hospital setting. Which of the following statements has not been supported by the literature?

- **a.** Patients in an intensive care unit (ICU) with lower levels of nurse staffing had an increased risk for ventilator-associated pneumonia
- **b.** The use of nonpermanent staff significantly increases a patient's infection risk
- **c.** A specific evidence-based nurse staffing level benchmark has been determined that is associated with decreased risk for HAI
- **d.** There is a relationship between adequate numbers of direct care providers (nurses) and the likelihood that CDC guidelines will be followed

10. The Director of Infection Prevention and Control is leading a process improvement project to decrease the rates of central line-associated bloodstream infections (CLABSI) in one of the hospital's ICUs. The multidisciplinary team has discussed multiple process improvement strategies to decrease these bloodstream infections. In developing the final improvement plan which of the choices below is most likely to help decrease the rates of these infections?

- **a.** Performing a gap analysis each month
- **b.** Performing a failure mode effect analysis immediately
- **c.** Incorporating the use of a CLABSI bundle and a checklist to ensure that all aspects of the plan are followed
- **d.** Perform a strengths, weaknesses, opportunities, and threats (SWOT) analysis

NOTES

11. The Director of Infection Prevention and Control has been asked to develop a business plan to potentially expand the scope of the organization's infection prevention program. The objective in developing a business plan for leadership is to:

- **a.** Provide a detailed synopsis of the impact of new services
- **b.** Demonstrate whether the expanded program will be worth the investment
- **c.** Summarize the infrastructure needs to support an expanded program
- **d.** Analyze program costs during the past 5 years

12. Which statement about organizational conflict is correct?

- **a.** Conflict resolution should focus on people, not issues
- **b.** Openness and transparency by management leads to conflict
- **c.** Conflict is a natural process within systems and fosters a search for alternatives
- **d.** Conflict is an immediate sign of dysfunctional work teams

13. The lead IP has proposed using an electronic surveillance system. Senior leadership at the healthcare organization now wants to know what the expected return on this investment will be. What is the IP's next step?

- **a.** Describe the project cost baseline developed from previous department budgets
- **b.** Provide a synopsis of the investment and direct and indirect costs, including factors such as capital expenses, depreciation, and inflation
- **c.** Project the impact of the surveillance system on hospital net revenue
- **d.** Calculate the amount of time needed to pay back the initial costs of the system

NOTES

14. An IP is updating the organization's infection prevention plan, which includes writing clearly stated goals and objectives. Which of the following statements might she consider including?

a. Vaccinate employees and volunteers for influenza every year

b. Serve as leader for facility safety rounds as needed

c. Achieve a 20 percent improvement in hand hygiene practice in the Emergency Department within 30 days

d. Collaborate with the laboratory to improve turnaround time for culture results

15. The Infection Prevention Manager observes increasing fatigue and burnout among the infection prevention team. What should the manager do first?

a. Contact Human Resources for assistance

b. Gather the team to identify issues and share concerns

c. Initiate a corrective action plan for the group

d. Recommend incentives to increase job satisfaction

16. Many external forces can impact the performance of an infection prevention team. Which of the following is *not* an example of an external force?

a. A mandate from the Chief Executive Officer to reduce costs by 8 percent

b. Changes in regulatory and accrediting standards

c. Increasing costs of supplies used for patient isolation

d. Department expenses to support IP certification

17. The Director of Infection Prevention and Control has been asked to participate in the organization's strategic planning. Which of the following might be a strategic goal for the Infection Prevention and Control program?

a. Implement an electronic surveillance system in the next 3 years

b. Fill the vacant IP position in the department within 45 days

c. Participate more actively in the organization's Value Analysis Committee

d. Share key HAI reports with senior managers every month

NOTES

18. A newly hired Infection Prevention Manager is addressing program deficits that occurred during the months the facility sought to fill the vacant position. The new manager must focus on many specific tasks, including working closely with others to clarify roles and responsibilities. This type of management approach is known as:

a. Charismatic

b. Situational

c. Functional

d. Motivational

19. The manager notices that a novice IP has misapplied the CDC definitions at least five times when conducting catheter-associated urinary tract infection surveillance recently. How should the manager respond?

a. Schedule the IP for additional training and competency-based testing

b. Speak with the IP to obtain additional information about the situation

c. Use the organization's disciplinary action process to correct poor performance

d. Refer the IP to the employee assistance program for personal counseling

20. Which of the following milestones indicates that the IP has achieved proficient status according to the APIC Competency Model?

a. After successfully completing his or her Certification in Infection Control®

b. Upon obtaining a graduate degree in a healthcare-related field

c. When continuously employed as an IP for more than 2 years

d. After 10 years of experience as the manager of an infection prevention and control program

NOTES

21. Obstacles for building a culture of patient safety in healthcare include all of the following *except*:

- **a.** Assignment of blame on healthcare providers
- **b.** High staff turnover rates
- **c.** Lack of resources for needed change
- **d.** Placement of accountability on healthcare systems

22. Which of the following statements best describes human factors?

- **a.** Ability to identify the many and various factors that impact upon a complex situation or event
- **b.** Prevention of errors and adverse effects to patients associated with healthcare use
- **c.** Environmental, organizational, and job elements and human and individual characteristics that influence behavior at work in a way that can affect health and safety
- **d.** The attitudes, beliefs, perceptions, and vales that employees share in relation to safety

23. When an error does not result in an adverse event for a patient because the error was caught, it is called a(n):

- **a.** Adverse event
- **b.** No-harm event
- **c.** Near-miss event
- **d.** Error report

24. In 1997, the Joint Commission on Accreditation of Healthcare Organizations (TJC) mandated the use of root cause analysis to:

- **a.** Document instances of medical malpractice
- **b.** Predict the occurrence of an incident
- **c.** Improve staffing issues
- **d.** Investigate sentinel events in accredited hospitals

25. The IP initiates a new program to encourage compliance with hand hygiene. One element to the program includes randomly distributing coupons for free coffee to employees who are seen adhering to hand hygiene recommendations. This is an example of which type of power?

- **a.** Coercive
- **b.** Reward
- **c.** Legitimate
- **d.** Expert

ANSWERS AND RATIONALES

NOTES

1. **(A) Adverse event**

Rationale: An adverse event is an unintended consequence of healthcare or services that results in a negative patient outcome (e.g., infection or physical or psychological injury). Incidents such as patient falls or improper administration of medications are also considered adverse events even if there is no permanent effect on the patient.

References: *APIC Text*, 4th edition, Chapter 18 - Patient Safety; *APIC Text*, 4th edition, Chapter 16 - Quality Concepts

2. **(B) Laboratory**

Rationale: Many hospital laboratories routinely perform antimicrobial susceptibility testing on bacterial pathogens. Cumulative susceptibility testing results are often organized into a summary table, or antibiogram, which may be used by clinicians, pharmacists, infection control personnel, and microbiologists as a reference guide to community or hospital-specific resistance patterns. Antibiograms lend information that can be used to raise awareness of resistance problems, support the use of optimal empiric therapy, and identify opportunities to reduce inappropriate antibiotic usage and to ascertain success of such efforts. Antibiograms are generally prepared by the laboratory according to the Clinical Laboratory Standards Institute guidelines.

References: *APIC Text*, 4th edition, Chapter 26 - Antimicrobials and Resistance; Appendix D. In: Brooks K. *Ready Reference for Microbes*, 3rd edition. Washington, DC: Association for Professionals in Infection Control and Epidemiology, 2012.

3. **(B) Food and Drug Administration (FDA)**

Rationale: The FDA falls within the executive branch of the U.S. government under the Department of Health and Human Services. The FDA develops, implements, monitors, and enforces standards for the safety, effectiveness, and labeling of all drugs and biologics, including food, blood and blood products, medical and radiological devices, antimicrobial products, and chemical germicides used in conjunction with medical devices.

Reference: *APIC Text*, 4th edition, Chapter 4 - Accrediting and Regulatory Agencies

4. **(D) Specific staffing requirement of one infection preventionist (IP) for every 100 beds in the facility**

Rationale: The Joint Commission lists five standards for infection prevention and control, which include minimizing the risk for development of an HAI through an organization-wide infection prevention program, identification of risk for the acquisition and transmission of infectious agents on an ongoing basis, effective management of the infection prevention and control program, collaboration of representatives from relevant components and functions within the organization in the implementation of the program, and allocation of adequate resources to the infection prevention and control programs. However, there is no specific staffing requirement.

Reference: *APIC Text*, 4th edition, Chapter 9 - Staffing

NOTES

5. (B) 4 percent

Rationale: In March 2014, the CDC released new data on healthcare-associated infection rates in the United States hospitals. According to the Multistate Point-Prevalence Survey of Health Care-Associated Infections, 1 in 25 patients (722,000 infections) in the U.S. acquire HAIs each year, and approximately 75,000 patients who have an HAI will die during hospitalization. The report notes that pneumonia is now the most common HAI in the United States, accounting for 22 percent of infections. The second most common infections are surgical site (22 percent), followed by gastrointestinal (17 percent), urinary tract (13 percent), and bloodstream infections (10 percent). The report also notes that the top organisms leading to HAIs are *Clostridium difficile* (12 percent), *Staphylococcus* (11 percent), *Klebsiella* (10 percent), *Escherichia coli* (9 percent), *Enterococcus* (9 percent), and *Pseudomonas* (7 percent).

Reference: Magill SS, Edwards JR, Bamberg W, et al. Multistate Point-Prevalence Survey of Health Care-Associated Infections. *N Engl J Med* 2014; 370:1198-1208. Available at: http://www.nejm.org/doi/full/10.1056/NEJMoa1306801

6. (C) 1, 3, 4

Rationale: Human factors refer to environmental, organizational and job factors, and human and individual characteristics, which influence behavior at work in a way that can affect health and safety. Human factor limitations that contribute to errors include:

- Limited memory capacity: five to seven pieces of information are typical for short-term memory
- Negative effects of stress and associated cognitive tunnel vision used to compensate and focus in highly intense situations
- Negative influence of fatigue and sensory overload
- Overdependence on multitasking skills of staff in complex work environments

Reference: *APIC Text*, 4th edition, Chapter 18 - Patient Safety

7. (A) 1, 2

Rationale: The first part of the Model for Improvement includes setting aims (asking what are we trying to accomplish), establishing measures (how to know that the change leads to an improvement), and selecting changes that will make an improvement. The second part of the Model for Improvement involves testing the selected changes in a plan-do-study-act cycle. Small-scale testing is followed by refinement and more testing until the changes are ready to be rolled out on a larger scale.

References: Institute for Healthcare Improvement. *Science of Improvement: How to Improve*. IHI website. 2014. Available at: www.ihi.org/resources/Pages/HowtoImprove/ScienceofImprovementHowtoImprove.aspx; *APIC Text*, 4th edition, Chapter 1 - Infection Prevention and Control Programs; *APIC Text*, 4th edition, Chapter 16 - Quality Concepts

NOTES

8. **A The way of operating or using a system or process, or a way or manner in which a thing is done**

Rationale: The FMEA tool is a proactive, preventive approach to identify potential failures and opportunities for error. The mode is described as the way of operating or using a system or process, or a way or manner in which a thing is done. A mode is the way or manner in which something, such as a failure, can happen. Combining the words "failure" and "mode," a failure mode is the manner by which something can fail. A failure mode generally describes the way the failure occurs and its impact on a process. Any step in a process can fail, and each failure may have many failure mode.

Reference: *APIC Text*, 4th edition, Chapter 18 - Patient Safety

9. **C A specific evidence-based nurse staffing level benchmark has been determined that is associated with decreased risk for HAI**

Rationale: Hospitals with low nurse staffing levels tend to have higher rates of poor patient outcomes such as pneumonia, shock, cardiac arrest, and urinary tract infections. Furthermore, a number of researchers have found the level and/or the use of nonpermanent staff also significantly increases a patient's infection risk. Despite these data, determination of a specific evidence-based nurse staffing level benchmark that is associated with decreased risk for HAI has not been determined.

Reference: *APIC Text*, 4th edition, Chapter 9 - Staffing

10. **C Incorporating the use of a CLABSI bundle and a checklist to ensure that all aspects of the plan are followed**

Rationale: Implementing a formalized process reduces errors caused by lack of information and inconsistent procedures. Checklists and best practice bundles can promote process improvement and increase patient safety. By applying checklists to the prevention of infection within an organization and using simple steps such as washing hands and cleaning the skin with antiseptic, organizations can eliminate hazards and problems that affect patients every day. Bundles can create standardized and simplified processes and procedures, and the checklist provides an organized way to incorporate best practices.

Reference: *APIC Text*, 4th edition, Chapter 16 - Quality Concepts

11. **B Demonstrate whether the expanded program will be worth the investment**

Rationale: A business plan is a formal statement of a set of business goals, the reasons they are believed attainable, and the plan for reaching those goals. Business plans are decision-making tools and cost and revenue estimates are central to any business plan for deciding the viability of the planned venture.

Reference: *APIC Text*, 4th edition, Chapter 1 - Infection Prevention and Control Programs

NOTES

12. (C) Conflict is a natural process within systems and fosters a search for alternatives

Rationale: Organizational conflict is a state of discord caused by the actual or perceived opposition of needs, values, and interests between people working together. Organizational conflict stimulates a search for alternatives and can represent an opportunity for productive change. Acknowledging the existence of the conflict and investigating the source of it can lead to creative solutions.

References: *APIC Text*, 4th edition, Chapter 1 - Infection Prevention and Control Programs; *APIC Text*, 4th edition, Chapter 16 - Quality Concepts

13. (B) Provide a synopsis of the investment and direct and indirect costs, including factors such as capital expenses, depreciation, and inflation

Rationale: Return on investment (ROI) is a financial ratio intended to measure the benefit obtained from an investment. A high ROI means the investment gains compare favorably to investment cost. As a performance measure, ROI is used to evaluate the efficiency of an investment or to compare the efficiency of a number of different investments.

Reference: *APIC Text*, 4th edition, Chapter 1 - Infection Prevention and Control Programs

14. (C) Achieve a 20 percent improvement in hand hygiene practice in the Emergency Department within 30 days

Rationale: Goals are statements about general aims or purposes that are broad and long-range intended outcomes and concepts. Specific measurable objectives, however, describe the desired learning outcomes. Answer C is an example of a specific, measurable objective and includes a time component.

Reference: *APIC Text*, 4th edition, Chapter 3 - Education and Training

15. (B) Gather the team to identify issues and share concerns

Rationale: Although some workplace stress is normal, excessive stress can result in increased absenteeism and turnover rates, as well as decreased productivity. Workplace stress can, however, be successfully reduced through organizational and worker-focused interventions. The first step involves identifying the problems and stressors in the organization. It is critical to collaborate with the team to identify problems and discuss the opportunities that exist for improvement and change.

Reference: *APIC Text*, 4th edition, Chapter 3 - Education and Training

16. (D) Department expenses to support IP certification

Rationale: Managers must recognize and respond to all factors that affect their organizations. Organizational change is driven through fluctuations in the internal and external environments. The external environment includes factors that occur outside of the department that cause changes within and are, for the most part, beyond the control of the department. Common external factors include competition, the economy, technology, political and social conditions, and resource.

References: *APIC Text*, 4th edition, Chapter 1 - Infection Prevention and Control Programs; *APIC Text*, 4th edition, Chapter 9 - Staffing

NOTES

17. (A) **Implement an electronic surveillance system in the next 3 years**

Rationale: Strategic planning is an organization's process of defining its strategy, or direction, and making decisions on allocating its resources to pursue this strategy. The process includes setting goals, determining actions to achieve the goals, and mobilizing resources to execute the actions. Strategic goals are planned objectives that a department or organization strives to achieve. Answer A is an example of a clear measurable goal that is focused on the future and provides direction for the departmen.

References: *APIC Text*, 4th edition, Chapter 1 - Infection Prevention and Control Programs; *APIC Text*, 4th edition, Chapter 16 - Quality Concepts; *APIC Text*, 4th edition, Chapter 6 - Healthcare Informatics and Information Technology

18. (C) **Functional**

Rationale: Functional management is the most common type of organizational management. A functional manager is a person who has management authority over an organizational unit—such as a department—within a business, company, or other organization. Functional managers have ongoing responsibilities and are not usually directly affiliated with project teams, other than ensuring that goals and objectives are aligned with the organization's overall strategy and vision.

References: *APIC Text*, 4th edition, Chapter 1 - Infection Prevention and Control Programs; *APIC Text*, 4th edition, Chapter 2 - Competency and Certification of the Infection Preventionist

19. (B) **Speak with the IP to obtain additional information about the situation**

Rationale: Discrepancies between current and desired job performance as well as gaps between existing and desired competencies and skills should be investigated and clarified before identifying a corrective action.

References: *APIC Text*, 4th edition, Chapter 1 - Infection Prevention and Control Programs; *APIC Text*, 4th edition, Chapter 9 - Staffing

20. (A) **After successfully completing his or her Certification in Infection Control®**

Rationale: The Certification in Infection Control® credential identifies healthcare professionals who have shown mastery in knowledge of infection prevention and control by sitting for and passing the certification exam. According to APIC's competency model, the proficient IP has earned an undergraduate degree and is often pursuing post-baccalaureate education. The proficient IP may have management or supervisory responsibility. This IP has earned certification and may serve as a mentor for those pursuing the credential. Proficient IPs have a diverse skill set, demonstrate critical thinking, and function successfully in team-based, collaborative situations. They have further developed and are refining their leadership skills and are effectively managing their IPC program. Proficient IPs are highly skilled and professionally confident in their roles as preventionists and patient safety advocates.

References: *APIC Text*, 4th edition, Chapter 2 - Competency and Certification of the Infection Preventionist; Murphy DM, Hanchett M, Olmsted RN, et al. Competency in infection prevention: a conceptual approach to guide current and future practice. *Am J Infect Control* 2012 May;40(4):296-303.

NOTES

21. **D Placement of accountability on healthcare systems**

Rationale: The creation, maintenance, and periodic measurement of a culture of safety are now health system regulatory requirements. Attributes of a safety culture include placing a high priority on safety; allocating the appropriate resources, structure, and accountability to promote a culture of safety; encouraging and rewarding the identification, communication, and resolution of safety issues; and providing a structure and process to learning from mistakes. Management has a set of responsibilities that include educating staff on event reporting, making continuous safety improvements, and identifying system flaws and potential corrective actions. Managers must focus on the "how," not the "who" of an event, while underscoring individual accountability and responsibility.

Reference: *APIC Text*, 4th edition, Chapter 18 - Patient Safety

22. **C Environmental, organizational, and job elements and human and individual characteristics that influence behavior at work in a way that can affect health and safety**

Rationale: Human factors examine the relationship between people, the tools and equipment they use in the workplace, and the systems with which they interact. The goal of human factors is to minimize errors by focusing on improving efficiency, creativity, productivity, and job satisfaction. The application of human factors knowledge to healthcare can help design processes to improve patient safety.

Reference: *APIC Text*, 4th edition, Chapter 18 - Patient Safety

23. **C Near-miss event**

Rationale: A near-miss event is an unplanned event that could have resulted in injury, illness, or damage but did not, either by chance or through timely intervention.

Reference: *APIC Text*, 4th edition, Chapter 18 - Patient Safety

24. **D Investigate sentinel events in accredited hospitals**

Rationale: A sentinel event is defined by TJC as any unanticipated event in a healthcare setting resulting in death or serious physical or psychological injury to a patient or patients that is not related to the natural course of the patient's illness. Sentinel events specifically include loss of a limb or gross motor function and any event for which a recurrence would carry a risk of a serious adverse outcome. Sentinel events are identified under TJC accreditation policies to help aid in root cause analysis and to assist in development of preventative measures.

References: *APIC Text*, 4th edition, Chapter 18 - Patient Safety; *APIC Text*, 4th edition, Chapter 16 - Quality Concepts

25. **B Reward**

Rationale: Power is an integral part of management and leadership. The five main types of power include coercive, expert, legitimate, referent, and reward. Reward power refers to the ability to grant another person something that they desire or to remove or decrease things that the person does not desire.

References: *APIC Text*, 4th edition, Chapter 1 - Infection Prevention and Control Programs; *APIC Text*, 4th edition, Chapter 3 - Education and Training

Chapter 8
EDUCATION AND RESEARCH

The CIC® exam will have a total of eleven (11) questions addressing Education and Research. The content will test knowledge of the following:

A. Education

1. Assess needs, develop goals and measurable objectives for preparing educational offerings
2. Prepare, present, or coordinate educational content that is appropriate for the audience
3. Provide immediate feedback, education, and/or training when lapses in practice are observed
4. Evaluate the effectiveness of education and learner outcomes (e.g., observation of practice, process measures)
5. Facilitate effective education of patients, families, and others regarding prevention and control measures
6. Implement strategies that engage the patient, family, and others in activities aimed at preventing infection

B. Research

1. Conduct a literature review
2. Critically appraise the literature
3. Facilitate incorporation of applicable research findings into practice

NOTES

NOTES

KEY CONCEPTS

- The most basic goal of healthcare education and training is to improve job skills and competence
- Healthcare's complexity and rapid changes require that training activities also address issues of literacy, diversity, cultural competency, cross-training, and technological advances
- Successful educational activities in healthcare should be informed by learning theories and the educational needs of the learner population, the institution, and the community as they relate to infection prevention
- The critical evaluation of published research is necessary to assess the usefulness and validity of research findings
- Incorporating evidence-based research findings into practice serves to improve safety, quality care, and outcomes of individuals, providers and organizations

RESOURCES FOR STUDY

Nearly all questions on Education and Research are based on chapters in the primary references, but secondary references may be useful to help clarify more detailed issues.

Primary Reference:

1. Grota P, ed. *APIC Text of Infection Control and Epidemiology*, 4th edition. Washington, DC: Association for Professionals in Infection Control and Epidemiology, 2014. Also available online at http://text.apic.org [subscription required].

Notable Chapters

3 Education and Training

5 Infection Prevention and Behavioral Interventions

19 Qualitative Research Methods

20 Research Study Design

NOTES

2. Brooks K. *Ready Reference for Microbes*, 3rd edition. Washington, DC: Association for Professionals in Infection Control and Epidemiology, 2012.

3. Heymann D, ed. *Control of Communicable Diseases Manual*, 19th edition. Washington, DC: American Public Health Association, 2008.

4. Kulich P, Taylor D, eds. *The Infection Preventionist's Guide to the Lab*. Washington, DC: Association for Professionals in Infection Control and Epidemiology, 2012.

Secondary Reference:

1. Current Recommendations of the Advisory Committee on Immunization Practices (ACIP).

2. Current guidelines, standards, and recommendations from CDC, APIC, SHEA, and Public Health Agency of Canada.

3. Pickering, Larry K, ed. *Red Book*, 29th ed., Elk Grove Village, IL: American Academy of Pediatrics; 2012.

NOTES

PRACTICE QUESTIONS

1. Adult learners are often motivated to learn by:

1) The need for new skills
2) Professional standard mandates
3) Desire for promotion and increased salary
4) Changing cultural expectations

   a. 2, 4
   b. 1, 3
   c. 3, 4
   d. 1, 4

2. The healthcare facility has established a goal of improving infection prevention competency with hand hygiene among all staff. Which of the following education and training approaches should the infection preventionist (IP) recommend as a priority?

   a. Analysis of human factors that may present unrecognized obstacles for compliance
   b. Attending local/state health department educational programs on hand hygiene
   c. Implementation of a mentoring program based on peer- to-peer instruction and coaching
   d. Intensified disciplinary actions for employees who do not follow hand hygiene procedures

3. Which of the following should be used as a quality improvement measure for infection prevention education programs?

   a. The frequency of classes offered through the year
   b. The average number of attendees per class offered
   c. Summary of pre-/post-test scores for each class
   d. Analysis of program evaluation scores for all classes

NOTES

4. The IP is asked to provide content for a hybrid education program. This model is most often based on:

a. Attendance at a live event with assigned online follow-up activities

b. Combination of online and independent study for a specific topic

c. Independent study with concurrent mentoring from a local expert

d. Self-assessment of learning needs that is used to develop an instructional plan

5. Which of the following situations would be best for the IP to apply just-in-time learning principles?

a. During a 30-minute orientation session for new employees

b. With staff who repeatedly have problems applying infection definitions

c. In a medical staff meeting where surveillance priorities are being discussed

d. For nurse managers evaluating monthly infection trend reports

6. A form of interactive training is often preferred among adult learners. However, in some situations a lecture may represent the best approach. In which of the following situations should the IP consider using a lecture?

a. When reviewing accreditation survey results for the infection prevention program with managers

b. When addressing inaccurate data entry of reportable infections by a health data analyst

c. After observing unsafe disposal of contaminated syringes in the Emergency Department

d. When discovering employees with influenza-like symptoms providing patient care

NOTES

7. Programs to build infection prevention competency have traditionally focused on a combination of skill and ability. Today, however, competency may include which of the following additional components?

1) Emotional intelligence
2) Cultural diversity
3) Communication methods
4) Effectiveness within a team

a. 1, 2, 3

b. 2, 3, 4

c. 1, 3, 4

d. 1, 2, 4

8. The director has requested that the IP summarize the results of an education program presented to five different groups within the institution. The director specifically requests that the method used not only indicate the overall mean score for each group but also aid a simple comparative analysis for all who participated. The best data display technique to summarize these fi would be:

a. A line list

b. A pie chart

c. A bar chart

d. A spreadsheet

9. Many infection prevention educational programs address behavioral change. To achieve sustainable success following initial training, the IP must focus on which aspect of behavior?

a. Avoidance of behavior change

b. Repetition and reinforcement

c. Need for approval and recognition

d. Critical thinking and judgment

NOTES

10. In which of the following infection prevention topics is the required educational content for employees most clearly described by a U.S. regulatory agency?

- **a.** Hand hygiene monitoring systems
- **b.** Environmental cleaning of hard surfaces
- **c.** Active surveillance for methicillin-resistant *Staphylococcus aureus* in hospitals
- **d.** Preventing employee exposure to bloodborne pathogens

11. All of the following are features of well-written research methods sections *except*:

- **a.** Time period of the study
- **b.** Clear criteria for defining cases and controls
- **c.** Questions the research will answer
- **d.** Methods of quality assurance

12. What of the following questions should be asked when evaluating results from a research study?

1) Were the instruments valid for the study?
2) Is this a peer-reviewed research journal?
3) Was the sample representative of the intended population?
4) Do the conclusions prove the hypothesis?

- **a.** 1, 2, 3
- **b.** 2, 3, 4
- **c.** 1, 3, 4
- **d.** 1, 2, 4

13. An assessment of internal validity and the influence of bias can be found in which section of a research study?

- **a.** Introduction
- **b.** Results
- **c.** Discussion
- **d.** Methods

NOTES

14. The abstract in a research study must include:

a. A review of the literature

b. A biographical profile of the principal investigator

c. The intent or objective of the study

d. Conflict of interest disclosures

15. Which of the following refers to the statistical technique that combines the results of a large number of studies?

a. Linear regression analysis

b. Inferential statistics

c. Meta-analysis

d. Axiomatic approach

16. The IP is reviewing a research study to assess the association between needleless connector (NC) change frequency and central line–associated bloodstream infection (CLABSI) rate. In multivariate analysis, the CLABSI rate was significantly higher ($p = 0.001$) among patients that had NC changed every 24 hours compared to patients with NC that were changed at 96-hour intervals. The IP knows that this p value indicates more evidence in support of which of the following?

a. The alternative hypothesis

b. The quality of the analysis

c. The null hypothesis

d. The statistical hypothesis

17. An employee has scored below the minimal acceptable level on the annual review of infection prevention competencies. The employee has attempted to pass the written test three times and has now been referred to the IP for additional help. What should the IP evaluate first?

a. The employee's motivation to learn or review the material

b. The length of time the individual has been employed in healthcare

c. The employee's anxiety regarding test taking

d. The employee's literacy and reading ability

NOTES

18. During an infection prevention class, one person repeatedly interrupts, contradicts the guest instructor, and makes negative comments. The most important thing that the IP can do in this situation is:

a. Request that the individual be removed by security

b. Insist that the individual interrupting the class remain silent

c. Remain calm and assess the best way to intervene

d. Dismiss the class and apologize to the instructor

19. The need to include employee education for infection prevention is included in all of the following programs components *except*:

a. The facility infection prevention risk assessment

b. The facility's infection prevention program plan

c. The annual facility budget and allocation of resources

d. The facility's 5-year strategic plan

20. The IP has received feedback from course attendees that the didactic component of the program is too lengthy and difficult Which training component should the IP now re-evaluate for its effectiveness?

a. Laboratory-based simulation training

b. Supervised clinical practice in patient care areas

c. The classroom portions of the program

d. The testing requirements for course completion

21. Direct observation of performance by an individual of a specific skill may yield a temporary and artificial high result. This phenomenon is known as the:

a. Hawthorne effect

b. Measure of success

c. Score inflation risk

d. Robertson's rule

NOTES

22. The IP wants to ensure that educational programs are based on the most rigorous and reliable sources of clinical evidence. Which of the following sources would best meet this need?

a. Standards issued by national or international authoritative sources

b. Best-practice guidelines from professional organizations

c. Consensus statements published by leading subject matter experts

d. Literature review of publications during the past 5 years

23. The process of evaluating learner response to individual test questions in order to determine the quality and accuracy of those questions is known as:

a. Validity testing

b. Correlation

c. Item analysis

d. Risk adjustment

24. After holding a housewide education session on hand hygiene, the IP want to find out how effective the sessions were in changing hand hygiene behavior. The most common way to assess hand hygiene behavior is to:

a. Give participants a post-test to find out how much information they retained about hand hygiene

b. Monitor job performance reviews for 1 year after the session to identify deficiencies related to hand hygiene

c. Send an anonymous observer to the floors to assess hand hygiene compliance

d. Conduct a survey to find out whether participants have changed their hand hygiene behavior

25. Which of the following would be an enabling factor to increase hand hygiene compliance with staff in the Intensive Care Unit?

a. Easy access to hand sanitizer, sinks, and soap

b. Staff rewards for good hand hygiene

c. Staff knowledge of contact transmission of infections

d. Counseling for staff members who are observed not performing hand hygiene

ANSWERS AND RATIONALES

NOTES

1. **(B) 1, 3**

Rationale: Adult learning is often a response to current situations and tends to be problem-centered. A majority of adult learners can be characterized as having a readiness to learn and preferring practical rather than academic knowledge. Learning is often motivated by job needs, such as the need for new skills or the desire for promotion and increased salary.

Reference: *APIC Text*, 4th edition, Chapter 3 - Education and Training

2. **(C) Implementation of a mentoring program based on peer-to-peer instruction and coaching**

Rationale: Hand hygiene is among the simplest and most effective preventive measures to reduce healthcare-associated infections. However, compliance with hand hygiene among healthcare personnel is consistently suboptimal. The Centers for Disease Control and Prevention's hand hygiene guideline describes the importance of role models. Numerous studies have suggested that healthcare personnel hand hygiene compliance is influenced significantly by the behavior of other healthcare personnel. The IP should emphasize the importance of role modeling to set high standards and to contribute to a culture of safety within a healthcare environment.

References: Boyce JM, Pittet D. Guideline for hand hygiene in health-care settings. *Morbid Mortal Weekly Rev* 2002;51(RR1):1-44; *APIC Text*, 4th edition, Chapter 27 - Hand Hygiene

3. **(D) Analysis of program evaluation scores for all classes**

Rationale: Quality improvement (QI) consists of systematic and continuous actions that lead to measurable improvement in healthcare services and the health status of targeted patient groups. Data is the cornerstone of QI. It is used to describe how well current systems are working and what happens when changes are applied and to document successful performance. Both quantitative and qualitative methods of data collection are helpful in QI efforts. Whatever evaluation methodology is used, the data must be gathered, tabulated, and analyzed to assess impact and make recommendations for curriculum revision before the next presentation.

References: *APIC Text*, 4th edition, Chapter 3 - Education and Training; *APIC Text*, 4th edition, Chapter 16 - Quality Concepts

4. **(A) Attendance at a live event with assigned online follow-up activities**

Rationale: "Hybrid" or "blended" learning is a formal education course in which some of the traditional face-to-face classroom methods have been replaced by online learning activities. Proponents of blended learning cite the opportunity for data collection and customization of instruction and assessment as two major benefits of this approach.

Reference: *APIC Text*, 4th edition, Chapter 3 - Education and Training

NOTES

5. **(B) With staff who repeatedly have problems applying infection definitions**

Rationale: Just-in-time teaching (JiTT) is a methodology that uses feedback between classroom activities and work that students do at home, in preparation for the classroom meeting. The goals are to increase learning during classroom time, to enhance student motivation, to encourage students to prepare for class, and to enable the instructor to fine-tune the classroom activities to best meet students' needs. JiTT assignments and classroom activities are designed to motivate the students to examine their present knowledge and get ready to modify such knowledge, add to it, and then apply the newly constructed knowledge. These tasks are accomplished as students and instructors work as a team.

Reference: *APIC Text*, 4th edition, Chapter 3 - Education and Training

6. **(A) When reviewing accreditation survey results for the infection prevention program with managers**

Rationale: Lectures are used to convey critical information, teach new knowledge and skills, promote reflection, and stimulate further work and learning. In the appropriate context, and assuming a certain quality standard, the lecture is an effective means of teaching. In this scenario, the IP is presenting the results of an accreditation survey, which does not require an interactive approach. Data are being presented, and there is no collaboration or training required.

Reference: *APIC Text*, 4th edition, Chapter 3 - Education and Training

7. **(C) 1, 3, 4**

Rationale: Professional competency has traditionally been divided into two essential components: knowledge and skill. More recent definitions have recommended additional components such as communication, values, reasoning, and teamwork.

Reference: *APIC Text*, 4th edition, Chapter 2 - Competency and Certification of the Infection Preventionist

8. **(B) A pie chart**

Rationale: A pie chart is a circular chart divided into sectors, illustrating proportion. In a pie chart, the arc length of each sector (and consequently its central angle and area), is proportional to the quantity it represents. A pie chart is best suited for visually representing the overall mean score and allowing viewers to rapidly compare one group to another.

Reference: *APIC Text*, 4th edition, Chapter 13 - Use of Statistics in Infection Prevention

9. **(B) Repetition and reinforcement**

Rationale: Behaviorism is an approach to psychology that combines elements of philosophy, methodology, and theory. Behaviorism focuses on one particular view of learning: a change in external behavior achieved through a large amount of repetition of desired actions, the reward of good habits, and the discouragement of bad habits.

References: *APIC Text*, 4th edition, Chapter 3 - Education and Training; *APIC Text*, 4th edition, Chapter 5 - Infection Prevention and Behavioral Interventions

NOTES

10. D Preventing employee exposure to bloodborne pathogens

Rationale: The Occupational Safety and Health Administration's (OSHA's) Bloodborne Pathogens standard prescribes safeguards to protect workers against the health hazards caused by bloodborne pathogens. Its requirements address items such as exposure control plans, Universal Precautions, engineering and work practice controls, personal protective equipment, housekeeping, laboratories, Hepatitis B vaccination, postexposure follow-up, hazard communication and training, and recordkeeping. The standard places requirements on employers whose workers can be reasonably anticipated to contact blood or other potentially infectious materials, such as unfixed human tissues and certain body fluids.

Reference: *APIC Text*, 4th edition, Chapter 101 - Occupational Exposure to Bloodborne Pathogens

11. C Questions the research will answer

Rationale: Questions the research will answer should be stated in the Introduction section of a research article. The Method section provides a detailed description of how the study was conducted, information on participants/subjects, information on materials/apparatus/measures, and a description of the procedure.

References: *APIC Text*, 4th edition, Chapter 20 - Research Study Design; *APIC Text*, 4th edition, Chapter 19 - Qualitative Research Methods

12. A 1, 2, 3

Rationale: Many factors should be considered in critically reviewing an article in the scientific literature. To evaluate articles that report original research, the reader should ask certain questions about each component of the paper.

The following questions may serve as a basic guide:

- *Introduction:* Is the study question important, appropriate, and stated clearly?
- *Materials and methods:* Is the study population appropriate and adequately described? Is the choice of study design applicable to the purpose of the study? Are selection and exclusion criteria described? Were outcomes of groups evaluated equally and by persons blinded to the study treatment arm? What were the proportions lost to follow-up in each study arm described?
- *Results:* Are the statistical tests appropriate for the study design? Is the sample size adequate? Are there factors that could have confounded results and were these taken into account? Do the data that are presented in the text, tables, and figures provide an answer to the stated research question(s)?
- *Discussion:* Are the conclusions that are drawn reasonable and justified? Could other explanations account for the observed results?

References: *APIC Text*, 4th edition, Chapter 20 - Research Study Design; *APIC Text*, 4th edition, Chapter 19 - Qualitative Research Methods

NOTES

13. (C) Discussion

Rationale: Internal validity refers to how well an experiment is done, especially whether it avoids systematic errors. If a study shows a high degree of internal validity, then one can conclude that there is strong evidence for causality. The methods section of a research article describes what procedures were followed to minimize threats to internal validity, the results section reports the relevant data, and the discussion section assesses the influence of bias.

References: *APIC Text*, 4th edition, Chapter 20 - Research Study Design; *APIC Text*, 4th edition, Chapter 19 - Qualitative Research Methods

14. (C) The intent or objective of the study

Rationale: The abstract is a brief summary of the purposes of the study and of its methods, main findings, and conclusions. A structured approach to abstracts is now used by many journals.

Reference: *APIC Text*, 4th edition, Chapter 20 - Research Study Design

15. (C) Meta-analysis

Rationale: A meta-analysis is a statistical method that combines the results of independent studies. Statistically combining the results of similar studies provides a precise estimate of treatment effect, giving due weight to the size of the different studies included.

Reference: *APIC Text,* 4th edition, Chapter 20 - Research Study Design

16. (A) The alternative hypothesis

Rationale: The p value is the probability of obtaining the observed sample results (or a more extreme result) when the null hypothesis is actually true. If the p value is small ($\leq$ the significance level), it suggests that the observed data is inconsistent with the assumption that the null hypothesis is true, and thus that hypothesis must be rejected and the alternative hypothesis accepted as true.

Reference: *APIC Text*, 4th edition, Chapter 13 - Use of Statistics in Infection Prevention

17. (D) The employee's literacy and reading ability

Rationale: The learning environment in healthcare settings is unique because of the diversity of healthcare personnel. Diversity includes characteristics such as age, cultural background, ethnicity, education level, and learning styles. Basic principles of adult learning have applied to the IP in the role of clinical educator with all types of healthcare personnel. Healthcare's complexity and rapid changes require that training activities also address issues of literacy, cultural diversity, cross-training, and technological advances. Successful educational activities in healthcare should be informed by learning theories and the educational needs of the learner population, the institution, and the community as they relate to infection prevention. IPs should provide an appropriate climate for learning as well as demonstrate creativity and flexibility.

Reference: *APIC Text*, 4th edition, Chapter 3 - Education and Training

NOTES

18. (C) Remain calm and asses the best way to intervene

Rationale: Classroom management techniques refers to the wide variety of skills and methods that teachers use to keep students organized, orderly, focused, attentive, on task, and productive. The use of effective classroom-management strategies can minimize the behaviors that impede learning for both individual students and groups of students, while maximizing the behaviors that facilitate or enhance learning. The early establishment of rules, standards, and expectations can minimize disruptions. For persistent disruptions and unruly behavior, the IP should first remain calm and consider which options will best resolve the conflict.

Reference: *APIC Text*, 4th edition, Chapter 3 - Education and Training

19. (D) The facility's 5-year strategic plan

Rationale: Strategic plans determine the direction an organization will go in the future and what the organization must do in order to reach the goal, mission, or vision. Strategic planning involves several important steps: (1) an analysis of the organization, (2) forming conclusions about what an organization must do as a result of issues facing the organization, and (3) action planning. Action plans determine what tactic the organization will use to accomplish goals, who will take responsibility to carry out the action, the timeline of action, and resources and evaluation criteria. A facility's strategic plan does not include department-specific goal.

References: *APIC Text*, 4th edition, Chapter 3 - Education and Training; *APIC Text*, 4th edition, Chapter 16 - Quality Concepts

20. (C) The classroom portions of the program

Rationale: Didactics is a theory of teaching, and in a wider sense, a theory and practical application of teaching and learning. The term "didactic" is often used to refer to lectures that are overburdened with instructive or factual material.

Reference: *APIC Text*, 4th edition, Chapter 3 - Education and Training

21. (A) Hawthorne effect

Rationale: The Hawthorne effect refers to a phenomenon whereby workers improve or modify an aspect of their behavior in response to the fact of a change in their environment (e.g., workers are aware they are being observed), rather than in response to the nature of the change itself.

Reference: *APIC Text*, 4th edition, Chapter 3 - Education and Training

22. (A) Standards issued by national or international authoritative sources

Rationale: Standards issued by national or international authoritative sources represent the penultimate standard of care used to guide practice, reduce variation, and improve the quality of patient care.

References: *APIC Text*, 4th edition, Chapter 1 - Infection Prevention and Control Programs; *APIC Text*, 4th edition, Chapter 4 - Accrediting and Regulatory Agencies

NOTES

23. (C) Item analysis

Rationale: Item analysis is the process of examining student's test scores in order to assess the quality of the individual test questions as well as the test itself. Item analysis is useful for improving the quality of the test and is valuable for increasing the instructors' skill in test construction and identifying areas that need improvement or greater emphasis.

Reference: *APIC Text*, 4th edition, Chapter 3 - Education and Training

24. (C) Send an anonymous observer to the floors to assess hand hygiene compliance

Rationale: The best way to assess behavioral change is by observing that behavior. Hand hygiene behavior can be assessed most effectively by sending a trained observer to units to monitor how often healthcare personnel comply with hand hygiene recommendations.

Reference: *APIC Text*, 4th edition, Chapter 3 - Education and Training

25. (A) Easy access to hand sanitizer, sinks, and soap

Rationale: Once people are motivated to begin the change process, the enabling factors will capture their capacity to change. This usually boils down to two issues: (1) do they have necessary skills and capability and (2) do they have the necessary resources? For example, if the objective is for staff to use best-practice gloving procedures, are they able to perform the techniques? If the objective is for family visitors to the hospital to carry out best-practice hand hygiene, do they have ready access to hand sanitizer? Enabling factors may be managed by training and coaching for skill development or by helping people obtain access to needed resources.

Reference: *APIC Text*, 4th edition, Chapter 5 - Infection Prevention and Behavioral Interventions

Chapter 9
ENVIRONMENT OF CARE

The CIC® exam will have a total of fourteen (14) questions addressing Environment of Care. The content will test knowledge of the following:

A. Recognize and monitor elements important for a safe care environment (e.g., Heating, Ventilation, and Air Conditioning, water standards, construction)

B. Assess infection risks of design, construction, and renovation that impact patient care settings

C. Provide recommendations to reduce the risk of infection as part of the design, construction, and renovation process

D. Collaborate on the evaluation and monitoring of environmental cleaning and disinfection practices and technologies

E. Collaborate with others to select and evaluate environmental disinfectant products

KEY CONCEPTS

- The environment is an important source of healthcare-associated infections
- Adherence to established environmental infection prevention practices must be followed to maintain a safe environment of care for both patients and providers
- Effective management plans are essential for taking charge of the environment of care

RESOURCES FOR STUDY

Nearly all questions on Environment of Care are based on chapters in the primary references, but secondary references may be useful to clarify more detailed issues.

NOTES

NOTES

Primary Reference:

1. Grota P, ed. *APIC Text of Infection Control and Epidemiology*, 4th edition. Washington, DC: Association for Professionals in Infection Control and Epidemiology, 2014. Also available online at http://text.apic.org [subscription required].

Notable Chapters

31 Cleaning, Disinfection, and Sterilization

84 Legionella pneumophila

107 Environmental Services

111 Laundry, Patient Linens, Textiles, and Uniforms

112 Maintenance and Engineering

113 Waste Management

114 Heating, Ventilation and Air Conditioning

115 Water Systems Issues and Prevention of Waterborne Infectious Disease in Healthcare Facilities

116 Construction and Renovation

2. Heymann, D., ed. *Control of Communicable Diseases Manual*, 19th ed., Washington, DC: American Public Health Association; 2008.

3. Brooks, Kathy. *Ready Reference for Microbes*, 3rd ed., APIC; 2012.

4. Heymann, D., ed. *Control of Communicable Diseases Manual*, 19th ed., Washington, DC: American Public Health Association; 2008.

5. Kulich P, Taylor D, eds. *The Infection Preventionist's Guide to the Lab*, APIC, Washington, DC, 2012.

Secondary Reference:

1. Current Recommendations of the Advisory Committee on Immunization Practices (ACIP).

2. Current guidelines, standards, and recommendations from CDC, APIC, SHEA, and Public Health Agency of Canada.

3. Pickering, Larry K, ed. *Red Book*, 29th ed., Elk Grove Village, IL: American Academy of Pediatrics; 2012.

PRACTICE QUESTIONS

NOTES

1. The director of EVS has notified you that the organization will be changing cleaning products due to a change in contract requirements. When selecting a new product, you should consider which of the following?

   1) What other organizations are using this product
   2) Ease of use
   3) Efficacy
   4) The preference of the EVS director

      a. 2, 3
      b. 3, 4
      c. 3, 4
      d. 1, 2

2. Your organization is planning a major construction project. You have been asked to complete the Infection Control Risk Assessment (IRCA) by the project manager. You explain that:

   a. It is his job to complete the ICRA
   b. The construction company will complete the ICRA
   c. An ICRA is not needed for the project
   d. The IRCA must be conducted by a committee with expertise in a variety of areas

3. The appropriate hot water temperature for laundering linen is:

   a. 160°F
   b. 140°F
   c. 165°F
   d. 145°F

4. Which of the following minimum efficiency reporting values (MERV) is sufficient to meet minimum OR standards for air filtration?

   a. MERV 10
   b. MERV 12
   c. MERV 14
   d. MERV 16

NOTES

5. The manager of linen services has contacted you for guidance regarding transporting clean and soiled linens in the same vehicle. Your response is:

a. Clean and dirty linens should never be transported in the same vehicle

b. Clean and dirty linens can be transported together in the same vehicle if they are clearly separated

c. Clean and dirty linens can be transported together without the need to separate the items

d. The health department must give permission to transport clean and dirty linen together

6. Which of the following would be an acceptable route for diffusion of air in an OR?

a. Laminar airflow with a supply over the surgical table and an exhaust in the floor at the center of the room

b. Laminar airflow with a supply over the surgical table and an exhaust near the floor at the periphery of the room

c. Noninductional unidirectional infusion of air with a supply over the surgical table and an exhaust in the floor at the center of the room

d. Noninductional unidirectional infusion of air with a supply over the surgical table and an exhaust near the floor at the periphery of the room

7. According to the OSHA Bloodborne Pathogen requirements, the appropriate concentration for household bleach used to clean up a blood spill on a nonporous surface is:

a. 1:10

b. 1:100

c. 1:150

d. 1:50

NOTES

8. You have been asked to advise the design team of a new healthcare facility on the planning for an airborne infection isolation room (AIIR). Which of the following are correct recommendations for this type of room in a new facility?

1) The AIIR must have an audible alarm to indicate when negative airflow is not being maintained
2) If the AIIR is a permanent, dedicated negative airflow room, then the air should exhaust to the outside
3) The AIIR must have at least 12 air changes per hour
4) The AIIR is required to have an anteroom

a. 1, 2
b. 2, 3
c. 1, 2, 3
d. 1, 2, 3, 4

9. During infection prevention rounds, you discover a small bucket filled with liquid inside the cart used by an EVS staff member. The staff person tells you that she pours her cleaning solution into the bucket because it is easier than pouring it from the product's container. Your response is:

a. Tell her that this practice is acceptable
b. Talk to the EVS manager and ask that she be placed in corrective action
c. Explain that as long as she writes the name of the product on the bucket, the practice is acceptable
d. Explain that the cleaning solution container must be labeled with the chemical content, name, and expiration date

10. The water temperature range recommended by the CDC for prevention of growth of *Legionella bacteria* is:

a. Hot water at 124°F and above and cold water at 68°F
b. Hot water at 108°F and above and cold water at 77°F
c. Hot water at 110°F and above and cold water at 80°F
d. Hot water at 77°F and above and cold water at 50°F

NOTES

11. The director of facilities at your organization does not feel it is necessary to include infection prevention in the design phase of a construction project planned for your facility. Your response to him is:

a. Request that all blueprints and committee minutes be shared with you

b. Agree with him, but request that he call if questions arise

c. Ignore his comment and attend anyway

d. Explain why it is important for you to participate at all levels of a construction project

12. Which of the following is the most reliable method of monitoring the effectiveness of environmental cleaning in a healthcare facility?

a. Visual inspection of the room after cleaning

b. An adenosine triphosphate bioluminescence test after cleaning

c. Fluorescent marking of a surface prior to cleaning with follow up after cleaning to determine if the mark was removed

d. Environmental cultures using Rodac plates

13. The Food and Drug Administration (FDA) approves which of the following:

a. Liquid disinfectants used for cleaning and disinfectants

b. Medications only

c. Antiseptics

d. Disinfectant and cleaning wipes

14. An infection preventionist should be involved in which of the following phases of construction and renovation?

1) The design phase

2) The construction phase

3) The clean-up phase

4) The return to use phase

a. 1

b. 1, 2

c. 1, 2, 3

d. 1, 2, 3, 4

NOTES

15. In a cost saving effort, staff has requested that they be allowed to "top off" cleaning products from a larger bottle. Your response is:

a. This a really good idea and offer to take the idea to the infection control committee for approval

b. The "topping off" of nearly empty containers of cleaning products is prohibited

c. "Topping off" is acceptable for cleaning products only

d. There is no evidence that this practice will results in harm

16. You are experiencing an outbreak of *Clostridium difficile* infection (CDI) in your facility. Which of the following practices related to environmental cleaning should you recommend that the environmental services director evaluate first to determine the cause of the outbreak?

a. Whether quaternary ammonium compounds are being mixed properly before being used to clean patient rooms

b. Whether EVS personnel are changing gloves in between cleaning patient care rooms

c. Whether rooms where a patient had CDI infection or known colonization are being terminally cleaned with bleach

d. Whether high touch surfaces in a room where a patient has CDI infection or known colonization are being cleaned at least once daily with detergent

17. Construction and renovation policies should include which elements:

1) Phasing and commissioning of projects

2) List of construction companies allowed to work in the facility

3) Authority for determining unit closure issues

4) Start and stop dates of projects

a. 1, 2

b. 2, 3

c. 3, 4

d. 1, 3

NOTES

18. Environmental Services is interested in using the most environmentally friendly product for cleaning a patient care room whenever possible. Which of the following are your recommendations to help accommodate this request?

a. All room surfaces should be cleaned with a disinfectant only

b. All room surfaces should be cleaned with a detergent only

c. Horizontal and high touch surfaces may be cleaned with a detergent provided that the contact time is at least 10 minutes

d. Floors may be cleaned with a detergent if the room was not last being used as an isolation room

19. Healthcare workers in your facility have requested that environmental services purchase a hydrogen peroxide vapor unit to decontaminate patient care rooms. The administrators would like you to work with the director of environmental services to determine the pros and cons of this technology. Which of the following is an accurate argument in favor of using the technology?

a. It is effective at disinfecting all surfaces and supplies in the room

b. It cuts down on room turnaround time because personnel don't need to clean the room before disinfection

c. The room can be occupied during the process so it is useful for daily cleaning

d. The heating, ventilation, and air condition (HVAC) system does not need to be turned off while the unit is being used

20. Which of the following is most critical in selecting a cleaning agent for use on patient care equipment?

a. The product should be one that is already in use in the facility

b. The product should be selected based on the manufacturer's guidelines for cleaning the equipment

c. The product should be the best disinfectant available regardless of other factors

d. The product should be environmentally friendly

NOTES

21. The director of environmental services (EVS) has asked for your assistance in collecting data related to process measures involving cleaning of high touch surfaces in patient care rooms. Which of the following monitoring methods would be most accurate for collecting this data?

a. Administer a survey to EVS personnel to ask about consistency of cleaning high touch surfaces

b. Survey patients to determine how clean the high touch surfaces were in their rooms

c. Ask EVS personnel to observe and report on each other's practices related to cleaning high touch surfaces

d. Use a secret shopper to observe cleaning practices related to high touch surfaces

22. Which of the following recommendations should be made to reduce the risk of infection from sinks in patient care areas?

a. Sink basins should be deep enough to prevent splashing of water onto nearby patient care items

b. Sinks faucets should be located such that the flow of water hits the drain directly

c. Sinks should be placed within two feet of the point of care to encourage frequent hand hygiene

d. Aerators should be installed on faucets to minimize the amount of splash in the sink

NOTES

23. The planning committee for your new healthcare facility would like to include a water feature just inside the entrance of the new building. Which of the following recommendations should you make to ensure that this does not put patients, staff, and visitors at risk of infection:

1) The water feature must include underwater lighting to allow personnel to visualize whether it is being properly maintained
2) The water feature should be designed so that water does not remain stagnant in any part of the feature, and should include built-in methods of filtering or disinfecting the water
3) The water feature should be designed to prevent aerosolizing of water
4) The water feature must have routine maintenance

a. 2

b. 2, 4

c. 2, 3, 4

d. 1, 2, 3, 4

24. In a construction zone in a healthcare facility that is occupied, airflow should be:

a. Negative in the construction zone

b. Positive in the construction zone

c. Neutral in the construction zone

d. Negative outside the construction zone

25. Which of the following is an Infection Control Risk Assessment (ICRA) element related to building design features?

a. An assessment of the specific construction hazards and the determination of protection levels for those hazards

b. The impact of a water outage during construction activity

c. The number of airborne infectious isolation (AII) rooms and where they will be located in the facility

d. A plan on where to relocate patients during construction

ANSWERS AND RATIONALES

NOTES

1. **(A) 2, 3**

   Rationale: When selecting disinfectants or cleaning products, factors to consider include ease of use, efficacy, acceptability, safety, and cost.

   Reference: *APIC Text*, 4th edition, Chapter 107 - Environmental Services

2. **(D) The IRCA must be conducted by a committee with expertise in a variety of areas**

   Rationale: The ICRA shall be conducted by a committee with expertise in infection control, direct patient care, risk management, facility design, construction, ventilation, safety, and epidemiology. The committee shall provide documentation of the risk assessment together with updated mitigation planning throughout construction.

   References: *APIC Text*, 4th edition, Chapter 116 - Construction and Renovation

3. **(A) 160°F**

   Rationale: Hot water also provides an effective means of destroying organisms. A temperature of at least 160°F (71°C) for a minimum of 25 minutes is recommended for hot water washing.

   References: *APIC Text*, 4th edition, Chapter 111 - Laundry, Patient Linens, Textiles, and Uniforms

4. **(C) MERV 14**

   Rationale: Heating, ventilation, and air condition (HVAC) systems include filtration systems to remove particulate matter, including airborne microbes. The American Society of Heating, Refrigeration, and Air-Conditioning Engineers (ASHRAE) created a numerical system to rate filtration based on the particle size that the filter could remove. This system runs on a scale of 1 to 16, with 1 being a filtration system that removes only larger particulate matter and 16 being a filtration system that removes greater than 95 percent of particulate matter. The minimum standard for air filtration in an OR is 90 percent, which equates to a MERV of 14.

   Reference: *APIC Text*, 4th edition, Chapter 114 - Heating, Ventilation and Air Conditioning

5. **(B) Clean and dirty linens can be transported together in the same vehicle if they are clearly separated**

   Rationale: Clean and soiled textiles may be transported in the same vehicle if functional separation is maintained using physical barriers and/or space separation sufficient to protect clean textiles from soiled textiles.

   Reference: *APIC Text*, 4th edition, Chapter 111 - Laundry, Patient Linens, Textiles, and Uniforms

NOTES

6. **D Noninductional unidirectional infusion of air with a supply over the surgical table and an exhaust near the floor at the periphery of the room**

Rationale: Airflow in a healthcare facility should move from a clean area to one that is considered to be less clean. In the OR, the air supply should be from the ceiling near the center of the room, and the air exhaust should be near the floor on the periphery of the room. Laminar airflow is not appropriate for an OR setting, as there is evidence that this high rate of airflow may induce hypothermia in the patient. A lower rate of air supply flow termed noninductional unidirectional infusion is used in the OR.

Reference: *APIC Text*, 4th edition, Chapter 114 - Heating, Ventilation and Air Conditioning

7. **B 1:100**

Rationale: If a spill occurs on a nonporous surface, a 1:100 dilution of household bleach (one part plus 99 parts water or 0.25 cup of bleach in a gallon of water) is a highly effective disinfectant and is the least expensive. A 1:10 dilution of household bleach (one part household bleach plus nine parts bleach water or 1.5 cups of bleach in one gallon of water) is required for porous surfaces and large surfaces.

Reference: *APIC Text*, 4th edition, Chapter 107 - Environmental Services

8. **B 2, 3**

Rationale: Airborne infection isolation rooms (AIIR) should be maintained under negative air pressure to ensure that airborne infectious organisms are not ventilated into the facility's corridor. These rooms must have at least 12 air changes per hour and newly constructed AIIR's must have a visible means of monitoring air flow. Anterooms are not required but there must be an area outside the room that allows for hand washing and for storage and disposal of personal protective equipment. If an AIIR is a dedicated negative airflow room then it should be designed to allow for air to exhaust directly outside the facility.

Reference: *APIC Text*, 4th edition, Chapter 116 - Construction and Renovation

9. **D Explain that the cleaning solution container must be labeled with the chemical content, name, and expiration date**

Rationale: Containers for cleaning agents must be labeled in accordance with regulatory requirements (e.g. chemical content, name, expiration date).

Reference: *APIC Text*, 4th edition, Chapter 107 - Environmental Services

10. **A Hot water at 124°F and above and cold water at 68°F**

Rationale: *Legionella* species are bacteria that are naturally found in water sources, including municipal drinking water. Infection with *Legionella* can occur through inhalation of aerosols containing the bacteria, and can result in pneumonia. The optimum temperature range for growth of *Legionella* is between 25°C and 42.2°C (77°F to 108°F) so the CDC recommendations have been made to maintain water temperatures that fall outside that range and are therefore not optimal for growth of *Legionella*.

Reference: *APIC Text*, 4th edition, Chapter 115 - Water Systems Issues and Prevention of Waterborne Infectious Disease in Healthcare Facilities

NOTES

11. **D Explain why it is important for you to participate at all levels of a construction project**

Rationale: Issues frequently addressed in the design phase include budget, space constraints, appropriate finishes, specific products with infectious implications, and applicable regulations. IPs should be prepared and support their position and recommendations with published citations whenever feasible, but particularly if a recommendation is not budget neutral.

References: *APIC Text*, 4th edition, Chapter 116 - Construction and Renovation

12. **D Environmental cultures using Rodac plates**

Rationale: Cleaning of the patient care environment with special attention to high touch surface is important for the prevention of healthcare-associated infections. The effectiveness of cleaning may be assessed in several ways, and this should be carried out in conjunction with timely feedback to environmental services personnel. The most reliable method to monitor cleaning is to use environmental cultures with Replicate Organism Detection and Counting (RODAC) plates. This method allows direct detection and counting of organisms from environmental surfaces, rather than relying on a proxy that may detect cleanliness but not whether there has been an acceptable reduction in bio burden after cleaning

Reference: *APIC Text*, 4th edition, Chapter 107 - Environmental Services

13. **C Antiseptics**

Rationale: Antiseptics are approved by the FDA as antimicrobial agents safe for use on skin. They are not to be used for cleaning inanimate objects or environmental surfaces because of their unproven efficacy on nonhuman surfaces.

Reference: *APIC Text*, 4th edition, Chapter 107 - Environmental Services

14. **D 1, 2, 3, 4**

Rationale: It is critical that an Infection Preventionist is involved in all phases of construction. Involvement during the design phase will ensure proper selection of materials, placement of products, and oversight of air and water quality. Involvement during the construction phase will ensure that design plans are being implemented properly and that the patient care environment is being protected from construction materials and dust. Involvement during the clean up phase will ensure that any existing dust and debris are properly removed and involvement during the return to use phase will ensure that the area is functional and is being utilized in the manner in which it was intended.

Reference: *APIC Text*, 4th edition, Chapter 116 - Construction and Renovation

15. **B The "topping off" of nearly empty containers of cleaning products is prohibited**

Rationale: It is important to prevent the extrinsic contamination of disinfectants and detergents. The practice of "topping off" nearly empty containers of disinfectants and detergents creates a risk for introducing unwanted microorganisms.

Reference: *APIC Text,* 4th edition, Chapter 107 - Environmental Services

NOTES

16. (C) Whether rooms where a patient had CDI infection or known colonization are being terminally cleaned with bleach

Rationale: CDI can be acquired from the environment and is a serious cause of healthcare- associated infections. Patient rooms that were occupied by a person with known CDI or colonization with *Clostridium difficile* should be terminally cleaned with bleach or with an appropriate sporicidal disinfectant. This practice is critical to remove *Clostridium difficile* vegetative cells and spores and prevent transmission to the next room occupant. Also important in preventing the spread of *Clostridium difficile* is that EVS personnel change gloves and perform hand hygiene in between cleaning patient room and that high touch surfaces are cleaned at least daily.

Reference: *APIC Text*, 4th edition, Chapter 107 - Environmental Services

17. (D) 1, 3

Rationale: Elements of the construction and renovation policy should include key issues, beginning with ensuring at least annual review and approval by the infection control committee and governing board of trustees. Broadly applicable elements should include the following as appropriate: Authority for closing units and phasing and commission in addition to several other elements.

Reference: *APIC Text*, 4th edition, Chapter 116 - Construction and Renovation

18. (D) Floors may be cleaned with a detergent if the room was not last being used as an isolation room

Rationale: Detergents tends to be more environmentally friendly, less toxic, and less likely to cause respiratory reactions than disinfectants. Disinfectants must be used on horizontal surfaces and high touch surfaces in the patient room, but detergents are acceptable for cleaning the floor provided that the most recent occupant of the room was not on isolation precautions during their stay.

Reference: *APIC Text*, 4th edition, Chapter 107 - Environmental Services

19. (A) It is effective at disinfecting all surfaces and supplies in the room

Rationale: Vaporized hydrogen peroxide units are useful for room disinfection after terminal cleaning, especially if there is concern for environmental contamination with *Clostridium difficile*. The hydrogen peroxide vapor easily reaches all surfaces in the room, including fabrics and wall behind furniture. It is also useful for disinfecting patient care items in the room and is safe for use in the presence of patient care equipment. However, the patient room must be cleaned prior to disinfection in order to remove organic material and the hydrogen peroxide vapor must be contained in the patient room during the disinfection process.

Reference: *APIC Text*, 4th edition, Chapter 107 - Environmental Services

NOTES

20. Ⓑ **The product should be selected based on the manufacturer's guidelines for cleaning the equipment**

Rationale: Patient care equipment can have many different components and material and not all cleaning and disinfecting agents will be appropriate for use on the equipment. It is important to follow manufacturer's guidelines when selecting a cleaning and disinfecting agent.

Reference: *APIC Text*, 4th edition, Chapter 107 - Environmental Services

21. Ⓓ **Use a secret shopper to observe cleaning practices related to high touch surfaces**

Rationale: Frequent cleaning of high touch surfaces with the correct cleaning and disinfecting agents is critical to reduce the occurrence of healthcare-associated infections. The most reliable way to collect data on the process of cleaning high touch surfaces is to enlist a secret shopper, a person who is unknown to EVS personnel, to discreetly observe the practice and gather data related to it. EVS personnel should receive timely feedback on the process being observed and should receive further education and training as needed.

Reference: *APIC Text*, 4th edition, Chapter 107 - Environmental Services

22. Ⓐ **Sink basins should be deep enough to prevent splashing of water onto nearby patient care items**

Rationale: Sink placement and design have been implicated in several outbreaks of healthcare- associated infections. Sinks should be far enough away from patients and patient care areas to prevent splashing of water onto these areas. The sink basin should be deep enough to help prevent this splashing and the stream of water should not be directed immediately over the drain because of the potential for aerosolization of microbes that can contaminate the drain. Use of aerators should be discouraged because of the potential for biofilm development.

Reference: *APIC Text*, 4th edition, Chapter 115 - Water Systems Issues and Prevention of Waterborne Infectious Disease in Healthcare Facilities

23. Ⓒ **2, 3, 4**

Rationale: Although water features can create a relaxing ambiance inside or outside a facility, they are associated with a risk of infection from pathogens that grow in water and can be aerosolized in the environment, such as Legionella. Water features are not prohibited in healthcare facilities but they must be carefully planned and maintained. These features should include filtration and/or ozone systems to remove pathogens from the water. Water should not be allowed to stagnate in any area of the feature because of the risk of biofilm development, and routine maintenance of the water feature must be followed. Underwater lighting may increase the water temperature to within a range that is optimal for growth of some pathogens, and has been implicated in at least one outbreak of Legionellosis.

Reference: *APIC Text*, 4th edition, Chapter 115 - Water Systems Issues and Prevention of Waterborne Infectious Disease in Healthcare Facilities

NOTES

24. Ⓐ Negative in the construction zone

Rationale: Because of the potential in a construction area to generate dust that may contain harmful pathogens such as *Aspergillus*, it is critical that airflow in a construction zone that is in an occupied facility is negative. This will pull air into the construction zone whenever someone enters it rather than allowing air to escape from the construction zone into areas where patients and healthcare workers might be exposed.

Reference: *APIC Text*, 4th edition, Chapter 116 - Construction and Renovation

25. Ⓒ The number of airborne infectious isolation (AII) rooms and where they will be located in the facility

Rationale: An ICRA should be utilized for the design phase of a healthcare facility and for the active construction phase. ICRA elements to be included in the design phase are how many AII rooms and protective environments rooms will be in the facility and where they will be located, the needs and locations for air ventilation, the types of water systems to include, and which finishes and surfaces are appropriate.

Reference: *APIC Text*, 4th edition, Chapter 116 - Construction and Renovation

Chapter 10
CLEANING, STERILIZATION, DISINFECTION, ASEPSIS

The CIC® exam will have a total of fifteen (15) questions addressing Cleaning, Sterilization, Disinfection, Asepsis. The content will test knowledge of the following:

A. Identify and evaluate appropriate cleaning, sterilization, and disinfection practices

B. Collaborate with others to assess products under evaluation for their ability to be reprocessed

C. Identify and evaluate critical steps of cleaning, high-level disinfection, and sterilization

KEY CONCEPTS

- Disinfection and sterilization are essential to reduce the risk of transmitting infectious pathogens to patients
- Failure to comply with scientifically based guidelines has led to numerous outbreaks
- Adherence to evidence-based recommendations on the preferred methods for cleaning, disinfection, and sterilization of patient care medical devices and for cleaning and disinfecting the healthcare environment are critical components of infection prevention and control programs

NOTES

NOTES

RESOURCES FOR STUDY

Nearly all questions on Environment of Care are based on chapters in the primary references, but secondary references may be useful to clarify more detailed issues.

Primary Reference:

1. Grota P, ed. *APIC Text of Infection Control and Epidemiology*, 4th edition. Washington, DC: Association for Professionals in Infection Control and Epidemiology, 2014. Also available online at http://text.apic.org [subscription required].

Notable Chapters

7	Product Evaluation
30	Aseptic Technique
31	Cleaning, Disinfection and Sterilization
32	Reprocessing Single Use Devices
106	Sterile Processing (was Central Services)

2. Brooks, Kathy. *Ready Reference for Microbes*, 3rd ed., APIC; 2012.
3. Heymann, D., ed. *Control of Communicable Diseases Manual*, 19th ed., Washington, DC: American Public Health Association; 2008.
4. Kulich P, Taylor D, eds. *The Infection Preventionist's Guide to the Lab*, APIC, Washington, DC, 2012.

Secondary Reference:

1. Current Recommendations of the Advisory Committee on Immunization Practices (ACIP).
2. Current guidelines, standards, and recommendations from CDC, APIC, SHEA, and Public Health Agency of Canada.
3. Pickering, Larry K, ed. *Red Book*, 29th ed., Elk Grove Village, IL: American Academy of Pediatrics; 2012.

PRACTICE QUESTIONS

NOTES

1. Which of the following is likely to result in the highest efficacy of medical instrument cleaning:
   - **a.** Use of a central reprocessing area for all instrument cleaning
   - **b.** Local instrument reprocessing within the area of care
   - **c.** Use of an acidic pH cleaner
   - **d.** Allowing the instrument to dry after use and before cleaning

2. Inadequate sterilization of surgical instruments and tubing may result in which of the following adverse events after cataract surgery?
   - **a.** Toxic Shock Syndrome
   - **b.** Posterior Segment Syndrome
   - **c.** Anterior Syndrome
   - **d.** Toxic Anterior Segment Syndrome

3. One disadvantage of liquid sterilization is:
   - **a.** Liquid sterilants are highly toxic and items must be aerated before use
   - **b.** It is a high heat process so it may not be used on heat-labile items
   - **c.** It is not an appropriate process for critical items
   - **d.** Items cannot be wrapped during the sterilization process so sterility cannot be maintained during storage

4. During infection control rounds in the emergency department, the manager tells you that they will be doing endovaginal ultrasounds soon and would like to use probe covers to speed up the cleaning process. You inform the manager that:
   - **a.** Using a probe cover will eliminate the need to high level disinfect the probe
   - **b.** Using a probe cover will reduce the amount of time needed to clean the probe
   - **c.** Using a probe cover is acceptable, but high level disinfection is still required
   - **d.** Using a probe cover is acceptable, but this device requires steam sterilization

NOTES

5. Which of the following practices have studies shown is most likely to result in improved infection prevention?

a. Strictly adhering to the EPA-registered product label contact time for low level disinfection of environmental surfaces

b. Utilizing a one minute contact time for low level disinfection of environmental surfaces regardless of the EPA-registered product label contact time

c. Thoroughly cleaning and disinfecting all surfaces in a room that have potentially come into contact with hands

d. Thoroughly cleaning and disinfecting all high touch surfaces in a room

6. The director of surgical services has received a call from a neurosurgeon who would like to schedule a brain biopsy on a person suspected of having Creutzfeldt-Jakob Disease (CJD). The staff have expressed concern cleaning and sterilizing the surgical instruments. You response is:

a. Surgical instruments are very expensive and should be cleaned and sterilized after the procedure

b. The recommendations are unclear as to how to clean and sterilize instruments

c. There are no special requirements for cleaning and sterilization of surgical instruments

d. The instrument used in these cases require special processing

NOTES

7. You have been asked to do an in-service for Environmental Services on cleaning procedures. Which of the following is the best practice for cleaning a patient room?

1) Clean the patient zone first, and then the perimeter of the room
2) Clean the perimeter of the room first, and then the patient zone
3) Clean items that are low to the floor first and then work your way up to higher items
4) Clean items that are higher up first, and then work your way down to lower items

a. 1, 3

b. 2, 3

c. 1, 4

d. 2, 4

8. The purpose of cleaning medical devices before sterilization or high level disinfection is to:

a. Reduce bio-burden

b. Add an additional step to the process

c. Replace the sterilization process

d. Increase the amount of time it takes to clean an endoscope

9. The purpose of including a biological indicator (BI) in an autoclave load is:

a. To determine whether the items being autoclaved are properly sterilized, which is indicated by a positive BI result

b. To determine whether the items being autoclaved are properly sterilized, which is indicated by a negative BI result

c. To determine whether the items being autoclaved are properly cleaned, which is indicated by a positive BI result

d. To determine whether the items being autoclaved are properly cleaned, which is indicated by a negative BI result

NOTES

10. In an effort to reduce cost and decrease turn around time, the endoscopy manager has asked if the enzymatic detergent can be used for multiple patients. Your response is:

a. It is acceptable to reuse the detergent

b. The enzymatic detergent must be discarded after each use

c. There are no recommendations on reuse of the detergent

d. It is not necessary to use an enzymatic detergent for endoscopes

11. An OR team was using a unique surgical instrument on a patient and the instrument was accidentally dropped on the floor. The team needs to reprocess it as quickly as possible to finish the surgery and would like to use Immediate-Use Steam Sterilization (IUSS). Which of the following is the best recommendation for this?

a. The team must clean and inspect the instrument before proceeding with IUSS

b. The team can proceed with IUSS without prior cleaning and inspection of the instrument since it will be used on the same patient

c. There is no need to use IUSS as the team can simply soak the instrument in ten percent bleach for 10 minutes

d. There is no situation in which IUSS is acceptable

12. Types of tissue consider at high risk for CJD include:

1) Heart

2) Blood

3) Eye

4) Brain

a. 1, 4

b. 1, 3

c. 3, 4

d. 2, 4

NOTES

13. Which of the following describes the correct storage to maintain sterility of reprocessed items?

- **a.** At least 12 inches below the ceiling, at least six inches above the floor, at least one inch from the outside wall, and on a rack with a solid bottom
- **b.** At least 18 inches below the ceiling, at least six inches above the floor, at least one inch from the outside wall, and on a rack with a solid bottom
- **c.** At least 18 inches below the ceiling, at least eight inches above the floor, at least two inches from the outside wall, and on a rack with a solid bottom
- **d.** At least 18 inches below the ceiling, at least eight inches above the floor, at least one inch from the outside wall, and on a rack with a solid bottom

14. Prior to opening a sterile package, the end user should inspect the package for:

1) Tears
2) Moisture
3) Date of manufacture
4) The name of the person who packaged the kit

- **a.** 1, 2
- **b.** 2, 4
- **c.** 3, 4
- **d.** 1, 3

15. Ultrasonic cleaners are used for:

- **a.** Removing gross soil from an instrument
- **b.** High-level disinfection of instruments
- **c.** Sterilization of instruments
- **d.** Fine cleaning of instruments

16. Aseptic technique is defined as:

- **a.** No touch technique
- **b.** A process used in the operating room
- **c.** An absence of organisms
- **d.** The process for keeping away disease producing organisms

NOTES

17. Which of the following indicators is most accurate for assessing whether surgical instruments have been processed correctly in a steam sterilization cycle:

a. Autoclave tape

b. Chemical indicator

c. Biological indicator

d. The cycle indicator on the steam sterilizer

18. You have recently accepted a position at a free standing endoscopy center. After reviewing the policy and procedures, you discover that the last time staff competency for cleaning and disinfecting endoscopes was completed was three years ago. Your next step is:

1) Schedule a meeting with the facility administrator to discuss your findings

2) Do not worry about it because this happened before you worked there

3) Develop competencies for cleaning and disinfection of endoscopes

4) Assume that it is not a problem because there have been no outbreaks at the center

a. 1, 3

b. 2, 4

c. 3, 4

d. 2, 3

19. A technician in the OR has reported an infestation of fruit flies in the sterile instrument storage room. The sterile packs were temporarily removed and pest management was called in to eradicate the flies. The OR staff want to know whether they can use the sterile packs. Which of the following is the best response?

a. The OR staff can use the packs without any reprocessing because there are no flies visible on the outside of the packs

b. The OR staff can use the packs without any reprocessing if they open a test pack and don't find any flies inside it

c. The OR staff don't need to repack the items but they do need to run the packs through the sterilizer again

d. They need to completely reprocess all of the items that were in the affected room

NOTES

20. Which of the following items can generally be reprocessed by only using low-level disinfectant:

a. Blood pressure cuffs

b. Anesthesia equipment

c. Bronchoscopes

d. Surgical instruments

21. Your endoscopy unit has experienced an outbreak associated with bronchoscopes. The CDC recommends that outbreaks in this setting be reported to which agencies:

1) The Joint Commission

2) Centers for Medicaid/Medicare Services

3) The Food and Drug Administration

4) The bronchoscope manufacturer

a. 1, 2

b. 2, 3

c. 3, 4

d. 2, 4

22. According to AAMI ST79, which of the following are among the recommendations for testing of mechanical cleaning equipment in order to verify adequate cleaning?

1) Verification should be carried out monthly

2) Verification should be carried out upon installation

3) Verification should be carried out after major repairs

4) Verification should be carried out when changing cleaning chemistry

a. 1, 2, 3, 4

b. 1, 2, 4

c. 1, 2, 3

d. 2, 3, 4

NOTES

23. A biological indicator that was included in a load of surgical implantables has indicated a failure. You are able to deduce that this was due to operator error, as this one load was not run on the correct cycle. Which of the following actions should you take?

a. No action is needed as the implantables did go through a sterilizer cycle

b. The load with the positive indicator must be reprocessed

c. A recall must be initiated; any loads of implantables run by the technician who ran this load must be reprocessed

d. A recall must be initiated; any loads of implantables run by any technician must be reprocessed

24. Which of the following are used for sterilization of medical instruments?

1) Gravity-displacement steam sterilizer

2) Pasteurizer

3) Ethylene oxide sterilizer

4) Ultrasonic cleaner

a. 1, 2

b. 1, 3

c. 1, 2, 3

d. 1, 2, 3, 4

25. The endoscopy manager has asked for your guidance in finding a location to store sterile supplies. Your response is:

a. The room must be positive pressure with a temperature of no greater than 65°F, with a relative humidity of less than 70 percent

b. The room must be positive pressure with a temperature of approximately no greater than 75°F, with a relative humidity not to exceed 70 percent

c. The room must be negative pressure with a temperature of 65°F, and a relative humidity of greater than 70 percent

d. There are no specific requirements for storing sterile supplies

NOTES

ANSWERS AND RATIONALES

1. **(A) Use of a central reprocessing area for all instrument cleaning**

Rationale: A central reprocessing area will have the highest efficacy of medical instrument cleaning because it will often have specialized cleaning equipment and because employees in this area specialize in cleaning equipment; they even may be certified in doing this.

Reference: *APIC Text*, 4th edition, Chapter 31 - Cleaning, Disinfection and Sterilization

2. **(D) Toxic Anterior Segment Syndrome**

Rationale: Toxic Anterior Segment Syndrome (TASS) is an acute inflammation of the eye that can occur following cataract surgery. A variety of substances have been implicated as causes of TASS and include impurities of autoclave steam, heat stable endotoxin, and irritants on the surfaces of intraocular surgical instruments. General principles of cleaning and sterilizing intraocular surgical instruments have been published and should be followed.

Reference: *APIC Text*, 4th edition, Chapter 63 - Opthamology Services

3. **(D) Items cannot be wrapped during the sterilization process so sterility cannot be maintained during storage**

Rationale: Liquid sterilization uses glutaraldehyde, hydrogen peroxide, or peracetic acid to sterilize items that are critical and are heat-sensitive. This is a liquid immersion process so items cannot be wrapped during the sterilization process. In addition, items may need to be rinsed after the process so sterility is not maintained in the rinsing, drying, and storage phases. Therefore, this method of sterilization is used only when an item cannot be sterilized in any other manner.

Reference: *APIC Text*, 4th edition, Chapter 31 - Cleaning, Disinfection and Sterilization

4. **(C) Using a probe cover is acceptable, but high level disinfection is still required**

Rationale: A recent study showed that a considerable number of ultrasound probes are contaminated with human papilloma virus (HPV). Endovaginal ultrasound probes are consider semicritical items (even if covered with a sheath or probe cover) and require high level disinfection.

References: *APIC Text*, 4th edition, Chapter 31 Cleaning, Disinfection and Sterilization; Rutala WA, Weber DJ, Healthcare Infection Control Practices Advisory Committee. Guidelines for disinfection and sterilization in healthcare facilities, 2008. CDC website. 2008. Available at: http://www.cdc.gov/hicpac/pdf/guidelines/Disinfection_Nov_2008.pdf

5. **(C) Thoroughly cleaning and disinfecting all surfaces in a room that have potentially come into contact with hands**

Rationale: Studies have shown that less than half of all surfaces and equipment that may be contaminated are properly cleaned during a terminal cleaning. Any surfaces or equipment that may have come into contact with hands have the potential to be contaminated; this is inclusive of but also beyond surfaces designated as "high touch."

Reference: *APIC Text*, 4th edition, Chapter 31 - Cleaning, Disinfection and Sterilization

NOTES

6. **D The instrument used in these cases require special processing**

Rationale: Contaminated surgical equipment or electrodes in the brain have transmitted infectious prions from one patient to another. In these instances, standard sterilization methods have been inadequate. Instruments used in these cases will require special processing; environmental cleaning and disinfection in surgery.

Reference: *APIC Text*, 4th edition, Chapter 73 - Creutzfeldt Jakob Disease and other Prion Infections

7. **D 2, 4**

Rationale: Cleaning should be carried out starting from the least soiled area (outside of the patient zone) and moving toward the most soiled area. Surfaces that are higher up should be cleaned first so that the dust from those surfaces does not contaminate items underneath that had already been cleaned.

Reference: *APIC Text*, 4th edition, Chapter 107 - Environmental Services

8. **A Reduce bio-burden**

Rationale: Items must be cleaned with water and detergents or enzymatic cleaners before processing. Cleaning reduces the bio-burden and removes foreign material that interferes with the sterilization process by acting as a barrier to the sterilization agent.

Reference: *APIC Text*, 4th edition, Chapter 31 - Cleaning, Disinfection and Sterilization

9. **B To determine whether the items being autoclaved are properly sterilized, which is indicated by a negative BI result**

Rationale: A biological indicator is a standardized, contained population of microbes that is included in a sterilization cycle to indicate whether the cycle was successful. The BI may contain spore-forming bacteria or other highly resistant microbes, and sterilization should render these microbes inactive. After sterilization, a BI is incubated at the optimum temperature and time for growth of the microbe. A positive result occurs from microbial growth, which indicates that the sterilization cycle was not optimal for inactivation of all microbes.

Reference: *APIC Text*, 4th edition, Chapter 106 - Sterile Processing

10. **B The enzymatic detergent must be discarded after each use**

Rationale: The CDC recommends that the enzymatic detergent be discarded after each use since these products are not antimicrobial and will not retard microbial growth.

Reference: *APIC Text*, 4th edition, Chapter 55 - Endoscopy

NOTES

11. **(A) They must clean and inspect the instrument before proceeding with IUSS**

Rationale: Immediate-Use Steam Sterilization (IUSS) allows for rapid reprocessing of an instrument in the event that a replacement that underwent standard sterilization is not available. This method is not intended to be used regularly to cut down on turnaround time of instrument reprocessing or to replace the need for back-up instruments. Instruments that will be processed by IUSS must be cleaned thoroughly and inspected, as they would if they were undergoing standard processing.

References: *APIC Text*, 4th edition, Chapter 106 - Sterile Processing

12. **(C) 3, 4**

Rationale: Tissues known to be highly infectious include brain, dura matter, pituitary tissue spinal cord and eye; tissues with low infectivity include lung, liver, kidney, spleen, lymph and CSF.

Reference: *APIC Text*, 4th edition, Chapter 73 - Creutzfeldt Jakob Disease and other Prion Infections

13. **(C) At least 18 inches below the ceiling, at least eight inches above the floor, at least two inches from the outside wall, and on a rack with a solid bottom**

Rationale: Proper storage of sterile, reprocessed items is critical for maintaining sterility. Items should be stored at least 18 inches below the ceiling and eight to ten inches above the floor. Storage should be at least two inches from the wall and if a rack is used then it should have a solid bottom to avoid contamination of items from dust on the floor.

Reference: *APIC Text*, 4th edition, Chapter 106 - Sterile Processing

14. **(A) 1, 2**

Rationale: Before use, sterile packages should always be inspected for signs of contamination such as moisture, tears, or discoloration in addition to the expiration date.

Reference: *APIC Text*, 4th edition, Chapter 30 - Aseptic Technique

15. **(D) Fine cleaning of instruments**

Rationale: Ultrasonic cleaners use sound waves to create bubbles that disrupt small particles that may exist in hard-to-clean places on instruments. Ultrasonic cleaners may be used after initial cleaning that removes all visible and accessible soiling is carried out and before final disinfection or sterilization, following manufacturer's recommendations.

Reference: *APIC Text,* 4th edition, Chapter 106 - Sterile Processing

16. **(D) The process for keeping away disease-producing organisms**

Rationale: Aseptic techniques, defined as the process for keeping away disease-producing micro-organisms, may be used in any clinical setting. It is implemented to protect the patient by minimizing contamination to reduce the risk for infection.

Reference: *APIC Text*, 4th edition, Chapter 30 - Aseptic Technique

NOTES

17. (C) Biological indicator

Rationale: A biological indicator is the only method of assuring that a steam sterilizer has reached the correct conditions to ensure sterility of products. Use of a biological indicator provides reliable, qualitative evidence that all spore-forming organisms have been inactivated during the sterilization cycle.

Reference: *APIC Text*, 4th edition, Chapter 106 - Sterile Processing

18. (A) 1, 3

Rationale: Staff should receive training on the safe use and reprocessing of the equipment and be competency tested. Infection control rounds and audits should be done annually. The CDC recommends that competency testing pf personnel reprocessing endoscopes should be done on a regular basis for example on hire and annually.

Reference: *APIC Text*, 4th edition, Chapter 31 - Cleaning, Disinfection and Sterilization, Chapter 55 Endoscopy

19. (D) They need to completely reprocess all of the items that were in the affected room

Rationale: The presence of any type of vermin can affect the integrity of the packaging and contaminate the contents. Fruit flies are small enough to crawl into the sterile packs and potentially contaminate the instruments. They could also become trapped in the packs and leave debris on the instruments. The instruments should be unwrapped, visible inspected, cleaned if necessary, and reprocessed.

Reference: *APIC Text*, 4th edition, Chapter 106 - Sterile Processing

20. (A) Blood pressure cuffs

Rationale: Non-critical items may generally be reused after being cleaned with a low-level disinfectant. These are items that only come into contact with intact skin and not mucous membranes. Low level disinfectants include 70 to 90 percent alcohol, improved hydrogen peroxide, and quaternary ammonium compounds.

Reference: *APIC Text*, 4th edition, Chapter 106 - Sterile Processing

21. (C) 3, 4

Rationale: The CDC recommends that endoscopy-associated infections be reported to the person responsible for infection prevention at the facility; the physician responsible for the care of the patient; the appropriate public health agency (which is the FDC or CDC); and the manufacturer(s) of the endoscope, disinfectant/sterilant, and automated endoscope washer-disinfector (if used).

Reference: *APIC Text*, 4th edition, Chapter 55 - Endoscopy

22. (D) 2, 3, 4

Rationale: Mechanical cleaning equipment uses automated cleaning and rinsing to remove soiling from items. According to AAMI ST79, verification of mechanical cleaners should be carried out weekly, and preferably daily. It should also be carried out upon installation of the equipment, after major repairs, and all cycles should be tested when changing cleaning chemistry.

Reference: *APIC Text*, 4th edition, Chapter 106 - Sterile Processing

NOTES

23. **B The load with the positive indicator must be reprocessed**

Rationale: When a biological indicator shows a sterilization process failure, it is important to try to deduce the source of the failure. If the failure is the result of a single load that was not run on the correct cycle, then no recall is needed. The load that was not processed correctly must be reprocessed.

Reference: *APIC Text*, 4th edition, Chapter 106 - Sterile Processing

24. **B 1, 3**

Rationale: Sterilization of instruments results in the instruments being free of all microbes, including spores. This can be achieved through the use of various types of steam sterilizers; gas sterilizers including those that use ethylene oxide gas, ozone, and hydrogen peroxide gas or vapor; and liquid immersion in chemical sterilants.

Reference: *APIC Text*, 4th edition, Chapter 106 - Sterile Processing

25. **B The room must be positive pressure with a temperature of approximately 75°F, with a relative humidity not to exceed 70 percent**

Rationale: The sterile storage area should be a limited access area with a controlled temperature (may be as high as 75°F) and relative humidity (30 to 60 percent in all work areas except sterile storage, where the relative humidity should not exceed 70 percent).

Reference: *APIC Text*, 4th edition, Chapter 106 - Sterile Processing

SECTION III. PRACTICE EXAMINATIONS

PRACTICE EXAM 1

QUESTIONS

NOTES

Instructions: Select the correct answer for each question.

1. The bacterium most likely to be transmitted from mother to infant during labor and cause neonatal sepsis is:

a. *Escherichia coli*

b. *Staphylococcus aureus*

c. Group B *Streptococcus*

d. Group A *Streptococcus*

2. Which of the following is an example of the criterion of "Strength of the Association" from Hill's criteria for causation?

a. In a study of the association between antibiotic exposure and development of *C. difficile* infection, the odds ratio was 2:3

b. In a study of the association between antibiotic exposure and development of *C. difficile* infection, the authors' conclusions are consistent with those of three other studies

c. In a study of the association between antibiotic exposure and development of *C. difficile* infection, antibiotic therapy began an average of 3 weeks before *C. difficile* infection developed

d. In a study of the association between antibiotic exposure and development of *C. difficile* infection, prolonged antibiotic therapy was a greater risk factor for *C. difficile* infection than short-term antibiotic therapy

NOTES

3. Which of the following rules should be followed when collecting a stool sample for *C. difficile* testing?

1) Stool sample should be freshly passed within 1-2 hours
2) 10-20mL. of formed stool should be collected
3) Stool should be passed into a clean, dry container
4) Specimens should be obtained before antimicrobial agents have been administered

a. 1, 2

b. 2, 3

c. 1, 3

d. 1, 4

4. What type of meningitis would be most consistent with the following cerebrospinal fluid (CSF) report result:

Glucose	Decreased
Protein	Elevated
WBC counts	1,000/mm^3

a. Bacterial

b. Viral

c. Fungal

d. Tuberculosis

5. The following blood culture result should be considered a potential contaminant:

a. A positive result of coagulase-negative staphylococci from two sets, 2 days apart, without symptoms

b. A positive result of *S. aureus* from one bottle in a patient with a temperature of 38.6°C

c. A positive result of *E. coli* from one bottle in an afebrile patient with diarrhea

d. A positive result of *Candida albicans* in a fungal blood culture in a patient with a urinary tract infection

NOTES

6. Which of the following organisms have been associated with the transmission of infections after body piercing?

1) *Atypical Mycobacterium* species
2) *Staphylococcus* species
3) *Pseudomonas* species
4) *Haemophilus* species

a. 1, 2, 3

b. 2, 3, 4

c. 1, 3, 4

d. 1, 2, 4

7. The Director of the Operating Room (OR) requests that the OR surfaces be routinely environmentally cultured. The IP's best response should be:

a. A schedule for routine culturing of the OR should be arranged so that each room is cultured at a set interval

b. Routine culturing of the OR should be done in the absence of any epidemiologic investigations in that area

c. Routine culturing should not be done because it is too expensive

d. Routine environmental culturing should not be considered unless an epidemiologic investigation is being conducted

8. All of the following may be indications of a heating, ventilation, and air conditioning (HVAC) malfunction *except*:

a. An increase in the postoperative surgical site infection (SSI) rates

b. A single case of aspergillosis in a severely immunosuppressed patient

c. Healthcare-associated varicella infections

d. An outbreak of ventilator-associated *Acinetobacter* infections in the Intensive Care Unit (ICU)

NOTES

9. A patient who underwent intraocular surgery was diagnosed with a noninfectious endopthalmitis after the procedure. The IP initiates an investigation to identify the possible cause. Which of the following factors should be considered?

1) Improper handling, cleaning, and rinsing of the instruments
2) Improper labeling of the solutions
3) Gloves and powder
4) Prophylactic antibiotics administered 2 hours before the procedure

   a. 1, 3
   b. 1, 2
   c. 3, 4
   d. 2, 4

10. Sensitivity may be defined as:

a. The ability of a test to detect true positives (persons with the disease) when applied to a population with the disease

b. The ability of a test to detect the true negatives (persons without the disease) when applied to a population without the disease

c. The ability of a test to detect true positives (persons with disease) when applied to a population without the disease

d. The percentage of persons with true positive results when the test is applied to persons without the disease

11. The IP is monitoring blood work in order to differentiate between bacterial or viral infection in a newly admitted ICU patient. Which of the following components of a complete blood count (CBC) should the IP examine in order to determine this information?

a. Hematocrit

b. White blood cell count

c. Platelet (thrombocyte count)

d. Red blood cell indices

NOTES

12. A nurse manager from a Rehabilitation Unit is requesting that aerators be installed on the sinks in the patient rooms on her unit. The IP should explain that:

a. Aerators should be placed on all sinks in the ICU only

b. Aerators are more effective when combined with an ultraviolet water disinfection method

c. Aerators increase the risk of HAIs

d. Low-flow aerators are suitable for use with this population

13. Herpes simplex virus (HSV) keratitis is suspected in an oncology patient. Aerobic eye cultures are negative to date. A single serum sample is sent for enzyme-linked immunosorbent assay (ELISA) antibody testing. The following titers are reported: HSV titer 1:128, cytomegalovirus (CMV) titer <1:8, Epstein-Barr virus (EBV) titer <1:8. These results indicate:

a. Immunity to HSV

b. Confirmation of acute HSV infection

c. Presumptive identification of HSV infection

d. Immunity to CMV and EBV

14. A patient is suspected of having Pertussis. A nasopharyngeal aspirate is collected for direct fluorescent antibody (DFA) testing and for culture eight hours after antimicrobial therapy is started. The DFA test is negative but the culture test is positive. Does this patient have Pertussis?

a. No, because the DFA test is highly specific and it was negative

b. No, because culture of *Bordatella pertussis* has very low sensitivity

c. No, because all testing is unreliable if antimicrobial therapy has been initiated prior to specimen collection

d. Yes, because the culture test is 100 percent specific for identification of *Bordatella pertussis*

NOTES

15. An ambulatory clinic will be transporting equipment to the local hospital for sterilization. The IP at the clinic has been askedto write a policy to ensure safe handling of the equipment by staff. The policy should include which of the following points on handling the instruments at the point of use?

1) Devices are to be cleaned before biofilm can form
2) Keep instrumentation moist to prevent bio-burden from drying
3) Instruments with lumens should be flushed with saline
4) Contaminated devices are to be placed in a sealed container to prevent exposure to staff and patients

   a. 1, 3, 4
   b. 2, 3, 4
   c. 1, 2, 4
   d. 1, 2, 3

16. A patient is admitted for a skin infection after swimming in the ocean. Which of the following organisms is the most likely cause?

a. *Mycobacterium marinum*
b. *Mycobacterium avium*
c. *Mycobacterium leprae*
d. *Mycobacterium tuberculosis*

17. What is the probability of committing a Type I error if the *p* value is 0.10?

a. 1 in 10
b. 1 in 100
c. 1 in 5
d. 1 in 20

18. Which of the following is an example of the principle of emergency management called "mitigation?"

a. Implementation of the hospital's emergency management plan during a hurricane
b. Recovery efforts after a major flood has subsided
c. A facility-wide bioterrorism disaster drill
d. Funding a program that will provide ring vaccination of exposed people against smallpox during an outbreak

NOTES

19. The purpose of the antibiogram is to:

a. Provide a monthly report on new and emerging antimicrobials

b. Give IPs another metric to track

c. Provide information on antimicrobial usage and resistance patterns in the community

d. Give hospitals information needed for reporting data through the National Healthcare Safety Network (NHSN)

20. The most common organism associated with pneumonia in school-aged children and young adults is:

a. *Neisseria meningitidis*

b. *Streptococcus pneumoniae*

c. *Staphylococcus aureus*

d. *Mycoplasma pneumoniae*

21. The purpose of a root cause analysis is to:

a. Determine which individual made an error so that the employee may be disciplined or terminated

b. Review the basic processes that are in place and then turn that review over to a unit-specific team so that they can determine how they should modify their practices

c. Provide a process that requires little time or training but allows employees to identify culpability after an adverse event

d. Include participants from diverse areas of the organization to delve into the cause of an error or systems failure and identify changes in practice and/or policy that will prevent a repeat of that error or event

22. A pediatric patient has been diagnosed with pediculosis. What is the most appropriate follow-up to prevent it from spreading to other patients or healthcare professionals?

a. Place the patient on Contact Precautions until 24 hours after appropriate treatment has been initiated

b. Require all visitors and HCP who enter the room to wear a disposable scrub cap for any patient contact

c. Use an insecticidal spray in the room after the patent is discharged

d. Prophylactically treat all family members and anyone with close physical contact with the patient

NOTES

23. An employee has experienced an accidental needlestick injury while providing care to a patient. All of the following lab tests would be appropriate for the source patient except:

a. Human immunodeficiency virus (HIV)

b. Hepatitis B antibody

c. Hepatitis B surface antigen

d. Hepatitis C Antibody (Anti-HCV)

24. The IP receives a call from a physician who is concerned that there is an outbreak of Acinetobacter baumannii, because he has cared for four patients in the past week who are infected with the organism. What is the IP's first step in responding to this call?

a. Contact the lab to ask them to create an alert for any *A. baumannii* cases

b. Contact hospital administration to request additional resources to investigate the outbreak

c. Confirm that there is an outbreak by using her own surveillance data and lab records to compare the rates of *Acinetobacter baumannii* over the past year

d. Initiate a case-control study to determine risk factors for *A. baumanii* infection

25. The IP receives a call from the Food and Drug Administration (FDA) with an official request for private health information (PHI) about a patient who was admitted to the facility with botulism. How should the IP respond to this call?

a. Tell the FDA officer that she cannot share PHI with the FDA due to Health Insurance Portability and Accountability Act (HIPAA) regulations

b. Ask the FDA to contact the local health department to obtain information about the patient

c. Provide the FDA officer with the minimum amount of information necessary related to the patient

d. Transfer the call to the Risk Management Department

NOTES

26. A measles exposure from a patient in a clinic was identified and an exposure workup was initiated. A staff exposure was defined as "nonimmune HCP with more than 5 minutes of same-room contact or face-to-face contact with the index patient." Forty-eight HCP were identified as possible exposures. Of these, 44 had documented immunity to measles. Of the remaining HCP, three did not have the same room or face-to-face contact. How many HCP were at risk of developing measles because of this exposure?

a. 4

b. 45

c. 1

d. 48

27. Which of the following recommendations related to disinfection and sterilization in healthcare facilities is a CDC category 1A recommendation?

1) "Before use on each patient, sterilize critical medical and surgical devices and instruments that enter normally sterile tissue or the vascular system or through which a sterile body fluid flows"
2) "Meticulously clean patient-care items with water and detergent, or with water and enzymatic cleaners before high-level disinfection or sterilization procedures"
3) "In hospitals, perform most cleaning, disinfection, and sterilization of patient-care devices in a central processing department in order to more easily control quality"
4) "Perform low-level disinfection for noncritical patient-care surfaces (e.g., bedrails, over-the-bed table) and equipment (e.g., blood pressure cuff) that touch intact skin"

a. 1

b. 1, 3

c. 1, 2, 4

d. 1, 2, 3, 4

28. Vaginal probes with probe covers require which type of disinfection:

a. Low-level disinfection

b. Intermediate-level disinfection

c. High-level disinfection

d. Sterilization

NOTES

29. The IP is reviewing the facility's performance measures, which are used to benchmark against national data. The IP ensures that each performance measure includes which of the following characteristics:

1) Measure is reliable
2) Measure targets improvement in a health population
3) Measure is defined according to physician preference
4) Measure can be easily interpreted by the users of the data

a. 1, 2, 3
b. 1, 2, 4
c. 2, 3, 4
d. 1, 3, 4

30. A preliminary microbiology report states that a patient's blood culture grew aerobic, Gram-negative bacilli. Which of the following is the most likely genus and species of the organism:

a. *Enterococcus faecalis*
b. *Bacteroides fragilis*
c. *Acinetobacter baumanii*
d. *Neisseria meningitides*

31. Urinary tract infections in the postpartum period have three important risk factors. Which of the following is *not* one of them:

a. Induction of labor
b. Tocolysis
c. Cesarean delivery
d. Twin births

32. If chance is a likely explanation for the difference between a sample statistic and the corresponding null hypothesis population value, then:

a. The difference is not statistically significant
b. The sample results are not compatible with the null hypothesis
c. The difference is statistically significant
d. The null hypothesis can be rejected

NOTES

33. Noninfectious postoperative endophthalmitis is most often associated with:

a. Wearing contact lens

b. Toxic anterior segment syndrome (TASS)

c. Conjunctivitis

d. Keratitis

34. An acute care facility experiences an outbreak of *Serratia marcescens* bloodstream infections. After the outbreak is under control and no new cases are being reported, the IP wants to find the source of the outbreak. The most appropriate epidemiology study design to use is:

a. Retrospective cohort study

b. Prospective cohort study

c. Case-control study

d. Cross-sectional study

35. To calculate the catheter-associated urinary tract infection (CAUTI) rate for a unit for one month, the denominator should be:

a. The number of patient days for the unit for the month

b. The number of admissions for the unit for the month

c. The number of patients with urinary catheters for the month

d. The number of urinary catheter insertions for the month

36. Which of the following is an example of surveillance on a process indicator?

a. The incidence rate of *Clostridium difficile* in the Bone Marrow Transplant Unit

b. The rate of hand hygiene compliance in the Bone Marrow Transplant Unit

c. The number of sharp object injuries in the month of May in the Bone Marrow Transplant Unit

d. The prevalence of vancomycin-resistant enterococci (VRE) in the Bone Marrow Transplant Unit

NOTES

37. Which of the following is not an advantage of a case-control study?

a. It takes less time than a cohort study

b. It requires fewer subjects

c. The data are more accurate because it is prospective

d. It is generally considered less expensive

38. You are working with the antimicrobial stewardship program in your facility to educate providers on appropriate use of antimicrobials. Which of the following would be an accurate recommendation from your group?

a. Metronidazole is an effective antimicrobial to use for MRSA skin infections

b. Consistent use of broad-spectrum antimicrobials regardless of susceptibility results will help reduce antimicrobial resistance in the facility

c. It is not always necessary to maintain antimicrobial concentration in the body above the level of the minimum inhibitory concentration of the pathogen being targeted

d. Cefepime is only useful for gram-negative bacterial infections

39. As a time-saving measure, hospital administrators in your facility have suggested that endocavitary probes do not need to undergo high-level disinfection because they are used with probe covers. How would you respond to this suggestion?

a. Agree, because the probe cover prevents contact with mucous membranes and non-intact skin

b. Disagree, because the probe covers are not 100 percent reliable

c. Agree, because even without covers the probes don't contact mucous membranes and non-intact skin during use

d. Disagree, because switching from high-level disinfection to low-level disinfection will not save time

NOTES

40. After reviewing the quarterly report, the manager of the adult ICU contacts the IP for assistance to create a plan to reduce central line infections. Which of the following should the IP recommend:

a. Wait for the next report to see if the rate has decreased

b. Create an Intravascular Team

c. Develop a multidisciplinary team to review and implement best practices

d. Send a referral to Medical Affairs for peer review

41. Important considerations regarding blood culture specimens include:

1) Collect prior to the initiation of antimicrobial therapy

2) Collect from a central venous catheter whenever possible

3) Ensure that the volume of the specimen collected is sufficient

4) Culture of specific sites is not recommended for surveillance

a. 1, 3

b. 2, 4

c. 1, 4

d. 3, 4

42. An IP subscribes to several peer-reviewed journals. As she reviews published articles describing research findings, what question should she ask before incorporating the conclusions/findings of the article into the infection prevention program:

a. Was the appropriate study design used and are the conclusions reasonable?

b. Is the author well known and well published?

c. Does the article state how to contact the author(s) with questions?

d. Are the findings described in tables or graphs and easily understandable?

NOTES

43. Which of the following is an accurate statement regarding the antibiogram for *Staphylococcus* isolates shown below?

	Total # of Isolates	Clindamycin	Tetracycline	Trimeth/ Sulfa	Vancomycin
Staphylococcus aureus	200	78	92	86	100
MRSA	147	69	93	88	100
***Staphylococcus*, coagulase-negative**	98				100

1) 50 percent of Staphylococcus aureus isolates were resistant to Vancomycin
2) 12 percent of MRSA isolates were resistant to Trimeth/Sulfa
3) Clindamycin should not be used for coagulase-negative Staphylococcus infections in this facility because 100% of isolates were resistant to it
4) There were no cases of Vancomycin-resistant *Staphylococcus aureus* in this facility

a. 2

b. 2, 4

c. 1, 2, 4

d. 1, 2, 3, 4

44. Which of the following scenarios would be most appropriate for immediate-use sterilization:

a. The vendor brings the instrument for the procedure the morning of the surgery, which does not allow for the full sterilization process

b. The instrument used for the procedure is dropped on the floor of the operating room and another instrument is not available

c. The turnaround time between procedures does not allow enough time for the full sterilization process

d. The OR does not have the needed instruments to meet the demand of surgeries so the instruments are flashed between procedures

NOTES

45. The Director of the Infection Prevention and Control Department has assigned one of her IPs to cofacilitate in a root cause analysis of an adverse event in collaboration with the Performance Improvement team. The IP plans to use process improvement tools and techniques during the analysis. Which of the following methods would best outline the possible causes of the event?

a. Brainstorming

b. Affinity diagrams

c. Fishbone diagram

d. Pareto chart

46. Which of the following is not an infection prevention objective of an occupational health program?

a. Contain costs by preventing infectious diseases that result in absenteeism and disability

b. Provide care to personnel for work-related illnesses or exposures

c. Educate patients about the principles of infection prevention

d. Collaborate with the Infection Prevention Department in monitoring and investigating potentially harmful infectious exposures and outbreaks

47. The biological indicator that was included in a steam sterilization load of non-implantable instruments has shown a positive result, as have biological indicators used in two additional follow-up tests of the sterilizer. The chemical indictor in the original load was reactive, as were the chemical indicators used in the follow-up tests. The log of all the runs indicates that the run conditions (temperature and time) were appropriate for the instrument load and there were no abnormalities in steam supply or electrical supply. Which of the following should be done next:

a. The load should be released for use in the facility

b. The sterilizer should be tested again with paired biological indicators from two different manufacturers

c. The items from the load should be immediately recalled and reprocessed

d. All items that were processed in that sterilizer since the time of the last negative biological indicator should be recalled and reprocessed.

NOTES

48. What action is indicated when the IP is asked to help determine if a worker has experienced occupational acquisition of an infectious agent or disease in order to receive workers' compensation benefit?

a. Provide enough information to prove or disprove the employee's claim

b. Notify the facility's attorney immediately

c. Review the workers' compensation system in place

d. Perform a root cause analysis to investigate

49. The safe temperature range for cold food storage is:

a. 41°F/5°C or lower

b. 42°F to 50°F/5.6°C to 10°C

c. 50°F to 55°F/10°C to 12.8°C

d. Less than 60°F/15.6°C

50. A robust Performance Improvement team should perform all of the following *except*:

a. Observational audits

b. Benchmark comparisons

c. Root cause analyses

d. Housewide infection rates

51. Toys used for inpatient pediatric patients should ideally be all of the following *except*:

a. New

b. Nonporous

c. Plush

d. Single-patient use

NOTES

52. Which of the following would be an appropriate method to evaluate the quality of an infection prevention program?

  a. The total number of areas where surveillance was carried out in the past year
  b. The average amount of time that elapsed between receiving reports from the lab about patients with multidrug-resistant infections and placing those patient on appropriate Isolation Precautions
  c. The number of IPs in the program per the number of beds
  d. The average amount of money spent on isolation gowns this year as compared to last year

53. On September 1, there were 30 surgical patients in the hospital. Two of these were postop patients with SSIs. A total of 75 surgeries were performed in September. Six additional SSIs occurred in patients who had surgery in September. What was the numerator for an incidence rate in September?

  a. 30
  b. 6
  c. 8
  d. 75

54. An employee is exposed to blood and body fluids from a patient whose baseline testing revealed positive results in a rapid HIV test. The most appropriate follow-up test for the patient would be:

  a. Western Blot
  b. Viral Load
  c. HIV polymerase chain reaction
  d. CD4

55. Which is an example of actions taken during the Study phase of the "Plan, Do, Study, Act" Performance Improvement Model?

  a. Identifying goals for the project
  b. Performing staff education sessions
  c. Trending and benchmarking of data collected
  d. Tweaking the program based on results

NOTES

56. An infant in the Neonatal ICU (NICU) has been diagnosed with *Malassezia furfur* fungemia. What is the most likely source of the infection?

a. Intravenous lipid infusions

b. A healthcare worker's false fingernails

c. Commercial powdered infant formula

d. Respiratory transmission from a colonized family member or healthcare worker

57. Which U.S. agency requires a respiratory program for HCP?

a. Food and Drug Administration (FDA)

b. The Joint Commission (TJC)

c. Centers for Disease Control and Prevention (CDC)

d. Occupational Safety and Health Administration (OSHA)

58. Which of the following must be reprocessed by high-level disinfection?

a. Non-critical items

b. Semi-critical items

c. Critical items

d. Non patient-care items

59. Which of the following are CDC requirements for storing endoscopes?

1) Store them coiled in the original case

2) Store them in a bin

3) Store hanging in a vertical position to facilitate drying

4) Store in a manner that protects the scope from contamination

a. 1, 4

b. 1, 2

c. 2, 3

d. 3, 4

NOTES

60. The following data on incidence rates of VAP in the Surgical ICU (SICU) were collected:

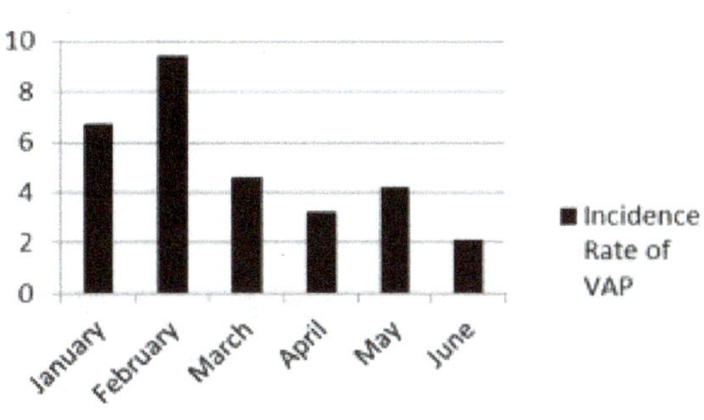

The best interpretation of the data in the graph is:

a. The number of cases of VAP was higher in January than in May

b. The number of cases of VAP was the same in January and February

c. Prevalence of VAP was lowest in June

d. The incidence rate of VAP was highest in February

61. A major difference between a prospective and a retrospective study is that the prospective study:

a. Requires a relatively small number of subjects

b. Is usually used for testing initial hypotheses

c. May require a long follow-up period

d. Is usually less costly

62. Program evaluation is necessary to measure change and growth in the learner. The following program elements should be evaluated in order to demonstrate efficacy and impact.

1) Appropriateness of the program design

2) Adequacy of the teaching and instructional resources

3) Knowledge, skills, and attitudes learned by the participants

4) Assessing the educational needs of the attendees

a. 1, 2, 3

b. 1, 3, 4

c. 2, 3, 4

d. 1, 2, 4

NOTES

63. An early-level (novice) IP in your department has set a goal of advancing to achieve middle-level (proficient) competency within the next year. Which of the following activities would be the most appropriate to include on her personal development plan for the year:

1) Nominating herself for the President-elect position of the local APIC chapter
2) Taking the Certification in Infection Control exam within six months
3) Requesting information about a Master of Science in Epidemiology degree
4) Learning the basics of CAUTI surveillance

a. 1

b. 1, 2

c. 1, 2, 3

d. 1, 2, 3, 4

64. Improved hydrogen peroxide contains:

a. Anionic and/or nonionic surfactants

b. Glutaraldehyde

c. Peracetic acid

d. Chlorine

65. The director of critical care has expressed a concern that there seems to be an increase in contaminated blood culture results in the ICU. An acceptable contamination level for blood cultures is:

a. Less than 10 percent

b. Greater than 3 percent

c. Greater than 5 percent

d. Less than 3 percent

66. Which of the following Transmission-based Precautions category requires a negative airflow room?

a. Contact Precautions

b. Airborne Precautions

c. Droplet Precautions

d. Standard Precautions

NOTES

67. A pregnant healthcare worker is concerned because she has been assigned to take care of a patient who has cytomegalovirus (CMV) infection. How should an IP respond to this concern?

a. Reassign her to another patient

b. Place the patient on Contact Precautions while the healthcare worker cares for him

c. Advise her that following Standard Precautions while caring for the patient will prevent transmission

d. Advise her that she is likely already infected with CMV and should not worry about transmission

68. In a published report on the risk of VRE infection in ICUs of a major teaching hospital, the authors report that the relative risk of infection is 1.9 for the Cardiac ICU (CICU) when compared to the SICU, and they conclude that a stay in the CICU is a risk factor for VRE infection. The authors have not controlled for age in their study despite the fact that their CICU patients average 20 years older than their SICU patients, and older age is a risk factor for VRE infection. The IP is concerned about the conclusions of this study because he suspects which of the following?

a. The study is affected by selection bias

b. The study is affected by standard error

c. The study is affected by confounding

d. The study is affected by causation

69. Inadequate refrigeration of food may permit the growth of potentially harmful microbes. Interventions to prevent the growth of pathogens due to inadequate refrigeration include:

1) Train personnel to recognize and implement safe maintenance of refrigerators

2) Establish a method to record temperature on a regular basis

3) Make daily rounds to ensure that the freezer and refrigerator are clean

4) Schedule and perform regular preventive maintenance of freezer and refrigerator

a. 1, 2, 3

b. 1, 2, 4

c. 2, 3, 4

d. 1, 3, 4

NOTES

70. Which of the following patient care units would be the best choice for conducting surveillance on wound infections with drug- resistant Gram-negative rod bacteria to prevent outbreaks?

a. The Burn Unit

b. The Orthopedic Medical/Surgical Unit

c. The CICU

d. The General Medical/Surgical Unit

71. While reviewing blood culture reports, you notice a note indicating that the specimen was received in the lab 3 hours after it was collected. You confirm with the microbiology supervisor. The acceptable transport time is:

a. Place specimen on ice and transport within one hour of collection

b. Within 24 hours of collection at room temperature

c. Equal to or less than 2 hours at room temperature

d. Equal to or greater than 4 hours if refrigerated

72. The "epidemiologic triangle" model for disease causation does *not* include:

a. Agent

b. Host

c. Time

d. Environment

73. A major hurricane is forecast for your area and you need to plan for the possible contamination of potable water that is supplied to your facility. Which of the following should be included in your planning?

a. You should have at least one day's worth of back up water supplies available

b. You will need one liter per day of drinking water for all patients and healthcare workers

c. All back up water must be stored on site for easy access

d. You will need at least 25 gallons of water per patient per day to maintain care

NOTES

74. Patients with mycoplasma pneumonia should be cared for in which type of precautions?

1) Standard Precautions
2) Airborne Precautions
3) Droplet Precautions
4) Contact Precautions

a. 1, 2
b. 3, 4
c. 1, 3
d. 1, 4

75. A case of healthcare-associated *Mycobacterium chelonae* respiratory infection has been identified in a patient. Of the following exposures that the patient had in the facility, which should be investigated as a potential source of the infection?

1) Bronchoscopes
2) Dialysis
3) Hydrotherapy pool
4) Ice from tap water used during surgery

a. 1
b. 1, 3
c. 1, 3, 4
d. 1, 2, 3, 4

76. Epidemic keratoconjunctivitis (EKC) is a viral conjunctivitis caused by a group of adenoviruses. EKC is highly contagious and can be problematic in ambulatory surgery settings. Recommended measures for control of these infections include:

1) Disinfection of tonometer tips in 3 percent hydrogen peroxide
2) Sterilize ophthalmoscopes between uses
3) Disinfection of the environment
4) Frequent hand hygiene

a. 2, 3, 4
b. 1, 2, 4
c. 1, 3, 4
d. 2, 3, 4

NOTES

77. All of the 72 patients in a chronic hemodialysis center were tested for Hepatitis C virus (HCV). Eight of the patients were identified as HCV positive. During the following year, two of the dialysis center's patients who previously tested negative for HCV converted to HCV positive. What was the incidence for that year?

a. 2.8 percent

b. 3.1 percent

c. 13.8 percent

d. 7.2 percent

78. The manufacturer of a wound dressing product has notified the hospital's Purchasing Department of possible contamination of one lot of dressings. The dressings were recently approved by the Product Standardization Committee and are used in all patient care areas. Which of the following actions should the IP take?

a. Instruct the Purchasing Department to remove all the manufacturer's dressings and like products from the hospital

b. Notify discharged patients who were using the product while in the hospital to be alert for signs of infection and notify their physician and the Infection Prevention and Control Department

c. Identify where the dressings are in the hospital, check the lot number and return them to the manufacturer, and assess the patients who used the product for signs of infection

d. Notify the Health Department of the recall and provide the names of the patients who used the product

79. An IP has completed the investigation of an increase in postdischarge SSIs following ambulatory surgical procedures. He identified some corrective measures that will require monitoring. Which of the following actions should the Infection Prevention team take?

a. Monitor the cleaning of the surgical suites

b. Ensure the effectiveness of the ventilation system

c. Revise the facility's surveillance plan

d. Ensure that patient care equipment is adequately cleaned

NOTES

80. All of the 72 patients in a chronic hemodialysis center were tested for Hepatitis C virus (HCV). Eight of the patients were identified as HCV positive. What is the prevalence?

a. 0.9 percent

b. 9 percent

c. 1 percent

d. 11 percent

81. The heating, ventilation, and air conditioning system will need to be shut down in one patient care unit of your hospital for repairs that are anticipated to take two hours. Which of the following protocols should be followed for this event?

a. Relocate all patients to other units while the shut down is in progress

b. Require all patients to wear a surgical mask while the shut-down is in progress

c. Relocate immunocompromised patients if necessary and provide emergency back up ventilation or portable units for other rooms

d. No protocol needs to be followed as the short shut down period will not affect any patients

82. An IP is asked to participate in the selection of a company to reprocess single-use devices (SUDs). Before a decision is made on which reprocessing company will be used, the IP reviews available information from a variety of resources to assist with the decision making. Which of the following activities should the IP recommend the hospital undertake?

a. Talk to other infection preventionists about which sterilizing methods to use on the SUDs

b. Visit reprocessing companies under consideration

c. Create quality control records for the SUDs

d. Identify the patients on which the reprocessed SUDs, as opposed to new devices, will be used

NOTES

83. What is the first action HCP should take after a needlestick exposure?

a. Contact the supervisor

b. Contact Occupational Health

c. Squeeze or milk the site

d. Wash the affected area

84. An IP collected the following data from the ICU for the month of March. How would she calculate the CAUTI rate the month of March?

March 2014
6 CAUTIs
240 patient days
180 catheter days

a. (6 ÷ 240) × 1,000 = 25 per 1,000 patient days

b. (6 ÷ 180) × 1,000 = 33.3 per 1,000 catheter days

c. (180 ÷ 240) × 1,000 = 750 per 1,000 patient days

d. (240 ÷ 180) × 1,000 = 1333.3 per 1,000 catheter days

85. The Director of Infection Prevention and Control is developing an educational program to provide annual bloodborne pathogen training to healthcare personnel in her facility. There are approximately 7,500 employees who need annual training, and her team of fi e IPs has to provide and document this training while still carrying out all other department duties. What is the best method of delivery for this training?

a. Web-based training sessions

b. Educational cart

c. Group lecture sessions

d. Role play training sessions

NOTES

86. Important elements of surveillance programs include:

1) Tracking diseases associated with the healthcare environment
2) Environmental sampling
3) Reviewing microbiology reports for antibiotic resistant organisms
4) Tracking and reporting HAIs as mandated by state/local public health requirements

a. 1, 2, 4

b. 1, 3, 4

c. 1, 2, 3

d. 2, 3, 4

87. Which of the following air filtration methods has the highest filtering efficiency compared to the others?

a. Diffusion

b. Straining

c. Impingement

d. Interception

88. The CDC has categorized bioterrorism agents according to priority. A disease that meets the criteria listed under Category B is:

a. Anthrax

b. Typhus

c. Hantavirus

d. Measles

89. Nursing Administration has announced the opening of a simulation lab at an acute care facility. The IP has been asked to develop a simulation setting dedicated to teaching infection prevention best practices. Which of the following is as example of a simulation activity?

a. Creating an isolation room to practice use of Isolation Precautions

b. Modeling proper hand hygiene techniques and having participants model back

c. Showing an interactive video of cleaning procedures and asking participants to identify correct and incorrect elements

d. Setting up a display of education materials concerning influenza vaccinations

NOTES

90. The IP at a long-term acute care (LTAC) facility is reviewing her surveillance data. Due to the high-risk nature of the LTAC's patient population, infection control data include a large number of outliers. Which measure of central tendency is least affected by outliers?

a. Proportions that include the population in the numerator and a subset of the population in the denominator

b. Proportions that include the population in the denominator and a subset of the population in the numerator

c. Arithmetic mean

d. Median

91. What is the acceptable upper limit for relative humidity in a facility to prevent fungal growth?

a. 40 percent

b. 50 percent

c. 60 percent

d. 70 percent

92. A staff nurse informs the IP that a patient with confirmed multidrug-resistant TB requires an immediate bronchoscopy. In which of the following rooms must the procedure be performed?

a. The operating room under positive pressure

b. Standard procedure room in the endoscopy suite

c. The ICU with direct exhaust to the outside

d. Airborne infection isolation room

93. In a Gram stain procedure, Gram-positive bacteria stain purple because:

a. They have a lipopolysaccharide layer in their cell wall that is decolorized with alcohol

b. Their cell walls contain long-chain fatty acids that take up crystal violet easily

c. They have a thick peptidoglycan cell wall that retains the primary stain during the alcohol decolorization

d. Gram-staining is simple staining so the only stain used is crystal violet

NOTES

94. Hepatitis A is diagnosed by the presence of:

a. Immunoglobulin G (IgG) for anti-Hepatitis D virus (HDV)

b. Hepatitis A virus (HAV) Immunoglobulin M (IgM)

c. Increase in anti-Hepatitis B virus (HBV)-related to previous Hepatitis B infection

d. HAV IgG

95. When using a medication vial that is intended to be discarded after a single procedure, it is acceptable to reuse the same syringe that was just used to access that vial and give that patient medication if:

a. The needle is replaced with a new needle

b. The medication vial is a single-use vial

c. The vial is only going to be used for that patient

d. It is not acceptable to reuse the syringe

96. Which method of face-to-face instruction is a useful option when large numbers of staff must be educated over a relatively short span of time?

a. Role play

b. Mentoring

c. Case studies

d. Train the trainer

97. An IP conducts an audit of the OR cleaning process. The action that would be most concerning would be:

a. The operating room is terminally cleaned at the end of each business day

b. The decontamination process starts on the floor of the OR and works upward toward the lighting

c. The cleaning solutions are prepared daily

d. A wet vacuum and microfiber mop head are used to clean the OR floors

NOTES

98. Strategies to prevent infection of a dialysis access site include the following:

1) Utilize an arteriovenous (AV) graft if a fistula cannot be established
2) Use a tunneled cuffed catheter for acute dialysis if use will be more than 3 weeks
3) Subclavian access is preferred over jugular options
4) Use femoral catheters only in bedbound patients for no more than 5 days

a. 1, 3, 4

b. 1, 2, 4

c. 2, 3, 4

d. 1, 2, 3

99. Fifteen persons were infected with *Salmonella* at a picnic where 75 ate egg salad sandwiches. What was the attack rate of *Salmonella* among those who ate the egg salad sandwiches?

a. 15 percent

b. 0.20 percent

c. 18 percent

d. 20 percent

100. A patient has been admitted with a wound infection. The lab reports that the stain of the wound culture is positive for AFB and the culture is positive for *Mycobacterium marinum*. Which of the following is the correct follow-up of this lab report?

a. No further follow-up is needed

b. Place the patient on airborne isolation

c. Contact the local health department to report the *Mycobacterium* infection

d. Place the patient on Contact Precautions

NOTES

101. Examples of efforts to improve patient safety in the healthcare setting include:

1) Encouraging patients to ask their healthcare providers if they have washed their hands
2) Medication safety programs that report medication errors and inform staff of efforts to prevent repeated errors
3) Encouraging patients to ask questions about their treatments and medications
4) Emphasizing punitive reactions to mistakes

a. 1, 2, 4

b. 1, 2, 3

c. 2, 3, 4

d. 1, 3, 4

102. Which short-term central lines are associated with a higher risk of infection?

1) Peripherally-inserted central venous catheters (PICC)
2) Femoral lines
3) Subclavian lines
4) Jugular lines

a. 1, 2

b. 2, 3

c. 2, 4

d. 1, 4

103. A technician finds out after obtaining an EKG on a patient that the patient may have varicella-zoster (shingles) on a dermatome on the upper body. The Occupational Health Nurse checks the employee's records and realizes that the employee was never tested for varicella on hire. The first thing the Occupational Health Nurse should do is:

a. Determine if the patient actually has an active case of varicella-zoster by involving the IP or checking with the patient's physician to verify the diagnosis

b. Test the employee for varicella immunity and, if not immune, exclude from work from day 10 through day 21 after the exposure

c. Give the varicella vaccine to the employee

d. Give varicella-zoster immune globulin (VZIG) to the employee

NOTES

104. A healthcare worker has had her uniform scrub top contaminated by a large blood spill that has penetrated the fabric. Choose her best option for follow-up from the choices below.

- **a.** She should be sent home immediately to take a shower
- **b.** She should remove the top by carefully pulling it over her head and then launder it in a washing machine with hot water and bleach
- **c.** She should remove the scrub top by using scissors to cut it off and discard it in a biohazard-labeled container
- **d.** She should remove the top by pulling it over her head and then discard it in the trash

105. There was contamination of a healthcare facility's potable water system with sewer water and there is high concern for the presence of *Cryptosporidium*. Which of the following should you recommend for corrective decontamination of the system?

- **a.** Use chlorination to disinfect the system
- **b.** Use high-temperature flushing to disinfect the system
- **c.** Use fluoridation to flush the system
- **d.** Use ultraviolet light to flush the system

106. During environmental rounds, the IP observes an environmental service worker cleaning up a blood spill on the floor. The best choice for cleaning blood and body fluids is:

- **a.** Alcohol
- **b.** Quaternary ammonium compound
- **c.** Phenolic
- **d.** Bleach

107. The Standardized Infection Ratio (SIR) for CLABSIs in the ICU is 0.8. Which of the following is correct?

- **a.** There were more CLABSIs in the ICU than expected
- **b.** There were fewer CLABSIs in the ICU than expected
- **c.** There were about the same number of CLABSIs in the ICU as the national baseline
- **d.** There was a 20% increase in CLABSI rates from the baseline period.

NOTES

108. Which of the following quality concepts will identify a pattern of observation points above and below the mean level?

a. Fishbone diagram

b. Run chart

c. Pareto chart

d. Process flow chart

109. Which agency or agencies has regulatory authority over some aspects of healthcare facility design, construction, and renovation related to Infection Prevention and Control?

1) Occupational Health and Safety Administration (OSHA)

2) National Institute for Occupational Safety and Health (NIOSH)

3) National Institutes of Health (NIH)

4) Centers for Disease Control and Prevention (CDC)

a. 1

b. 1, 2

c. 2, 3, 4

d. 1, 2, 3, 4

110. You are the IP in an ambulatory surgery center. During rounds, you discover that staff are using a single bag of saline to prepare saline flushes for multiple patients. Your immediate response is:

a. Clarify that saline bags must be labeled with time of use and discarded within 24 hours

b. Explain that single dose bottles of sterile water should be used to flush IVs

c. Remove the bag and send a follow-up email to the staff explain your actions

d. Remove the bag and teach staff how to follow safe injection practices

NOTES

111. An outbreak of Hepatitis C has occurred in the endoscopy clinic. Single-dose vials of medication are used in the clinic and observation of practice shows that the rubber stopper of each vial is wiped with alcohol before access. Medication is drawn up with a needle and syringe and administered to the patient. If an added dose is needed, the needle is replaced on the syringe and more medication is drawn up from the vial. If medication remains in the vial, then it is stored at the recommended temperature for use on another patient. HCP in the clinic had a 40 percent overall compliance with recommended hand hygiene practices. Which practice is the most likely cause of the outbreak?

a. Use of a single-dose mediation vial for more than one patient

b. Poor hand hygiene practices

c. Contamination of medication through the rubber stopper

d. Inadequate cleaning and disinfection of endoscopes

112. What is an advantage of experimental studies when identifying approaches to successfully interrupt the chain of infection?

a. Experimental studies can identify causative disease factors retrospectively

b. Experimental studies can establish association and causality if host factors such as disease susceptibility and other variables are strictly controlled

c. Experimental studies avoid the need to manipulate the independent variable, and therefore ethical issues associated with exposure to disease

d. Experimental studies do not require randomization, which is difficult to achieve in the healthcare environment

NOTES

113. The IP wants to calculate the surgeon-specific rate of infections associated with spinal fusion surgeries in the facility. Which of the following data elements will he need?

1) Number of spinal fusion procedures within the designated time frame
2) Number of spinal fusion SSIs within the designated time frame
3) Number of spinal fusion surgeries performed by each surgeon within the designated time frame
4) Number of spinal fusion infections for each surgeon within the designated time frame

a. 1, 2

b. 1, 4

c. 2, 3

d. 3, 4

114. A blood spill contaminated a pneumatic tube system and its contents. The leak was not identified for a period of time. After remediation of the contamination, the IP recommended the following to prevent a future incident:

a. Establish a method to recognize spills or leaks

b. Perform a hazard vulnerability analysis

c. Contract with an outside vendor to clean and maintain system

d. Restrict the use of pneumatic tube to nonhazardous material

115. A healthcare facility is undergoing extensive renovation. Surveillance for which of the following organisms would be particularly important during any construction or renovation project in a healthcare facility?

a. MRSA, VRE, and other MDROs

b. *Legionella* and *Aspergillus*

c. Gram-negative bacilli

d. *Mycobacterium abscessus*

NOTES

116. An outbreak of norovirus in an LTCF would most likely have an epidemiological curve (EPI curve) that:

a. Indicated a common source of infection

b. Indicated a propagated source of infection

c. Indicated a point source of infection

d. Indicated a common vehicle of infection

117. What is the term for an unexpected occurrence involving death or serious physical or psychological injury, or the risk there of?

a. Error

b. Adverse event

c. Near miss

d. Sentinel event

118. The incubation period for meningococcal meningitis is:

a. 10 to 14 days

b. 7 to 21 days

c. 2 to 10 days

d. 1 to 2 days

119. A patient in has been diagnosed with Legionnaires' disease that was possibly acquired during his stay in the hospital. What is the recommended firs t response to this incident?

a. All water sites in the healthcare facility to which the patient was exposed should be cultured for *L. pneumophila*

b. The patient should be placed on respiratory isolation until 24 hours after treatment has started

c. The water system should be superheated and flushed immediately

d. All patients should immediately be provided with bottled water for drinking

120. Properly written instructional objectives include:

a. Statements that communicate the intent of the curriculum

b. Directions and plans for the educational session

c. Learner outcomes in measurable terms using action verbs

d. Measures of change and growth in the learner

NOTES

121. The key to cleaning and disinfection of environmental surfaces is the:

a. Use of specific antiseptics for each surface

b. Physical removal of visible dirt, organic material, and debris

c. Assignment of trained staff to each department

d. Maintenance of equipment used for cleaning

122. What key strategy should the IP use to meet the administrative challenges of outpatient settings that are geographically dispersed?

a. Standardized measurement and definitions for HAIs consistent with those used for inpatient settings

b. HAI comparison with external benchmarks for all sites

c. Development of communication networks between sites, hospitals, and health departments

d. Standardized infection prevention policies and procedures

123. A hospital administrator has proposed that single-use angiography catheters be reprocessed and reused to cut costs. What is the best response to this request?

a. Single-use items are not allowed to be reprocessed

b. A cost-benefit analysis should be done before a decision is made

c. Single-use items can be reprocessed in the facility as long as administration, Risk Management, Legal Counsel, Supply Chain Administrator, and Infection Control representatives say it is allowable

d. Single-use items can be reprocessed in a third-party facility if FDA guidelines are followed

124. Which of the following need to be considered when updating the annual infection risk assessment?

1) An evaluation of the previous year's goals and objectives

2) An identification of risks based on geographic location, community, and population served

3) Risks related to the type of services that the facility provides

4) A broad assessment of all risks identified in the facility

a. 1, 2, 4

b. 1, 2, 3

c. 2, 3, 4

d. 1, 3, 4

NOTES

125. In 2013, 565 persons died from influenza-related illness in a large metropolitan area with a population of 1.8 million. What was the cause-specific mortality rate?

a. 31 per 100,000

b. 53 per 100,000

c. 31 percent

d. 0.03 percent

126. Which of the following would be considered biomedical waste?

a. Diaper soiled with feces

b. Blood-tinged suctioned fluids

c. Wound dressing that is not saturated

d. Isolation gown worn to deliver food tray

127. You are presenting an in-service to the Environmental Services group in your facility. Which of the following recommendations should you make related to mopping of patient rooms?

1) Standard mop heads should be disinfected with a disinfectant weekly
2) Floors should be mopped using the "S" stroke
3) Mop water should be changed after two hours of use.
4) The mops should never be redipped into the mopping solution.

a. 1, 2

b. 2, 3

c. 3, 4

d. 2, 4

128. The local Health Department informs the IP that a nurse in the CICU has been diagnosed with measles immediately after returning from a trip to Europe. His symptoms began 2 days ago, and he last worked in the unit 9 days ago. The incubation period for measles is 8 to 12 days, and the period of contagion is 1 to 2 days prior to onset of symptoms. How should the IP follow up on this report?

a. Determine the susceptibility to measles of all HCP and patients who had contact with the nurse in the past 12 days

b. Place all susceptible patients who were cared for by the nurse in Airborne Isolation

c. Inform Occupational Health about the infection so that they can furlough the employee for the appropriate amount of time

d. The IP does not need to conduct any follow-up

129. A patient who had neurosurgery was exposed to Creutzfeldt-Jakob disease (CJD) prions through surgical instruments that were not correctly processed after having been previously used on an infected patient. As a result, she has developed the disease herself. This is an example of which mode of infection?

a. Familial CJD

b. Iatrogenic CJD

c. Spontaneous CJD

d. Mutational CJD

130. List the following diseases in order of resistance of the disease agents to disinfection and sterilization, from high resistance to low resistance.

1) Staphylococcus aureus
2) *Clostridium difficile*
3) Creutzfeldt-Jakob Disease
4) Polio

a. 1, 2, 3, 4

b. 2, 3, 4, 1

c. 3, 4, 2, 1

d. 3, 2, 4, 1

131. When considering occupational health issues in healthcare settings, which individuals are covered under the term "healthcare personnel"?

1) All paid persons working in healthcare settings who have the potential for exposure to infectious materials
2) All paid and unpaid persons working in healthcare settings who have the potential for exposure to infectious materials
3) Any individual who has the potential to acquire or transmit infectious agents during the course of his or her work in healthcare
4) All paid and unpaid persons who work in healthcare settings and encounter patients
5) All workers employed by the healthcare organization

a. 1, 5

b. 2, 3

c. 1, 4

d. 4, 5

NOTES

NOTES

132. What is the positive predictive value of the following data?

	True Disease **Positive**	True Disease **Negative**
Test Result: **Positive**	100	3
Test Result: **Negative**	40	500

a. 97.0 percent
b. 92.5 percent
c. 96.2 percent
d. 99.4 percent

133. All of the following would be considered prevention strategies to reduce the transmission of infections in a healthcare setting *except*:

a. Implementing an influenza vaccine program for employees
b. Educating staff members in PPE usage
c. Decolonization of MRSA-positive patients prior to surgery
d. Instituting use of bleach for cleaning *C. difficile* patient rooms

134. Which of the following parameters affect(s) the effectiveness of ethylene oxide (ETO) sterilization?

1) Gas concentration
2) Temperature
3) Relative humidity
4) Exposure time

a. 1, 2
b. 1, 3, 4
c. 1, 2, 3, 4
d. 1, 4

135. Which of the following could be a result of a descriptive study on *C. difficile* in the healthcare setting?

a. The average age of a patient with *C. difficile*
b. The association between proton pump inhibitors and *C. difficile*
c. The likelihood of having *C. difficile* and being placed on a specific unit
d. The lack of hand hygiene by staff resulting in *C. difficile* acquisition

ANSWERS AND RATIONALES

NOTES

1. **(C) Group B *Streptococcus***

Rationale: In Group B *Streptococcus* (GBS) neonatal infections, heavy maternal colonization is associated with an increased risk for preterm labor, which in turn is a significant risk factor for neonatal infection. Intrauterine infection of the fetus therefore likely occurs via ascending spread of GBS from the vagina of a pregnant, asymptomatically colonized woman and subsequent rupture of membranes before 37 weeks' gestation.

Reference: *APIC Text*, 4th edition, Chapter 94 - Streptococci

CBIC Core Competency: Identification of Infectious Disease Processes

2. **(A) In a study of the association between antibiotic exposure and development of *C. difficile* infection, the odds ratio was 2:3**

Rationale: Causal associations exist when evidence indicates that one factor is clearly shown to increase the probability of the occurrence of a disease. In a causal relationship, the reduction or diminution of a factor decreases the frequency of the disease being studied. The criteria currently used for causality were developed by Austin Bradford Hill and are known as Hill's criteria. These criteria use modern epidemiological methods to determine whether a factor is causal for a given disease. Strength of association is the first criterion: The incidence of disease should be higher in those who are exposed to the factor under consideration than in those who are not exposed; that is, the stronger the association between an exposure and a disease, the more likely the exposure is to be causal. The odds ratio is a statistical measure that gives us an indication of how strongly the risk factor is associated with the disease outcome.

Reference: *APIC Text*, 4th edition, Chapter 10 - General Principles of Epidemiology

CBIC Core Competency: Education and Research

3. **(C) 1, 3**

Rationale: The accuracy of all tests depends on proper specimen handling and transport. The following rules should be followed when collecting samples for *C. difficile* testing:

- Stool samples should be freshly passed within 1-2 hours
- 10-20 mL of watery, soft, or unformed stool should be collected
- Stool should be passed into a clean, dry container

Reference: *APIC Text*, 4th edition, Chapter 72 - *Clostridium difficile* Infections and Colitis

CBIC Core Competency: Identification of Infectious Disease Processes

NOTES

4. **Ⓐ Bacterial**

Rationale: Culture of blood and CSF are indicated for patients with suspected invasive meningococcal disease. The CSF of patients with untreated meningococcal meningitis is usually cloudy and has pleocytosis with a predominance of neutrophils, low glucose, and high protein levels. In most of the cases, the organisms are seen on Gram stain or can be identified using latex agglutination assays. The culture is almost invariably positive as long as the sample was obtained before the administration of antibiotics.

Reference: *APIC Text*, 4th edition, Chapter 74 - Central Nervous System Infection

CBIC Core Competency: Identification of Infectious Disease Processes

5. **Ⓐ A positive result of coagulase-negative staphylococci from two sets, 2 days apart, without symptoms**

Rationale: According to the CDC CLABSI criteria, common commensals (such as coagulase-negative staphylococci) meet the criteria for a CLABSI if there are two positive cultures from two or more sets of blood cultures drawn less than 2 days apart and the patient has symptoms (fever greater than 38°C, chills, or hypotension).

CDC CLABSI criteria: Patient has at least one of the following signs or symptoms: fever (greater than 38°C), chills, or hypotension and positive laboratory results are not related to an infection at another site.

And the same common commensal (i.e., diphtheroids [*Corynebacterium* spp. not *C. diphtheriae*], *Bacillus* spp. [not *B. anthracis*], *Propionibacterium* spp., coagulase-negative staphylococci [including *S. epidermidis*], viridans group streptococci, *Aerococcus* spp., and *Micrococcus* spp.) is cultured from two or more blood cultures drawn on separate occasions.

Criterion elements must occur within a time frame that does not exceed a gap of 1 calendar day between two adjacent elements.

Reference: Centers for Disease Control and Prevention (CDC). Patient Safety Component Manual: Device-associated module - Central line-associated bloodstream infection (CLABSI) event. CDC website. January 2014. Available at: http://www.cdc.gov/nhsn/PDFs/pscManual/4PSC_CLABScurrent.pdf

CBIC Core Competency: Identification of Infectious Disease Processes

6. **Ⓐ 1, 2, 3**

Rationale: Body piercing activities can transmit infectious diseases. Bacterial infections may result from improper initial piercing technique or from poor hygiene. The organisms involved in most earlobe-piercing infections are often considered normal skin flora, including *Staphylococcus* and *Streptococcus* species. Higher ear piercings in the ear cartilage have been associated with more pathogenic organisms, including *Pseudomonas* species. Multiple cases of atypical *Mycobacterium* infections after piercing have been reported.

Reference: *APIC Text*, 4th edition, Chapter 123 - Body Piercing, Tattoos, and Electrolysis

CBIC Core Competency: Preventing/Controlling the Transmission of Infectious Agents

NOTES

7. **D Routine environmental culturing should not be considered unless an epidemiologic investigation is being conducted**

Rationale: Microbiological environmental testing is not generally recommended. Environmental culturing can be costly and may require special laboratory procedures. Additionally, in most cases no standards for comparison exist. Because of the lack of standards, environmental testing may generate inconclusive data that could result in the implementation of unnecessary procedures or treatment. Rationale for special environmental monitoring should be carefully planned and limited to epidemiological investigations. In limited situations, "routine" environmental sampling may be indicated.

Reference: *APIC Text*, 4th edition, Chapter 24 - Microbiology Basics

CBIC Core Competency: Environment of Care

8. **D An outbreak of ventilator-associated *Acinetobacter* infections in the Intensive Care Unit (ICU)**

Rationale: Detection and identification of certain HAIs may suggest HVAC malfunction (e.g., healthcare-associated tuberculosis, single case of aspergillosis in a severely immunosuppressed patient, healthcare-associated varicella infections). Analysis of postoperative SSI rates and associated infectious agents may offer important clues to problems in the OR air system(s). HVAC systems are usually not the immediate cause of device-associated HAIs.

Reference: *APIC Text*, 4th edition, Chapter 114 - Heating, Ventilation, and Air Conditioning

CBIC Core Competency: Environment of Care

9. **A 1,3**

Rationale: Endophthalmitis is an inflammatory condition of the intraocular cavities (aqueous and/or vitreous humor) usually caused by infection. Noninfectious (sterile) endophthalmitis may result from various causes such as retained native lens material after an operation or from toxic agents. Improper cleaning and rinsing of surgical instruments can leave a residue, which can irritate the eye and cause an inflammation. Gloves, especially those with powder, can also cause inflammation of the eye during surgery.

Reference: *APIC Text*, 4th edition, Chapter 63 - Ophthalmology Services

CBIC Core Competency: Identification of Infectious Disease Processes

10. **A The ability of a test to detect true positives (persons with the disease) when applied to a population with the disease**

Rationale: Sensitivity and specificity are common statistical measures to describe diagnostic tests or presence of disease. Sensitivity is the ability of a test to identify true cases or persons who have the disease or health condition of interest. In other words, it is the probability of getting positive test results among patients *with* disease. A high sensitivity test means that a negative result rules out the disease.

Reference: *APIC Text*, 4th edition, Chapter 13 - Use of Statistics in Infection Prevention

CBIC Core Competency: Surveillance and Epidemiologic Investigation

NOTES

11. **B** **White blood cell count**

Rationale: A white blood cell (WBC) count and differential provide information about the relative numbers (that is, the percentage) of each type of WBC. Evaluation of the WBC count can help to determine whether an illness has a bacterial or viral origin.

Reference: Urinalysis, Fluid Analysis, Chemistry, and Hematology. In: Kulich P, Taylor D, eds. *Infection Preventionists' Guide to the Lab*. Washington, DC: Association for Professionals in Infection Control and Epidemiology, 2012.

CBIC Core Competency: Identification of Infectious Disease Processes

12. **C** **Aerators increase the risk of HAIs**

Rationale: Various types of equipment and fixtures can promote the growth of water-associated pathogens. Important water reservoirs for these organisms include potable water systems and cooling towers, flush sinks, faucet aerators, hoppers and toilets, eyewash/drench shower stations, chests/ice machines, water baths used to thaw or warm blood products and other liquids, and whirlpool or spa-like baths. Faucet aerators on sinks can enhance growth of waterborne organisms. Aerators are not recommended, but if they must be used, especially in an area with immunocompromised patients, a systematic cleaning routine should be established.

Reference: *APIC Text*, 4th edition, Chapter 115 - Water Systems Issues and Prevention of Waterborne Infectious Diseases in Healthcare Facilities

CBIC Core Competency: Environment of Care

13. **C** **Presumptive identification of HSV infection**

Rationale: The herpesviruses are a family of eight DNA viruses that initiate acute, chronic, and latent infections of the skin, epithelial cells, lymphocytes, and neurons. These include herpes simplex type 1 (HSV-1), herpes simplex type 2 (HSV-2), varicella-zoster virus, EBV, CMV, human herpesvirus 6 (HHV-6), human herpesvirus 7 (HHV-7), and human herpesvirus 8 (HHV-8). Herpesviruses are transmitted by close intimate contact or exposure to virus-containing body fluids (saliva, urine, blood, breast milk, and contaminated respiratory or genital secretions). The reference range for HSV Type I or 2 IgM antibody is <1:10 negative; a result of 1:10 or greater is a positive result indicative of acute HSV infection.

Reference: *APIC Text*, 4th edition, Chapter 80 - Herpes Virus

CBIC Core Competency: Identification of Infectious Disease Processes

NOTES

14. **D Yes, because the culture test is 100 percent specific for identification of *Bordatella pertussis***

Rationale: Pertussis is caused by the bacterium *Bordatella pertussis*. Diagnosis may occur by culture, DFA, or polymerase chain reaction testing. Culture of B. pertussis is carried out on Bordet-Gengout or Regan-Lowe media with nasopharyngeal samples and has varying sensitivity depending on specimen handling and whether antimicrobial therapy was initiated prior to specimen collection. DFA testing is very specific but not very sensitive, and PCR testing has good sensitivity and variable specificity. A negative DFA test may not mean that a patient doesn't actually have pertussis because this test has low sensitivity and thus there is a chance of false negative tests, so a culture test must be performed to confirm DFA test results. If the culture test is negative then this cannot rule out pertussis because culture may have low sensitivity, but if a culture test is positive then the patient has pertussis because the 100 percent specificity of the test means that there are no false positive results.

References: *APIC Text,* 4th edition, Chapter 71 - Bordetella pertussis; CDC Website - Pertussis (http://www.cdc.gov/pertussis/clinical/diagnostic-testing/diagnosis-confirmation.html)

CBIC Core Competency: Identification of Infectious Disease Processes

15. **C 1,2,4**

Rationale: Reprocessing contaminated equipment or instruments for sterilization begins at point of use. The end user is responsible for removing gross soil and debris and for rinsing items at the site of use. Instruments with lumens should be flushed with water (not saline, as salt is corrosive to most instruments). Every attempt should be made to keep instrument or equipment surfaces moist until they can be cleaned to facilitate the removal of soil. Applying enzymatic foam or gel cleaner, using wet towels placed within the set of used instruments, or presoaking used items in water or cleaning solution may also be done. Contaminated items should be placed in puncture-proof sealable containers and visibly labeled as biohazardous.

Reference: *APIC Text*, 4th edition, Chapter 106 - Sterile Processing

CBIC Core Competency: Cleaning, Sterilization, Disinfection, Asepsis

16. **A *Mycobacterium marinum***

Rationale: *M. marinum* causes cutaneous lesions after exposure to swimming pools, fish tanks, or other water sources. The organisms may enter through previously unappreciated superficial nicks and abrasions. The lesions first appear as papules that later ulcerate. Because special culture conditions must be used to isolate the organism, the Microbiology Lab should be alerted if this is a diagnostic consideration.

Reference: *APIC Text*, 4th edition, Chapter 95 - Tuberculosis and Other Mycobacteria

CBIC Core Competency: Identification of Infectious Disease Processes

NOTES

17. (A) 1 in 10

Rationale: A Type I error occurs when one rejects the null hypothesis (H_0) when it is true. This is also called a false-positive result (we incorrectly conclude that the research hypothesis is true when in fact it is not). The *p* value or calculated probability is the estimated probability of rejecting the null hypothesis of a study question when that hypothesis is true. A *p* value of 0.10 indicates a 10 percent (or 1 in 10) chance of making a Type 1 error.

Reference: *APIC Text*, 4th edition, Chapter 13 - Use of Statistics in Infection Prevention

CBIC Core Competency: Surveillance and Epidemiologic Investigation

18. (D) Funding a program that will provide ring vaccination of exposed people against smallpox during an outbreak

Rationale: Disasters should be planned for and responded to using the principles of emergency management. Emergency management is composed of four principles: mitigation, preparedness, response, and recovery. Mitigation describes actions taken to decrease the potential impact of a situation. These include interventions to either prevent or reduce morbidity and mortality and ease the economic and social impact of the event on the affected community. Funding a program that will provide ring vaccination of exposed people against smallpox during an outbreak is an example of mitigation because the activity will help prevent further morbidity and mortality.

Reference: *APIC Text*, 4th edition, Chapter 119 - Emergency Management

CBIC Core Competency: Management and Communication

19. (C) Provide information on antimicrobial usage and resistance patterns in the community

Rationale: The surveillance of antimicrobial resistance is an essential first step in identifying priority areas for managing antimicrobial use from an infection prevention perspective versus a pharmacy or cost-containment perspective. An antibiogram simplifies multiple patients' antimicrobial sensitivity information at an institution into a single number for pathogens of interest in an effort to monitor trends emerging in drug resistance. An antibiogram is a useful tool for the IP to determine the status of strategies in place to reduce MDROs.

Reference: *APIC Text*, 4th edition, Chapter 26 - Antimicrobials and Resistance

CBIC Core Competency: Identification of Infectious Disease Processes

20. (D) *Mycoplasma pneumoniae*

Rationale: *Mycoplasma* is uncommon under the age of 5 but is the leading cause of pneumonia in school-aged children and young adults. It can occur during any season and occurs throughout the world.

Reference: *Mycoplasma pneumoniae* and Other *Mycoplasma* Species Infections. In: Pickering LK, ed. *Red Book: 2012 Report of the Committee on Infectious Diseases*, 29th edition. Elk Grove Village, IL: American Academy of Pediatrics, 2012.

CBIC Core Competency: Identification of Infectious Disease Processes

NOTES

21. **(D) Include participants from diverse areas of the organization to delve into the cause of an error or systems failure and identify changes in practice and/or policy that will prevent a repeat of that error or event**

Rationale: The root cause analysis process takes a retrospective look at adverse outcomes and determines what happened, why it happened, and what an organization can do to prevent the situation from recurring. Risk managers commonly use the root cause analysis to investigate major incidents, sentinel events, or errors in healthcare delivery. The root cause analysis process avoids individual blame, considers human factors engineering, and analyzes redesign for a safer system. When conducting root cause analysis, a multidisciplinary team discovers basic and contributing causes for what happened. The team includes frontline staff, and individuals most familiar with the situation to dig deep into the process, asking why something happens at each level of cause and effect. The entire root cause analysis process identifies changes to a particular process or system that improves safety or reduces process error. A thorough root cause analysis determines: (1) human and other factors; (2) the process or system involved; (3) underlying causes and effects of the process; and (4) the risks and potential contributions to failure or adverse results.

Reference: *APIC Text*, 4th edition, Chapter 16 – Quality Concepts

CBIC Core Competency: Management and Communication

22. **(A) Place the patient on Contact Precautions until 24 hours after appropriate treatment has been initiated**

Rationale: In addition to placing the patient on Contact Precautions, patient bedding, clothing, and waterproof personal items should be washed at high temperature.

Reference: *APIC Text*, 4th edition, Chapter 96 – Viral Hemorrhagic Fevers

CBIC Core Competency: Preventing/Controlling the Transmission of Infectious Agents

NOTES

23. Ⓑ **Hepatitis B antibody**

Rationale: A positive Hepatitis B antibody indicates past infection or immunity via vaccination. It does not indicate active infection. (See Table PE1-1)

Table PE1-1. Interpretation of Patterns of Hepatitis B Virus Serologic Markers

Serologic Markers				
HBsAg	Total Anti-HBc	IgM Anti-HBc	Anti-HBs	Interpretation
-	-	-	-	Susceptible, never infected
+	-	-	-	Acute infection, early incubation*
+	+	+	-	Acute resolving infection
+	-	-	-	Acute resolving infection
-	+	-	+	Past infection, recovered and immune
+	+	-	-	Chronic infection
-	+	-	-	False positive (i.e., susceptible), past infection, or "low-level" chronic infection
-	-	-	+	Immune if titer is ≥ 10 mIU/mL

Abbreviations: HBsAg , Hepatitis B surface antigen; Anti-HBc, Antibody to Hepatitis B core antigen. The total anti-HBc assay detects both IgM and IgG antibody; IgM, Immunoglobulin M; Anti-HBs, Antibody to Hepatitis B surface antigen.

*Transient HBsAg positivity (lasting 18 days or less) might be detected in some patients during vaccination.

+, Positive; -, Negative

Adapted from Table 1. Recommendations for preventing transmission of infections among chronic hemodialysis patients. *MMWR Recomm Rep* 2001 Apr 26;50(No. RR-05):1-43.

Reference: *APIC Text*, 4th edition, Chapter 101 - Occupational Exposure to Bloodborne Pathogens

CBIC Core Competency: Employee/Occupational Health

24. Ⓒ **Confirm that there is an outbreak by using her own surveillance data and lab records to compare the rates of *Acinetobacter baumannii* over the past year**

Rationale: Confirming the presence of an outbreak is a key first step in an outbreak investigation.

Reference: *APIC Text*, 4th edition, Chapter 12 - Outbreak Investigations

CBIC Core Competency: Surveillance and Epidemiologic Investigation

NOTES

25. **C Provide the FDA officer with the minimum amount of information necessary related to the patient**

Rationale: The FDA is a public health authority. HIPAA regulations cover disclosure to the FDA of the minimum amount of information is necessary to prevent or control disease.

References: *APIC Text*, 4th edition, Chapter 8 - Legal Issues; U.S. Department of Health & Human Services (HHS). Health Information Privacy: Public Health. HHS website. 2003. Available at: http://www.hhs.gov/ocr/privacy/hipaa/understanding/special/publichealth.

CBIC Core Competency: Cleaning, Sterilization, Disinfection, Asepsis

26. **C 1**

Rationale: Measles is a highly contagious febrile exanthem. In most immunocompetent individuals, measles is a self-limited condition with a distinct clinical prodrome of cough, coryza, and conjunctivitis followed by a morbilliform skin eruption. Measles is more severe in young, malnourished, and immunocompromised persons. Even healthy individuals may experience complications, however, such as otitis media, bronchopneumonia, encephalitis, and laryngotracheobronchitis. Because measles is so highly contagious, healthcare facilities need to be prepared to safely care for measles patients. Measles immunity (natural or vaccinated) among HCP and use of proper isolation guidelines and postexposure protocols need to be established to minimize the potential for healthcare-associated transmission of measles.

According to the definition of staff exposure, only one healthcare worker was nonimmune and had more than 5 minutes of same-room contact or face-to-face contact with the index patient. Susceptible personnel who have been exposed to an individual with measles should be furloughed (relieved from healthcare activities) from the fifth to the 21st day after exposure, regardless of whether they received measles vaccine or immunoglobulin after exposure or until 4 days after development of rash. Personnel who develop measles should be furloughed until they have had their rash for 4 days.

Reference: *APIC Text*, 4th edition, Chapter 86 - Measles, Mumps, Rubella

CBIC Core Competency: Employee/Occupational Health

27. **A 1**

Rationale: The CDC has established a system for cataloging recommendations based on the amount of data available to support the recommendation. Category 1A recommendations are strongly supported by epidemiologic, clinical data, or experimental data from well-designed studies. Sterilization of medical instruments that will come into contact with sterile tissue or the vascular system is a Category 1A recommendation.

Reference: CDC Guideline for Disinfection and Sterilization in Healthcare Facilities, 2008 Page: 83-84

CBIC Core Competency: Cleaning, Sterilization, Disinfection, Asepsis

NOTES

28. (C) High-level disinfection

Rationale: Vaginal probes are used in sonographic scanning. A vaginal probe and all endocavitary probes without a probe cover are semicritical devices because they have direct contact with mucous membranes. It is recommended that a new condom/probe cover should be used to cover the probe for each patient and, because condoms/probe covers may fail, high-level disinfection of the probe should also be performed. These medical devices should be free of all vegetative microorganisms (i.e., mycobacteria, fungi, viruses, bacteria), though small numbers of bacterial spores may be present.

Reference: *APIC Text*, 4th edition, Chapter 31 - Cleaning, Disinfection, and Sterilization

CBIC Core Competency: Cleaning, Sterilization, Disinfection, Asepsis

29. (B) 1, 2, 4

Rationale: Performance measures focus on outcomes or processes. They are used for internal improvement purposes, intra- or interorganizational comparisons, and by various external entities for making decisions about care. Performance measure should be designed to address improvement that is likely to have a significant impact to the health of a specified population. The measure should consistently track the events within an organization or across organizations and over time. The resulting data should be easily understood by the end-users (e.g., staff, facility leaders).

Reference: *APIC Text*, 4th edition, Chapter 17 - Performance Measures

CBIC Core Competency: Management and Communication

30. (C) *Acinetobacter baumanii*

Rationale: *Acinetobacter baumannii* is a Gram-negative bacterium. It is typically short, almost round, and rod-shaped (coccobacillus). It can be an opportunistic pathogen in humans, affecting people with compromised immune systems and is becoming increasingly important as an HAI. It has also been isolated from soil and water samples in the environment.

Reference: *APIC Text*, 4th edition, Chapter 77 - Environmental Gram-negative Bacilli

CBIC Core Competency: Identification of Infectious Disease Processes

31. (D) Twin births

Rationale: Urinary tract infections (UTIs) in the postpartum period have three important risk factors: cesarean delivery, tocolysis, and induction of labor. Twin births are not associated with an increased risk of UTI.

Reference: *APIC Text*, 4th edition, Chapter 33 - Urinary Tract Infection

CBIC Core Competency: Preventing/Controlling the Transmission of Infectious Agents

NOTES

32. (A) The difference is not statistically significant

Rationale: A common use of statistics is hypothesis testing. A hypothesis is a statement of expected results. Hypothesis testing uses the distribution of a known area in the normal curve and estimates the likelihood (probability) that a result did not occur by chance. Significance levels show how likely a result is due to chance. In statistics, if a result is significant, it means that it is not due to chance. If chance is a likely explanation for the difference between a sample statistic and the corresponding null hypothesis population value, then the difference is not statistically significant.

Reference: *APIC Text*, 4th edition, Chapter 13 - Use of Statistics in Infection Prevention

CBIC Core Competency: Surveillance and Epidemiologic Investigation

33. (B) Toxic anterior segment syndrome (TASS)

Rationale: Healthcare-associated endophthalmitis can be either noninfectious or infectious. Noninfectious endophthalmitis is an adverse event with several presenting causes, including retained lens material and other introduced toxic substances. Frequency is unknown, but occurrence is not rare. Noninfectious postoperative endophthalmitis is most often associated with TASS—an acute, rapid onset of sterile anterior segment inflammation that mimics infectious endophthalmitis. Outbreaks of TASS have been associated with breaches in handling, cleaning, and disinfecting surgical instruments; introduction of contaminated solutions, contaminated intraocular lenses, and toxic medications during surgery; powder from gloves; and irritants (dried blood, endotoxins, residual detergent) left on instruments.

Reference: *APIC Text*, 4th edition, Chapter 63 - Ophthalmology Services

CBIC Core Competency: Preventing/Controlling the Transmission of Infectious Agents

34. (C) Case-control study

Rationale: Case-control studies group people by disease status and then investigate past exposures with the objective of identifying exposures that are more common to cases than to controls. This is an appropriate study design for this example because there are existing cases, and the IP is trying to identify the exposures that are associated with the bloodstream infections.

References: *APIC Text*, 4th edition, Chapter 10 - General Principles of Epidemiology; *APIC Text*, 4th edition, Chapter 20 - Research Study Design

CBIC Core Competency: Surveillance and Epidemiologic Investigation

35. (C) The number of patients with urinary catheters for the month

Rationale: There are three important aspects of the formula in determining the CAUTI rate: (1) persons in the denominator must reflect the same population from which the numerator was taken; (2) counts in the numerator and denominator should cover the same time period; and (3) the persons in the denominator should have been at risk of the event or occurrence (that is, number of patients with urinary catheters.

Reference: *APIC Text*, 4th edition, Chapter 13 - Use of Statistics in Infection Prevention

CBIC Core Competency: Surveillance and Epidemiologic Investigation

NOTES

36. **(B) The rate of hand hygiene compliance in the Bone Marrow Transplant Unit**

Rationale: This is a process measure because it is measuring whether an action has taken place but not whether there is any effect of this action on outcomes.

Reference: *APIC Text*, 4th edition, Chapter 11 - Surveillance

CBIC Core Competency: Surveillance and Epidemiologic Investigation

37. **(C) The data is more accurate because it is prospective**

Rationale: Case-control studies collect data retrospectively. Retrospective studies are used to get information about past events and are subject to recall bias because they rely on the memory of subjects and others for information on exposure.

Reference: *APIC Text*, 4th edition, Chapter 10 - General Principles of Epidemiology

CBIC Core Competency: Education and Research

38. **(C) It is not always necessary to maintain antimicrobial concentration in the body above the level of the minimum inhibitory concentration of the pathogen being targeted**

Rationale: The minimum inhibitory concentration (MIC) of a drug is the lowest amount that can be used that will still be effective against the pathogen. The MIC is a quantitative measure of resistance of the microbe to a drug, obtained by some antimicrobial susceptibility testing methods, such as E-test. Drugs with concentration-dependent activity are most effective when they reach a high concentration in the blood over a short period of time. The concentration of these drugs will then fall below the MIC for a period of time but they are still effective, and they can be dosed once a day. This is in contrast to drugs with time-dependent activity that should be maintained consistently in concentrations above the MIC in the system and are administered with multiple or continuous doses.

Reference: *APIC Text*, 4th edition, Chapter 13 - Chapter 26 - Antimicrobials and Resistance

CBIC Core Competency: Identification of Infectious Disease Processes

39. **(B) Disagree, because the probe covers are not 100 percent reliable**

Rationale: Any patient care items that come into contact with mucous membranes and non-intact skin must undergo high-level disinfection. While probe covers are used for endocavitary probes like vaginal probes, the probe covers are prone to perforation before and during use, which can lead to contamination of the probe during the procedure.

Reference: CDC Guideline for Disinfection and Sterilization in Healthcare Facilities, 2008 Page: 19

CBIC Core Competency: Cleaning, Sterilization, Disinfection, Asepsis

NOTES

40. (C) Develop a multidisciplinary team to review and implement best practices

Rationale: Multidisciplinary teams are a valuable tool in deploying a quality-focused culture or process. Successful teams increase problem solving and efficiency, raise morale and productivity, use integrative rather than imposed solutions, increase acceptance of the solution, and tap the potential in people and their fundamental knowledge of the process.

Reference: *APIC Text*, 4th edition, Chapter 16 - Quality Concepts

CBIC Core Competency: Management and Communication

41. (A) 1,3

Rationale: The accuracy of a blood culture can be impacted by a wide variety of factors, many of which pertain to skin antisepsis and/or specimen collection techniques. The venipuncture site should be cleaned with an antiseptic first to minimize the risk of contaminating the blood specimen with common commensals. It is critical that blood cultures be drawn prior to initiation of antibiotic therapy. Blood may not be sterile immediately following antimicrobial therapy. If empiric antibiotic therapy is initiated on an emergency basis, cultures should be obtained as soon as possible following the first dose. The volume of blood obtained for culture is a critical variable in detecting bacteremia or fungemia. Specimen collection from a central venous catheter is not recommended due to the risk of intraluminal bacterial contamination of the device. Percutaneous venipuncture from two separate sites is preferred.

References: *APIC Text*, 4th edition, Chapter 24 - Microbiology Basics; Blood Cultures. In: Kulich P, Taylor D, eds. *Infection Preventionists' Guide to the Lab*. Washington, DC: Association for Professionals in Infection Control and Epidemiology, 2012.

CBIC Core Competency: Identification of Infectious Disease Processes

42. (A) Was the appropriate study design used and are the conclusions reasonable?

Rationale: Many study designs, observational or experimental, are available to investigators. Understanding the advantages and disadvantages of each study design should prepare the IP to critically evaluate published research studies so as to appropriately assign value to the findings.

Reference: *APIC Text*, 4th edition, Chapter 20 - Research Study Design

CBIC Core Competency: Education and Research

43. (B) 2, 4

Rationale: An antibiogram provides the percentage of samples for a given organism that were sensitive to certain antibiotics and can be unit-specific or reflect hospital-wide isolates. There should be at least 30 diagnostic isolates included in an antibiogram, with only the first isolate from each patient included. The greater the number of isolates, the more accurate the sensitivity results for the given organism. Therefore the antibiogram might not accurately reflect all resistant microbes isolated in the facility.

Reference: *APIC Text*, 4th edition, Chapter 26 - Antimicrobials and Resistance

CBIC Core Competency: Identification of Infectious Disease Processes

NOTES

44. (B) The instrument used for the procedure is dropped on the floor of the operating room and another instrument is not available

Rationale: Flash sterilization is a quick-steam sterilization cycle that does not use the full sterilization cycle of exposure and dry times. Exposure may be abbreviated in gravity steam sterilizers by eliminating wrapping material or using container systems that ensure that the steam has unrestricted access to the instruments. The Association of Perioperative Registered Nurses' (AORN) Recommended Practices are consistent with the Association of Advancement in Medical Instrumentation (AAMI), which recommended that flash sterilization should be used only when there is an urgent need for the items.

Reference: *APIC Text*, 4th edition, Chapter 68 - Surgical Services

CBIC Core Competency: Cleaning, Sterilization, Disinfection, Asepsis

45. (C) Fishbone diagram

Rationale: A fishbone diagram (also called a tree diagram or Ishikawa) allows a team to identify, explore, and graphically display all of the possible causes related to a problem to discover the root cause. See Figure PE1-1 for an example.

Figure PE1-1. Example of a Fishbone (Ishikawa) Diagram

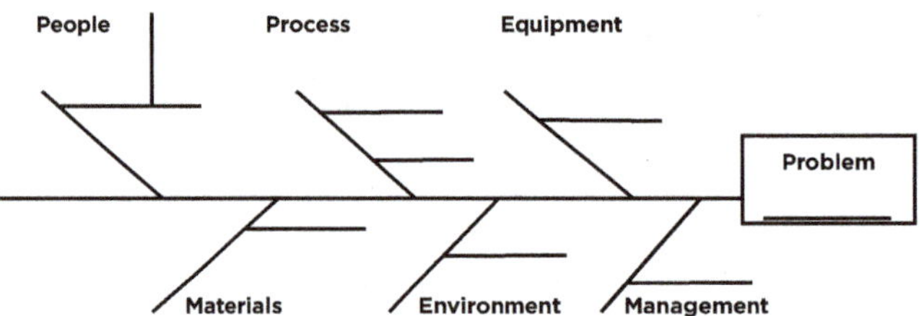

Source: Monsees E. Quality Concepts. In: Grota P, ed. *APIC Text of Infection Control and Epidemiology*, 4th edition. Washington, DC: Association for Professionals in Infection Control and Epidemiology, 2014.

Reference: *APIC Text*, 4th edition, Chapter 16 - Quality Concepts

CBIC Core Competency: Management and Communication

46. (C) Educate patients about the principles of infection prevention

Rationale: The healthcare organization's administration, medical staff, and other HCP need to support the infection prevention objectives of an occupational health program. These objectives are to (1) educate personnel about the principles of infection prevention and their individual responsibility for infection prevention, (2) collaborate with the Infection Prevention Department in monitoring and investigating potentially harmful infectious exposures and outbreaks, (3) provide care to personnel for work-related illnesses or exposures, (4) identify work-related infection risks and institute appropriate preventive measures, and (5) contain costs by preventing infectious diseases that result in absenteeism and disability.

Reference: *APIC Text*, 4th edition, Chapter 100 - Occupational Health

CBIC Core Competency: Employee/Occupational Health

NOTES

47. **B** **The sterilizer should be tested again with paired biological indicators from two different manufacturers**

Rationale: Biological indictors included in steam sterilization loads may show a positive result if the sterilization parameters are not met; if there is contamination of the growth medium in the indicator; or if the indicator was not manufactured properly. With steam sterilization, the instrument load does not need to be recalled for a single positive biological indicator test, with the exception of implantable objects. The log should be checked to ensure that the sterilizer was used correctly and maintenance should be contacted to determine if there was an interruption to steam or electrical supply. If there is no indication of abnormalities, then the sterilizer should be tested again in three consecutive cycles using paired biological indicators from different manufacturers to account for a possible defective biological indicator.

Reference: CDC Guideline for Disinfection and Sterilization in Healthcare Facilities, 2008 Page: 76-78, 117

CBIC Core Competency: Cleaning, Sterilization, Disinfection, Asepsis

48. **C** **Review the workers' compensation system in place**

Rationale: Disease that results from occupational exposure usually is eligible for compensation if the occupational exposure is the sole cause of disease; the occupational exposure is one of several causes of the disease; the occupational exposure aggravates a pre-existing disease (e.g., asthma); or the occupational exposure hastens the onset of disability. The burden of proving that disease was occupationally acquired lies with the workers. The IP's expertise may be needed to help assess this situation. Risk Management and Occupational Health provide the necessary follow-up. IPs should be familiar with the workers' compensation system in place within their country.

Reference: *APIC Text*, 4th edition, Chapter 100 - Occupational Health

CBIC Core Competency: Employee/Occupational Health

49. **A** **41°F/5°C or lower**

Rationale: Cold foods for serving must be held at 41°F/5°C or lower. The temperature danger zone is 41°F to 135°F/5°C to 57°C, which is the temperature range for rapid multiplication of virtually all bacteria associated with foodborne disease.

Reference: *APIC Text*, 4th edition, Chapter 109 - Nutrition Services

CBIC Core Competency: Preventing/Controlling the Transmission of Infectious Agents

50. **D** **Housewide infection rates**

Rationale: A robust performance improvement program should include the following basic elements: measuring how a facility or organization controls or complies with policies; documenting results of observational audits; performing root cause analyses; reporting individual physician or unit infection rates; and benchmarking the organization's infection rate against community, state, and national averages..

Reference: *APIC Text*, 4th edition, Chapter 16 - Quality Concepts

CBIC Core Competency: Management and Communication

NOTES

51. **C Plush**

Rationale: Strategies to minimize pediatric infection risk from toys include:

- Practice of hand hygiene by patients before and after handling toys
- Implementation of a process for appropriate toy acquisition to ensure suitability for cleaning/disinfection; toys should be nonporous and able to withstand rigorous mechanical cleaning. Avoid toys that are water-retaining, plush, and stuffed (an exception is therapeutic dolls, which should be single-patient use); and those that are difficult to clean and dry.
- Use of new toys

Reference: *APIC Text*, 4th edition, Chapter 42 - Pediatrics

CBIC Core Competency: Preventing/Controlling the Transmission of Infectious Agents

52. **B The average amount of time that elapsed between receiving reports from the lab about patients with multidrug-resistant infections and placing those patients on appropriate Isolation Precautions**

Rationale: The quality of the infection prevention program should be assessed routinely by evaluating customer satisfaction, appropriateness, efficacy, timeliness, availability, effectiveness, and efficiency. The average amount of time that elapsed between receiving reports from the lab about patients with multidrug-resistant infections and placing those patients on appropriate Isolation Precautions relates to timeliness of initiating appropriate interventions. Therefore, it can be used as a quality measure for the program.

Reference: *APIC Text*, 4th edition, Chapter 1 - Infection Prevention and Control Programs

CBIC Core Competency: Management and Communication

53. **B 6**

Rationale: An incidence rate is a measure of the frequency with which an event occurs in a population over a specified period of time. Incidence indicates the risk of disease in a population over a period of time. The numerator is the number of new cases of a disease during a specific time period. The denominator is the population at risk for the same time period. The incidence rate is equal to the numerator divided by the denominator and multiplied by a constant. Because there were six new cases after September 1, the numerator to calculate the incidence rate in this scenario is 6.

Reference: *APIC Text*, 4th edition, Chapter 13 - Use of Statistics in Infection Prevention

CBIC Core Competency: Surveillance and Epidemiologic Investigation

54. **A Western blot**

Rationale: Rapid HIV tests can offer a result in 15 minutes. A negative rapid test is reported as a definitive negative HIV test. A reactive test result needs to be confirmed with standard serologic tests. The most commonly used laboratory test for diagnosis of HIV infection is the serologic detection of antibodies to the virus. The standard serologic test consists of a screening enzyme immunoabsorbent assay (EIA) followed by a confirmatory Western blot (WB). In a patient with a positive EIA test, the test should be repeated. In a patient with a repeatedly positive EIA test, a confirmatory WB is performed. These serologic assays show sensitivity and specificity rates of 99.9 percent.

Reference: *APIC Text*, 4th edition, Chapter 81 - HIV/AIDS

CBIC Core Competency: Identification of Infectious Disease Processes

NOTES

55. (C) Trending and benchmarking of data collected

Rationale: TJC makes clear in the Infection Control and Prevention Standards that organizations should align the plan with the goal of improving infection rates. The organization must collect and display data to frontline staff about how well the organization actually achieves rate reduction. Data may include steps to increase staff influenza vaccination rates, reduce bloodstream infection and urinary catheter rates, and reduce rates of VAP. During the study phase of the cycle, data display, benchmarking, and trending become essential.

Reference: *APIC Text*, 4th edition, Chapter 16 - Quality Concepts

CBIC Core Competency: Management and Communication

56. (A) Intravenous lipid infusions

Rationale: *M. furfur* is fungemia that is most often associated with lipid infusions.

Reference: *APIC Text*, 4th edition, Chapter 10 - General Principles of Epidemiology

CBIC Core Competency: Preventing/Controlling the Transmission of Infectious Agents

57. (D) Occupational Safety and Health Administration (OSHA)

Rationale: The OSHA respiratory protection standard requires that the employer implement a respiratory protection program with a qualified administrator as the person who oversees the program, including evaluating the effectiveness of the program. The standard also requires that each worker assigned to wear a respirator receive a fit test before wearing the respirator in the workplace and perform a seal check with each use.

Reference: *APIC Text*, 4th edition, Chapter 100 - Occupational Health

CBIC Core Competency: Employee/Occupational Health

58. (B) Semi-critical items

Rationale: High-level disinfection must be used for processing of semi-critical items. These are items that will come into contact with non-intact skin or mucous membranes. High-level disinfection will inactivate all vegetative organisms but some spores may remain. High-level disinfection can be carried out by Pasteurization or by immersion in high-level disinfectants.

Reference: *APIC Text*, 4th edition, Chapter 106 - Sterile Processing

CBIC Core Competency: Cleaning, Sterilization, Disinfection, Asepsis

59. (D) 3,4

Rationale: Endoscopes should be stored in a manner that protects them from contamination. When storing the endoscope, hang it in a vertical position to facilitate drying (with caps, valves, and other detachable components removed as per manufacturer instructions).

Reference: *APIC Text*, 4th edition, Chapter 55 - Endoscopy

CBIC Core Competency: Preventing/Controlling the Transmission of Infectious Agents

NOTES

60. (D) The incidence rate of VAP was highest in February

Rationale: Incidence rate is calculated as the number of new cases divided by the population at risk. The graph presents the data as incidence rates, and the rate in February was higher than the rate for any other month.

Reference: *APIC Text*, 4th edition, Chapter 11 - Surveillance

CBIC Core Competency: Surveillance and Epidemiologic Investigation

61. (C) May require a long follow-up period

Rationale: A retrospective study looks backwards and examines exposures to suspected risk or protection factors in relation to an outcome that is established at the start of the study. Retrospective studies may be undertaken in a timelier and less-expensive manner than prospective cohort studies because cases may be identified retrospectively, and at least some exposure data are often available through medical record review.

A prospective cohort study watches for outcomes, such as the development of a disease, during the study period and relates this to other factors such as suspected risk or protection factor(s). The study usually involves taking a cohort of subjects and watching them over a long period. Prospective studies usually have fewer potential sources of bias and confounding than retrospective studies.

Reference: *APIC Text*, 4th edition, Chapter 20 - Research Study Design

CBIC Core Competency: Surveillance and Epidemiologic Investigation

62. (A) 1,2,3

Rationale: Program evaluation is a systematic method for collecting, analyzing, and using information to assess the effectiveness and efficiency of the educational offering. Specific program elements that must be evaluated include appropriateness of program design, adequacy of teaching and instructional resources, and the knowledge, skills, and attitudes learned by the participants. Needs assessments identify deficiencies in knowledge, skills, or attitude and should be conducted prior to the development of the program.

Reference: *APIC Text*, 4th edition, Chapter 3 - Education and Training

CBIC Core Competency: Education and Research

63. (C) 1,2,3

Rationale: APIC has created a competency model to help guide the advancement of infection preventionists in the field. The three levels of competency are early-level (novice), middle-level (proficient), and advanced-level (expert). The competency levels can be used to guide goal setting activities as part of the IP's personal development plan. Middle-level competencies include being Certified in Infection Control, considering an advanced degree in the field, and being active in the local APIC chapter by serving in a leadership position.

Reference: *APIC Text*, 4th edition, Chapter 2 - Competency and Certification of Infection Preventionists

CBIC Core Competency: Management and Communication

NOTES

64. (A) Anionic and/or nonionic surfactants

Rationale: Improved hydrogen peroxide contains very low levels of anionic and/or nonionic surfactant in an acidic product that act with hydrogen peroxide to produce microbial activity. This combination of ingredients speeds the antimicrobial activity of hydrogen peroxide and clean efficiency.

Reference: *APIC Text*, 4th edition, Chapter 31 - Cleaning, Disinfection, and Sterilization

CBIC Core Competency: Cleaning, Sterilization, Disinfection, Asepsis

65. (D) Less than 3 percent

Rationale: Bacteremia is a significant cause of morbidity and mortality in hospitalized patients. Accurate and timely identification of the causative organism is imperative. Blood cultures are considered the "gold standard" in the diagnosis and treatment of bacteremia. However, the prognostic value of blood cultures is limited by contamination. Contamination, or false positive blood cultures, occurs when organisms that are not present in the blood are grown in culture. Blood culture contamination rates of less than 3 percent are desired.

Reference: *The Infection Preventionist's Guide to the Lab*, Chapter: 3, Page: 39

CBIC Core Competency: Identification of Infectious Disease Processes

66. (B) Airborne Precautions

Rationale: Airborne Precautions are used to prevent transmission of infectious organisms that remain suspended in the air and travel great distances. These diseases include measles, smallpox, chickenpox, pulmonary tuberculosis, avian influenza and possibly severe acute respiratory syndrome-associated coronavirus. Patients should be placed in an airborne infection isolation (AII) room with negative air pressure relative to the corridor and at least 6 to 12 air exchanges with direct exhaust of air to the outside. Monitor the air pressure daily. Keep the door shut.

Reference: *APIC Text*, 4th edition, Chapter 29 - Isolation Precautions (Transmission-based Precautions)

CBIC Core Competency: Preventing/Controlling the Transmission of Infectious Agents

NOTES

67. (C) Advise her that following Standard Precautions while caring for the patient will prevent transmission

Rationale: CMV is transmitted through saliva, urine, and blood products and organs. The CDC recommends using Standard Precautions when caring for patients with CMV, with no additional precautions recommended for pregnant HCP.

References: *APIC Text*, 4th edition Chapter 104 - Pregnant Healthcare Personnel; *APIC Text*, 4th edition, Chapter 80 - Herpes Virus; *APIC Text*, 4th edition, Chapter 29 - Isolation Precautions (Transmission-Based Precautions)

CBIC Core Competency: Employee/Occupational Health

68. (C) The study is affected by confounding

Rationale: A confounding variable is an extraneous variable (i.e., a variable that is not a focus of the study) that is statistically related to (or correlated with) the independent variable. This means that as the independent variable changes, the confounding variable changes along with it. The result is that subjects in one condition are different in some unintended way from subjects in the other condition. Confounding can lead to the assumption that there are differences that do not really exist or to the observation that there is no difference when one truly exists. In this example, older age is associated with the risk factor of a CICU stay and with the outcome of VRE infection. The authors did not adjust for age in their study, so the IP should be concerned that the reported association is confounded by age.

Reference: *APIC Text*, 4th edition, Chapter 10 - General Principles of Epidemiology

CBIC Core Competency: Education and Research

69. (B) 1, 2, 4

Rationale: Interventions to prevent the growth of microbes include:

- When selecting/purchasing equipment for cooling or freezing, compare features that best meet the intended use, including operating range (e.g., an automatic defrost cycle can damage temperature-sensitive items), size, location of use, cleanable surfaces, durability, and maintenance needs.
- Provide accurate temperature monitoring for refrigerators and freezers; an alarm system may be required (e.g., blood bank refrigerator) or desired.
- Establish a method to record temperature on a regular basis (e.g., visualize and document daily or observe an automated recording chart each shift); include action to take if reading is not in the acceptable range.
- Schedule routine monitoring of refrigerator and freezer alarms where applicable.
- Test accuracy of thermometers; calibration may be required (e.g., blood bank, tissue freezer) by using standard regulations and/or recommendations.
- Schedule and perform regular preventive maintenance of all freezers and refrigerators; include air vents, gaskets, cooling coils, and fans.
- Walk-in refrigeration units may experience a condensation point if the building dehumidification is inadequate, resulting in mold proliferation.
- Provide training for personnel in recognizing and implementing safe maintenance of refrigerators to include appropriate cleaning methods.

Reference: *APIC Text*, 4th edition, Chapter 112 - Maintenance and Engineering

CBIC Core Competency: Preventing/Controlling the Transmission of Infectious Agents

NOTES

70. Ⓐ The Burn Unit

Rationale: Infection is the leading cause of morbidity and mortality in burn patients, despite improvements in care. Burns increase a patient's susceptibility to infection by damaging both the patient's physical and immunological defenses. Skin is the largest organ of the body, and constitutes the first defense against infection. When burned, the integrity of the skin barrier is broken and normally sterile sites become vulnerable to microbes. Recent studies have shown an increasing prevalence of *Acinetobacter, Klebsiella*, and other Gram-negative rods in burn wounds. Although all of these above patient populations might be susceptible to Gram-negative rod wound infections, burn patients have the highest risk of Gram-negative wound infections, and therefore this unit is most susceptible to outbreaks with those organisms.

Reference: *APIC Text*, 4th edition, Chapter 38 - Burns

CBIC Core Competency: Preventing/Controlling the Transmission of Infectious Agents

71. Ⓒ Equal to or less than 2 hours at room temperature

Rationale: The reliability and value of test results depends on numerous factors. Improper collection, transport, or processing of a specimen can decrease the quality of patient care or result in unnecessary additional testing or treatment. Blood Culture bottles must be transported to the Lab within a time frame equal to or less than two hours and must be maintained at room temperature.

Reference: *The Infection Preventionist's Guide to the Lab*, Chapter: 1, Page: 7

CBIC Core Competency: Identification of Infectious Disease Processes

72. Ⓒ Time

Rationale: The "epidemiological triangle" model of disease (see Fig. PE1-2) consists of three elements: host, agent, and environment. The host is the human, and the environment consists of all external factors associated with the host. The agent may be a bacteria, virus, fungus, protozoan, helminth, or prion. In this model of dynamic interaction, a change in any component alters the existing equilibrium. Change may increase or decrease the frequency of disease. Although this model is particularly useful in the study of infectious diseases, it is also applicable to other conditions.

Figure PE1-2. Epidemiologic triangle model of disease causation

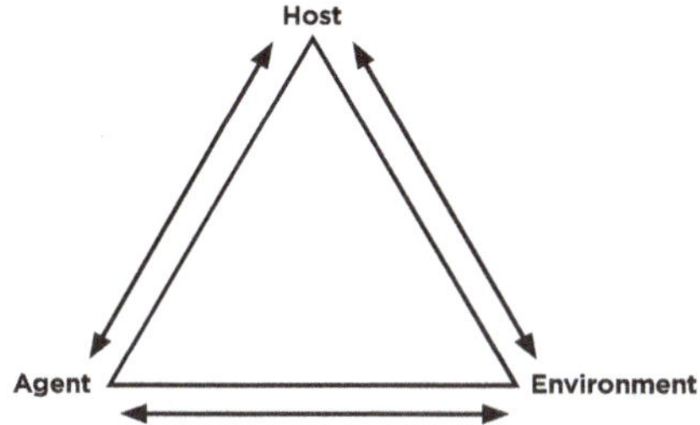

Source: Tweeten SM. General Principles of Epidemiology. In: Grota P, ed. *APIC Text of Infection Control and Epidemiology*, 4th edition. Washington, DC: Association for Professionals in Infection Control and Epidemiology, 2014.

Reference: *APIC Text*, 4th edition, Chapter 10 - General Principles of Epidemiology

CBIC Core Competency: Surveillance and Epidemiologic Investigation

NOTES

73. (D) You will need at least 25 gallons of water per patient per day to maintain care

Rationale: In the event of a disaster, it is critical to ensure that there is a reliable supply of water available for drinking and for patient care activities. Individuals in the facility will need at least 2 liters of drinking water per day per person, and additional water will be needed for bathing, flushing toilets, dialysis, cooking, and other activities. It is estimated that a facility will need 25 gallons of water per patient per day to maintain these patient care activities. Water may be stored on-site or off-site but it must be accessible in the event of an emergency.

Reference: *APIC Text*, 4th edition, Chapter 119 - Emergency Management

CBIC Core Competency: Environment of Care

74. (C) 1, 3

Rationale: Mycoplasma pneumonia is spread by respiratory droplets during close contact with a symptomatic person. In addition to Standard Precautions, Droplet Precautions are recommended for the duration of symptomatic illness.

References: Siegel JD, Rhinehart E, Jackson M, et al. *2007 Guideline for Isolation Precautions: Preventing Transmission of Infectious Agents in Healthcare Settings*. CDC website. 2007. Available at: http://www.cdc.gov/hicpac/pdf/isolation/isolation2007.pdf. *Mycoplasma pneumoniae* and Other *Mycoplasma* Species Infections. In: Pickering LK, ed. *Red Book: 2012 Report of the Committee on Infectious Diseases*, 29th edition. Elk Grove Village, IL: American Academy of Pediatrics, 2012.

CBIC Core Competency: Preventing/Controlling the Transmission of Infectious Agents

75. (B) 1, 3

Rationale: Mycobacterium chelonae belongs to the family of nontuberculous mycobacteria (NTM) classified in the rapidly growing mycobacteria (RGM), Runyon group IV. M chelonae are ubiquitous in the environment and have been isolated from both natural and potable freshwater sources, soil, contaminated solutions, and reptiles. The organism can grow in distilled and unsupplemented water. Likely sources of healthcare-related exposure may occur from bronchoscopes that were processed with tap water or from exposure to a hydrotherapy pool.

Reference: CDC Guidelines for Environmental Infection Control in Health-Care Facilities, 2003

CBIC Core Competency: Environment of Care

76. (C) 1, 3, 4

Rationale: Prevention of EKC requires meticulous attention to hand washing. Soap and water and/or an alcohol-based hand sanitizer should be used before and after each patient contact. Gloves should be worn and discarded appropriately during outbreaks and when exposure to patient's tears or excretions is likely. The current CDC recommendations for disinfection of tonometer tips include a 5 to 10 minute soak in 3 percent hydrogen peroxide, 70 percent isopropyl, 70 percent ethyl alcohol, or in 5,000 ppm bleach. Ophthalmoscopes should be wiped with 70 percent alcohol between patients.

Reference: *APIC Text*, 4th edition, Chapter 63 - Ophthalmology Services

CBIC Core Competency: Preventing/Controlling the Transmission of Infectious Agents

NOTES

77. **B** **3.1 percent**

Rationale: An incidence rate is a measure of the frequency with which an event occurs in a population over a specified period of time. Incidence indicates the risk of disease in a population over a period of time. The incidence rate equals the number of new cases of a disease for a specified time period divided by the population at risk for the same time period multiplied by a constant (k).

k = A constant used to transform the result of division into a uniform quantity so that it can be compared with other, similar quantities. A whole number (fractions are inconvenient) such as 100, 1,000, 10,000, or 100,000 is usually used (selection of k is usually made so that the smallest rate calculated has at least one digit to the left of the decimal point) or is determined by accepted practice (the magnitude of numerator compared with denominator).

The numerator for this scenario is 2—the number of new cases. The denominator would be the number of patients who are at risk for developing HCV, which would be 64. Patients already diagnosed with HCV would not be included.

Incidence rate in this scenario: $2 \div 64 \times 100 = 3.125$ percent

Reference: *APIC Text*, 4th edition, Chapter 13 - Use of Statistics in Infection Prevention

CBIC Core Competency: Surveillance and Epidemiologic Investigation

78. **C** **Identify where the dressings are in the hospital, check the lot number and return them to the manufacturer, and assess the patients who used the product for signs of infection**

Rationale: The U.S. FDA is the federal agency that is responsible for promoting public health through a number of activities, including the reasonable assurance that (1) food is safe, wholesome, sanitary, and properly labeled; (2) human drugs are safe and effective; (3) medical devices intended for human use are safe and effective; and (4) public health and safety are protected from electronic product radiation. Recalls are actions taken by a manufacturer/distributor to remove a product from the market. Recalls may be conducted on a manufacturer/distributor's own initiative (voluntary recall), by FDA request, or by FDA order. According to the FDA, a recall is a removal or correction of a product that is (1) defective; (2) a potential health risk; or (3) in violation of FDA regulations. The first step that the IP should take is to identify where the dressings are in the hospital, immediately remove them, and return them to the manufacturer. It is critical to assess the patients who used the product for signs of infection.

Reference: *APIC Text*, 4th edition, Chapter 106 - Sterile Processing

CBIC Core Competency: Preventing/Controlling the Transmission of Infectious Agents

79. **C** **Revise the facility's surveillance plan**

Rationale: Surveillance activities should support a system that can identify risk factors for infection and other adverse advents, implement risk-reduction measures, and monitor the effectiveness of interventions. The items noted in answers A, B, and D are rarely related to the development of SSIs. The facility's surveillance program should be revised to reflect the current risks and risk reduction measures.

Reference: *APIC Text*, 4th edition, Chapter 11 - Surveillance

CBIC Core Competency: Surveillance and Epidemiologic Investigation

NOTES

80. D 11 percent

Rationale: A prevalence rate is the proportion of persons in a population with a particular disease or attribute at a specific point in time (point prevalence) or over a specified time period (period prevalence). Prevalence depends on the duration of disease. The prevalence rate equals the number of existing cases of disease from a specified interval or point in time divided by the population at risk for same time period multiplied by a constant (k).

k = A constant used to transform the result of division into a uniform quantity so that it can be compared with other, similar quantities. A whole number (fractions are inconvenient) such as 100, 1,000, 10,000, or 100,000 is usually used (selection of k is usually made so that the smallest rate calculated has at least one digit to the left of the decimal point) or is determined by accepted practice (the magnitude of numerator compared with denominator).

This prevalence rate is calculated as: $8 \div 72 \times 100 = 11$ percent

Reference: *APIC Text*, 4th edition, Chapter 13 - Use of Statistics in Infection Prevention

CBIC Core Competency: Surveillance and Epidemiologic Investigation

81. C Relocate immunocompromised patients if necessary and provide emergency back-up ventilation or portable units for other rooms

Rationale: Any shut-down of the HVAC must be coordinated with Infection Control to protect patient safety. Immunocompromised patients should be moved from the area if possible and an alternate ventilation method (emergency back-up or portable ventilation) should be used to maintain proper air flow in all rooms, including airborne isolation rooms and protective environments. Infection preventionists should be aware of the potential for a burst of spores from the HVAC when it is brought back online. In addition, critical areas will need to be given time for the appropriate number of air changes per hour to occur before they can be put back into regular use.

Reference: CDC Guidelines for Environmental Infection Control in Health-Care Facilities, 2003

CBIC Core Competency: Environment of Care

82. B Visit reprocessing companies under consideration

Rationale: Healthcare facilities that are considering contracting with a commercial third-party reprocessor must verify that reprocessing an SUD presents no greater risk to their patients' health and safety than using a new SUD. The decision to contract with a reprocessing company should be based on a thorough review and FDA approval of their 510(k) application. An onsite visit should be scheduled, with the opportunity to meet with personnel involved in the process, and a review of the company's policies. The visit should also include an opportunity to view the cleaning and decontamination, inspection and testing, and sterilization load preparation process, and to review quality control records.

Reference: *APIC Text*, 4th edition, Chapter 32 - Reprocessing Single-Use Devices

CBIC Core Competency: Cleaning, Sterilization, Disinfection, Asepsis

NOTES

83. D Wash the affected area

Rationale: The first action after exposure involves an immediate cleaning of the exposed/injured site. A soap-and-water hand wash should be performed to remove visible soil. Alcohol is virucidal, so an alcohol-based hand hygiene agent can be used after soap-and-water hand wash has been performed. Caustic chemicals such as bleach should not be used in an attempt to disinfect or cleanse the skin. Squeezing or "milking" the injured site is not necessary. Once the area has been washed, evaluation by a skilled professional should be sought.

Reference: *APIC Text*, 4th edition, Chapter 81 - HIV/AIDS

CBIC Core Competency: Employee/Occupational Health

84. B (6 ÷ 180) × 1,000 = 33.3 per 1,000 catheter days

Rationale: A rate is calculated by dividing the numerator (number of occurrences) by the denominator (number of opportunities for that occurrence) and then multiplying by a constant.

Basic formula for all types of rates: Rate = $x/y \times k$

Where:

x = The numerator, which equals the number of times the event (e.g., infections) has occurred during a specified time interval.

y = The denominator, which equals a population (e.g., number of patients at risk) from which those experiencing the event were derived during the same time interval.

k = A constant used to transform the result of division into a uniform quantity so that it can be compared with other, similar quantities. A whole number (fractions are inconvenient) such as 100, 1,000, 10,000, or 100,000 is usually used (selection of k is usually made so that the smallest rate calculated has at least one digit to the left of the decimal point) or is determined by accepted practice (the magnitude of numerator compared with denominator).

There are three important aspects of the formula:

1. Persons in the denominator must reflect the same population from which the numerator was taken.
2. Counts in the numerator and denominator should cover the same time period.
3. At least in theory, the persons in the denominator should have been at risk of the event or occurrence.

Reference: *APIC Text*, 4th edition, Chapter 13 - Use of Statistics in Infection Prevention

CBIC Core Competency: Surveillance and Epidemiologic Investigation

85. A Web-based training sessions

Rationale: Although each of the delivery methods listed has benefits, the best method in this case is web-based training. It is easy to deliver to a large number of people, flexible so that people with varied schedules can complete the training at a time that is convenient for them, and easy to track by having employees register for training through an online system. Assessments can be built into web-based training so that learners can evaluate their understanding of the training while it is in progress and demonstrate their mastery of the material at the end of the training session.

Reference: *APIC Text*, 4th edition, Chapter 3 - Education and Training

CBIC Core Competency: Education and Research

NOTES

86. (B) 1, 3, 4

Rationale: Surveillance has been defined as the "ongoing collection, collation, and analysis of data and the ongoing dissemination of information to those who need to know so that action can be taken." It is an essential component of an effective infection prevention program. Surveillance programs should measure outcomes of healthcare, processes of healthcare, and selected events of importance to the organization. Routine or random, undirected microbiological culturing of air, water, and environmental surfaces in healthcare facilities is not recommended.

Reference: *APIC Text*, 4th edition, Chapter 11 - Surveillance

CBIC Core Competency: Surveillance and Epidemiologic Investigation

87. (A) Diffusion

Rationale: When air enters a facility's ventilation system from the outside it passes through a series of filters that remove particulate matter. The first bank of filters has low to medium efficiency for removing particles and can include straining, impingement, and interception filtration methods. This air is then mixed with the recirculated air from the facility and filtered again with high efficiency filtration methods including diffusion filtration.

Reference: CDC Guidelines for Environmental Infection Control in Health-Care Facilities, 2003

CBIC Core Competency: Environment of Care

88. (B) Typhus

Rationale: Agents classified by CDC as Category A are biological agents that have high potential for adverse public health impact, increased risk to national security, serious potential for large-scale dissemination, potential for public panic, social disruption, and high mortality rates. Category B agents have a moderate ease in disseminating, specific requirements for disease surveillance, moderate morbidity rates, and low mortality. Typhus (*Rickettsia prowazekii*) meets the Category B criteria.

Reference: Bioterrorism Agents. In: Brooks K. *Ready Reference for Microbes*, 3rd edition. Washington, DC: Association for Professionals in Infection Control and Epidemiology, 2012.

CBIC Core Competency: Preventing/Controlling the Transmission of Infectious Agents

89. (A) Creating an isolation room to practice use of Isolation Precautions

Rationale: The goal of simulation is to create a controlled learning environment that closely resembles the practice setting. This process facilitates use of practical and critical thinking skills on the part of the participant and serves to protect the safety of the patient. One example of a simulation room may be to create a mock isolation room. The goal may be to increase the awareness of the nursing staff regarding common infection prevention infractions that may occur during the provision of care. The simulation would enable participants to practice infection prevention activities necessary to care for patients.

Reference: *APIC Text*, 4th edition, Chapter 3 - Education and Training

CBIC Core Competency: Education and Research

NOTES

90. **(D) Median**

Rationale: The median is the point at which 50 percent of the values fall below a middle value and 50 percent of values occur above the middle value. It is the midpoint of the observations. The median ignores extreme values and is better at indicating values close to an average.

Reference: *APIC Text*, 4th edition, Chapter 11 - Surveillance

CBIC Core Competency: Surveillance and Epidemiologic Investigation

91. **(C) 60 percent**

Rationale: Building materials contain fungal spores that have the potential to germinate in the correct conditions. Fungi require high relative humidity for growth, with most species needing relative humidity above 70 percent. Healthcare facilities should maintain relative humidity below 60 percent to prevent the growth of fungus and to provide a comfortable patient care environment.

Reference: CDC Guidelines for Environmental Infection Control in Health-Care Facilities, 2003

CBIC Core Competency: Environment of Care

92. **(D) Airborne infection isolation room**

Rationale: Bronchoscopy permits direct visualization of airways using a fiberoptic bronchoscope and is used in the diagnosis and management of inflammatory, infectious, and malignant diseases of the chest. Bronchoscopy should not be performed on patients with TB unless absolutely necessary. If medically necessary, bronchoscopy should only be performed in a room that meets the ventilation requirements for an airborne infection isolation room (negative directional air flow, a minimum of 12 air exchanges per hour and direct exhaust to the outside more than 25 feet from an air intake or discharged through a high efficiency particulate air filtration system).

Reference: *APIC Text*, 4th edition, Chapter 55 - Endoscopy

CBIC Core Competency: Preventing/ Controlling the Transmission of Infectious Agents

93. **(C) They have a thick peptidoglycan cell wall that retains the primary stain during the alcohol decolorization**

Rationale: Gram-positive cells will take up the initial crystal violet stain and will not be decolorized with alcohol because their peptidoglycan cell walls are thick enough to resist decolorization.

Reference: *APIC Text*, 4th edition, Chapter 24 - Microbiology basics

CBIC Core Competency: Identification of Infectious Disease Processes

NOTES

94. (B) Hepatitis A virus (HAV) immunoglobulin M (IgM)

Rationale: The clinical case definition for acute viral hepatitis is (1) discrete onset of symptoms (e.g., nausea, anorexia, fever, malaise, or abdominal pain) and (2) jaundice or elevated serum aminotransferase levels. Because the clinical characteristics are the same for all types of acute viral hepatitis, Hepatitis A diagnosis must be confirmed by a positive serologic test for IgM antibody to HAV, or the case must meet the clinical case definition and occur in a person who has an epidemiologic link with a person who has laboratory-confirmed Hepatitis A (i.e., household or sexual contact with an infected person during the 15 to 50 days before the onset of symptoms). IgM is the first antibody built during immune response and is indicative of current disease.

Reference: *APIC Text*, 4th edition, Chapter 97 - Viral Hepatitis

CBIC Core Competency: Identification of Infectious Disease Processes

95. (D) It is not acceptable to reuse the syringe

Rationale: While the medication in this example is expected to only be used on one patient, a healthcare worker should still use a new, sterile syringe and needle to access the medication vial the second time. This is a precaution in the event that the vial does not get discarded after use on this one patient and instead is accidentally used on another patient.

References: *APIC Text*, 4th edition, Chapter 64 - Isolation Precautions (Transmission-based Precautions); CDC, Frequently Asked Questions (FAQs) regarding Safe Practices for Medical Injections; http://www.cdc.gov/injectionsafety/providers/provider_faqs_med-admin.html

CBIC Core Competency: Preventing/Controlling the Transmission of Infectious Agents

96. (D) Train the trainer

Rationale: Train the trainer is an option for face-to-face institutional training when large numbers of staff must be quickly educated. Leader guides are used to train those responsible for implementing the program and for providing staff inservice and continuing education. These leader guides should be simply written, concise, and systematic. They should include curriculum goals and objectives, the course outline, instructional methods, references, and evaluation. Role playing is often used to allow the learner to experience a professional dilemma firsthand. Mentors may be used as a way to upgrade and cross-train workforce. Case studies are viewed as an effective method to help bridge the learning gap between theory and actual practice.

Reference: *APIC Text*, 4th edition, Chapter 3 - Education and Training

CBIC Core Competency: Education and Research

97. (B) The decontamination process starts on the floor of the OR and works upward toward the lighting

Rationale: At the end of each day's operating schedule, a complete terminal cleaning program should be initiated to ensure that every operating room, scrub room, and service room is properly and thoroughly cleaned. The decontamination process begins at the highest level (i.e., light tracks, ceiling fixtures) and progresses downward (i.e., shelves, tables, kick buckets, and floor).

Reference: *APIC Text*, 4th edition, Chapter 68 - Surgical Services

CBIC Core Competency: Cleaning, Sterilization, Disinfection, Asepsis

NOTES

98. (B) **1, 2, 4**

Rationale: The risk of infection related to vascular access for hemodialysis varies with the type of vascular access used. Risk for bacteremia increases sevenfold in patients with a dialysis catheter compared to those with a primary arteriovenous (AV) fistula. It is recommended that an AV fistula be created and used for long-term hemodialysis treatment because of the lower incidence of infection. If an AV fistula cannot be established, an AV graft is the next preferred type of access. Because of infection risk, creation of the fistula in the upper arm is preferred over the thigh. For acute hemodialysis, where access for less than 3 weeks' duration is anticipated, vascular access may be obtained using a noncuffed or cuffed catheter. However, if a catheter must be used for access for longer than 3 weeks, a tunneled, cuffed venous catheter should be used. The preferred insertion site is the right internal jugular. Because there is a greater incidence of central venous thrombosis and stenosis when the subclavian is used, subclavian access should be used only when jugular options are not available and permanent vascular access is not required. In addition, tunneled cuffed catheters should not be placed on the same side as a maturing AV access if possible. Femoral catheters should be placed only in bedbound patients only with good exit site care and should be left in place for no more than 5 days because of associated infection rates.

Reference: *APIC Text*, 4th edition, Chapter 39 - Dialysis

CBIC Core Competency: Preventing/Controlling the Transmission of Infectious Agents

99. (D) **20 percent**

Rationale: An attack rate is a special form of incidence rate. In fact, it is not truly a rate but a proportion. It is the proportion of persons at risk who become infected over an entire period of exposure or a measure of the risk or probability of becoming a case. It is usually expressed as a percentage and is used almost exclusively for epidemics or outbreaks of disease where a specific population is exposed to a disease for a limited period of time.

The attack rate for this scenario is calculated as follows: $15 \div 75 \times 100 =$ 20 percent.

Reference: *APIC Text*, 4th edition, Chapter 13 - Use of Statistics in Infection Prevention

CBIC Core Competency: Surveillance and Epidemiologic Investigation

100. (A) **No further follow-up is needed**

Rationale: *M. marinum* is a bacterium found in water and may be the cause of wound infections. Infection with *M. marinum* is not transmissible, and infection with non-tuberculosis mycobacteria is not notifiable. No further infection control follow-up is needed.

References: Appendix A. In: Siegel J, Rhinehart E, Jackson M, et al. *2007 Guideline for Isolation Precautions: Preventing Transmission of Infectious Agents in Health Care Settings*. Available at: http://www.cdc.gov/hicpac/pdf/isolation/isolation2007.pdf; *APIC Text*, 4th edition, Chapter 95 - Tuberculosis and Other Mycobacteria

CBIC Core Competency: Preventing/Controlling the Transmission of Infectious Agents

NOTES

101. B 1, 2, 3

Rationale: In healthcare organizations, surveillance, reporting, and analysis are the foundation of risk prevention programs, but targeted interventions must be deployed if patient safety programs are to be successful in reducing harm from medical errors and other adverse events. The Agency for Healthcare Research and Quality recommends that all healthcare organizations focus on the following infection prevention initiatives:

1. Improving hand hygiene
2. Utilizing barrier precautions to prevent transmission of infection
3. Prudent antibiotic use to reduce *C. difficile* and VRE
4. Preventing urinary tract infections
5. Preventing central venous catheter-related bloodstream infections
6. Preventing VAP
7. Preventing SSIs

Medication errors are also common in healthcare and are addressed in TJC's list of sentinel events: "Any patient death, paralysis, coma, or other major permanent loss of function associated with a medication error."

A culture of safety must prevent punitive reactions to mistakes, and staff members must feel confident that if they speak out about risk, their leaders will respond. Providers involved in medical errors must know that leaders will look beyond the obvious and drill down until the root causes of accidents and errors are found and that they will routinely evaluate systems and processes during any accident investigation.

Reference: *APIC Text*, 4th edition, Chapter 18 - Patient Safety

CBIC Core Competency: Management and Communication

102. C 2, 4

Rationale: The CDC recommends using the subclavian site rather than a jugular or a femoral site in adult patients to minimize infection risk for nontunneled central venous catheter placement.

References: O'Grady NP, Alexander M, Burns LA, et al. *Guidelines for the Prevention of Intravascular Catheter-Related Infections*, 2011. Centers for Disease Control and Prevention website. 2011. Available at: http://www.cdc.gov/hicpac/pdf/guidelines/bsi-guidelines-2011.pdf; *APIC Text*, 4th edition, Chapter 34 - Intravascular Device Infections

CBIC Core Competency: Preventing/Controlling the Transmission of Infectious Agents

103. A Determine if the patient actually has an active case of varicella-zoster by involving the IP or checking with the patient's physician to verify the diagnosis

Rationale: The first step is to verify that the patient actually has the disease. If the patient does have confirmed varicella-zoster, the occupational health nurse should work this up as an exposure and exclude the employee from work.

References: *APIC Text*, 4th edition, Chapter 100 - Occupational Health; Advisory Committee on Immunization Practices (ACIP). ACIP Recommendations. ACIP website. Available at: http://www.cdc.gov/vaccines/acip/recs/index.html

CBIC Core Competency: Employee/Occupational Health

NOTES

104. **C** **She should remove the scrub top by using scissors to cut it off and discard it in a biohazard-labeled container**

Rationale: A scrub top that has been thoroughly soiled with blood should be removed immediately. If the scrub top is soiled through the top layer, there is potential for further exposure through contamination of mucus membranes if the employee pulls it over her head. She should use scissors to carefully cut off the top.

Reference: *APIC Text*, 4th edition, Chapter 111 - Laundry, Patient Linens, Textiles, and Uniforms

CBIC Core Competency: Preventing/Controlling the Transmission of Infectious Agents

105. **B** **Use high-temperature flushing to disinfect the system**

Rationale: If there is contamination of the potable water system with sewer water in a facility then it is necessary to flush the system. A variety of methods can be used to accomplish this and they may be used in combination, if necessary. As Cryptosporidium is highly resistant to chlorine and there is suspected contamination with this protozoa in this scenario, you would have to minimally recommend the use of high-temperature flushing to disinfect the system.

Reference: CDC Guidelines for Environmental Infection Control in Health-Care Facilities, 2003

CBIC Core Competency: Environment of Care

106. **D** **Bleach**

Rationale: Many disinfectants are inactivated by blood and other organic matter. If the spill is small, it can be cleaned and disinfected in one step by pouring the disinfectant directly on the spill and cleaning up after the appropriate contact time for the disinfectant has been reached. If the spill involves a higher concentration of microorganisms, such as a large body fluid spill or a blood spill in a laboratory, absorbent material can be placed over the spill until all of the fluid is absorbed. The disinfectant solution can be poured over the spill and the absorbent material until both are thoroughly soaked with the disinfectant for the designed contact time. Then the spill site is cleaned. Absorbent powders that solidify liquids are recommended for cleaning large spills.

Occupational Safety & Health Administration (OSHA) stipulates that blood and body fluid spills be decontaminated with one of the following: an EPA-registered disinfectant effective against HBV and HIV, a tuberculocidal disinfectant, or an appropriate dilution of household bleach (5.25 to 6.15 percent sodium hypochlorite solution). If the spill occurs on a nonporous surface, a 1:100 dilution of household bleach (one part household bleach plus 99 parts tap water or 0.25 cup of bleach in a gallon of water) is a highly effective disinfectant and is the least expensive. A 1:10 dilution of household bleach (one part household bleach plus nine parts water or 1.5 cups of bleach in a gallon of water) is required for porous surfaces and large spills. Large quantities of blood may inactivate the higher concentration of bleach. Higher concentrations of bleach may also be damaging or corrosive to surfaces.

Reference: *APIC Text*, 4th edition, Chapter 107 - Environmental Services

CBIC Core Competency: Cleaning, Sterilization, Disinfection, Asepsis

NOTES

107. (B) **There were fewer CLABSIs in the ICU than expected**

Rationale: If the SIR is less than 1, then there were fewer infections reported in 2011 than what we would have predicted given the baseline data. In other words, progress has been made since the baseline period.

SIR less than 1	SIR greater than 1
Fewer infections than what would have been predicted given baseline data	More infections than what would have been predicted given baseline data
Infections have been prevented since the baseline period.	Infections have increased since the baseline period.
1 minus the SIR = percent reduction:	SIR minus 1 = percent increase
For example, the SIR of 0.80 means that there was a 20 percent reduction in 2011 from the baseline period.	For example, the SIR of 1.25 means that there was a 25 percent increase in 2011 from the baseline period.

Reference: Centers for Disease Control and Prevention (CDC). *CDC's National Healthcare Safety Network (NHSN) Healthcare-associated Infections Summary Data Reports Q and A*. CDC website. Available at: http://www.cdc.gov/HAI/surveillance/QA_stateSummary.html#a6.

CBIC Core Competency: Surveillance and Epidemiologic Investigation

108. (B) **Run chart**

Rationale: Run charts are epidemiological tools used to identify how process specifications change over time. For example, if the organization examines the number of HAIs occurring within a hospital over a given period of time, clinicians will record each monthly value and graph the values, creating a chart that looks at trends and averages. Run charts allow for the mean or average to be determined and show changes in the mean/average. Run charts also demonstrate special-cause variation when there is a steady pattern of observation points falling above or below the mean/average line in an equal pattern.

Reference: *APIC Text*, 4th edition, Chapter 16 – Quality Concepts

CBIC Core Competency: Surveillance and Epidemiologic Investigation

109. (A) **1**

Rationale: OSHA is the only agency listed above that has regulatory authority over any aspect of healthcare facility design, construction, and renovation. OSHA has set regulations for engineering controls related to bloodborne pathogens and to isolation of suspected or confirmed cases of Tuberculosis in an airborne isolation room.

Reference: Occupational Health and Safety Administration (OSHA) https://www.osha.gov

CBIC Core Competency: Environment of Care

110. (D) **Remove bag and teach staff how to follow safe injection practices**

Rationale: Unsafe injection practices put patients and healthcare providers at risk of infectious and non-infectious adverse events and have been associated with a wide variety of procedures and settings. Use fluid infusion and administration sets for one patient only and dispose of appropriately after use. Do not use bags or bottles of IV solution as a common source of supply for multiple patients.

References: *APIC Text*, 4th edition, Chapter 64 – Ambulatory Surgery Centers; CDC One & Only Campaign http://www.oneandonlycampaign.org

CBIC Core Competency: Preventing/Controlling the Transmission of Infectious Agents

NOTES

111. (A) Use of a single-dose medication vial for more than one patient

Rationale: Vials that are labeled as single-dose or single-use should be used for a single patient and single case/procedure/injection. There have been multiple outbreaks resulting from healthcare personnel using single dose or single-use vials for multiple patients. Even if a single-dose or single-use vial appears to contain multiple doses or contains more medication than is needed for a single patient, that vial should not be used for more than one patient nor stored for future use on the same patient.

Reference: *APIC Text*, 4th edition, Chapter 110 - Pharmacy Services; CDC Injection Safety found at: http://www.cdc.gov/injectionsafety/CDCposition-SingleUseVial.html

CBIC Core Competency: Preventing/Controlling the Transmission of Infectious Agents

112. (B) Experimental studies can establish association and causality if host factors such as disease susceptibility and other variables are strictly controlled

Rationale: Epidemiology provides the background for interventions to reduce the transmission of infecting organisms. Selecting appropriate study design is an essential step in answering questions important to the IP. Experimental designs are always prospective. The investigator manipulates one or more factors (variables) while the others remain constant. In true experiments, randomization is used. Experimental studies can establish association and may establish causality, (when) other factors are strictly controlled.

References: *APIC Text*, 4th edition, Chapter 10 - General Principles of Epidemiology; Centers for Disease Control and Prevention (CDC). *TB Elimination Interferon-Gamma Release Assays (IGRAs) - Blood Tests for TB Infection*. CDC website. 2012. Available at: http://www.cdc.gov/tb/publications/factsheets/testing/igra.htm.

CBIC Core Competency: Education and Research

113. (D) 3, 4

Rationale: The IP will need to divide the number of spinal fusion infections for each surgeon by the number of spinal fusion surgeries performed by each surgeon.

Reference: *APIC Text*, 4th edition, Chapter 21 - Risk Factors Facilitating Transmission of Infectious Agents

CBIC Core Competency: Surveillance and Epidemiologic Investigation

114. (A) Establish a method to recognize spills or leaks

Rationale: Blood/body fluid (e.g., from specimens due to spill or leak) may contaminate transport system pathways (e.g., pneumatic tube system), receiver stations, transport carts, dumbwaiters, or elevators. Disruption caused by these spills can delay specimen transport and processing until the area is cleaned and disinfected. Personnel may also be exposed to bloodborne pathogens, other microbes (e.g., sputum specimen, tissue specimen), or chemicals (pharmaceuticals; preservatives such as formaldehyde). Establish a method to recognize spills or leaks; include communication protocol (e.g., notification to sender, system shutdown, alternative methods of transport), cleaning and decontamination, retrieval of "stuck" items, and restoration of system.

Reference: *APIC Text*, 4th edition, Chapter 112 - Maintenance and Engineering

CBIC Core Competency: Environment of Care

NOTES

115. (B) *Legionella* and *Aspergillus*

Rationale: The risk of HAIs increases significantly when hospitals are undergoing construction and renovation. Dust particles contaminated with bacteria and fungi are dispersed and pose a health risk for patients, staff, and visitors. Construction-related HAIs are primarily caused by fungi, and to a lesser extent by bacteria. The most common etiological agent is *Aspergillus*, in particular, *A. fumigatus, A. flavus, A. niger,* and *A. terreus*. *A. fumigatus* is considered the most pathogenic species and is responsible for more than 90 percent of all *Aspergillus* infections. The most common group of bacteria associated with construction-related nosocomial infections are *Legionella* species, including *L. pneumophila*. *Legionella* bacteria have been isolated from soil and dust but are more often associated with aquatic environments. Typical water sources in hospitals supporting colonization with *Legionella* bacteria are cooling towers, evaporative condensers, heated potable water systems, and heating and air conditioning systems. During construction and renovation processes, water systems are often disrupted. Potable water can become contaminated with *Legionella* when the water supply is restored. The introduction of contaminated soil into the plumbing system, as well as optimized growth conditions for bacteria in stagnant water, may increase the number of *Legionella* bacteria.

References: *APIC Text*, 4th edition, Chapter 11 - Surveillance; *APIC Text*, 4th edition, Chapter 116 - Construction and Renovation

CBIC Core Competency: Environment of Care

116. (B) Indicated a propagated source of infection

Rationale: An epidemic curve gives a graphical display of the numbers of incident cases in an outbreak or epidemic plotted over time. The form of the resulting distribution of cases can be used to propose hypotheses on the nature of the disease and its mode of transmission.

A propagated source means that infections are transmitted from person to person in such a way that cases identified cannot be attributed to agent(s) transmitted from a single source. Propagated (continuing) source cases occur over a longer period than in common source transmission. Explosive epidemics resulting from person-to-person transmission may occur (e.g., chickenpox). If secondary and tertiary cases occur, intervals between peaks usually approximate average incubation period.

Reference: *APIC Text*, 4th edition, Chapter 12 - Outbreak Investigations

CBIC Core Competency: Surveillance and Epidemiologic Investigation

117. (D) Sentinel event

Rationale: According to The Joint Commission, a sentinel event is an unexpected occurrence involving death or serious physical or psychological injury or the risk thereof. Serious injury specifically includes loss of limb or function. The phrase "or the risk thereof" includes any process variation for which a recurrence would carry a significant chance of a serious adverse outcome. Such events are called sentinel because they signal the need for immediate investigation and response.

Reference: *APIC Text*, 4th edition, Chapter 18 - Patient Safety

CBIC Core Competency: Management and Communication

NOTES

118. (C) 2 to 10 days

Rationale: The incubation period for meningococcal meningitis is between 2 to 10 days, commonly 3 to 4 days.

Reference: Meningococcal infection. In: Heymann D. *Control of Communicable Diseases Manual*, 19th edition. Washington, DC: American Public Health Association, 2008.

CBIC Core Competency: Identification of Infectious Disease Processes

119. (A) All water sites in the healthcare facility to which the patient was exposed should be cultured for *L. pneumophila*

Rationale: If there is suspicion of healthcare-associated *L. pneumophila*, the water system should be tested first to determine whether the microbe is present.

References: *APIC Text*, 4th edition, Chapter 84 - *Legionella pneumophila*; *APIC Text*, 4th edition, Chapter 115 - Water Systems Issues and Prevention of Waterborne Infectious Diseases in Healthcare Facilities

CBIC Core Competency: Environment of Care

120. (C) Learner outcomes in measurable terms using action verbs

Rationale: Instructional objectives include specific actions the learner will perform as a result of instruction. There is no single correct method or style, but properly written learning objectives describe the learner outcomes in measureable terms and use action verbs such as discuss, describe, or demonstrate. Statements that communicate the intent of the curriculum and directions and plans for the educational session (A and B) are more appropriate for learning goals. Measures of changes and growth in the learner (D) are used for evaluation of the learning program.

Reference: *APIC Text*, 4th edition, Chapter 3 - Education and Training

CBIC Core Competency: Education and Research

121. (B) Physical removal of visible dirt, organic material, and debris

Rationale: Accumulation of dust, soil, and microbial contaminants on environmental surfaces in healthcare facilities is not only aesthetically displeasing, but evidence indicates that it also plays a major role in the spread of HAIs. Studies have shown that many microorganisms survive on surfaces for long periods. The key to cleaning and disinfecting environmental surfaces is the use of friction to physically remove visible dirt, organic material, and debris, thereby removing microorganisms.

Reference: *APIC Text*, 4th edition, Chapter 107 - Environmental Services

CBIC Core Competency: Cleaning, Sterilization, Disinfection, Asepsis

122. (C) Development of communication networks between sites, hospitals, and health departments

Rationale: The establishment of communication networks and collaboration at all levels of the outpatient sites is essential to implement infection prevention practices more effectively and efficiently. For outpatient sites, the use of measurement and operational definitions for HAIs can be challenging due to the lack of standardized definitions. There are limited external benchmarks for HAIs in ambulatory care, and HAI rates are often internally compared over time to establish a benchmark. Infection prevention policies and procedures should be specific to each setting.

Reference: *APIC Text*, 4th edition, Chapter 48 - Ambulatory Care

CBIC Core Competency: Management and Communication

NOTES

123. (D) Single-use items can be reprocessed in a third-party facility if FDA guidelines are followed

Rationale: The decision to reprocess and reuse a single-use item should be made by representatives from Administration, Risk Management, Legal Counsel, the supply chain administrator, and Infection Control. Third-party reprocessors must be FDA-licensed to reprocess single-use devices. The reprocessing facility must maintain its own documentation, but it is recommended that the IP also review all documentation and records.

Reference: *APIC Text*, 4th edition, Chapter 7 - Product Evaluation

CBIC Core Competency: Environment of Care

124. (B) 1, 2, 3

Rationale: The risk assessment should be tailored to the risks in specific to a facility and must include identification of risks based on the facility's geographic location, community, and population served as well as the types of services the facility offers. The annual risk assessment should take into account the previous year's goals and objectives and whether the facility met the targets associated with those goals.

Reference: *APIC Text*, 4th edition, Chapter 1 - Infection Prevention and Control Programs

CBIC Core Competency: Management and Communication

125. (A) 31 per 100,000

Rationale: A mortality rate is the measure of the frequency of death in a defined population during a specified time (usually a year). The crude mortality rate measures the proportion of the population dying each year from all causes. The cause-specific mortality rate measures mortality from a specified cause for a population.

Mortality rate = $x/y \times k$

Where:

x = The number of people in a defined population during a specified interval of time who (1) die of any cause (crude rate) or (2) die of a specified cause (cause-specific rate)

y = Estimated population at midyear (i.e., July); crude rates use 1000 or 100,000

k = Usually an assigned value of 1,000 when calculating crude rates: 100,000 is used for cause-specific rates

The cause-specific mortality rate for this scenario is calculated as follows:

$565 \div 1,800,000 \times 100,000 = 31.38$

We round to 31 and state that the cause-specific mortality rate is 31 per 100,000.

Reference: *APIC Text*, 4th edition, Chapter 13 - Use of Statistics in Infection Prevention

CBIC Core Competency: Surveillance and Epidemiologic Investigation

NOTES

126. (B) Blood-tinged suctioned fluids

Rationale: Blood and blood products, as defined in the OSHA Bloodborne Pathogen Standard (e.g., serum, plasma, and other components known or suspected to be contaminated with a transmissible agent) must be handled carefully. Small amounts of these materials dried on dressings or other disposable items represent an insignificant hazard once they are properly contained because of the absence of a portal of entry and a means of transmission. Bulk blood, blood-tinged suctioned fluids, excretions, and secretions are considered infectious waste because they may be splashed onto mucous membranes or the container may break and become a contaminated sharp. These fluids may be carefully poured down a drain connected to a sanitary sewer that is designed for the disposal of human waste. Personnel must follow Standard Precautions due to splash and aerosolization potential. Alternative treatment methods for inactivation or handling prior to disposal are available.

Reference: *APIC Text*, 4th edition, Chapter 113 - Waste Management

CBIC Core Competency: Preventing/Controlling the Transmission of Infectious Agents

127. (D) 2, 4

Rationale: Cleaning of floors and carpets should start at the back of the room and move toward the door. Floors should be mopped using the "S" stroke, catching dirt and debris on the leading edge of the mop. Cleaning items (e.g., detergent and/or disinfectant solutions, water buckets, cleaning cloths, dusters, toilet brushes, and mops) must be changed routinely and after they are used to clean blood spills or highly contaminated areas such as isolation rooms or operating rooms. Using contaminated cloths and mops will result in cross-contamination of surfaces, equipment, and hands. CDC recommends changing floor mopping solutions every three rooms and at least every 60 minutes. Used mops and cleaning cloths should never be returned to containers of cleaning solution. They should be laundered or discarded after use.

Reference: *APIC Text*, 4th edition, Chapter 107 - Environmental Services

CBIC Core Competency: Cleaning, Sterilization, Disinfection, Asepsis

128. (C) Inform Occupational Health about the infection so they can furlough the employee for the appropriate amount of time

Rationale: This is an appropriate follow-up in this example. Occupational Health will need to furlough the nurse for 7 days after he developed a rash. There is no risk of exposure to coworkers or patients because the employee was not in the facility during the period of contagion, so determining susceptibility of HCP and patients who had contact with the nurse and placing susceptible patients on Airborne Isolation would be unnecessary in this example.

References: *APIC Text*, 4th edition, Chapter 86 - Measles, Mumps, Rubella; *APIC Text*, 4th edition, Chapter 100 - Occupational Health

CBIC Core Competency: Employee/Occupational Health

NOTES

129. (B) Iatrogenic CJD

Rationale: CJD is one of several neurologically degenerative diseases caused by a group of protein particles that are infectious by nature of their ability to replicate in the central nervous system and interrupt crucial neuron functioning. CJD and other prion diseases with demonstrated transmissibility remain a concern for the healthcare community because of their inherent resistance to traditional disinfection/sterilization methods and devastating clinical outcomes. Prion diseases occur sporadically in nature, by familial transmission (gene mutation), iatrogenically, and by ingestion of abnormal prions as in the case of the bovine encephalopathies. In this instance, the CJD developed as a result of medical treatment so it is termed iatrogenic.

Reference: *APIC Text*, 4th edition, Chapter 73 - Creutzfeldt-Jakob Disease and other Prion Diseases

CBIC Core Competency: Identification of Infectious Disease Processes

130. (D) 3, 2, 4, 1

Rationale: Microbes and other disease causing agents such as prions have differing resistance to disinfection and sterilization. Prions are the most resistant and special reprocessing is required for instruments that have come in contact with infectious tissue of a person with Creutzfeldt-Jakob Disease. Spore-forming microbes are less resistant than prions but sterilization is require to remove these agents from medical instruments. Non-lipid viruses such as Poliovirus and small viruses require intermediate-level disinfection and are more resistant than lipid-viruses or larger viruses. Vegetative bacteria such as *Staphylococcus aureus* have the lowest level of resistance to disinfection and sterilization.

Reference: CDC Guideline for Disinfection and Sterilization in Healthcare Facilities, 2008

CBIC Core Competency: Cleaning, Sterilization, Disinfection, Asepsis

131. (B) 2, 3

Rationale: According to the CDC, paid and unpaid personnel, as well as contracted workers or workers employed outside the healthcare organization (such as emergency medical service personnel) are included in the term HCP. Also included are laboratory and autopsy personnel as well as researchers and volunteers who may potentially be exposed to infectious agents.

Reference: *APIC Text*, 4th edition, Chapter 100 - Occupational Health

CBIC Core Competency: Employee/Occupational Health

NOTES

132. Ⓐ **97.1 percent**

Rationale: The positive and negative predictive values are the proportions of positive and negative results in statistics and diagnostic tests that are true positive and true negative results.

The positive predictive value is the proportion of people with positive test results who have the disease.

	Disease Positive	Disease Negative
Positive test	True positive (TP)	False positive (FP)
Negative test	Fals negative (FN)	True negative (TN)

Positive predictive value = TP/(TP + FP)

The positive predictive value for this question is calculated as follows:

100 ÷ (100 + 3) = 0.97 or 97 percent

Reference: *APIC Text*, 4th edition, Chapter 13 - Use of Statistics in Infection Prevention

CBIC Core Competency: Surveillance and Epidemiologic Investigation

133. Ⓒ **Decolonization of MRSA-positive patients prior to surgery**

Rationale: Prevention strategies in healthcare infection prevention are wide ranging and depend on the disease in question and what information is available to the practitioner. Prevention strategies to reduce the risk of transmission, including barrier precautions; immunizations of HCP; and cleaning, sterilization, and disinfection are designed to prevent the occurrence of disease and, therefore, form primary prevention measures. Current decolonization protocols using intranasal mupirocin and chlorhexidine body washes are effective for reducing MRSA colonization in surgical patients. The purpose of this treatment is to prevent SSIs in the individual patients. It is not designed to prevent the spread of MRSA to other patients.

Reference: *APIC Text*, 4th edition, Chapter 10 - General Principles of Epidemiology

CBIC Core Competency: Preventing/Controlling the Transmission of Infectious Agents

134. Ⓒ **1, 2, 3, 4**

Rationale: Ethylene oxide (ETO) sterilization is affected by four parameters. The concentration of gas should be between 450 and 1200 mg/L, the temperature range should be between 37 and 63°C, the relative humidity should be between 40 and 80 percent, and the exposure time should be between1 and 6 hours.

Reference: CDC Guideline for Disinfection and Sterilization in Healthcare Facilities, 2008 Page: 61-62

CBIC Core Competency: Cleaning, Sterilization, Disinfection, Asepsis

NOTES

135. (A) The average age of a patient with *C. difficile*

Rationale: Epidemiological studies can be divided by levels of data and analysis. The first level of distinction is between observational and experimental studies. Observational studies involve gathering data on existing subjects with no intervention. In experimental studies, the researcher provides one or more interventions and determines differences before and after the intervention. The simplest type of observational study is the descriptive study. This type of study seeks to describe a population in terms of person, place, and time: who gets disease, when, and in what kind of geographical location. Examples of "person" variables include age, sex or gender, occupation, marital status, ethnicity, and health status. These studies also describe "place" variables, such as urban/rural differences, socioeconomic differences across areas, interfacility locations, and others. For these studies, time may involve an epidemic period, month, quarter, season, or periods of consecutive years or months. Descriptive studies can be used to generate rates and identify populations at risk but cannot be used to show causality.

Reference: *APIC Text*, 4th edition, Chapter 10 - General Principles of Epidemiology

CBIC Core Competency: Education and Research

PRACTICE EXAM 1 ASSESSEMENT

Category	Total Questions	Number Correct	Percent Correct
Identification of Infectious Disease Processes	22		
Surveillance and Epidemiologic Investigation	24		
Preventing/Controlling the Transmission of Infectious Agents	25		
Employee/Occupational Health	11		
Management and Communication	13		
Education and Research	11		
Environment of Care	14		
Cleaning, Sterilization, Disinfection, Asepsis	15		
Total	135		

The purpose of this assessment is to help the user evaluate his or her strengths and weaknesses by content area, in order to identify topics that may need further study. This practice exam employs similar, but not identical methodology that CBIC uses to score their computer-based tests, and it should not be used as a predictor of actual performance on the CBIC exam.

PRACTICE EXAM 2

QUESTIONS

NOTES

Instructions: Select the correct answer for each question.

1. The infection preventionist (IP) on the Antimicrobial Stewardship Team is thinking of ways that he can support efforts and add to the success of the team in decreasing antimicrobial resistance. Some of the activities that he can do to help with the mission of the team include:

1) Calculate multidrug-resistant organism (MDRO) infection rates
2) Detect asymptomatic carriers using active surveillance cultures
3) Use molecular typing for investigating outbreaks
4) Collect environmental cultures of isolation rooms

a. 2, 3, 4
b. 1, 3, 4
c. 1, 2, 4
d. 1, 2, 3

2. A classic sign of measles is:

a. Kaposi sarcoma
b. Stiff neck
c. Koplik spots
d. Bull's-eye rash

NOTES

3. The IP has been notified that three patients with possible pneumonic plague have been admitted to the Emergency Department. The IP recommends which of the following strategies?

a. A surgical mask worn within 3 feet of patient, door may be open

b. Negative pressure isolation room with use of N95 respirators

c. Normal ventilation, but door must remain closed and N95 respirator mask worn

d. No masks are required, but patient must be placed in private room and contacts should be treated for exposure

4. Using the surgical risk index to stratify the identified infections for the previous quarter, an IP would report which of the following case(s) as having a higher risk for developing a surgical site infection (SSI)?

1) An 80-year-old male with poor circulation who develops a donor site infection after a coronary artery bypass graft surgery that took 4 hours to perform

2) A 30-year-old female who has knee surgery to repair a torn anterior cruciate ligament (ACL) after a skiing accident

3) A 90-year-old female with insulin-dependent diabetes who has hip replacement surgery that takes 2.5 hours to perform

4) A 27-year-old male with Crohn's disease who has colon resection that takes more than 4 hours to perform due to adhesions

a. 1, 2

b. 2, 3

c. 3, 4

d. 1, 4

NOTES

5. A 47-year-old female bus driver is brought to the Emergency Department (ED) with a two-day history of fever, shortness of breath, and chest pain. She is diaphoretic and appears acutely ill. She is confused as to place and time. Temperature is 38°C (100.4°F), blood pressure is 88/60 mm Hg, pulse rate is 110/min, and respiration rate is 28/min. Coarse bronchial breath sounds are heard. She has had no recent known contact with ill persons. The leukocyte count is 15,000/QL (15 × 109/L). A chest radiograph shows a widened mediastinum and bilateral pleural effusions. Gram stain of a peripheral blood smear shows box car–shaped Gram-positive bacilli. A bioterrorism agent is suspected. Which of the following agents is most likely?
   - **a.** Typhus fever
   - **b.** Smallpox
   - **c.** Tularemia
   - **d.** Anthrax

6. Phlebotomists within an organization are complaining that the new blood collection device introduced 6 months ago is difficult to use for blood draws and has resulted in an increase in needlestick injuries (NSIs). The IP is working with Occupational Health to evaluate the problem and would like to compare NSI rates before and after implementation of the device. Which of the following would be the most useful denominator in order to calculate useful data?
   - **a.** Phlebotomist employee hours at work (full-time equivalents)
   - **b.** Number of occupied beds (or licensed beds)
   - **c.** Number of patients (average daily census)
   - **d.** Number of blood collection devices used or purchased

7. Which of the following processes should be used for contaminated endotracheal blades?
   - **a.** Cleaning followed by high-level disinfection
   - **b.** Cleaning with chlorhexidine followed by soaking in an enzymatic solution for 20 minutes
   - **c.** Cleaning followed by ultrasonic washer
   - **d.** Cleaning followed by alcohol disinfection

NOTES

8. A new Environmental Services employee has been asked to clean up a large blood spill on the floor in the OR. How should he proceed?

a. He should mix an EPA-registered disinfectant with water in a bucket and mop up the spill

b. He should place absorbent material over the spill and pour the correct dilution of disinfectant over the material for the recommended contact time

c. He should pour undiluted bleach directly on the blood spill, wait 10 minutes, and then mop up the spill

d. He should place absorbent material over the spill, dispose of the material after absorption, and then mop the floor with an EPA-registered disinfectant

9. Which of the following statements is *true* regarding an asymptomatic employee with a newly positive tuberculin skin test (TST) of 10 mm induration in a medium to high risk setting?

1) The employee has latent tuberculosis (TB) infection

2) The employee is capable of transmitting TB to others

3) The employee is not infectious

4) The employee has TB disease

a. 3, 4

b. 2, 4

c. 1, 3

d. 1, 2

10. While rounding in an ambulatory care center, an IP discovers that healthcare personnel (HCP) have been using single-dose vials (SDVs) of lidocaine for multiple patients. She informs the clinic manager that the practice must end immediately. Which of the following statements about SDVs should the IP include in her explanation to the clinic manager?

1) SDVs lack antimicrobial preservatives

2) Inappropriate use of SDVs can lead to contamination

3) A needleless access device (spike) must be applied when reusing an SDV

4) All medications from an SDV must be prepared in a pharmacy

a. 1, 2

b. 2, 3

c. 3, 4

d. 2, 4

NOTES

11. A patient is admitted with measles and placed on Airborne Isolation. How many days after symptom onset would the characteristic blotchy red rash appear?

a. On days 1–2

b. On days 7–10

c. On days 3–7

d. On days 21–25

12. The annual education budget for the Infection Prevention Department is $1,650.00. In October, the Infection Prevention Manager allocated 20 percent of the department education budget towards resources for the annual flu shot program. However, in November, the financial report indicates that only 15 percent was spent. How much of the budgeted amount remains unspent?

a. $330.00

b. $247.50

c. $82.50

d. $66.00

13. An IP is assisting local public health with a Hepatitis A outbreak in the community. She has been asked to contact the Health Department with any patients who are admitted to her facility with a test positive for Hepatitis A virus (HAV). Patients who test positive in the acute phase of the illness will have a positive:

a. Immunoglobulin G (IgG) anti-HAV

b. Immunoglobulin M (IgM) anti-HAV

c. Immunoglobulin A (IgA) anti-HAV

d. IgG, IgM anti-HAV

14. A patient from a long-term acute care (LTAC) facility is being transferred to an acute care facility for an outpatient procedure. The patient has a history of cryptococcal meningitis. The outpatient department asks the IP what type of Isolation Precautions the patient requires. The IP informs them that the patient requires:

a. Airborne Precautions

b. Droplet Precautions

c. Standard Precautions

d. Contact Precautions

NOTES

15. Which of the following statements are *true* regarding consent to immunization?

1) Some states allow personal belief exemptions
2) Federal regulations require Informed consent
3) All states allow medical exemptions for persons with medical contraindications to vaccination
4) Vaccine recipients must receive Vaccine Information Statements (VISs)

a. 1, 2, 3
b. 2, 3, 4
c. 1, 3, 4
d. 1, 2, 4

16. An inspection of the Sterile Processing Department reveals several incorrect practices. Which of the following would be a *correct* practice?

a. Ensuring hinged instruments are cleaned with the hinge closed
b. Flushing instruments with saline
c. Daily use of a biological indicator in the sterilizer
d. Transporting contaminated instruments in a permeable container

NOTES

17. An IP is asked to report on compliance with a methicillin-resistant *Staphylococcus aureus* (MRSA) screening program in place at the facility. The report that is available lists all possible patients in each category that should have been screened on admission. The goal of the facility is to be at least 90 percent compliant with the MRSA screening program. Using the reported data in the table, the IP and the facility leadership need to focus on what groups of patients?

High Risk Category	Total number of patients screened	Total number of patients in category
Pre-op patients for high-risk surgery	180	194
Transfers into Intensive Care Unit	237	268
Transfers from other facilities	164	186
Previous MRSA diagnosis	211	225
Total screening compliance	800	873

1) Preoperative patients for high-risk surgery
2) Transfers into Intensive Care Unit
3) Transfers from other facilities
4) Previous MRSA diagnosis

a. 1, 2
b. 2, 3
c. 1, 3
d. 2, 4

18. The Hemodialysis Department at a hospital completes a monthly water culture testing. The results are over the limit for colony-forming unit (CFU)/mL. Which of the following actions should be done first?

a. Notify the physician
b. Initiate daily water culture testing
c. Disinfect the system
d. Notify the Infection Control Department

NOTES

19. Which of the following is an example of an effective performance measure?

a. A measure that has been developed based on observation of practices in a facility

b. A measure that is based on a definition that can easily be understood and applied in a facility

c. A measure that demonstrates a return on investment (ROI)

d. A measure that takes into consideration customer satisfaction

20. The Product Evaluation Committee has asked the IP to assess a new preoperative skin preparation product that is less expensive than the one the facility is currently using. In researching the background information on the product, the IP reviews several sources of literature. Which of the following sources provides the best evidence for effectiveness of the product?

a. The vendor representative's assurance that the new product has been tested and works at least as well as the product currently being used

b. An independent, randomized trial that shows with statistical significance that the new product is comparable to the current product in preventing infections when used as a surgical skin prep

c. The vendor-sponsored laboratory research showing that skin flora is reduced by the same magnitude with the new product as with the current product

d. The testimonial of another IP whose hospital has been using the new product for 6 months

21. Which of the following is an example of infectious waste?

a. An unused syringe and needle that were discarded after accidentally being dropped on the floor

b. A gauze pad with a small amount of blood on it

c. Gloves that were worn to administer a Hepatitis B vaccine

d. Agar plates used for testing sputum samples in the microbiology lab

NOTES

22. Contact Precautions for a patient with scabies can be discontinued when the patient has received effective treatment for:

a. 10 days

b. 7 days

c. 48 hours

d. 24 hours

23. Infection prevention challenges related to body piercings and tattooing include all of the following *except*:

a. There have not been uniform licensure requirements for body art studios

b. Reporting of infections to the Public Health Department is limited to bloodborne diseases

c. The popularity of tattooing and body piercing has made it more socially acceptable

d. Inspectors may not receive adequate training to conduct site inspections

24. Which of the following statements is correct regarding the efficacy of a disinfectant product on a microbe?

a. For all disinfectants, the greater the concentration of the disinfectant, the shorter the contact time is for effective cidal activity

b. For all disinfectants, the activity of the disinfectant increases as temperature increases

c. For all disinfectants, the greater the number of microbes on an object or surface, the greater the amount of time that's needed for a disinfectant to have effective cidal activity

d. For all disinfectants, the existence of a biofilm does not affect cidal activity

25. Which of the following scenarios is an example of the preparation phase of the transtheoretical model?

a. Auditing reveals that staff compliance with personal protective equipment (PPE) use has increased in the last month

b. Data is showing a 96 percent compliance rate for PPE use in the last 10 months

c. Staff are discussing strategies to increase PPE use at the monthly staff meeting

d. Staff are questioning why they need to wear PPE when caring for patients in isolation

NOTES

26. The Director of Facilities informs the IP that water testing of the hospital's hot water tanks and distal sites was positive for *Legionella*. The IP should consider disinfection of the hospital's water system if:

a. There have not had any prior cases of healthcare-associated legionellosis

b. The IP conducts prospective surveillance of healthcare-associated legionellosis and there are no cases

c. The colonization rate for distal water sites in the hospital is greater than 30 percent

d. The hospital Risk Manager asks for the disinfection to be completed

27. The IP is planning an educational program for the nursing staff. The IP knows that in order to increase retention and motivate the nurses to change practice behaviors, she should do which of the following?

1) Assume a facilitator role

2) Utilize monologues to provide critical information

3) Incorporate an interactive approach

4) Use a computer-based learning module

a. 1, 3

b. 1, 4

c. 2, 3

d. 1, 2

28. Which of the following is an advantage of orthophthalaldehyde (OPA) over glutaraldehyde?

a. OPA does not require activation

b. OPA is compatible with many more materials than glutaraldehyde

c. It does not stain skin

d. No personal protective equipment is needed to handle OPA

NOTES

29. The purpose of the annual infection prevention program risk assessment is to:

a. Determine goals and objectives for the following year

b. Describe support requirements of the program

c. Outline the achievements and activities of the program

d. Document the facility's risks of infection

30. A seriously ill patient has two positive blood cultures showing Gram-positive cocci in pairs and chains and has been started on ampicillin. This bacteremia is most likely secondary to a urinary tract infection. The antibiogram for the healthcare facility is shown below. Assuming that the organism causing the bacteremia is one that is listed below, is ampicillin the most appropriate antimicrobial therapy for this patient?

Organism	Number of Isolates Tested	Percent Susceptible					
		Oxacillin	Erythromycin	Clindamycin	Vancomycin	Ampicillin	Gentamicin
Staphylococcus aureus - MRSA	926	100	3	51	100		
Coagulase-negative Staphylococci	668	26	19	43	100		
Enterococcus faecium	21				26	12	100
Escherichia coli	87					52	92
Klebsiella sp.	403						97

a. No, the patient should be treated with vancomycin for coagulase-negative staphylococci

b. No, the patient should be treated with oxacillin for MRSA

c. No, the patient should be treated with gentamicin for *Enterococcus faecium*

d. No, the patient should be treated with gentamicin for *Klebsiella* sp

NOTES

31. The Director of Infection Prevention and Control has just received information about a bioterrorist threat in her county with an agent spread primarily by contaminated food/water. Which of the following agents should she include in her emergency response plan?

a. Tularemia

b. *Vibrio cholerae*

c. Q fever

d. Brucellosis

32. A patient is admitted to rule out TB. All of the following would be noted as a risk factor for transmission of infection to the staff *except*:

a. Improper N95 respirator use by the staff

b. Surgical mask placed on the patient during transport

c. Acid-fast bacilli (AFB) smear positive sputum culture from the patient

d. Patient placed in a regular exam room in the emergency room

33. In the event of a disaster with a prolonged power outage, how should you prioritize use of food stored in the facility?

a. You should continue to use food from a variety of refrigerators and freezers as usual

b. You should prepare food that is in unpowered refrigerators first

c. You should prepare food that is in unpowered freezers first

d. You should immediately use disaster reserve supplies

34. Which of the following diseases are preventable by immunization?

1) Diphtheria

2) Varicella

3) Pertussis

4) Cytomegalovirus

a. 1, 2, 3

b. 1, 2, 4

c. 1, 4, 5

d. 2, 4, 5

NOTES

35. According to the Centers for Disease Control and Prevention (CDC) and the Advisory Committee on Immunization Practices (ACIP), which of the following groups should receive the Hepatitis B vaccine?

1) Unvaccinated adults receiving chemotherapy
2) Residents and staff of facilities for developmentally delayed disabled persons
3) People with more than one sexual partner
4) Unvaccinated adults <60 years of age with diabetes mellitus

   a. 1, 2, 3
   b. 2, 3, 4
   c. 1, 3, 4
   d. 1, 2, 4

36. When performing an audit of the Endoscopy Department, the IP observes the following practices. Which one is cause for concern?

a. Single-use brushes are used to clean the scopes
b. Equipment is immersed in enzymatic cleaner that is discarded every 24 hours
c. Leak testing performed on scopes after each use
d. Scopes stored vertically in a closed cabinet

37. While conducting rounds in the Intensive Care Unit (ICU), the IP is approached by a nurse who wants to know what the best practice standards are for drawing blood cultures from an existing central line. The correct response is:

a. Drawing blood cultures from an established central line reduces the contamination rate
b. Blood samples should be obtained in pairs (two sets) from different peripheral sites
c. The site is unimportant as long as the hub is cleaned thoroughly
d. The tip of the catheter is also cultured if bacteremia is suspected

NOTES

38. Which of the following organisms is most likely to be associated with contaminated disinfectants?

a. *Pseudomonas* species

b. Hepatitis C

c. *Clostridium difficile*

d. *Cryptosporidium parvum*

39. In 2013, 3,254 persons died of all causes in a large metropolitan area with a population of 1.8 million. What was the crude mortality rate?

a. 18 per 100,000

b. 18 per 1,000

c. 180 per 1,000

d. 180 per 100,000

40. In a published study of the risk factors associated with an outbreak of *Serratia marcescens* in a Neonatal ICU (NICU), the authors present the following table:

Risk Factor	P Value*	Odds Ratio (Confidence Interval)
Birth weight <1000 g	0.07	1.93 (1.62-4.86)
Mechanical ventilation	<0.001	4.24 (2.76-6.33)
Central venous catheter	0.008	3.38 (1.97-9.74)
Previous antibiotic use	0.02	1.32 (0.079-5.97)

*$p < 0.05$ considered significant

Given the list of risk factors below, which ones are statistically significant for *Serratia* infection in this outbreak?

1) Birth weight

2) Mechanical ventilation

3) Central venous catheter

4) Previous antibiotic use

a. 1, 2

b. 1, 3

c. 2, 3

d. 3, 4

NOTES

41. Methods to prevent the transmission of *C. difficile* infections include:

1) Hand washing with soap and water
2) Environmental cleaning and disinfection
3) Closing the unit for deep cleaning
4) Laundry and waste management controls

a. 1, 2

b. 2, 4

c. 1, 3

d. 3, 4

42. When using heat to treat a room for bed bugs, the temperature must be:

a. 85°F or 29°C for one hour

b. 110°F or 43°C for 90 minutes

c. 125°F or 51°C for two hours

d. 118°F or 48°C for one hour

43. Event-related storage of sterile items allows packaged, sterile items to be used any time after processing provided that:

1) The expiration date has not passed
2) The packing wrapper is intact
3) The item has not gotten wet
4) The storage area is well-ventilated, dry, and free of dust and insects

a. 1

b. 1, 2, 3

c. 2, 3, 4

d. 1, 2, 3, 4

NOTES

44. The Infection Prevention Manager is analyzing the department's overall performance. The ratio of output to input will produce a measure of the department's:

a. Productivity

b. Effectiveness

c. Quality control

d. Throughput

45. There is a flu outbreak in a community, and the IP at the local hospital is interested in accurately identifying infected patients as quickly as possible so that they can be placed on Isolation Precautions. The IP has a choice between two rapid flu tests. Test A has a sensitivity of 98 percent and a specificity of 85 percent. Test B has a sensitivity of 92 percent and a specificity of 89 percent. Which test will be most accurate in correctly identifying patients who are infected with flu?

a. Test A, because it has higher sensitivity

b. Test A, because it has a higher predictive value negative

c. Test B, because it has higher specificity

d. Test B, because it has higher predictive value negative

46. Of the recommendations for reprocessing flexible gastrointestinal endoscopes listed below, the one that is most strongly supported by well-designed experimental, clinical, or epidemiologic studies is:

a. Cleaning of endoscopes is essential before manual or automated disinfection

b. Brushes used to clean endoscopes should be thoroughly cleaned and disinfected or sterilized between uses

c. Ultrasonic cleaning of reusable endoscopic components should be used to remove soil and organic material

d. Routine environmental microbiological testing of endoscopes should be carried out

NOTES

47. What is the negative predictive value of the following data?

	True Disease **Positive**	True Disease **Negative**
Test Result **Positive**	100	3
Test Result **Negative**	40	500

a. 82.9 percent
b. 83.3 percent
c. 92.5 percent
d. 71.4 percent

48. When a test has a higher specificity than sensitivity, it means the test:

a. Will be more accurate when predicting who is ill
b. A negative result will be more accurate than a positive
c. A positive result will be more accurate than a negative
d. It should only be done as a secondary testing procedure to rule out disease

49. A healthcare worker has called the IP to ask the reasoning behind the policy that prohibits employees who have patient contact from wearing artificial fingernails. Which of the following reasons would she give to this employee?

a. There is strong evidence that artificial nails are associated with HAIs
b. HCP with artificial nails are more likely to have more Gram-negative bacteria under their nails than HCP with natural nails
c. Artificial nails often puncture gloves, exposing the healthcare worker to blood and body fluids
d. HCP with artificial nails do not perform hand hygiene as often as HCP with natural nails

50. Managing infection prevention outcomes, analyzing variance trends, and evaluating corrective actions taken to reduce infection risks are components of:

a. Case management
b. Utilization review
c. Performance improvement
d. Medical review

NOTES

51. What recommendation should an IP give regarding mask use by a staff member who has documented immunity to varicella (chickenpox) while caring for a patient who is on Airborne Precautions for varicella (chickenpox)?

a. Wear an N95 respirator whenever entering the room

b. Wear a regular surgical mask whenever entering the room

c. No mask is needed

d. The patient should don a surgical mask

52. Diluted bleach solutions stored in an open container must be changed every:

a. 30 days

b. 28 days

c. 24 hours

d. 12 hours

53. A patient in Droplet Precautions is scheduled for a procedure in Endoscopy. In addition to following respiratory hygiene and cough etiquette, which of the following is the most appropriate method to reduce the transmission of infectious organisms during transportation of the patient?

a. Instruct patient to wear an N95 respirator

b. Cover or contain potentially infectious body fluids

c. Place a surgical mask on the patient

d. Provide respiratory protection for transport personnel

54. A pregnant environmental services worker, who is nonimmune to varicella, enters the room of a patient with confirmed varicella (chickenpox) before an isolation sign is posted. She spends 6 minutes in the room with the patient (who is not wearing a mask). This exposure happened on January 11. After giving the employee varicella-zoster immune globulin (VZIG), it is determined that that she should be excluded from work. What day can she return to work?

a. January 31

b. February 1

c. February 8

d. February 9

NOTES

55. This process destroys all forms of microbial life:

a. High-level disinfection

b. Cleaning

c. Sterilization

d. Antisepsis

56. A patient was admitted to the Emergency Department with severe headache, fever, and photophobia. The results of the lumbar puncture are pending. A staff member who cared for the patient is requesting antibiotics because the patient may have meningitis. If meningococcal meningitis is confirmed, chemoprophylaxis would be indicated for all of the following individuals *except*:

a. The licensed practical nurse who did not have direct contact with the patient's oral secretions

b. The emergency medical technician who performed mouth-to-mouth resuscitation

c. The resident who did not wear appropriate PPE during intubation

d. The registered nurse who suctioned the patient without wearing a mask

57. Which of the following statements about testing for statistical significance is *true*?

a. A *p* value of 0.05 means that the probability that the observation occurred by chance alone is 1 in 20

b. A *p* value of 0.05 increases the likelihood of making a Type 2 error

c. The size of the *p* value indicates the power of the results

d. The research hypothesis is the basis of significance

58. An IP is writing instructional objectives for a learning module on catheter-associated bloodstream infections. He wants to focus on the cognitive level of "Analysis" from Bloom's taxonomy. Which of the following choices contains the verbs he should use to describe his learning objectives?

a. Compare, discriminate, and differentiate

b. Define, identify, and select

c. Discuss, explain, and paraphrase

d. Judge, summarize, and recommend

NOTES

59. During rounds in several patient care areas, the IP discovers several cardboard boxes being used to store patient care supplies. She informs the unit manager that another method of storing supplies must be implemented because:

a. The boxes cause clutter in the storeroom

b. Cardboard can only be used to store supplies in soiled utility rooms

c. The boxes may harbor dust, bacteria, and insects

d. The boxes are a fire hazard

60. An IP is evaluating her control chart and notices that several points in a row are above the mean line. This probably indicates:

a. The mean is incorrectly calculated

b. She should investigate potential sources of special cause variation

c. There is common cause variation in her process, and it requires no correction

d. She is using the incorrect type of control chart

61. Which of the following organisms are most likely to be the cause of outbreaks of healthcare-associated infections due to improper reprocessing of bronchoscopes?

1) Mycobacterium tuberculosis

2) Carbapenem-resistant Enterobacteriaceae

3) Pseudomonas aeruginosa

4) Staphylococcus aureus

a. 1, 2, 3, 4

b. 1, 3, 4

c. 1, 3

d. 2, 4

62. This type of sterilizer works by forcing steam into the chamber from the top and pushing the air in the chamber out the bottom of the chamber:

a. Steam sterilizer

b. Ethylene oxide sterilizer

c. Dynamic air removal steam sterilizer

d. Gravity displacement steam sterilizer

NOTES

63. Which of the following organisms is most likely to contaminate a urine specimen if the collection process is not done correctly:

a. *Staphylococcus aureus*

b. *Pseudomonas aeruginosa*

c. *Candida albicans*

d. *Klebsiella pneumonia*

64. Which of the following environmental infection prevention measures are recommended for inpatient units that house hematopoietic stem cell transplant (HSCT) patients?

1) Providing sterile linens

2) Prohibiting live plants and dried or fresh flowers in rooms of HSCT patients

3) Avoiding items that collect or trap dust

4) Providing laminar air flow

a. 1, 2

b. 3, 4

c. 2, 3

d. 1, 3

65. Which of the following is the primary method to prevent influenza?

a. Annual vaccination

b. Hand washing

c. Droplet Precautions

d. Promotion of respiratory hygiene/cough etiquette

66. Which of the sterility assurance levels (SAL) listed below is appropriate for critical items?

a. zero

b. 10^{-4}

c. 10^{-6}

d. 10^{-8}

NOTES

67. Green cleaning is a new approach to environmental cleaning that aims at reducing harm to human health and the environment while maintaining or improving the hygiene of the healthcare environment. Which of the following green strategies would be appropriate to implement?

1) Replacing floor strippers and finishes that contain heavy metals and asthmagens
2) Substituting disinfectant room cleaners with less toxic detergents
3) Employing carcinogen-free carpet cleaners
4) Introducing high-filtration vacuum cleaners

a. 1, 2, 4
b. 2, 3, 4
c. 1, 3, 4
d. 1, 2, 4

68. Which of the following would be evidence of CAUTI in an adult patient with an indwelling urinary catheter in place for more than 2 days?

1) Fever greater than 38°C
2) A positive dipstick for leukocyte esterase
3) A positive urine culture with 104 CFU/ml of *E. coli*
4) A positive urinary catheter tip for *E. coli*

a. 1, 3, 4
b. 1, 2, 4
c. 1, 2, 3
d. 2, 3, 4

69. Case-control studies are useful for studying:

a. Rare outcomes or outcomes that develop over a long time after exposure
b. Individuals with and without exposure to a potential risk factor
c. Specific exposure incidents
d. The availability of a risk exposure

NOTES

70. The existence of an outbreak is most often determined by:

a. The identification of more than 10 new cases per week

b. An incidence rate that is more than two standard deviations higher than the previous year

c. Detection of a cluster of organisms within more than one population.

d. An incidence of disease that is clearly in excess of that expected

71. Decontamination is the process by which an item is:

a. Cleaned of all soil and germs

b. Rendered free from all pathogens and infectious organisms

c. Sterilized and ready for reuse

d. Rendered safe for handling without protective attire

72. While caring for a patient with suspected or confirmed Ebola, if during patient care a partial or total breach in PPE (gloves separate from sleeves leaving exposed skin, a tear develops in an outer glove, a needlestick) occurs, the healthcare worker must:

a. Quickly remove PPE to reduce the risk of exposure

b. Immediately perform disinfection of gloved hands using an ABHR

c. Move immediately to the doffing area to assess the exposure

d. Immerse exposed areas with a bleach solution

NOTES

73. While making rounds on a nursing unit, the IP encounters a nurse who has just incurred a needlestick after giving an injection to a patient. The nurse tells the IP that the patient's recent laboratory results indicate that he has Hepatitis B, and the nurse has not completed her Hepatitis B vaccination series. She requests the IP's advice. In reviewing the patient's record, the IP finds that the patient's antibody to Hepatitis B is positive and his Hepatitis B surface antigen (HBsAg) is negative. The IP's explanation of the patient's laboratory results indicates which of the following?

a. The patient is in the early incubation period of the disease and has a low probability of transmitting Hepatitis B; the nurse should report to Occupational Health

b. The patient had Hepatitis B in the past and does not have active disease now; the nurse should complete her Hepatitis B series as scheduled, but no additional treatment is needed

c. The results indicate a possible error in the results and another blood sample should be submitted

d. The patient does have Hepatitis B but the disease is resolving; the nurse should report to Occupational Health

74. Measures of dispersion to consider for surveillance reporting include which of the following?

a. Rates

b. Ratios and proportions

c. Percentiles

d. Range and standard deviation

75. Infection of short-term intravenous devices is associated with all of the following *except*:

a. Percutaneous transmission during insertion

b. Colonization of the catheter hub

c. Extraluminal transmission

d. Contamination of intravenous (IV) fluids

NOTES

76. The IP is asked to review with a group of staff nurses how to interpret antibiotic susceptibility tests. The susceptibility test that allows a determination of the least amount of antibiotic per milliliter that impedes the growth of an organism is known as a:

- **a.** Minimum inhibitory concentration
- **b.** Kirby-Bauer disc method
- **c.** Minimum bactericidal concentration
- **d.** Serum-cidal level

77. Under what circumstances should human immunodeficiency virus (HIV)-infected HCP be placed under work restrictions?

1) When viral burden measurements of <5 x 102 GE/mL for HIV infection and techniques for eliminating transmission risks cannot be identified
2) No work restrictions necessary if Standard Precautions are followed
3) When required by state or regional regulations
4) Whenever performing exposure-prone, noninvasive procedures
5) After counsel from an expert review panel is sought

- **a.** 2, 5
- **b.** 1, 3
- **c.** 3, 5
- **d.** 4, 5

78. Poor planning during a construction project can lead to an increase risk of infection related to:

1) Construction delays
2) Compromised air quality
3) Contaminated water
4) Increase in construction-related traffic

- **a.** 1, 3
- **b.** 2, 4
- **c.** 2, 3
- **d.** 1, 4

NOTES

79. The following factors should be considered when preparing the environment for an educational program:

1) Providing an atmosphere of mutual respect and support
2) Establishing a comfortable environment conducive to learning
3) Encouraging interaction by arranging desks in straight rows
4) Having a person control and troubleshoot the environment as needed

a. 1, 2, 4
b. 2, 3, 4
c. 1, 3, 4
d. 1, 2, 3

80. Which of the following is an example of syndromic surveillance?

1) Analyzing Emergency Department records for reports of influenza-like illness (ILI)
2) Monitoring sentinel chickens in the community for antibodies to arboviruses
3) Tracking all laboratory orders for respiratory cultures
4) Monitoring over-the-counter drug sales for cough medicine

a. 2, 3, 4
b. 1, 2, 4
c. 1, 2, 3
d. 1, 3, 4

81. The IP is performing the annual evaluation of the infection prevention and control program. Components of this document should include:

1) The achievements and activities of the program
2) Results from the latest accreditation survey
3) Stress the value of the program to the organization
4) Satisfy the legal requirements for reporting infections

a. 1, 2
b. 2, 3
c. 1, 3
d. 3, 4

NOTES

82. A bacterium that is decolorized with alcohol during a Gram stain and retains the counterstain is:
   a. Gram-positive
   b. Gram-negative
   c. Stained purple
   d. Acid-fast positive

83. Which type of room would be the most appropriate to place a patient who is immunocompromised and has disseminated herpes zoster disease?
   a. A shared, standard room
   b. A private, standard room
   c. An airborne infection isolation (AII) room
   d. A protective environment room

84. Seventy-five patients were admitted to the Medical-Surgical ICU. Forty were on the surgical service and 35 were on the medical service. Fifteen patients developed a healthcare-associated MRSA infection. Nine of the patients with MRSA infection were on the surgical service. There were 230 patient days in the ICU for the surgical patients in January, and 325 patient days for medical patients. What was the overall MRSA attack rate?
   a. 20 percent
   b. 2 percent
   c. 53 percent
   d. 5 percent

85. All of the following are examples of risk-adjusted stratification *except*:
   a. CLABSI rates by birth weight in the NICU
   b. Needlestick injuries by profession
   c. CAUTI rate for the ICU
   d. CLABSI rates by type of line

NOTES

86. The IP hears that one of the nursing units in his facility will soon be renovated. After verifying the information, he contacts the newly hired Director of Design and Construction to explain how important it is for the IP to be included in the planning and design of all renovation projects. Which of the following is the most compelling argument?

a. The IP supplies necessary maintenance for critical utility systems that deliver ventilation and water to patient care areas

b. The IP provides essential input into preventing hazardous risks to patients, HCP, and visitors during design and construction projects

c. The IP will ensure compliance with various compliance-, regulatory standard-, and guideline-setting agencies

d. The IP is responsible for facilitating the transport and approval for disposal of waste materials

87. Viral infections are difficult to treat because:

a. Viruses can suspend their metabolism in the presence of antivirals

b. Viruses use the host's cells to replicate

c. Synthesis of enzymes that inactivate the drug

d. Viruses may block viral mRNA transcription

88. The Infection and Prevention Control Team has adopted the reduction of healthcare-associated MRSA as an annual goal. It has implemented improved processes and plans to monitor the effectiveness of these processes. Which of the following performance improvement tools will assist in identifying effectiveness?

a. Affinity diagram

b. Run chart

c. Process flow chart

d. Pareto chart

89. A patient is admitted with skin and soft tissue injury from a cat bite. The most likely organism involved in the infection would be:

a. *Pasteurella*

b. *Pseudomonas*

c. *E. coli*

d. *Mycobacterium*

NOTES

90. The OR notifies the IP that a patient is scheduled for a brain biopsy. After reviewing the results of diagnostic tests, possible diagnosis, and the reason for biopsy, the IP assesses the patient to be high risk for Creutzfeldt-Jakob disease (CJD). The next step is to:

a. Determine the instruments to be used and the processing to be done

b. Notify the staff to quarantine the patient after the procedure

c. Advise the OR staff to disinfect the instruments in the OR

d. Incinerate all equipment used to perform the biopsy

91. The CDC lists 18 drug-resistant threats to the United States. These threats are categorized based on level of concern: urgent, serious, and concerning. Which of the following belong to the "Urgent" threat category?

1) Neisseria gonorrhea

2) Vancomycin-resistant Staphylococcus aureus

3) Drug-resistant Tuberculosis

4) *Clostridium difficile*

a. 1, 2

b. 2, 3

c. 1, 4

d. 3, 4

92. The Infection Prevention Manager must apply principles of conflict resolution to resolve growing tension about how best to apply limited department resources in the coming year. For maximum success, the IP manager should use all of the following approaches *except*:

a. Active listening

b. Accept responsibility

c. Use indirect communication

d. Identify points of agreement

NOTES

93. The IP is designing a new hand hygiene intervention for HCP based on the Health Belief Model. According to that model, which of the following is/are examples of "modifying factors" in the hand hygiene intervention?

a. The ages and genders of the people for whom the intervention is being designed

b. Signs posted in the unit that remind HCP to perform hand hygiene

c. The perception of how much time it will take HCP to perform hand hygiene compared to the potential for hand hygiene to prevent infection in patients

d. The belief among the target audience that they will be able to comply with hand hygiene 100 percent of the time

94. A patient in your facility has been diagnosed with naturally-acquired inhalational Anthrax, and Environmental Services need to know how to terminally clean the patient's room. Which protocol should they follow?

a. They should clean the room with a protocol similar to the one used for patients with *C. difficile*

b. They should only use an EPA-registered disinfectant with proven effectiveness against Anthrax

c. The should call the Centers for Disease Control and Prevention to come clean the room

d. They should use the standard terminal cleaning protocol

95. A healthcare facility is experiencing its first case of carbapenem-resistant Enterobacteriaceae (CRE) infection. The IP plans to intensify the facility's MDRO control efforts and is implementing an active surveillance culture (ASC) program for CRE. Which of the following strategies should the IP implement?

1) Screen all patients for CRE on admission

2) Place all colonized or infected CRE patients on Contact Precautions

3) Minimize invasive devices

4) Communicate results to healthcare providers

a. 1, 2, 3

b. 2, 3, 4

c. 1, 3, 4

d. 1, 2, 4

NOTES

96. A patient is receiving eye drops to treat conjunctivitis. The drops are only available in a multi-dose vials. Which of the following is/are acceptable practices for this use of this medication?

1) This vial of medication may not be used on multiple patients
2) This vial of medication may be used on multiple patients if it has not come into contact with tears or the conjunctiva
3) This vial of medication may be used on multiple patients if it is used within 28 days of being opened
4) This vial of medication should be stored away from the patient care area

a. 1

b. 1, 4

c. 2, 3

d. 2, 3, 4

97. The IP has just reviewed the current public health recommendations concerning influenza vaccines before developing an educational program for employees. The report indicates that the most important problem in developing a long-term vaccine for influenza is:

a. Potential toxicity of the vaccine if the dosage is increased

b. Lack of potency

c. Antigenic drift of the viruses

d. Short storage life of the vaccine

98. During routine infection prevention rounds in the Cardiac Catheterization Department, the IP notices that the air vents are dusty. The Nurse Manager is unsure of the cleaning schedule. The best action to take is:

1) Contact Environmental Services and request that the air vents be cleaned as soon as the room is available
2) Ask the nurse caring for the patient to dust the vents immediately
3) Reduce the number of air exchanges per hour until vent has been cleaned
4) Establish a monthly cleaning schedule

a. 1, 2

b. 1, 4

c. 2, 3

d. 3, 4

NOTES

99. Five cases of prosthetic valve endocarditis caused by *Staphylococcus epidermidis* are observed in one hospital. Of the following available methods, which is best for determining whether all five isolates were derived from a single source?

a. Serotyping

b. Pulsed-field gel electrophoresis

c. Antimicrobial susceptibility testing

d. Bacteriophage typing

100. One of the units in an LTAC facility is experiencing an outbreak of crusted scabies. In this situation, when is HCP prophylaxis indicated?

a. Prolonged skin-to-skin contact with suspected and confirmed cases

b. Evidence of infestation such as pruritic cutaneous rash

c. All staff, volunteers, and visitors who may have been exposed to a patient with crusted scabies

d. Treatment is indicated for all staff on affected units

101. A biological indicator from one of the sterilizers in Sterile Processing turns positive. The first action should be:

a. Retrieve unused items from the load

b. Conduct surveillance of involved patients

c. Evaluate the sterilizer

d. Evaluate staff education of using the sterilizers

102. An advantage of a case-control study over a cohort study is that a case-control study:

a. Is considered less biased than a cohort study

b. Provides stronger evidence for a causal association

c. Is less time consuming and less expensive

d. Is more valid

103. Which of the following statements is accurate about adult learners?

a. They do not readily speak out if their learning needs are not being met

b. They have a preference for academic knowledge rather than practical knowledge

c. Most older adults have the same technological capabilities as younger adults

d. They are more likely to transfer knowledge to practice if education sessions are interactive

104. An IP has data on the number of bloodstream infections per central line days in the Cardiac ICU. This is an example of which type of data?

1) Discrete data

2) Categorical data

3) Noncategorical data

4) Continuous data

a. 1, 2

b. 1, 3

c. 1, 4

d. 2, 4

105. Which of the following would be a good tool to prepare for a Joint Commission visit?

a. Root cause analysis

b. Gap analysis

c. Multivoting

d. Plan, Do, Study, Act

NOTES

NOTES

106. A patient has been admitted to an acute care facility with a diagnosis of rule-out pulmonary TB. Below is the lab report for the sputum testing on this patient.

Date and time of sputum collection	AFB stain result
03/04 11:43 a.m.	Negative for AFB
03/04 8:26 p.m.	Negative for AFB
03/05 11:13 a.m.	Negative for AFB

Can this patient be removed from Airborne Precautions for rule-out pulmonary TB?

a. Yes, the patient can be removed from Airborne Precautions, as TB can be ruled out

b. No, the patient cannot be removed from Airborne Precautions, because he is infectious

c. Yes, the patient can be removed from Airborne Precautions, as he has latent TB and is not infectious

d. No, the patient cannot be removed from Airborne Precautions, because the sample collection was not sufficient to rule out pulmonary TB

107. Unused alcohol swabs that are placed on top of a dialysis machine in an active dialysis unit:

a. Should be discarded

b. May be returned to the common area

c. Must be cleaned before being used on another patient

d. Should only be used on patients with that dialysis machine

108. Which interventions are designed to limit the spread of respiratory illnesses in outpatient settings?

a. Sterilization monitors

b. Aseptic technique

c. Respiratory hygiene/cough etiquette

d. Symptom-based evaluation

NOTES

109. In preparing for the first meeting of the year for the Infection Prevention and Control Committee, the IP develops an annual report to include HAI trends. Of the choices below, this report should also address:

a. A summary of injuries and risk factors for injuries in personnel during the previous year

b. Staffing needs of the department to optimize efficiency

c. An evaluation of the surveillance program providing an assessment of its usefulness to the healthcare facility in preventing and controlling infections

d. A line list of all HAIs for the previous year and risk-reduction strategies

110. The IP has identified a cluster of *Candida* bloodstream infections in two adjoining ICUs. She wants to look at risk factors that these patients may have had in common. Which study design would she use?

a. Cross-sectional study

b. Cohort study

c. Case-control study

d. Clinical trial

111. An IP is planning an educational program for hospital nursing staff to improve compliance with infection prevention strategies. Please choose the approach that should be used to ensure an effective learning experience for those who attend.

a. Provide food and drinks to all who attend as well as sufficient breaks and have a raffle to entice attendance

b. Plan the educational offering by developing goals and objectives and determining the teaching method to use

c. Use a slide presentation that periodically provides humor to the presentation to ensure attention

d. Provide continuing educational credits and handouts for future reference

NOTES

112. Which of the four clinical variables that determine the probability of infection would the IP be targeting when reviewing preoperative chlorhexidine gluconate (CHG) bathing instructions that have been given to the preoperative patient population?

a. Inoculum of bacteria

b. Virulence of bacteria

c. Adjuvants in the microenvironment

d. Efficiency of host defenses

113. Which of the following processes should take place after an adverse event has occurred?

a. Failure mode effect analysis (FMEA)

b. Root cause analysis (RCA)

c. Strengths-weaknesses-opportunities-threats analysis (SWOT)

d. Infection control risk assessment (ICRA)

114. What is the annual sharps injury rate per 100 full-time equivalents (FTEs) in a facility that has 18 sharp injuries and 800 full-time employees?

a. 0.02

b. 0.23

c. 2.25

d. 22.5

115. An adult patient is admitted through the Emergency Department with a 1-day history of rash, fever, and cough. The attending physician is concerned that the patient has measles, as the patient cannot recall whether he has had measles disease or vaccine in the past. The serum sample does not contain measles-specific IgG or IgM antibodies. What is the significance of this finding?

a. The patient does not have measles infection

b. The patient has had the measles vaccine in the past

c. The patient has a history of measles disease

d. The patient might be infected with measles

NOTES

116. Primary components of an initial outbreak investigation are:

1) Preparing a line list and epidemic curve
2) Notifying key partners about the investigation
3) Continuing case finding
4) Initiating an analytic study

a. 1, 4
b. 2, 3
c. 1, 2
d. 3, 4

117. An IP has been asked to present an educational program to a group of HCP who are culturally different from him. What is the best approach to developing an effective program in this case?

a. Develop the program without taking cultural diversity into account, but allow the learners to ask questions while he is teaching
b. Be aware of potential cultural differences, but do not incorporate them into the program
c. Outline the major points of the educational program, and ask the audience to work together to identify culturally appropriate examples of the major points
d. There is no need to take cultural diversity into account because that does not change the learning objectives of the educational program

118. The IP is helping develop a large-scale project to address SSIs. Which of the following tools will the IP utilize that helps secure expert judgment prior to launching the project?

a. Delphi technique
b. Peer review
c. Fisher exact test
d. Meta-analysis

119. The use of influenza vaccines in school-aged children to decrease the number of cases in the community uses the principle of:

a. Innate immunity
b. Passive immunity
c. Herd immunity
d. Epidemic immunity

NOTES

120. Several HCP have been exposed to a patient with untreated, active pulmonary TB. Which is the best option for follow-up after this exposure?

a. TSTs should be administered at the time of exposure; If these are negative, then no further follow-up is needed

b. TSTs should be administered at the time of exposure and repeated at 12 weeks postexposure; converters without symptoms should be excluded from work and treated immediately

c. TSTs should be administered at the time of exposure and repeated at 12 weeks postexposure; converters with symptoms should follow up with a chest x-ray

d. TSTs and chest x-rays should be administered at the time of exposure and repeated at 12 weeks postexposure

121. Microorganisms are grown on culture media made of an agar base. Additives to media vary according to growth requirements of organisms and/or the desire to select out a specific organism. Fastidious organisms require __________ media and __________ media are used to inhibit normal commensals.

1) Differential

2) Enrichment

3) Selective

4) Nutrient broth

5) Synthetic sheep blood agar

a. 1, 3

b. 2, 3

c. 3, 4

d. 5, 1

NOTES

122. A patient is concerned that there might be microbes in the facility that are resistant to the environmental disinfection products in use. How do you respond to this concern?

- **a.** Inform her that while microbes can develop resistance to antimicrobials, they cannot become resistant to disinfectants
- **b.** Assure her that the disinfection products in use are ones that microbes have not developed resistance to yet
- **c.** Inform her that while reduced susceptibility of microbes to disinfectants can occur, the antimicrobial level of disinfectants used is still sufficient to inactivate those microbes
- **d.** Assure her that your facility uses special environmental disinfection procedures for all antimicrobial resistant organisms

123. An IP has monitored the rate of hand hygiene compliance among different nursing units. She finds that the ICU staff's compliance is less than satisfactory even after providing conveniently located hand hygiene dispensers. She shares this feedback with the staff. Of the choices below, what other information should be included in her discussion with the staff to improve hand hygiene compliance?

1) The number of patients on the unit during the monitoring period compared to the number of staff, as well as the nurse to patient ratio
2) Information about hand contamination
3) Information about the association between hand hygiene practices and the transmission of infection
4) The effects of hand hygiene products on skin

- **a.** 1, 2, 3
- **b.** 2, 3, 4
- **c.** 1, 3, 4
- **d.** 1, 2, 4

NOTES

124. The IP is called to the day care center for a possible outbreak of Hepatitis A. The Public Health Nurse is assisting her in investigating the outbreak. Prophylactic administration of immunoglobulin to the day-care workers and noninfected children would be an example of:

a. Passive immunity

b. Active immunity

c. Herd immunity

d. Nonspecific immunity

125. Which of the following would be an acceptable use of immediate-use sterilization for a surgical instrument?

a. To resterilize a surgical instrument that was dropped on the floor and for which no replacement is available

b. To sterilize an expensive surgical tool so that additional tools do not need to be purchased

c. To sterilize instruments that are not heat tolerant

d. To sterilize an instrument quickly so that a surgeon does not have to wait for a replacement to be brought to the OR

126. The IP has implemented a new educational program focusing on teaching safe injection practices to the staff nurses. Several months after the program is initiated, the IP is notified of a potential outbreak issue—a nurse used a medication vial for more than one patient. Which of the following quality tools would be most useful to investigate this incident?

a. Value stream mapping (VSM)

b. RCA

c. SWOT

d. FMEA

127. A patient is admitted to the hospital with severe community-acquired pneumonia (CAP). His symptoms include hemoptysis and a multilobar infiltrate seen on chest radiograph. The patient is recovering from a recent influenza virus infection. What organism should be suspected?

a. *Moraxella catarrhalis*

b. *Streptococcus pneumoniae*

c. MRSA

d. *Haemophilus influenzae*

NOTES

128. An IP notes that there appears to be an increase in positive AFB results for a 2-week time period. She recalls that there had been a confirmed case of *Mycobacterium tuberculosis* in a college student at the beginning of the time period. In all, six patients have culture results that confirm TB. After conferring with the Microbiology supervisor, a break in the lab's procedure is identified. The buffer solution that is used in these tests was contaminated with the initial patient's TB. This conclusion is confirmed with polymerase chain reaction (PCR) testing of the isolates. What would this type of outbreak be called?

a. TB outbreak

b. Pseudo-outbreak

c. Epidemic

d. Propagated outbreak

129. Which of the following would be best studied via qualitative research?

a. The effect of preoperative bathing with CHG on SSI rates

b. Declining influenza vaccination rates in HCP

c. MRSA colonization rates in dialysis patients

d. Reoccurrence of *C. difficile* in nursing home patients

130. A facility has decided to engage in animal-assisted activities/animal-assisted therapy, and the IP has been asked to develop infection prevention guidelines related to these activities. Of the choices below, which should be included in the guidelines?

a. The types of animals visiting a patient must be limited to small dogs less than 20 lbs. with the proper temperament

b. Animals must be screened to ensure that they are healthy and that their immunizations are current

c. A patient's personal pet may interact with other patients

d. Service animals may enter the operating room

131. The IP lives in a community of 100,000 persons. There have been more than 1,000 cases of Hepatitis C with 200 resultant deaths in 1 year. The case fatality rate for this is:

a. 10 percent

b. 800 per 10,000

c. 20 percent

d. 200 per 100,000

NOTES

132. Which of the following is *not* an example of syndromic surveillance?

a. Number of patients seen in the Emergency Room with influenza-like illness

b. Number of purchases of over-the-county flu remedy medications

c. Number of school absences related to illness

d. Number of new cancer diagnoses reported to the cancer registry

133. Which of the following is used to determine efficacy of antimicrobials on a particular pathogen?

a. KOH preparation

b. Methylene blue stain

c. Rapid Plasma Reagin

d. Kirby-Bauer test

134. The IP must prepare a cost-benefit analysis (CBA) for the proposed purchase of a new electronic surveillance system for the hospital. Which statement about the CBA is correct?

a. All measures are expressed in monetary (US dollar) terms

b. Only costs are expressed in monetary (US dollar) terms

c. CBA is never based on existing financial data

d. The monetary value of possible benefits is often highly speculative

135. A dialysis patient who is known to be positive for Hepatitis B has been admitted to the surgical floor for a surgical procedure. The patient will require dialysis three times a week while he is in the hospital. The inpatient dialysis unit does not have an isolation room and is very small. The dialysis nurse has requested the IP's assistance in identifying the best location to dialyze the patient. Which of the following should the IP recommend?

a. Transfer the patient to an isolation room in the outpatient unit

b. Perform the treatment in the inpatient unit

c. Perform the treatment in the patient's hospital room

d. Transfer the patient to an isolation room in the ICU

ANSWERS AND RATIONALES

NOTES

1. **(D) 1, 2, 3**

Rationale: Surveillance of MDROs is critical to an antimicrobial stewardship program. IPs monitoring microbiology isolates to detect prevalence and emergence of MDROs. IPs may also support antimicrobial stewardship efforts in the following ways:

- Calculate MDRO incidence on the basis of clinical culture results
- Calculate MDRO infection rates
- Use molecular typing for investigating outbreaks
- Detect asymptomatic carriers using active surveillance cultures

References: *APIC Text*, 4th edition, Chapter 26 - Antimicrobials and Resistance

CBIC Core Competency: Preventing/Controlling the Transmission of Infectious Agents

2. **(C) Koplik spots**

Rationale: Measles is a highly communicable viral illness with prodromal fever, conjunctivitis, coryza, cough, and small spots with white or bluish-white centers on an erythematous base on the buccal mucosa. These small spots are called Koplik spots.

Reference: Measles. In: Heymann D. *Control of Communicable Diseases Manual*, 19th edition. Washington, DC: American Public Health Association, 2008.

CBIC Core Competency: Identification of Infectious Disease Processes

NOTES

3. (A) A surgical mask worn within 3 feet of patient, door may be open

Rationale: Pneumonic plague is the least common form of naturally occurring disease and also the most severe. The mortality rate is nearly 100 percent in untreated cases and almost 60 percent even when treated. In a bioterrorism event, primary pneumonic plague is most likely to occur because it results from the inhalation of aerosolized bacterial particles. The incubation period for pneumonic plague is 1 to 6 days, but most commonly occurs 2 to 4 days after exposure. Clinical features for pneumonic plague are similar to symptoms for the other forms of plague: nonspecific influenza-like symptoms such as fever, chills, body aches, malaise, headache, and gastrointestinal distress such as nausea, vomiting, diarrhea, and abdominal pain. Patients typically progress from feeling well to having severe pneumonia with cough, chest pain, shortness of breath, and stridor within 24 hours. Pneumonic plague can be spread from person to person. Transmission occurs by respiratory droplets. Patients with pneumonic plague require Droplet Precautions. Special air handling or negative pressure rooms are not indicated. Droplet Precautions (in addition to Standard Precautions) require that patients be placed in private rooms or cohorted, wearing a mask when working within 3 feet of the patient (logistically, some hospitals may want to implement the wearing of a mask to enter the room). Patient transport should be minimized to essential purposes only, and if movement is necessary, the patient should wear a surgical mask to minimize dispersal of droplets. Isolation generally can be discontinued after 48 hours of appropriate antimicrobial therapy. However, isolation should never be discontinued if the patient is not clinically improving. It is possible that the terrorists will genetically alter the strain of plague they release and make it antibiotic resistant. If an antibiotic-resistant strain is used in a bioterrorism attack and isolation is discontinued after 48 hours, the patient would remain infectious and thus constitute a risk to staff, patients, and visitors. Isolation should not be discontinued until 48 hours of appropriate therapy and when the patient is showing signs of clinical improvement.

Reference: *APIC Text*, 4th edition, Chapter 120 - Infectious Disease Disasters: Bioterrorism, Emerging Infections, and Pandemics

CBIC Core Competency: Preventing/Controlling the Transmission of Infectious Agents

NOTES

4. **C 3, 4**

Rationale: A surgical risk index is a score used to predict a surgical patient's risk of acquiring an SSI. The risk index score, ranging from 0 to 3, is the sum of the number of risk factors present among the following:

- A patient with an ASA physical status classification score of 3, 4, or 5
- An operation classified as contaminated or dirty/infected
- An operation lasting longer than the duration cut point in minutes, where the duration cut point varies by the type of operative procedure performed

The higher the score by this index, the greater is the risk for subsequent SSI (see Table PE2-1).

Patient 1 has a risk index of 1 and an ASA score of 3. Patient 2 has a risk index of 0. Patient 3 has an ASA score of 3 and an operation lasting longer than the duration cut point in minutes; her risk index would be 2. Patient 4 has a Class II procedure (contaminated) and an operation lasting longer than the duration cut point in minutes; his risk index is 2.

Table PE2-1. Rates of Surgical Site Infection and NHSN Risk Index for Six Commonly Performed Operations*

			NNIS Risk Index		
Procedure	**Cut Point (min)**	**0 (%)**	**1 (%)**	**2 (%)**	**3 (%)**
Colon resection	187	3.99	5.59	7.06	9.47
Coronary artery bypass with donor incision	301	0.35	2.55	4.26	8.49
Spinal fusion	239	0.70	1.84	4.15†	—
Herniorrhaphy	124	0.74	2.42	5.25†	—
Hip prosthesis	120	0.67	1.44	2.40†	—
Abdominal hysterectomy	143	1.1	2.2	4.05†	—

*The cut point is identified in minutes. Procedures that exceed the cut point in duration have one risk point added to the NNIS risk index.

†Indicates that risk index groups 2 and 3 have been pooled together because of small total cases

Source: Edwards JR, Peterson KD, Mu Y, et al. National Healthcare Safety Network (NHSN) report: data summary for 2006 through 2008, issued December 2009. *Am J Infect Control* 2009;37:783-805.

Reference: *APIC Text*, 4th edition, Chapter 37 - Surgical Site Infection

CBIC Core Competency: Surveillance and Epidemiologic Investigation

NOTES

5. **D Anthrax**

Rationale: A biological attack, or bioterrorism, is the intentional release of viruses, bacteria, or other germs that can sicken or kill people, livestock, or crops. *Bacillus anthracis*, the bacteria that causes anthrax, is one of the most likely agents to be used in a biological attack because:

- Anthrax spores are easily found in nature, can be produced in a lab, and can last for a long time in the environment
- Anthrax makes a good weapon because it can be released quietly and without anyone knowing. The microscopic spores could be put into powders, sprays, food, and water. Because they are so small, individuals may not be able to see, smell, or taste them.
- Anthrax has been used as a weapon before

There are three types of anthrax: cutaneous, gastrointestinal, and inhalational. Symptoms of inhalation anthrax include:

- Fever and chills
- Chest discomfort
- Shortness of breath
- Confusion or dizziness
- Cough
- Nausea, vomiting, or stomach pains
- Headache
- Sweats (often drenching)
- Extreme tiredness
- Body aches

If inhalation anthrax is suspected, chest X-rays or computed tomography scans can confirm if the patient has mediastinal widening or pleural effusion, which are X-ray findings typically seen in patients with inhalation anthrax. The only way to confirm a diagnosis of anthrax is to either test directly for B. anthracis in a sample (blood, skin lesion swab, spinal fluid, or respiratory secretions) or measure antibodies or toxin in blood.

Samples must be taken before the patient begins taking antibiotics.

Reference: *APIC Text*, 4th edition, Chapter 120 - Infectious Disease Disasters: Bioterrorism, Emerging Infections, and Pandemics

CBIC Core Competency: Preventing/Controlling the Transmission of Infectious Agents

6. **D Number of blood collection devices used or purchased**

Rationale: The denominator should represent the potential for exposure to sharps. There are many possible denominators that may be used, and each will provide a different view of the sharps injury situation in the facility. A device-based rate can be used to compare needlestick risk from different devices and to evaluate the effectiveness of the product design. Because blood draws may be performed by nurses, phlebotomists, or physicians, total device-associated needlestick injuries since implementation of the new product will provide the most useful data.

Reference: *APIC Text*, 4th edition, Chapter 100 - Occupational Health

CBIC Core Competency: Employee/Occupational Health

NOTES

7. **(A) Cleaning followed by high-level disinfection**

Rationale: Semicritical items are those items that will contact mucous membranes or nonintact skin. Respiratory therapy and anesthesia equipment, some endoscopes, laryngoscope blades, esophageal manometry probes, anorectal manometry catheters, and diaphragm fitting rings are included in this category. These medical devices should be free of all vegetative microorganisms (i.e., mycobacteria, fungi, viruses, bacteria), though small numbers of bacterial spores may be present. Intact mucous membranes, such as those of the lungs or the gastrointestinal tract, generally are resistant to infection by common bacterial spores but are susceptible to other organisms, such as bacteria, mycobacteria, and viruses. Semicritical items minimally require high-level disinfection using chemical disinfectants.

Reference: *APIC Text*, 4th edition, Chapter 31 - Cleaning, Disinfection, Sterilization

CBIC Core Competency: Environment of Care

8. **(B) He should place absorbent material over the spill and pour the correct dilution of disinfectant over the material for the recommended contact time**

Rationale: Cleaning of a large blood spill may be a risk for acquisition of bloodborne pathogens, so immediate inactivation of any pathogens before cleaning is important to reduce this risk. Absorbent material may be placed over the spill to contain it and the correct dilution of an EPA-registered disinfectant can be poured on the absorbent material to reduce the bioburden. After this, the absorbent materials can be gathered up and disposed of and the area can be cleaned.

Reference: *APIC Text*, 4th edition, Chapter 107 - Environmental Services

CBIC Core Competency: Cleaning, Sterilization, Disinfection, Asepsis

9. **(C) 1, 3**

Rationale: Latent tuberculosis infection (LTBI) is the presence of *M. tuberculosis* organisms (tubercle bacilli) without symptoms or radiographic or bacteriologic evidence of TB. Approximately 90 to 95 percent of those infected are able to mount an immune response that halts the progression from LTBI to TB. Persons with LTBI are asymptomatic (they have no symptoms of TB) and are not infectious.

Reference: Jensen PA, Lambert LA, Iademarco MF, et al. Guidelines for Preventing the Transmission of Mycobacterium tuberculosis in Health-Care Settings, 2005. *MMWR* 2005 December 30. 41(RR-17). 1-141. Available at: http://www.cdc.gov/mmwr/preview/mmwrhtml/rr5417a1.htm?s_cid=rr5417a1_e.

CBIC Core Competency: Identification of Infectious Disease Processes

10. **(A) 1, 2**

Rationale: The CDC's guidelines call for medications labeled as "single dose" or "single use" to be used for only one patient. This practice protects patients from life-threatening infections that occur when medications get contaminated from unsafe use. Vials labeled by the manufacturer as "single dose" or "single use" should only be used for a single patient. These medications typically lack antimicrobial preservatives and can become contaminated and serve as a source of infection when they are used inappropriately.

Reference: *APIC Text*, 4th edition, Chapter 48 - Ambulatory Care

CBIC Core Competency: Preventing/Controlling the Transmission of Infectious Agents

NOTES

11. **C On days 3-7**

Rationale: Measles symptoms generally appear in two stages. In the first stage, which lasts 2 to 4 days, the individual may have a runny nose, cough, and a slight fever. The eyes may become reddened and sensitive to light, while the fever gradually rises each day, often peaking as high as 103° to 105°F. Koplik spots (small bluish white spots surrounded by a reddish area) may also appear on the gums and inside of the cheeks. The second stage begins on the third to seventh day and consists of a red blotchy rash lasting 5 to 6 days. The rash usually begins on the face and then spreads downward and outward, reaching the hands and feet. The rash fades in the same order that it appeared, from head to extremities.

Reference: Measles. In: Heymann D. *Control of Communicable Diseases Manual*, 19th edition. Washington, DC: American Public Health Association, 2008.

CBIC Core Competency: Identification of Infectious Disease Processes

12. **C $82.50**

Rationale: A budget is a quantitative expression of a plan for a defined period of time. It may include planned sales volumes and revenues, resource quantities, costs and expenses, assets, liabilities, and cash flows. It expresses strategic plans of business units, organizations, activities, or events in measurable terms. The manager's budget for the flu shot program is 20 percent of $1,650 (1,650 × 0.20), or $330. However, only 15 percent (1,650 × 0.15), or $247.50 was spent. This leaves a remainder of $82.50.

Reference: *APIC Text*, 4th edition, Chapter 1 – Infection Prevention and Control Programs

CBIC Core Competency: Management and Communication

13. **B Immunoglobulin M (IgM) anti-HAV**

Rationale: HAV is of the genus *Hepatovirus* in the family Picornaviridae of enteroviruses. It is a nonenveloped, 27-nm single-stranded RNA virus. HAV is transmitted primarily by the fecal-oral route, facilitated by intimate personal contact (household, sexual, etc.), poor hygiene, unsanitary conditions, or contaminated water, milk, or food, especially raw shellfish. Clinical features of acute hepatitis are not specific for HAV infection, so serological diagnosis is necessary. Demonstration of the IgM antibodies against HAV (IgM anti-HAV) in the serum of acutely or recently ill patients establishes the diagnosis.

Reference: Hepatitis A. In: Heymann D, ed. *Control of Communicable Diseases Manual*, 19th edition. Washington, DC: American Public Health Association, 2008.

CBIC Core Competency: Identification of Infectious Disease Processes

14. **C Standard Precautions**

Rationale: Cryptococcal meningitis is caused by the fungus *Cryptococcus neoformans*. This fungus is found in soil around the world. Unlike bacterial meningitis, this form of meningitis comes on more slowly over a few days to a few weeks. Patients with cryptococcal meningitis do not require Isolation Precautions. Standard Precautions should be followed on all patients.

Reference: Cryptococcosis. In: Heymann D, ed. *Control of Communicable Diseases Manual*, 19th edition. Washington, DC: American Public Health Association, 2008.

CBIC Core Competency: Preventing/Controlling the Transmission of Infectious Agents

NOTES

15. **C** **1, 3, 4**

Rationale: HCP are required by the National Childhood Vaccine Injury Act (NCVIA) to provide a copy of the Vaccine Information Statement to either the adult recipient or to the child's parent/legal representative. All states allow medical exemptions for persons who have medical contraindication to vaccination. Most states allow religious exemptions and some allow philosophical/personal belief exemptions. There is no federal requirement for informed consent relating to immunization.

Reference: *APIC Text*, 4th edition, Chapter 100 - Occupational Health

CBIC Core Competency: Employee/Occupational Health

16. **C** **Daily use of a biological indicator in the sterilizer**

Rationale: Steam sterilizers should be routinely tested at least weekly—preferably daily—with a biological indicator process challenge device. If a sterilizer is used frequently (e.g., several loads per day), daily use of biological indicators allows earlier discovery of equipment malfunctions or procedural errors and thus minimizes the extent of patient surveillance and product recall needed in the event of a positive biological indicator.

Reference: *APIC Text*, 4th edition, Chapter 106 - Sterile Processing

CBIC Core Competency: Cleaning, Sterilization, Disinfection, Asepsis

17. **B** **2, 3**

Rationale: By dividing the total number of patients screened by the total number of patients in each respective category, the resulting compliance rate is less than 90 percent for *Transfers into ICU* and *Transfers from other facilities*. The IP should focus on improving performance related to these two risk categories.

Reference: *APIC Text*, 4th edition, Chapter 13 - Use of Statistics in Infection Prevention

CBIC Core Competency: Surveillance and Epidemiologic Investigation

18. **C** **Disinfect the system**

Rationale: According to the Conditions for Coverage document from Centers for Medicare & Medicaid Services (CMS), product water used to prepare dialysate or concentrates from powder at a dialysis facility, or to process dialyzers for reuse, shall contain a total viable microbial count lower than 200 CFU/mL and an endotoxin concentration lower than 2 EU/mL. Measures must be performed promptly when results exceed the action level or the maximum allowable level. Dialysis may continue when bacteria/endotoxin is found to be at the action level, but retesting and/or disinfection of the system should be performed promptly. *Promptly* has been defined by CMS regulation as within 48 hours of receiving the report.

Reference: *APIC Text*, 4th edition, Chapter 39 - Dialysis

CBIC Core Competency: Preventing/Controlling the Transmission of Infectious Agents

NOTES

19. (B) A measure that is based on a definition that can easily be understood and applied in a facility

Rationale: Performance measures should be evidence-based, well-defined, clinically important for patient populations, and broadly applicable in different types of facilities. Selection of performance measures will be based on both external and internal measurement requirements.

Reference: *APIC Text*, 4th edition, Chapter 17 - Performance Measures

CBIC Core Competency: Management and Communication

20. (B) An independent, randomized trial that shows with statistical significance that the new product is comparable to the current product in preventing infections when used as a surgical skin prep

Rationale: In randomized clinical trials (RCTs), the participants are randomly assigned to treatment or control groups to ensure that the allocation is unbiased. The RCT design minimizes bias and provides the best evidence for direct causal relationships between the experimental factor and the outcome. A randomized trial that was conducted by someone with no financial interest in the product and that was conducted under clinical conditions will provide the best evidence for effectiveness.

Reference: *APIC Text*, 4th edition, Chapter 7 - Product Evaluation

CBIC Core Competency: Management and Communication

21. (D) Agar plates used for testing sputum samples in the microbiology lab

Rationale: Any objects with the potential to have sufficient dose of a pathogen, a portal of entry, and a method of being transmitted are considered to be infectious waste. Bacterial cultures that have amplified potential pathogens may also have sharp edges and should be considered infectious waste. Nonpenetrating objects with minimal blood and body fluid contamination are not infectious waste. Unused sharps are not infectious waste but must be disposed of in a sharps container because of the high risk of puncture injuries and inability to know that the object was not contaminated.

Reference: *APIC Text*, 4th edition, Chapter 113 - Waste Management

CBIC Core Competency: Preventing/Controlling the Transmission of Infectious Agents

22. (D) 24 hours

Rationale: For hospitalized patients, Contact Precautions are required for 24 hours after the start of effective treatment. Twenty-four hours may be insufficient in cases of crusted scabies because viable mites can remain on the patient after a single treatment; in this case an alternative isolation approach is suggested in institutional outbreaks: 10-day quarantine of the index patient.

References: Scabies. In: Heymann D. *Control of Communicable Diseases Manual*, 19th edition. Washington, DC: American Public Health Association, 2008; *APIC Text*, 4th edition, Chapter 99 - Parasites

CBIC Core Competency: Identification of Infectious Disease Processes

NOTES

23. **C The popularity of tattooing and body piercing has made it more socially acceptable**

Rationale: Tattooing and body piercing activities can transmit infectious diseases. It is difficult to describe the epidemiology of disease transmission after tattooing and body piercing procedures. There have not been uniform licensure requirements for body art studios or for individuals performing the procedures, so the reporting of infections to a public health agency is generally limited to bloodborne diseases identified by the healthcare system. The licensure varies greatly by state. Regulations may address the age of the client, client histories, sterilization processes, single-use items, apprenticeships/training, and bloodborne pathogens training. Some states leave the regulations up to local ordinances and some have no regulations whatsoever. The enforcement of the various regulations is dependent on funding of the programs, which is also variable. Many local health departments may inspect the business sites, but it is questionable whether inspectors receive adequate training about the appropriate infection prevention practices they should monitor in these nontraditional settings. Also, the frequency by which the sites are inspected is variable. Sometimes it takes an adverse event for a site to be inspected. There are many opportunities for contamination, particularly for tattooing. Many of the practices being adopted by piercing studios worldwide are based on a common sense approach, as well as guidelines offered by professional organizations such as the Association of Professional Piercers or the Piercing Association of the United Kingdom.

Reference: *APIC Text*, 4th edition, Chapter 123 - Body Piercing, Tattoos, and Electrolysis

CBIC Core Competency: Preventing/Controlling the Transmission of Infectious Agents

24. **C For all disinfectants, the greater the number of microbes on an object or surface, the greater the amount of time that is needed for a disinfectant to have effective cidal activity**

Rationale: Without exception, a higher bioburden of organisms on an object or surface will require higher contact time for a disinfectant to kill the organisms. Prior cleaning of a surface or instrument will reduce the bioburden, which will decrease the necessary contact time for the disinfection process.

Reference: CDC Guideline for Disinfection and Sterilization in Healthcare Facilities, 2008, Page: 33-35

CBIC Core Competency: Environment of Care

25. **C Staff are discussing strategies to increase PPE use at the monthly staff meeting**

Rationale: The principal concept behind the Transtheoretical Model (or Stage Theory) is readiness. For any given health-associated behavior, people will have diverse orientations to change. Some will be unaware that a particular change is a desirable option, whereas others will have already completed the change but remain at risk of reversing their progress or relapsing. The stages include Precontemplation, Contemplation, Preparation, Action, and Maintenance. The preparation phase is when a person or group of people starts planning for the behavior change.

Reference: *APIC Text*, 4th edition, Chapter 5 - Infection Prevention and Behavioral Interventions

CBIC Core Competency: Education and Research

NOTES

26. C The colonization rate for distal water sites in the hospital is greater than 30 percent

Rationale: *Legionella pneumophila* is a common cause of both community-acquired and healthcare-associated pneumonia. Clinical manifestations are nonspecific, but high fever, diarrhea, and hyponatremia are often distinctive. Infection has been linked to drinking water distribution systems of acute care and extended care facilities. Health departments and public agencies have issued infection prevention guidelines aimed at preventing outbreaks. These guidelines include diagnostic testing for *Legionella* infection and culturing of the drinking water distribution system. Disinfection of the water distribution system includes superheating and flushing with hyperchlorination as a short-term approach to terminating an outbreak. Copper-silver ionization has been validated for long-term systemic disinfection. Chlorine dioxide is a promising alternative disinfection method. Disinfection of the facility's water system should be considered if there is evidence of a prior case(s) of healthcare-associated legionellosis, greater than 30 percent colonization of distal sites in the water system, or prospective surveillance for legionellosis detects a healthcare-associated case.

Reference: *APIC Text*, 4th edition, Chapter 84 - *Legionella pneumophila*

CBIC Core Competency: Environment of Care

27. A 1, 3

Rationale: To increase retention and motivate the learner to change practice behaviors, the educator should assume a facilitator role, limit monologues or lectures, and opt for more interactive classroom approaches. A rule of thumb for the active/passive ratio is a minimum of 60/40. This mix of activities and presentation methods will also help to hold the adult learner's interest. Providing a safe, low-risk, nonthreatening learning environment can facilitate class interaction.

Reference: *APIC Text*, 4th edition, Chapter 3 - Education and Training

CBIC Core Competency: Education and Research

28. A OPA does not require activation

Rationale: There are several advantages of OPA over glutaraldehyde. OPA requires no activation, is stable over a range of pH values, does not irritate the eyes and nose, and does not have a strong odor. Both OPA and glutaraldehyde are compatible with many types of materials.

Reference: CDC Guideline for Disinfection and Sterilization in Healthcare Facilities, 2008, Page 48-49

CBIC Core Competency: Environment of Care

29. A Determine goals and objectives for the following year

Rationale: An annual risk assessment must be performed to determine goals and objectives for the infection prevention program. These should be based on the institution's strategic goals and institutional data and findings from the previous year's activities. Infection prevention resources and data systems needs should be evaluated in the context of these goals and objectives.

Reference: *APIC Text*, 4th edition, Chapter 1 - Infection Prevention and Control Programs

CBIC Core Competency: Management and Communication

NOTES

30. Ⓒ No, the patient should be treated with gentamicin for *Enterococcus faecium*

Rationale: Given the arrangement and morphology of the bacteria and the probable origin of the infection, the patient most likely has *E. faecium*. Only 12 percent of the *E. faecium* isolates in the facility are susceptible to ampicillin, but 100 percent are susceptible to gentamicin. Therefore, gentamicin is a better choice of antimicrobial therapy for this patient.

Reference: *APIC Text*, 4th edition, Chapter 26 - Antimicrobials and Resistance; Antimicrobial Testing. In: Kulich P, Taylor D, eds. *The Infection Preventionist's Guide to the Lab*. Washington, DC: Association for Professionals in Infection Control and Epidemiology, 2012.

CBIC Core Competency: Identification of Infectious Disease Processes

31. Ⓑ *Vibrio cholerae*

Rationale: Bioterrorism refers to the use of biological agents on civilian or military populations, animals, or crops. There are a broad range of potential bioterrorism agents, including bacteria, viruses, and toxins (of microbial, plant, or animal origin). Common characteristics of this diverse group of agents include (1) the ability to be dispersed in aerosols of 1 to 5 μm particles, which can penetrate the distal bronchioles; (2) the ability to deliver these aerosols with simple technology; (3) the feasibility of these agents, if delivered from a line source (e.g., an airplane) upwind from the target, to infect large numbers of the population; and (4) the ability to spread infection, disease, panic, and fear. The U.S. public health system and primary healthcare providers must be prepared to address various biological agents, including pathogens that are rarely seen in the United States. The CDC classifies high-priority agents as Category A. This category includes organisms that pose a risk to national security because they have the following characteristics:

- Can be easily disseminated or transmitted from person to person
- Result in high mortality rates and have the potential for major public health impact
- Might cause public panic and social disruption
- Require special action for public health preparedness

Second highest priority agents (Category B) include those that have the following characteristics:

- Are moderately easy to disseminate
- Result in moderate morbidity rates and low mortality rates
- Require specific enhancements of the CDC's diagnostic capacity and enhanced disease surveillance

Category B diseases/agents include:

- Brucellosis (*Brucella* species)
- Epsilon toxin of *Clostridium perfringens*
- Food safety threats (e.g., *Salmonella* species, *E. coli* O157:H7, *Shigella*)
- Glanders (*Burkholderia mallei*)
- Melioidosis (*Burkholderia pseudomallei*)
- Psittacosis (*Chlamydia psittaci*)
- Q fever (*Coxiella burnetii*)

NOTES

- Ricin toxin from *Ricinus communis* (castor beans)
- Staphylococcal enterotoxin B
- Typhus fever (*Rickettsia prowazekii*)
- Viral encephalitis (alphaviruses [e.g., Venezuelan equine encephalitis, eastern equine encephalitis, western equine encephalitis])
- Water safety threats (e.g., *Vibrio cholerae, Cryptosporidium parvum*)

Reference: *APIC Text*, 4th edition, Chapter 120 - Infectious Disease Disasters: Bioterrorism, Emerging Infections, and Pandemics

CBIC Core Competency: Preventing/Controlling the Transmission of Infectious Agents

32. (B) Surgical mask placed on the patient during transport

Rationale: The risk of infection transmission is related to the number of organisms that are aerosolized. Increased risk of infection is associated with patients with cavitary disease, smear-positive sputum, or a cough. Risk is also increased if patients are placed in poorly or improperly ventilated rooms. The emergency room (ER) and clinic areas should have plans for appropriately isolating patients with suspected TB who are being seen as outpatients. These plans should include details on placing the patient in a separate area from other patients and placing a surgical mask on him or her until appropriate isolation can be arranged.

Reference: *APIC Text*, 4th edition, Chapter 95 - Tuberculosis and Other Mycobacteria

CBIC Core Competency: Preventing/Controlling the Transmission of Infectious Agents

33. (B) You should prepare food that is in unpowered refrigerators first

Rationale: In the event of an emergency where there is a power outage, the use of food should be prioritized to maximize supplies and to prevent the occurrence of foodborne illnesses. Food in an unpowered refrigerator should be used first because the temperature in this appliance will drop most rapidly below the critical temperature for food safety. If food is held at room temperature for more than two hours or above 90°F for more than an hour, it should be discarded because of the risk of microbial growth.

Reference: *APIC Text*, 4th edition, Chapter 119 - Emergency Management

CBIC Core Competency: Environment of Care

34. (A) 1, 2, 3

Rationale: The ACIP immunization schedule for HCP includes vaccines for diphtheria, varicella, and pertussis. There is no available vaccine for preventing congenital (present at birth) CMV disease. However, a few CMV vaccines are being tested in humans, including live attenuated (weakened) virus vaccines and vaccines that contain only pieces of the virus. The Institute of Medicine has ranked the development of a CMV vaccine as a highest priority because of the lives it would save and the disabilities it would prevent.

Reference: *APIC Text*, 4th edition, Chapter 100 - Occupational Health

CBIC Core Competency: Employee/Occupational Health

NOTES

35. Ⓑ **2, 3, 4**

Rationale: Hepatitis B vaccination is the most effective measure to prevent HBV infection and its consequences, including cirrhosis of the liver, liver cancer, liver failure, and death. In adults, ongoing HBV transmission occurs primarily among unvaccinated persons with behavioral risks for HBV transmission, such as heterosexuals with multiple sex partners and men who have sex with men. Developmentally disabled persons in residential and nonresidential facilities also have had high rates of HBV infection, but the prevalence of infection has declined since the implementation of routine Hepatitis B vaccination in these settings. However, since Hepatitis B surface antigen-positive persons reside in such facilities, clients and staff continue to be at risk for infection. In response to multiple outbreaks of HBV among persons receiving assisted blood glucose monitoring, it is now recommended that all previously unvaccinated adults aged 19 through 59 years with diabetes mellitus (type 1 and type 2) be vaccinated against Hepatitis B as soon as possible after a diagnosis of diabetes is made.

References: Centers for Disease Control and Prevention. Use of Hepatitis B Vaccination for Adults with Diabetes Mellitus: Recommendations of the Advisory Committee on Immunization Practices (ACIP). *MMWR* 2011 Dec 23; 60(50);1709-1711. Mast EE, Weinbaum CM, Fiore AE, et al. A Comprehensive Immunization Strategy to Eliminate Transmission of Hepatitis B Virus Infection in the United States: Recommendations of the Advisory Committee on Immunization Practices (ACIP) Part II: Immunization of Adults. *MMWR Rec Rep* 2006 Dec 8;55(RR-16) 1-33.

CBIC Core Competency: Preventing/Controlling the Transmission of Infectious Agents

36. Ⓑ **Equipment is immersed in enzymatic cleaner that is discarded every 24 hours**

Rationale: Infection prevention is dependent on the education, training, and skill of the practitioner, the integrity of the device (ensuring that the equipment is free of defects), and strict adherence to reprocessing protocols. Flexible endoscopes are considered semicritical devices because they come into contact with mucous membranes but do not usually enter sterile tissue or the vascular system. Endoscopes should, at a minimum, receive high-level disinfection. Enzymatic detergents must be discarded after each use, as these products are not microbicidal and will not retard microbial growth.

Reference: *APIC Text*, 4th edition, Chapter 55 - Endoscopy

CBIC Core Competency: Cleaning, Sterilization, Disinfection, Asepsis

37. Ⓑ **Blood samples should be obtained in pairs (two sets) from different peripheral sites**

Rationale: Specimen collection from central catheters is not recommended due to the possibility of intraluminal bacterial contamination of the device. Percutaneous venipuncture from two separate sites is preferred.

Reference: Blood Cultures. In: Kulich P, Taylor D, eds. *The Infection Preventionist's Guide to the Lab*. Washington, DC: Association for Professionals in Infection Control and Epidemiology, 2012.

CBIC Core Competency: Identification of Infectious Disease Processes

NOTES

38. (A) *Pseudomonas* species

Rationale: Although disinfectants are formulated to kill microbes, they can become contaminated during use and can spread the contaminating microbe in the environment. Species of the genus *Pseudomonas* have been isolated in over 80 percent of contaminated products. To prevent contamination of disinfectants, the products should not be diluted unless specified by the manufacturer, workers who prepare and use disinfectant solutions should be trained on the common ways that these solutions become contaminated, and disinfectant solutions should be stored per the manufacturer's recommendations.

Reference: CDC Guideline for Disinfection and Sterilization in Healthcare Facilities, 2008, Page 31-32

CBIC Core Competency: Cleaning, Sterilization, Disinfection, Asepsis

39. (D) 180 per 100,000

Rationale: A mortality rate is the measure of the frequency of death in a defined population during a specified time (usually a year). The crude mortality rate measures the proportion of the population dying each year from all causes. The cause-specific mortality rate measures mortality from a specified cause for a population.

Mortality rate = $x/y \times k$

Where:

x = The number of people in a defined population during a specified interval of time who (1) die of any cause (crude rate) or (2) die of a specified cause (cause-specific rate)

y = Estimated population at midyear (i.e., July); crude rates use 1,000 or 100,000

k = Usually an assigned value of 1,000 when calculating crude rates: 100,000 is used for cause-specific rates

In this scenario the crude mortality rate is calculated as 3.254 ÷ 1,800,000 × 100,000 = 180 per 100,000 population.

Reference: *APIC Text*, 4th edition, Chapter 13 - Use of Statistics in Infection Prevention

CBIC Core Competency: Surveillance and Epidemiologic Investigation

40. (C) 2, 3

Rationale: The odds ratio (OR) is the probability of having a particular risk factor if a condition or disease is present divided by the probability of having the risk factor if the disease or condition is not present. If there is no association between the variables, the OR equals one. An OR either greater than one or less than one indicates a possible statistical relationship (or association) between the variables. Confidence intervals may be used to determine the statistical significance of the relationship. If the confidence interval does not contain the value 1.0, the association is statistically significant at $\alpha = 0.05$. If the p value is less than or equal to α, reject the null hypothesis that there is no relationship between the variables.

In this table, Mechanical ventilation and Central venous catheter have p values below 0.05 and have confidence intervals that do not contain the value 1.0. The conclusion is that there is a statistical association between these variables and outbreak of *Serratia marcescens*.

References: *APIC Text*, 4th edition, Chapter 10 - General Principles of Epidemiology; *APIC Text*, 4th edition, Chapter 13 - Use of Statistics in Infection Prevention

CBIC Core Competency: Education and Research

NOTES

41. Ⓐ **1, 2**

Rationale: *C. difficile* is a Gram-positive, spore-forming anaerobic bacillus that produces two large toxins—A and B—that cause diarrhea and colitis in susceptible patients whose normal colonic bacterial flora has been disrupted by prior antimicrobial treatment. Measures directed at the interruption of horizontal transmission include barrier precautions (hand hygiene/washing, gloving, isolation, and cohorting), and environmental cleaning and disinfection.

Reference: *APIC Text*, 4th edition, Chapter 72 - *Clostridium difficile* Infections and Pseudomembranous Colitis

CBIC Core Competency: Preventing/Controlling the Transmission of Infectious Agents

42. Ⓓ **118°F or 48°C for one hour**

Rationale: Bed bugs are challenging to eradicate. Some pest control firms utilize specialized heating equipment to de-infest furnishings, rooms, and entire dwellings. The procedure involves heating up the infested item or area to temperatures lethal to bed bugs. Portable heaters and fans are used to treat the room with high heat (118°F or 48°C for one hour).

Reference: *APIC Text*, 4th edition, Chapter 107 - Environmental Services

CBIC Core Competency: Environment of Care

43. Ⓒ **2, 3, 4**

Rationale: Event-related storage of sterile items allows for items to be used at any time after processing, provided the sterile packaging has not been compromised. Items must be stored in a dry, well-ventilated, dust-free, insect-free, and temperature controlled area. Packages must be inspected before use to ensure that the wrapping is still intact, with no tears, punctures, or evidence of water intrusion.

Reference: CDC Guideline for Disinfection and Sterilization in Healthcare Facilities, 2008, Page 91-92

CBIC Core Competency: Cleaning, Sterilization, Disinfection, Asepsis

44. Ⓐ **Productivity**

Rationale: Productivity is the ratio of output to inputs in production. It is an average measure of the efficiency of production. Efficiency of production means production's capability to create incomes, which are measured by subtracting real input value from real output value.

References: *APIC Text*, 4th edition, Chapter 1 - Infection Prevention and Control Programs; *APIC Text*, 4th edition, Chapter 19 - Qualitative Research Methods

CBIC Core Competency: Management and Communication

45. Ⓐ **Test A, because it has higher sensitivity**

Rationale: Test A is the best choice. It will correctly identify 98 percent of people who have flu because it has 98 percent sensitivity. The specificity of Test A is 85 percent, so 15 percent of patients who do not have flu will be identified as positive (15 percent false positives [FPs]). In this case the IP is most interested in isolating infected patients, so the false-positive rate is an acceptable trade-off in this example.

Reference: *APIC Text*, 4th edition, Chapter 13 - Use of Statistics in Infection Prevention

CBIC Core Competency: Identification of Infectious Disease Processes

NOTES

46. (A) Cleaning of endoscopes is essential before manual or automated disinfection

Rationale: Cleaning of endoscopes before manual or automated disinfection is a category 1A recommendation by the CDC's HICPAC and is critical for prevention of endoscopy-related HAIs. There is no strong evidence to show that cleaning and disinfecting brushes or that ultrasonic cleaning will prevent endoscopy-related HAIs. These are both Category II recommendations. There is no recommendation for the use of routine environmental microbiological testing of endoscopes (see Table PE2-2).

Table PE2-2. HICPAC Categorization Scheme for Recommendations

Category IA	A strong recommendation supported by high to moderate-quality evidence suggesting net clinical benefits or harms.
Category IB	A strong recommendation supported by low-quality evidence suggesting net clinical benefits or harms, or an accepted practice (e.g., aseptic technique) supported by low- to very low-quality evidence.
Category IC	A strong recommendation required by state or federal regulation.
Category II	A weak recommendation supported by any quality evidence suggesting a trade-off between clinical benefits and harms.
No Recommendation	An unresolved issue for which there is low- to very low-quality evidence with uncertain trade-offs between benefits and harms.

Source: Table 3. Updated HICPAC Categorization Scheme for Recommendations. In: Umscheid CA, Agarwal RK, Brennan PJ. Updating the Guideline Methodology of the Healthcare Infection Control Practices Advisory Committee (HICPAC). *Am J Infect Control* 2010;38: 264-273. Available at: http://www.ajicjournal.org/article/S0196-6553(09)00953-5/fulltext

Reference: *APIC Text*, 4th edition, Chapter 55 - Endoscopy

CBIC Core Competency: Cleaning, Disinfection, Sterilization, Asepsis

47. (C) 92.5 percent

Rationale: The positive and negative predictive values are the proportions of positive and negative results in statistics and diagnostic tests that are true positive (TP) and true negative (TN) results. The negative predictive value is the proportion of people with negative test results who do *not* have the disease.

Negative predictive value = TN/(FN + TN)

The negative predictive value for this question is calculated as follows:

500 ÷ (40 + 500) = 0.9259 = 92.5 percent

Reference: *APIC Text*, 4th edition, Chapter 13 - Use of Statistics in Infection Prevention

CBIC Core Competency: Surveillance and Epidemiologic Investigation

NOTES

48. (B) A negative result will be more accurate than a positive

Rationale: Sensitivity (also called the true positive rate) measures the proportion of actual positives that are correctly identified as such (e.g., the percentage of sick people who are correctly identified as having the condition). Specificity (sometimes called the true negative rate) measures the proportion of negatives that are correctly identified as such (e.g., the percentage of healthy people who are correctly identified as not having the condition).

Specificity = TN/(TN+FP)

Therefore, a test with 100 percent specificity correctly identifies all patients without the disease.

Reference: *APIC Text*, 4th edition, Chapter 13 - Use of Statistics in Infection Prevention

CBIC Core Competency: Surveillance and Epidemiologic Investigation

49. (B) HCP with artificial nails are more likely to have more Gram-negative bacteria under their nails than HCP with natural nails

Rationale: Whether artificial nails contribute to the spread of HAIs is unknown. However, HCP with artificial nails are more likely to harbor Gram-negative organisms on their fingertips than are those with natural nails. This holds true both before and after hand washing.

References: *APIC Text*, 4th edition, Chapter 27 - Hand Hygiene; Boyce JM, Pittet D. Guideline for hand hygiene in health-care settings. *Morbid Mortal Weekly Rev* 2002;51(RR1):1-44.

CBIC Core Competency: Preventing/Controlling the Transmission of Infectious Agents

50. (C) Performance improvement

Rationale: Performance improvement is measuring the output of a particular process or procedure, then modifying the process or procedure to increase the output, increase efficiency, or increase the effectiveness of the process or procedure. Performance improvement is an ongoing cycle that focuses on patient clinical outcomes and customer satisfaction and service. Measuring performance determines program effectiveness and efficiency and whether proactive approaches or retrospective analysis of high-risk processes can further improve the infection prevention program.

Reference: *APIC Text*, 4th edition, Chapter 16 - Quality Concepts

CBIC Core Competency: Management and Communication

51. (C) No mask is needed

Rationale: According to the HICPAC *2007 Guideline for Isolation Precautions*, there are no recommendations for HCP who are immune to measles and chickenpox (varicella) to wear respiratory PPE. There are also no recommendations for susceptible HCP to wear a surgical mask versus an N95 respirator when caring for patients with measles or chickenpox (varicella).

References: *APIC Text*, 4th edition, Chapter 29 - Isolation Precautions (Transmission-based Precautions); Siegel J, Rhinehart E, Jackson M, et al., and the Healthcare Infection Control Practices Advisory Committee (HICPAC). 2007 Guideline for Isolation Precautions: Preventing Transmission of Infectious Agents in Health Care Settings. *Am J Infect Control* 2007;35(10 Suppl 2): S65- S164. Available at: www.cdc.gov/infectioncontrol/guidelines/isolation/index.html

CBIC Core Competency: Preventing/Controlling the Transmission of Infectious Agents

NOTES

52. **C 24 hours**

Rationale: If a diluted bleach solution is stored in an open container, the chlorine rapidly dissipates and therefore must be prepared daily. When stored in a spray or wash bottle or in a closed, brown opaque container, the bleach solution remains stable for 30 days and will retain 50 percent of its initial value.

Reference: *APIC Text*, 4th edition, Chapter 107 - Environmental Services

CBIC Core Competency: Environment of Care

53. **C Place a surgical mask on the patient**

Rationale: According to the CDC's *2007 Isolation Guidelines*, patient transport outside the room should be limited to medically necessary purposes. If the patient must leave the room, instruct the patient to wear a surgical mask and follow respiratory hygiene and cough etiquette. Once the patient is masked, the patient transporter does not need to wear a surgical mask. Notify the receiving department of the Isolation Precautions status.

References: *APIC Text*, 4th edition, Chapter 29 - Isolation Precautions (Transmission-based Precautions); Siegel JD, Rhinehart E, Jackson M, et al. *2007 Guideline for Isolation Precautions: Preventing Transmission of Infectious Agents in Healthcare Settings.* CDC website. 2007. Available at: http://www.cdc.gov/hicpac/pdf/isolation/isolation2007.pdf.

CBIC Core Competency: Preventing/Controlling the Transmission of Infectious Agents

54. **D February 9**

Rationale: The healthcare worker was given VZIG. Normal time off would be from day 10 through day 21 after exposure, but because VZIG was given, it is recommended to keep the employee off through day 28 (able to return on the 29th day after the exposure).

References: *APIC Text*, 4th edition, Chapter 100 - Occupational Health; Advisory Committee on Immunization Practices (ACIP). *ACIP Recommendations*. ACIP Website. Available at: http://www.cdc.gov/vaccines/acip/recs/index.html

CBIC Core Competency: Employee/Occupational Health

55. **C Sterilization**

Rationale: Sterilization is the term for the process where all microbial life including spores is destroyed. Sterilization may be carried out using steam, hydrogen peroxide gas, ethylene oxide gas, and liquid sterilants.

Reference: CDC Guideline for Disinfection and Sterilization in Healthcare Facilities, 2008, Page 8-9

CBIC Core Competency: Cleaning, Sterilization, Disinfection, Asepsis

NOTES

56. (A) The licensed practical nurse who did not have direct contact with the patient's oral secretions

Rationale: HCP without direct exposure to the patient's oral secretions are considered low risk and chemoprophylaxis is not recommended.

Reference: Meningococcal Infections. In: Pickering LK, ed. *Red Book: 2012 Report of the Committee on Infectious Diseases*, 29th edition. Elk Grove Village, IL: American Academy of Pediatrics, 2012.

CBIC Core Competency: Identification of Infectious Disease Processes

57. (A) A *p* value of 0.05 means that the probability that the observation occurred by chance alone is 1 in 20

Rationale: The level of significance is the probability value arbitrarily chosen by the researcher as the desired level of probability at which one may feel secure in rejecting the null hypothesis. When using sample data, it is not possible to be absolutely certain that the hypothesis being accepted is true. Therefore, a probability that the finding is due to chance is stated. This probability of rejecting a null hypothesis when it is true is the level of significance or α level. Most researchers use 0.05 (5 percent) or 0.01 (1 percent) values for α to minimize the chances of incorrectly rejecting the null hypothesis. This specified level states a sufficiently small likelihood that the given observation could occur by chance variation alone (e.g., 0.05 or a 1-in-20 chance). The researcher finds the appropriate rejection region for a test statistic at a given α level and rejects the null hypothesis for values of the test statistic that lie beyond the specified value. Simply stated, α level is the level of risk of being wrong that a researcher is willing to take. The *p* value is commonly compared to α—the specified significance level of the test. A *p* value of 0.05 indicates that the probability that the observation occurred by chance alone is 0.05 or 1 in 20. That is, a true null hypothesis will be rejected one out of every 20 times.

Reference: *APIC Text*, 4th edition, Chapter 13 - Use of Statistics in Infection Prevention

CBIC Core Competency: Surveillance and Epidemiologic Investigation

58. (A) Compare, discriminate, and differentiate

Rationale: Bloom's taxonomy was developed in the 1950s and is still used today to categorize ways of learning and thinking in a hierarchical structure. A revised model was developed in the 1990s to better fit educational practices of the 21st century. The "Analysis" level refers to the process of breaking material into constituent parts, determining how the parts relate to one another and to an overall structure or purpose through differentiating, organizing, and attributing. Applicable verbs include analyze, appraise, break down, calculate, categorize, classify, compare, contrast, criticize, derive, diagram, differentiate, discriminate, distinguish, examine, experiment, identify, illustrate, infer, interpret, model, outline, point out, question, relate, select, separate, subdivide, test.

Reference: *APIC Text*, 4th edition, Chapter 3 - Education and Training

CBIC Core Competency: Education and Research

NOTES

59. (C) The boxes may harbor dust, bacteria, and insects

Rationale: Corrugated cardboard boxes are not appropriate as storage units in medical or clean supply rooms because the boxes may harbor dust, bacteria, and small insects that have entered during shipping.

Reference: *APIC Text*, 4th edition, Chapter 106 - Sterile Processing

CBIC Core Competency: Environment of Care

60. (B) She should investigate potential sources of special cause variation

Rationale: Statistical process control (SPC) is a method used to monitor both processes and outcomes in a systematic and statistically valid manner. It is a decision-making tool that shows when a process is working correctly and when it is not. This information can then be used to improve quality. Control charts show if a process is in control or out of control. There are eight major rules used to detect special cause variation on a control chart:

1. Any point above the Upper Control Limit or below the Lower Control Limit
2. One of two points above +2 Standard Deviation (SD) or below -2 SD
3. Four of five points above +1 SD or below -1 SD
4. Eight consecutive points above or below the CL
5. Six consecutive points increasing or decreasing
6. Fifteen consecutive points between +1 SD and -1 SD
7. Fourteen consecutive points alternating up and down.
8. Eight consecutive points above +1 SD and/or below -1 SD

Figure PE2-1 depicts an SPC chart where the first and second rules were violated (hollow square data points), indicating special cause variation is present.

Figure PE2-1. Control chart with special cause variation

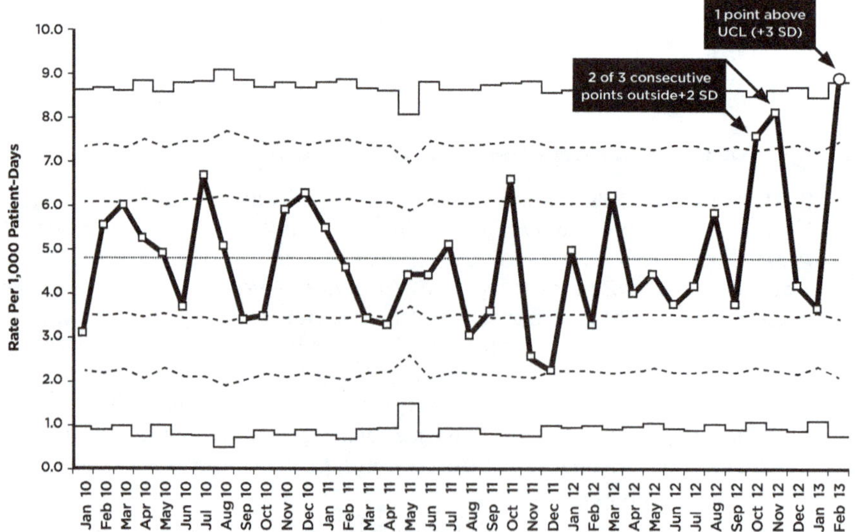

Source: Weimken TL, Kelley RR. Process Control Charts. In: Grota P, ed. *APIC Text of Infection Control and Epidemiology*, 4th edition. Washington, DC: Association for Professionals in Infection Control and Epidemiology, 2014.

Reference: *APIC Text*, 4th edition, Chapter 14 - Process Control Charts

CBIC Core Competency: Surveillance and Epidemiologic Investigation

NOTES

61. **C** **1, 3**

Rationale: Improperly processed bronchoscopes have been associated with outbreaks of infections in healthcare settings. These incidents have been due to inadequate cleaning of the scope, incorrect selection of disinfecting agents, and lapses in following the manufacturer's protocol for cleaning. The organisms that have been most highly associated with improperly processed bronchoscopes are *Mycobacterium tuberculosis* and *Pseudomonas aeruginosa*.

Reference: CDC Guideline for Disinfection and Sterilization in Healthcare Facilities, 2008, Page 15

CBIC Core Competency: Cleaning, Sterilization, Disinfection, Asepsis

62. **D** **Gravity displacement steam sterilizer**

Rationale: A gravity displacement sterilizer works by admitting steam into the sterilizer chamber. The steam has lower density than the air in the chamber, so the steam initially stays at the top of the chamber and then pushes the air out of a drain vent in the bottom of the chamber.

Reference: *APIC Text*, 4th edition, Chapter 106 - Sterile Processing

CBIC Core Competency: Cleaning, Sterilization, Disinfection, Asepsis

63. **C** ***Candida albicans***

Rationale: Fungi are eukaryotic organisms with cell walls containing chitin, cellulose, or both. Yeasts are unicellular organisms that reproduce by budding and typically, but not always, produce circular, mucoid colonies upon culture. Clinically, the most frequently isolated yeasts are *Candida*, of which there are more than 80 species. *Candida* is a normal commensal of the human gastrointestinal and female genital tracts.

Reference: *APIC Text*, 4th edition, Chapter 78 - Fungi

CBIC Core Competency: Identification of Infectious Disease Processes

64. **C** **2, 3**

Rationale: Infectious complications are a common occurrence among patients receiving HSCT. Preventive measures should emphasize provision of a protective environment, appropriate use of prophylactic anti-infective agents, and meticulous attention to infection prevention practices, such as hand hygiene, device management, and the regulation of visitors. Furnishings and fixtures in patient rooms should be easy to clean, and items that trap or collect dust should be avoided. Flowers/plants or their potting materials may harbor large numbers of *Aspergillus* spores and other microorganisms and should be restricted from the patient environment.

Reference: *APIC Text*, 4th edition, Chapter 46 - Hematopoietic Stem Cell Transplantation

CBIC Core Competency: Environment of Care

NOTES

65. Ⓐ **Annual vaccination**

Rationale: Vaccination is the primary method for preventing influenza and its complications. Recommendations for vaccine and antiviral drug use are published regularly by the ACIP. All persons aged 6 months and older should be vaccinated annually unless specific medical contraindications exist.

References: *APIC Text*, 4th edition, Chapter 82 - Influenza; Appendix C. In: Brooks K. *Ready Reference for Microbes*, 3rd edition. Washington, DC: Association for Professionals in Infection Control and Epidemiology, 2012.

CBIC Core Competency: Preventing/Controlling the Transmission of Infectious Agents

66. Ⓒ **10^{-6}**

Rationale: The sterility assurance level (SAL) is the probability of a microbe surviving on an item after sterilization. A SAL of 10^{-6} means that there is at most a 1 in one million chance of an organism having survived. This SAL is considered to be appropriate for critical items.

Reference: CDC Guideline for Disinfection and Sterilization in Healthcare Facilities, 2008, Page 101

CBIC Core Competency: Cleaning, Sterilization, Disinfection, Asepsis

67. Ⓒ **1, 3, 4**

Rationale: The effective use of disinfectants is part of a multibarrier strategy to prevent healthcare-associated infections. CDC Guidelines recommend that noncritical medical equipment surfaces should be disinfected with an EPA-registered low- or intermediate-level disinfectant. Current certification programs for green cleaning products and equipment do not cover EPA-registered disinfectants.

Reference: *APIC Text*, 4th edition, Chapter 107- Environmental Services

CBIC Core Competency: Environment of Care

68. Ⓒ **1, 2, 3**

Rationale: Virtually all healthcare-associated urinary tract infections are caused by instrumentation of the urinary tract. For patients with an indwelling urinary catheter at the time of specimen collection, NHSN criteria for a symptomatic urinary tract infection (SUTI) include:

- Patient had an indwelling urinary catheter in place for > 2 calendar days, with day of device placement being Day 1, and catheter was in place on the date of event
  and
- At least 1 of the following findings:
  - Positive dipstick for leukocyte esterase and/or nitrite
  - Pyuria (urine specimen with ≥ 10 white blood cells [WBC]/mm^3 of unspun urine or >5 WBC/high power field of spun urine)
  - Microorganisms seen on Gram stain of unspun urine
    and
- A positive urine culture of ≥ 10^3 and < 10^5 CFU/mL and with no more than two species of microorganisms. Elements of the criterion must occur within a time frame that does not exceed a gap of one calendar day between two adjacent elements.

References: Centers for Disease Control and Prevention. *Device-Associated Module: CAUTI*. CDC website. January 2014. Available at: http://www.cdc.gov/nhsn/pdfs/pscmanual/7psccauticurrent.pdf; *APIC Text*, 4th edition, Chapter 33 - Urinary Tract Infection

CBIC Core Competency: Identification of Infectious Disease Processes

NOTES

69. (A) Rare outcomes or outcomes that develop over a long time after exposure

Rationale: Case-control studies may be undertaken in a timelier and less-expensive manner than prospective cohort studies because cases may be identified retrospectively, and at least some exposure data are often available through medical record review.

Reference: *APIC Text*, 4th edition, Chapter 20 - Research Study Design

CBIC Core Competency: Education and Research

70. (D) An incidence of disease that is clearly in excess of that expected

Rationale: Outbreaks in healthcare should be suspected when HAIs or adverse events occur above the background rate or when an unusual microbe or adverse event is recognized. Healthcare-associated outbreaks often have multiple causes, but almost all are due to one or more of the following: lapses in infection prevention or clinical practices, colonization or infection of HCP, or defects in or contamination of a product or device, either at the time of production (intrinsic contamination) or during use (extrinsic contamination). Outbreaks in healthcare settings may also be caused by visitors who have, or are harboring, an infectious disease (e.g., influenza or chickenpox).

Reference: *APIC Text*, 4th edition, Chapter 11 - Surveillance

CBIC Core Competency: Surveillance and Epidemiologic Investigation

71. (D) Rendered safe for handling without protective attire

Rationale: Decontamination renders an area, device, item, or material safe to handle (i.e., safe in the context of being reasonably free from a risk of disease transmission). The primary objective is to reduce the level of microbial contamination so that infection transmission is eliminated.

Reference: *APIC Text*, 4th edition, Chapter 31 - Cleaning, Disinfection, and Sterilization

CBIC Core Competency: Cleaning, Sterilization, Disinfection, Asepsis

72. (C) Move immediately to the doffing area to assess the exposure

Rationale: Prior to working with patients with EVD, all healthcare workers must have received repeated training and have demonstrated competency in performing all Ebola-related infection control practices and procedures, and specifically in donning/doffing proper PPE. While working in PPE, healthcare workers caring for patients with EVD should have no skin exposed. If during patient care a partial or total breach in PPE (gloves separate from sleeves leaving exposed skin, a tear develops in an outer glove, a needlestick) occurs, the healthcare worker must move immediately to the doffing area to assess the exposure. Implement the facility exposure plan, if indicated by assessment.

Reference: CDC, Guidance on Personal Protective Equipment To Be Used by Healthcare Workers During Management of Patients with Ebola Virus Disease in U.S. Hospitals, Including Procedures for Putting On (Donning) and Removing (Doffing). Available at: http://www.cdc.gov/vhf/ebola/healthcare-us/ppe/guidance.html

CBIC Core Competency: Employee/Occupational Health

NOTES

73. (B) The patient had Hepatitis B in the past and does not have active disease now; the nurse should complete her Hepatitis B series as scheduled, but no additional treatment is needed

Rationale: HBsAg is a protein on the surface of HBV; it can be detected in high levels in serum during acute or chronic HBV infection. The presence of HBsAg indicates that the person is infectious. The presence of Hepatitis B surface antibody (anti-HBs) is generally interpreted as indicating recovery and immunity from HBV infection. This patient's surface antibody is positive and the surface antigen is negative, indicating that he is immune due to a natural infection. The nurse does not have to take any action.

Reference: *APIC Text*, 4th edition, Chapter 101 - Occupational Exposure to Bloodborne Pathogens

CBIC Core Competency: Employee/Occupational Health

74. (D) Range and standard deviation

Rationale: Measures of dispersion are important for describing the spread of the data or its variation around a central value (mean). Commonly used measures of dispersion are the range, deviation, variance, and standard deviation. The range is the difference between the highest value in a data set and the lowest value. The standard deviation is a measure of how much the data are scattered around the mean and is the square root of the sample variance.

Reference: *APIC Text*, 4th edition, Chapter 11 - Surveillance

CBIC Core Competency: Surveillance and Epidemiologic Investigation

75. (B) Colonization of the catheter hub

Rationale: With short-term intravenous devices (IVDs) (in place fewer than 10 days), such as peripheral IV catheters, arterial catheters, and noncuffed, nontunneled CVCs, most device-associated bloodstream infections (BSIs) are of cutaneous origin, from the insertion site, and gain access extraluminally, occasionally intraluminally. In contrast, contamination of the catheter hub and luminal fluid is the predominant mode of BSI with long-term IVDs (e.g., in place more than 10 days), such as cuffed Hickman- and Broviac-type catheters, subcutaneous central ports, and PICCs.

Reference: *APIC Text*, 4th edition, Chapter 34 - Intravascular Device Infection

CBIC Core Competency: Preventing/Controlling the Transmission of Infectious Agents

76. (A) Minimum inhibitory concentration

Rationale: Minimum inhibitory concentration is the lowest concentration of an antimicrobial that will inhibit the visible growth of a microorganism after overnight incubation. Minimum inhibitory concentrations are important in diagnostic laboratories to confirm resistance of microorganisms to an antimicrobial agent and to monitor the activity of new antimicrobial agents.

Reference: *APIC Text*, 4th edition, Chapter 24 - Microbiology Basics

CBIC Core Competency: Identification of Infectious Disease Processes

NOTES

77. **C** **3, 5**

Rationale: The CDC recommends that exposure-prone invasive procedures should not be performed by HCP with HIV until counsel from an expert review panel is sought. Risks during noninvasive procedures would be minimized with the use of Standard Precautions, but this may not be true for high-risk invasive procedures. An expert review panel can make these determinations and recommendations. State or regional recommendations must be followed. In addition to CDC, the Society for Healthcare Epidemiology of America and the Association for Professionals in Infection Control and Epidemiology provide guidance on this issue.

Reference: *APIC Text*, 4th edition, Chapter 100 - Occupational Health

CBIC Core Competency: Employee/Occupational Health

78. **C** **2, 3**

Rationale: Insufficient planning can lead to compromised air quality and potential for continued environmental contamination from fungi (e.g., *Aspergillus* spp.) or water contaminated with water-associated microorganisms (e.g., *Legionella* spp.) during construction or renovation.

Reference: *APIC Text*, 4th edition, Chapter 116 - Construction and Renovation

CBIC Core Competency: Environment of Care

79. **A** **1, 2, 4**

Rationale: One of the most important roles of the educator is to provide an atmosphere of mutual respect, as well as one that is friendly, informal, and supportive. Eye contact, addressing students by name, listening without interrupting, and acknowledging the validity of problems or opinions expressed are characteristics of an effective educator. The educator must also take steps to create an environment that is comfortable and conducive to learning. The learning space should be private and congenial with careful consideration to seating, room temperature, and lighting. There should be a contact person at the learning site to troubleshoot any facility or technical problems should they occur. The traditional classroom setup with straight rows of desks does not promote interaction.

Reference: *APIC Text*, 4th edition, Chapter 3 - Education and Training

CBIC Core Competency: Education and Research

80. **D** **1, 3, 4**

Rationale: Syndromic surveillance is used for early detection of outbreaks; to follow the size, spread, and tempo of outbreaks; to monitor disease trends; and to provide reassurance that an outbreak has not occurred. Syndromic surveillance systems use existing health data in real time to provide immediate analysis and feedback to those charged with investigation and follow-up of potential outbreaks. The fundamental objective of syndromic surveillance is to identify illness clusters early, before diagnoses are confirmed and reported to public health agencies, and to mobilize a rapid response, thereby reducing morbidity and mortality. Answers 1, 3, and 4 are all examples of syndromic surveillance. The monitoring of chickens for antibodies to arboviruses is an example of sentinel surveillance, which is an alternative to population-based surveillance and involves collecting data from a sample of reporting sites (sentinel sites).

Reference: *APIC Text*, 4th edition, Chapter 11 - Surveillance

CBIC Core Competency: Surveillance and Epidemiologic Investigation

NOTES

81. **C 1, 3**

Rationale: An annual evaluation of the infection prevention program is important to outline achievements and activities of the program and describe support requirements. The value of the infection prevention program to the organization should be emphasized, along with patient outcomes and cost savings.

Reference: *APIC Text*, 4th edition, Chapter 1 – Infection Prevention and Control Programs

CBIC Core Competency: Management and Communication

82. **B Gram-negative**

Rationale: In the Gram stain technique, bacteria are fixed on a slide and a primary stain, crystal violet, is added to the slide. All bacteria will stain purple at this point regardless of their Gram-reaction category. Iodine is added to fix the crystal violet stain to the peptidoglycan layer of the cell wall of the bacteria, and then alcohol is used as a decolorizing agent. Gram-positive bacteria have a thick peptidoglycan layer that will retain the crystal violet stain even after alcohol is added, whereas Gram-negative bacteria have a lipopolysaccharide layer and a thin peptidoglycan layer. The lipopolysaccharide layer will be dissolved with alcohol and the peptidoglycan layer will be decolorized. The counterstain, safranin, will then stain the decolorized Gram-negative bacteria red; the Gram-positive bacteria will continue to appear purple.

Reference: *APIC Text*, 4th edition, Chapter 24 – Microbiology Basics

CBIC Core Competency: Identification of Infectious Disease Processes

83. **C An airborne infection isolation (AII) room**

Rationale: Herpes zoster, also known as zoster and shingles, is caused by the reactivation of the varicella-zoster virus (VZV), the same virus that causes varicella (chickenpox). People with herpes zoster most commonly have a rash in one or two adjacent dermatomes (localized zoster). The rash most commonly appears on the trunk along a thoracic dermatome. The rash does not usually cross the body's midline. However, approximately 20 percent of people have rash that overlaps adjacent dermatomes. Less commonly, the rash can be more widespread and affect three or more dermatomes. This condition is called disseminated zoster. This generally occurs only in people with compromised immune systems. Disseminated herpes zoster can be transmitted by an airborne route, so the patient needs to be placed in an airborne isolation room with negative airflow for the duration of the illness.

Reference: Siegel JD, Rhinehart E, Jackson M, et al. *2007 Guideline for Isolation Precautions: Preventing Transmission of Infectious Agents in Healthcare Settings*. CDC website. 2007. Available at: http://www.cdc.gov/hicpac/pdf/isolation/isolation2007.pdf.

CBIC Core Competency: Preventing/Controlling the Transmission of Infectious Agents

NOTES

84. (A) 20 percent

Rationale: An attack rate is a special form of incidence rate. It is not truly a rate, but a proportion. It is the proportion of persons at risk who become infected over an entire period of exposure or a measure of the risk or probability of becoming a case. It is usually expressed as a percentage and is used almost exclusively for epidemics or outbreaks of disease where a specific population is exposed to a disease for a limited time. The attack rate equals the number of new cases of disease (for a specified time period) divided by the population at risk for the same time period multiplied by 100. Attack rate is the same as incidence rate, except that attack rates are always expressed as cases per 100 populations or as a percentage. The attack rate for this scenario is calculated as follows: 15 ÷ 75 × 100= 20 percent.

Reference: *APIC Text*, 4th edition, Chapter 13 – Use of Statistics in Infection Prevention

CBIC Core Competency: Surveillance and Epidemiologic Investigation

85. (C) CAUTI rate for the ICU

Rationale: Stratification is a form of risk adjustment that involves classifying data into subgroups based on one or more characteristics, variables, or other categories. For example, a measure's population might be stratified by gender before calculating rates, resulting in separate rates for males and females. In infection prevention, it is common to stratify infants by birth weight when assessing infections and infection risk or to stratify sharps injuries by time of day, role, and unit. Each subgroup becomes a separate denominator (population of interest), with the numerator event of interest the same for the subgroups; separate rates are then calculated for each subgroup.

Reference: *APIC Text*, 4th edition, Chapter 17 – Performance Measures

CBIC Core Competency: Surveillance and Epidemiologic Investigation

86. (B) The IP provides essential input into preventing hazardous risks to patients, HCP, and visitors during design and construction projects

Rationale: A key element that IPs bring to the construction and renovation process is creating an environment of care that supports prevention of infection and promotes safety of patients and personnel.

Reference: *APIC Text*, 4th edition, Chapter 116 – Construction and Renovation

CBIC Core Competency: Environment of Care

87. (B) Viruses use the host's cells to replicate

Rationale: It is difficult to designing safe and effective antiviral drugs because viruses use the host's cells to replicate. This makes it challenging to find targets for the drug that would interfere with the virus without also harming the host organism's cells.

Reference: *APIC Text*, 4th edition, Chapter 25 – Laboratory Testing and Diagnostics

CBIC Core Competency: Identification of Infectious Disease Processes

NOTES

88. Ⓑ **Run chart**

Rationale: Run charts are useful for identifying variations and trends, especially when assumptions for construction of control charts are not met. Run charts display observed data that can reveal trends or patterns over a specified period of time. They can be used with any type of data (discrete, continuous, etc.), and do not use any statistical calculations aside from measures of central tendency. They require at least 20 data points for reliability.

Reference: *APIC Text*, 4th edition, Chapter 16 - Quality Concepts

CBIC Core Competency: Surveillance and Epidemiologic Investigation

89. Ⓐ ***Pasteurella***

Rationale: Cat bites are more likely to become infected (28 to 80 percent) than dog bites (3 to 18 percent), and *Pasteurella* spp. (primarily *P. multocida*) is the most common isolate from dogs as well as cats. *Pasteurella* spp. is highly pathogenic, inducing progressive soft tissue infections with a typically rapid onset (often < 24 hours). Streptococci, staphylococci, *Moraxella* spp., *Corynebacterium* spp., and *Neisseria* spp. were the next most common aerobic isolates derived from cat bites.

Reference: *APIC Text*, 4th edition, Chapter 92 - Skin and Soft Tissue Infections

CBIC Core Competency: Identification of Infectious Disease Processes

90. Ⓐ **Determine the instruments to be used and the processing to be done**

Rationale: The OR, Sterile Processing Department, and the IP should meet to review the policy and recommendations for disinfecting and sterilization of the instruments as outlined by the World Health Organization (WHO) and the CDC.

Reference: *APIC Text*, 4th edition, Chapter 73 - Creutzfeldt-Jakob Disease and Other Prion Diseases

CBIC Core Competency: Cleaning, Sterilization, Disinfection, Asepsis

91. Ⓒ **1, 4**

Rationale: Infections classified as urgent threats include carbapenem-resistant Enterobacteriaceae (CRE), drug-resistant gonorrhea, and *Clostridium difficile*, a serious diarrheal infection usually associated with antibiotic use. These are high-consequence threats due to the significant risks identified across several criteria. These threats have the potential to become widespread and require urgent public health attention to identify infections and limit transmission.

Reference: CDC, Antibiotic Resistance Threats in the United States, 2013. http://www.cdc.gov/drugresistance/threat-report-2013

CBIC Core Competency: Identification of Infectious Disease Processes

NOTES

92. (C) Use indirect communication

Rationale: Conflict resolution refers to the methods and processes involved in facilitating the peaceful ending of conflict and preventing retribution. A wide range of methods and procedures for addressing conflict exist and include negotiation, mediation, diplomacy, and creative peace building. Principles of conflict resolution include:

- Use direct communication
- Listen actively
- Think before reacting
- Attack the problem, don't make it personal
- Accept responsibility
- Look for common interests
- Focus on the future

Reference: *APIC Text*, 4th edition, Chapter 3 - Education and Training

CBIC Core Competency: Management and Communication

93. (A) The ages and genders of the people for whom the intervention in being designed

Rationale: The health belief model (HBM) is the oldest theory specifically developed to understand and predict health-associated behavior. An IP can use this model as a theoretical framework to motivate and influence infection prevention behaviors of HCP. The HBM includes key components of perceived susceptibility, perceived severity, perceived benefits, and perceived barriers. According to the HBM, HCP would adhere to hand hygiene if they believed that they were susceptible to infection if they neglected to wash their hands. Education on infection prevention measures may influence HCP's perceived risk of contracting and spreading infection. HCP may perceive severity by understanding the serious consequences of infection caused by poor hand hygiene compliance, such as prolonged hospital stay, expensive medical cost, and increased morbidity. HCP may perceive benefits regarding the effectiveness of hand hygiene practice when it comes to decreasing infection among patients and thereby decreasing HCP's heavy workload.

Reference: *APIC Text*, 4th edition, Chapter 5 - Infection Prevention and Behavioral Interventions

CBIC Core Competency: Education and Research

94. (D) They should use the standard terminal cleaning protocol

Rationale: Anthrax is an illness caused by *Bacillus anthracis*, a spore-forming bacterium. Infection with *Bacillus anthracis* can be acquired through exposure to contaminated soil, water, or animals, including imported animal skin drums. It can also be acquired as a consequence of a bioterrorism event, where the spore form of the agent might be released into the environment. In the case of a naturally-acquired case of anthrax, there is no person-to-person transmission of the agent and no environmental contamination of the patient room with the spores. Therefore, no special cleaning protocol is needed in this case. However, a bioterrorism event with release of spores in the facility would warrant higher level decontamination and would warrant higher level decontamination and cleaning.

Reference: CDC 2007 Guideline for Isolation Precautions: Preventing Transmission of Infectious Agents in Healthcare Settings, Appendix A

CBIC Core Competency: Environment of Care

NOTES

95. (B) 2, 3, 4

Rationale: The emergence and dissemination of carbapenem resistance among Enterobacteriaceae in the United States represent a serious threat to public health. These organisms are associated with high mortality rates and have the potential to spread widely. Clinicians play a critical role in slowing the spread of CRE. Rapidly identifying patients colonized or infected with these organisms and placing them in Contact Precautions when appropriate, using antibiotics wisely, and minimizing device use are all important parts of preventing CRE transmission. Rather than screening all patients on admission, the CDC recommends focusing surveillance testing on patients admitted to certain high-risk settings (e.g., ICUs, long-term acute care) or specific patients (i.e., patients with risk factors, patients admitted from high-risk settings like long-term acute care or transferred from areas with high CRE prevalence).

Reference: *APIC Text*, 4th edition, Chapter 29 - Isolation Precautions (Transmission-based Precautions)

CBIC Core Competency: Preventing/Controlling the Transmission of Infectious Agents

96. (A) 1

Rationale: Multidose eye drops or creams are not acceptable for reuse on other patients if they have been used on a patient with an infectious disease of the eye. If the patient does not have an infectious disease of the eye, then the multidose vial may be used for other patients provided that it has not come into contact with the conjunctiva or tears of a patient. This medication must be used within 28 days of being opened or per the manufacturer's recommendations. Multidose medications that will be used on more than one patient must be stored away from the patient care area.

Reference: *APIC Text*, 4th edition, Chapter 64 - Ambulatory Surgery Centers

CBIC Core Competency: Preventing/Controlling the Transmission of Infectious Agents

97. (C) Antigenic drift of the viruses

Rationale: Antigenic drift refers to small changes in the influenza virus that happen continually over time. Antigenic drift produces new virus strains that may not be recognized by the body's immune system. When such a change occurs, people who have had the illness in the past will lose their immunity to the new strain, and vaccines against the original virus will also become less effective.

Reference: *APIC Text*, 4th edition, Chapter 82 - Influenza

CBIC Core Competency: Employee/Occupational Health

98. (B) 1, 4

Rationale: Cardiac catheterization and associated diagnostic or therapeutic procedures bypass natural host defenses and thereby introduce the risk of infection. The air vent should be cleaned as soon as the room is empty to reduce the exposure of the patient to organisms. Air exchanges should provide three fresh air per 15 total air exchanges per hour. The air vents should be cleaned at least monthly.

Reference: *APIC Text*, 4th edition, Chapter 50 - Cardiac Catheterization and Electrophysiology

CBIC Core Competency: Preventing/Controlling the Transmission of Infectious Agents

NOTES

99. (B) Pulsed-field gel electrophoresis

Rationale: Pulsed-field gel electrophoresis (PFGE) begins with the lysis of organisms and digestion of their chromosomal DNA with restriction enzymes. The fragments are separated into a pattern of discrete bands by switching the direction of the electrical current. This pattern serves as a "bar code" of the bacterial chromosome that can be used to assess the relatedness of different clinical isolates. This test method may be used with any organism from which chromosomal DNA can be properly isolated; it has been used with a wide variety of bacterial pathogens to assess epidemiological interrelationships. PFGE is probably the most widely used method for molecular epidemiology and is generally considered to be the gold standard for most clinically important organisms.

Reference: *APIC Text*, 4th edition, Chapter 24 - Microbiology Basics

CBIC Core Competency: Identification of Infectious Disease Processes

100. (B) Evidence of infestation such as pruritic cutaneous rash

Rationale: Control measures for an outbreak involving one or more cases of crusted scabies should involve rapid and aggressive detection, diagnosis, infection control, and treatment measures because this form of scabies is so highly transmissible. Unrecognized crusted scabies often is the source of institutional outbreaks of scabies. All staff, volunteers, and visitors who may have been exposed to a patient with crusted scabies, or to clothing, bedding, or furniture used by the patient, should be identified and treated.

References: *APIC Text*, 4th edition, Chapter 100 - Occupational Health; Scabies. In: Heymann D, ed. *Control of Communicable Diseases Manual*, 19th edition. Washington, DC: American Public Health Association, 2008.

CBIC Core Competency: Employee/Occupational Health

101. (A) Retrieve unused items from the load

Rationale: Recalling unused items would prevent further possibility of infection in patients and, therefore, should be done first. A written policy and procedure is needed to address who, when, and how to recall reprocessed items. Evidence of sterilization failures (e.g., positive biological indicators) is the most common reason for a recall. In addition, the policy may include compliance components of the Safe Medical Device Act if failure is noted in the reuse of reprocessed items. At a minimum, a log of items within the sterilized load should be reviewed, unused items in the load should be retrieved for reprocessing, functional evaluation of the involved sterilizer should be completed, and surveillance of involved patients should be initiated.

Reference: *APIC Text*, 4th edition, Chapter 106 - Sterile Processing

CBIC Core Competency: Cleaning, Sterilization, Disinfection, Asepsis

102. (C) Is less time consuming and less expensive

Rationale: Case-control studies begin with the identification of persons who have the outcome of interest. Then a control group of individuals without the outcome is selected for comparison. Case-control studies are quicker, easier, and cheaper than cohort studies, especially if outcome is rare or has long latency period.

Reference: *APIC Text*, 4th edition, Chapter 20 - Research Study Design

CBIC Core Competency: Surveillance and Epidemiologic Investigation

NOTES

103. (D) They are more likely to transfer knowledge to practice if education sessions are interactive

Rationale: Research shows that adult learners retain and use more of the knowledge they gain if they are encouraged to apply what they learned. Learning is facilitated when:

- There is immediate application for the learning.
- They participate actively in the learning process.
- They can practice new skills or test new knowledge before leaving a learning session

When participants are involved in their learning, rather then being passive observers, they are more likely to master the information or concepts presented, apply them to their practice, and retain the information presented.

Reference: *APIC Text*, 4th edition, Chapter 3 - Education and Training

CBIC Core Competency: Education and Research

104. (B) 1, 3

Rationale: Discrete data contain whole numbers and are mutually exclusive (e.g., infected or not infected, male or female, blood type). Discrete data can be categorical or noncategorical. Categorical data can count both the number of events/occurrences and the number of nonevents/nonoccurrences (e.g., for 10 SSIs in 100 surgical cases, there are 10 events [SSIs] and 90 nonevents [no SSIs]). Noncategorical data can count the events/occurrences but not the nonevents/nonoccurrences (e.g., number of patient falls per 1,000 patient days). With noncategorical data, the number at risk can be identified, but the actual number of "no infections" or "no falls" among those at risk cannot be identified. Continuous data contain information that can be measured on a continuum or scale and can have numeric values between the minimum and maximum value (a continuum) (e.g., age; serum cholesterol level; temperature, such as 98.6°F, 98.7°F, and 98.8°F; infection rates); continuous data require the process of measuring, rather than counting, and may contain whole numbers, decimals, or percentages. The type of data in this scenario is an example of both discrete data because it contains whole numbers and noncategorical data because it is only counting the events (i.e. infections), not the nonevents.

Reference: *APIC Text*, 4th edition, Chapter 13 - Use of Statistics in Infection Prevention

CBIC Core Competency: Surveillance and Epidemiologic Investigation

NOTES

105. (B) Gap analysis

Rationale: Business and quality professionals describe a gap analysis as a technique to determine the steps to take to move from a current state to a desired future state. A gap analysis begins with (1) listing characteristic factors, such as attributes, competencies, or performance levels of the present situation (what is); (2) listing factors required to achieve the future objectives (what should be); and (3) identifying the highlights or "gaps" that exist within the process and that must be filled to meet a goal or achieve standard compliance. Literature also refers to a gap analysis as a need-gap analysis, needs analysis, and needs assessment (see Table PE2-3 for sample).

Table PE2-3. Sample Gap Analysis

Duty Number	Description	Evidence	Gap/Compliance/ Action
1	To protect patients, staff, and others from HAIs	Joint Commission standard IP.01.05.01 2009 EP: 7	Yes
2	Assess risks of acquiring HAIs and take action to reduce or control such risks	Joint Commission standard IP IP.01.03.01 2009 EP: 5	No; Review risk assessment quarterly and communicate to infection prevention program committee

Reference: *APIC Text*, 4th edition, Chapter 16 – Quality Concepts

CBIC Core Competency: Management and Communication

106. (D) No, the patient cannot be removed from Airborne Precautions, because the sample collection was not sufficient to rule out pulmonary TB

Rationale: Sputum samples for AFB testing for active pulmonary TB must be collected between 8 and 24 hours apart and at least one sample must be an early morning sample. There must be three negative AFB stains to rule out communicable pulmonary TB. In this example the three sample collections are spaced appropriately but there was no early morning sample collected. Therefore, the patient cannot yet be removed from Airborne Precautions.

Reference: Jensen PA, Lambert LA, Iademarco MF, et al. Guidelines for Preventing the Transmission of Mycobacterium tuberculosis in Health-Care Settings, 2005. *MMWR* 2005 December 30. 41(RR-17). 1-141. Available at: http://www.cdc.gov/mmwr/preview/mmwrhtml/rr5417a1.htm?s_cid=rr5417a1_e.

CBIC Core Competency: Identification of Infectious Disease Processes

107. (A) Should be discarded

Rationale: There has been transmission of Hepatitis B and Hepatitis C in dialysis settings, which necessitates rigorous infection control practices. Any medications or patient care supplies such as tape, alcohol swabs, and syringes that come into contact with a dialysis machine should be discarded. Other items should be cleaned if possible before being returned to a common area or used on another patient. If cleaning is not possible, then those items should also be discarded.

Reference: *APIC Text*, 4th edition, Chapter 39 – Dialysis

CBIC Core Competency: Cleaning, Sterilization, Disinfection, Asepsis

NOTES

108. C Respiratory hygiene/cough etiquette

Rationale: Although all options are used to prevent infections, respiratory hygiene/respiratory etiquette measures are specifically designed to limit the spread of respiratory diseases such as influenza. Respiratory hygiene/cough etiquette is an element of Standard Precautions that highlights the need for prompt implementation of infection prevention measures at the first point of encounter with the facility/ambulatory settings (e.g., reception and triage areas). Key recommendations from the CDC for respiratory hygiene/cough etiquette in ambulatory settings include:

- Post signs at entrances with instructions to patients with symptoms of respiratory infection to:
  - Cover their mouths/noses when coughing or sneezing
  - Use and dispose of tissues
  - Perform hand hygiene after hands have been in contact with respiratory secretions
- Provide tissues and no-touch receptacles for disposal of tissues
- Provide resources for performing hand hygiene in or near waiting areas
- Offer masks to coughing patients and other symptomatic persons upon entry to the facility

Provide space and encourage persons with symptoms of respiratory infections to sit as far away from others as possible. If available, facilities may wish to place these patients in a separate area while waiting for care.

Reference: *APIC Text*, 4th edition, Chapter 48 - Ambulatory Care

CBIC Core Competency: Preventing/Controlling the Transmission of Infectious Agents

109. C An evaluation of the surveillance program providing an assessment of its usefulness to the healthcare facility in preventing and controlling infections

Rationale: An annual evaluation of the infection prevention program is important to outline achievements and activities of the program and describe support requirements. The value of the infection prevention program to the organization should be emphasized, along with patient outcomes and cost savings.

Reference: *APIC Text*, 4th edition, Chapter 11 - Surveillance

CBIC Core Competency: Surveillance and Epidemiologic Investigation

110. C Case-control study

Rationale: A case-control study is designed to help determine if an exposure is associated with an outcome (i.e., disease or condition of interest). Case-control studies begin with the identification of persons who have the outcome of interest. Then a control group of individuals without the outcome is selected for comparison. For example, in a study to determine risk factors for healthcare-associated bacteremia, patients with bacteremia are identified and compared with a control group of hospitalized patients without bacteremia; medical records are reviewed to determine exposures to various factors, such as IV devices, invasive monitoring devices, prior infections, and immunocompetence.

Reference: *APIC Text*, 4th edition, Chapter 20 - Research Study Design

CBIC Core Competency: Surveillance and Epidemiologic Investigation

NOTES

111. (B) Plan the educational offering by developing goals and objectives and determining the teaching method to use

Rationale: The educator controls the learning experience with a well-defined plan using goals, objectives, and appropriate teaching methods. Goals are statements that communicate the intent of the curriculum and provide a direction for planning the education session. Expectations are clearly defined in terms of time and available resources.

Reference: *APIC Text*, 4th edition, Chapter 3 - Education and Training

CBIC Core Competency: Education and Research

112. (A) Inoculum of bacteria

Rationale: The probability of infection is determined by the interaction of four clinical variables: (1) inoculum of bacteria, (2) virulence of bacteria, (3) adjuvants in the microenvironment, and (4) efficiency of host defenses. The risk for SSI is related to the number of microorganisms contaminating the wound. A preoperative antiseptic shower or bath decreases skin microbial colony counts. Clinical studies have documented that multiple applications of 2 or 4 percent CHG using a standardized protocol results in high skin surface concentrations sufficient to inhibit/kill skin colonizing flora, including MRSA.

Reference: *APIC Text*, 4th edition, Chapter 37 - Surgical Site Infection

CBIC Core Competency: Preventing/Controlling the Transmission of Infectious Agents

113. (B) Root cause analysis (RCA)

Rationale: The RCA process takes a retrospective look at adverse outcomes and determines what happened, why it happened, and what an organization can do to prevent the situation from recurring. A thorough RCA determines: (1) human and other factors; (2) the process or system involved; (3) underlying causes and effects of the process; and (4) the risks and potential contributions to failure or adverse results.

Reference: *APIC Text*, 4th edition, Chapter 16 - Quality Concepts

CBIC Core Competency: Management and Communication

NOTES

114. (C) 2.25

Rationale: A rate measures the probability of occurrence (i.e., frequency) in a population of some particular event, such as cases of disease or deaths. A rate provides a means of comparing the occurrence of an event in one population to similar populations by adjusting for differences in population sizes.

Basic Formula for All Types of Rates

Rate = x/y × k

Where:

x = The numerator, which equals the number of times the event has occurred during a specified time interval.

y = The denominator, which equals a population from which those experiencing the event were derived during the same time interval.

k = A constant used to transform the result of division into a uniform quantity so that it can be compared with other, similar quantities. A whole number (fractions are inconvenient) such as 100, 1,000, 10,000, or 100,000 is usually used (selection of k is usually made so that the smallest rate calculated has at least one digit to the left of the decimal point) or is determined by accepted practice (the magnitude of numerator compared with denominator).

The annual sharps injury rate per 100 FTE in a facility that has 18 sharp injuries and 800 full-time employees is calculated as follows: (18 ÷ 800) × 100= 2.25. There are 2.25 sharps injuries per 100 FTE per year.

Reference: *APIC Text*, 4th edition, Chapter 13 - Use of Statistics in Infection Prevention

CBIC Core Competency: Employee/Occupational Health

115. (D) The patient might be infected with measles

Rationale: If the patient had been vaccinated or had a history of measles disease, his serum sample would most likely have contained measles-specific IgG antibody. We cannot assume that the patient does not have measles infection at only 24 hours after the onset of rash, as there might not have been enough time yet for the immune response to develop. It can take up to 72 hours after the onset of rash for IgM to be produced in response to measles infection, so this patient might be infected.

Reference: *APIC Text*, 4th edition, Chapter 86 - Measles, Mumps, Rubella

CBIC Core Competency: Identification of Infectious Disease Processes

NOTES

116. **C** **1, 2**

Rationale: In general, outbreak investigations can be divided into two major sections, the initial investigation and the follow-up investigation, each with multiple components.

The primary components of the initial investigation include the following:

- Confirming the presence of an outbreak
- Alerting key partners about the investigation
- Performing a literature review
- Establishing a preliminary case definition
- Developing a methodology for case finding
- Preparing an initial line list and epidemic curve
- Observing and reviewing potentially implicated patient care activities
- Considering whether environmental sampling should be preformed
- Implementing initial control measures

Reference: *APIC Text*, 4th edition, Chapter 12 - Outbreak Investigations

CBIC Core Competency: Surveillance and Epidemiologic Investigation

117. **C** **Outline the major points of the educational program, and ask the audience to work together to identify culturally appropriate examples of the major points**

Rationale: An increasingly diverse workforce has driven the need for increased attention to transcultural competence in training programs. Cultural diversity and a mixed workforce are regarded as organizational strengths. People who do not think alike help to create a competitive advantage when problem solving. Concepts of transcultural care need to be incorporated into successful educational activities. Cultural backgrounds will affect the ability of the learner to participate in learning activities and accommodate new skills and ideas. Transcultural education will encompass different perceptions based on geography, gender, religion, social status, age, sexual orientation, and ethnic diversity. Answer C is correct, as this will allow participants to apply the educational content in a manner that is culturally familiar to them.

Reference: *APIC Text*, 4th edition, Chapter 3 - Education and Training

CBIC Core Competency: Education and Research

118. **A** **Delphi technique**

Rationale: The Delphi technique is a structured communication method that solicits opinions from a panel of experts who answer questionnaires in two or more rounds. After each round, the responses are summarized and redistributed for discussion. The experts are encouraged to revise their earlier answers in light of the replies of other members of their panel. Common trends are identified, outliers are examined and a consensus is reached. Delphi is based on the principle that forecasts (or decisions) from a structured group of individuals are more accurate than those from unstructured groups.

References: *APIC Text*, 4th edition, Chapter 5 - Infection Prevention and Behavioral Interventions; *APIC Text*, 4th edition, Chapter 3 - Education and Training

CBIC Core Competency: Management and Communication

NOTES

119. (C) Herd immunity

Rationale: Herd or community immunity describes a situation in which a sufficient proportion of a population is immune to an infectious disease (through vaccination and/or prior illness) to make its spread from person to person unlikely. Even individuals not vaccinated are offered some protection because the disease has little opportunity to spread within the community.

Reference: *APIC Text*, 4th edition, Chapter 10 - General Principles of Epidemiology

CBIC Core Competency: Surveillance and Epidemiologic Investigation

120. (C) TSTs should be administered at the time of exposure and repeated at 12 weeks postexposure; converters with symptoms should follow up with a chest X-ray

Rationale: TSTs should be administered at the time of exposure to establish the baseline TST reaction. Follow-up TST should occur at 12 weeks postexposure to determine whether infection has occurred. If HCP are symptomatic in conjunction with a TST conversion, they should be screened for active TB by chest X-ray.

Reference: *APIC Text*, 4th edition, Chapter 100 - Occupational Health

CBIC Core Competency: Employee/Occupational Health

121. (B) 2, 3

Rationale: A growth medium or culture medium is a liquid or gel designed to support the growth of microorganisms or cells. There are several categories of growth media, including (1) nutrient agar, a general-purpose growth medium that supports the growth of a wide variety of bacteria (e.g., trypticase soy agar with 5 percent sheep blood); (2) enrichment medium, which contains special nutrients necessary for the growth of hard-to-grow (fastidious) bacteria (e.g., chocolate agar for the growth of *Neisseria meningitidis*); (3) selective media that contain chemicals or antibiotics designed to inhibit normal commensals, allowing organisms of interest to grow (e.g., bismuth sulfate agar for the isolation of *Salmonella spp.*); and (4) differential media that promote the differentiation of specific organisms while inhibiting others (e.g., acetate agar to differentiate *E. coli* from *Shigella*).

Reference: *APIC Text*, 4th edition, Chapter 24 - Microbiology Basics

CBIC Core Competency: Identification of Infectious Disease Processes

122. (C) Inform her that while reduced susceptibility of microbes to disinfectants can occur, the level of disinfectant used is still sufficient to inactivate those microbes

Rationale: As with resistance to antibiotics, microbes can develop altered sensitivity to environmental disinfectant products though spontaneous mutation in the bacterial genome, transmission of transposable resistance genes to the chromosome from a plasmid and vice versa, and transfer of resistance genes on plasmids between microbes. However, decreased sensitivity or increased tolerance to environmental disinfectant products does not render the microbes resistant to these products and the concentrations of product used in the healthcare facility remain cidal for even less sensitive organisms.

Reference: CDC Guideline for Disinfection and Sterilization in Healthcare Facilities, 2008, Page 28

CBIC Core Competency: Environment of Care

NOTES

123. (B) 2, 3, 4

Rationale: To improve hand hygiene compliance, HCP should be provided with evidence-based information about hand contamination, the effects of hand hygiene products on the physiology of normal skin, and the association between hand hygiene practices and transmission of infection. The process of change is complex, and single interventions often fail; therefore, a multimodal, multidisciplinary strategy is necessary to change and improve hand hygiene practices.

Reference: *APIC Text*, 4th edition, Chapter 27 - Hand Hygiene

CBIC Core Competency: Preventing/Controlling the Transmission of Infectious Agents

124. (A) Passive immunity

Rationale: Hepatitis A, caused by infection with HAV, has an incubation period of approximately 28 days (range: 15 to 50 days). HAV replicates in the liver and is shed in high concentrations in feces from 2 weeks before to 1 week after the onset of clinical illness. HAV infection produces a self-limited disease that does not result in chronic infection or chronic liver disease. Current CDC guidelines recommend that persons who have recently been exposed to HAV and who have not been vaccinated previously be administered a single dose of single-antigen Hepatitis A vaccine or Immunoglobulin (IG) (0.02 mL/kg) as soon as possible, within 2 weeks after exposure. IG is an example of passive immunity, which is provided when a person is given antibodies to a disease rather than producing them through his or her own immune system.

Reference: *APIC Text*, 4th edition, Chapter 103 - Immunization of Healthcare Personnel

CBIC Core Competency: Surveillance and Epidemiologic Investigation

125. (A) To resterilize a surgical instrument that was dropped on the floor and for which no replacement is available

Rationale: The Association for the Advancement of Medical Instrumentation (AAMI) defines immediate-use steam sterilization (IUSS) as the "Process designed for cleaning, steam sterilization, and delivery of patient care items for immediate use previously known as flash sterilization." The Association for Operating Room Nurses (AORN) states that IUSS should be kept to a minimum and should only be used in select clinical situations and in a controlled manner. IUSS should only be used when there is insufficient time to process the preferred wrapped or container methods intended for terminal sterilization, and it should not be used as a substitute for sufficient instrument inventory.

Reference: *APIC Text*, 4th edition, Chapter 31 - Cleaning, Disinfection, and Sterilization

CBIC Core Competency: Cleaning, Sterilization, Disinfection, Asepsis

NOTES

126. B RCA

Rationale: The RCA process takes a retrospective look at adverse outcomes and determines what happened, why it happened, and what an organization can do to prevent the situation from recurring. The RCA process avoids individual blame, considers human factors engineering, and analyzes redesign for a safer system. A thorough RCA determines (1) human and other factors; (2) the process or system involved; (3) underlying causes and effects of the process; and (4) the risks and potential contributions to failure or adverse results.

Reference: *APIC Text*, 4th edition, Chapter 16 - Quality Concepts

CBIC Core Competency: Management and Communication

127. C MRSA

Rationale: Community-associated MRSA (CA-MRSA) strains are primarily associated with skin and soft tissue infections; however, they are increasingly causing more invasive infections, including severe CAP. CA-MRSA should be suspected in patients with severe CAP plus hemoptysis, multilobar or cavitary infiltrate seen on chest radiograph, or neutropenia.

Reference: *APIC Text*, 4th edition, Chapter 36 - Pneumonia

CBIC Core Competency: Identification of Infectious Disease Processes

128. B Pseudo-outbreak

Rationale: A pseudo-outbreak is defined as an episode of increased disease incidence due to enhanced surveillance or other factor not related to the disease under study. It is generally applied to situations in which there is a rise in test results (e.g., positive microbiology cultures) without actual clinical disease.

Reference: *APIC Text*, 4th edition, Chapter 12 - Outbreak Investigations

CBIC Core Competency: Surveillance and Epidemiologic Investigation

129. B Declining influenza vaccination rates in HCP

Rationale: Qualitative research methods can be used to study phenomena of interest to IPs, including HCP adherence to infection prevention recommendations (e.g., immunization schedules, hand hygiene, and safe surgical techniques). By using qualitative methods, IPs can systematically identify variables and relationships among variables that influence the practices and behavior of HCP. Qualitative research can be used to determine why HCP are not receiving the flu vaccine.

Reference: *APIC Text*, 4th edition, Chapter 19 - Qualitative Research Methods

CBIC Core Competency: Education and Research

NOTES

130. (B) Animals must be screened to ensure that they are healthy and that their immunizations are current

Rationale: People benefit from the human-animal interaction socially, psychologically, and physiologically. In healthcare-related situations, programs for animal visitation, animal-assisted activities, animal-assisted therapy, and service animals are intended to assist in returning patients to wellness and independence. Healthcare facilities must establish animal and handler guidelines and program-specific infection prevention policies to provide a safe environment for animals, handlers, and patients. Infection prevention policies should stipulate that animals participating in animal-assisted therapy and interventions must be healthy and current with immunizations, including rabies vaccination and others required in the state in which the healthcare facility is located. An annual physical examination by a licensed veterinarian should include dental and dermatological evaluation. Animals should be free of communicable diseases and parasites and be on a flea control program prior to visiting. Animals participating is animal-assisted activities/animal-assisted therapy must be screened and trained to ensure that they have the temperament to tolerate the equipment and environment in a healthcare setting. Personal pets should not be allowed to interact with other patients because of uncertainty regarding temperament and obedience. Service animals are not pets and are defined under the Americans with Disabilities act as "dogs that are individually trained to do work or perform tasks for a person with a disability." Hospitals may exclude service animals from areas such as ORs and burn units if the animal's presence could compromise a sterile environment.

Reference: *APIC Text*, 4th edition, Chapter 122 - Animals Visiting Healthcare Facilities

CBIC Core Competency: Preventing/Controlling the Transmission of Infectious Agents

131. (C) 20 percent

Rationale: The case-fatality rate (CFR) is the proportion of persons with a particular condition (cases) who die from that condition. It is a measure of the severity of the condition. The formula is:

CFR = x/y × k

Where:

x = Number of cause-specific deaths among the incident cases

y = Number of cause-specific deaths among the incident cases

k = Usually an assigned value of 100 when calculating CFR

A CFR is conventionally expressed as a percentage and represents a measure of risk. CFRs are most often used for diseases with discrete, limited time courses, such as outbreaks of acute infections.

The CFR for this scenario is calculated as (200 ÷ 1000) × 100 = 20 percent

Reference: *APIC Text*, 4th edition, Chapter 13 - Use of Statistics in Infection Prevention

CBIC Core Competency: Surveillance and Epidemiologic Investigation

NOTES

132. (D) Number of new cancer diagnoses reported to the cancer registry

Rationale: Syndromic surveillance now includes any indicator that might signal an increase in illness in the community. Some examples of data that could be collected and analyzed as part of a syndromic surveillance program include (1) number of patients seen in an emergency department; (2) number of patients presenting to the emergency department with influenza-like illness as their chief symptom; (3) number of patients admitted to a hospital; (4) number of emergency medical services or ambulance runs performed each day, week, month, or other time period; (5) number of purchases of over-the-counter flu remedies; (6) number of purchases of over-the-counter diarrhea medications; or (7) other data available from healthcare facilities or agencies that may indicate a change or trend in the community.

Reference: *APIC Text*, 4th edition, Chapter 117 - Public Health

CBIC Core Competency: Surveillance and Epidemiologic Investigation

133. (D) Kirby-Bauer test

Rationale: Kirby-Bauer antibiotic testing (KB testing or disc diffusion antibiotic sensitivity testing) is a method to determine the sensitivity of microorganisms to specific antimicrobial drugs; greater drug efficacy yields larger microbe-free zones surrounding drug-containing disks after overnight growth on solid media.

Reference: *APIC Text*, 4th edition, Chapter 25 - Laboratory Testing and Diagnostics

CBIC Core Competency: Identification of Infectious Disease Processes

134. (A) All measures are expressed in monetary (US dollar) terms

Rationale: CBA is a systematic method of estimating the strengths and weaknesses of alternatives that satisfy transactions, activities, or functional requirements for a business. It is a technique that is used to determine options that provide the best approach for adoption and practice in terms of benefits such as labor, time, and cost savings. CBAs can help determine which alternative is a sound investment or decision by comparing the total expected cost of each option against the total expected benefits. The comparison shows whether the benefits outweigh the costs and by how much.

Reference: *APIC Text*, 4th edition, Chapter 1 - Infection Prevention and Control Programs

CBIC Core Competency: Management and Communication

NOTES

135. (C) Perform the treatment in the patient's hospital room

Rationale: While hospitalized, HBsAg-positive chronic hemodialysis patients should undergo dialysis in a separate room and use separate machines, equipment, instruments, supplies, and medications designed only for HBsAg-positive patients. While HBsAg-positive patients are receiving dialysis, staff members who are caring for them should not care for susceptible patients.

References: *APIC Text*, 4th edition, Chapter 39 - Dialysis; Centers for Disease Control and Prevention (CDC). Recommendations for Preventing Transmission of Infections Among Chronic Hemodialysis Patients. *MMWR* 2001 April 27;50(RR05):1-43.

CBIC Core Competency: Preventing/Controlling the Transmission of Infectious Agents

PRACTICE EXAM 2 ASSESSMENT

Category	Total Questions	Number Correct	Percent Correct
Identification of Infectious Disease Processes	22		
Surveillance and Epidemiologic Investigation	24		
Preventing/Controlling the Transmission of Infectious Agents	25		
Employee/Occupational Health	11		
Management and Communication	13		
Education and Research	11		
Environment of Care	14		
Cleaning, Sterilization, Disinfection, Asepsis	15		
Total	135		

The purpose of this assessment is to help the user evaluate his or her strengths and weaknesses by content area, in order to identify topics that may need further study. This practice exam employs similar, but not identical methodology that CBIC uses to score their computer-based tests, and it should not be used as a predictor of actual performance on the CBIC exam.

PRACTICE EXAM 3

QUESTIONS

NOTES

Instructions: Select the correct answer for each question.

1. Which of the following is an accurate statement regarding the antibiogram for *Staphylococcus* isolates shown below?

	Total # of Isolates	Clindamycin	Tetracycline	Trimeth/Sulfa	Vancomycin
Staphylococcus aureus	200	78	92	86	100
MRSA	147	69	93	88	100
Staphylococcus, coagulase-negative	98				100

1) 50 percent of *Staphylococcus aureus* isolates were resistant to Vancomycin
2) 12 percent of MRSA isolates were resistant to Trimeth/Sulfa
3) Clindamycin should not be used for coagulase-negative *Staphylococcus* infections in this facility because 100 percent of isolates were resistant to it
4) There were no cases of Vancomycin-resistant *Staphylococcus aureus* in this facility

a. 2

b. 2, 4

c. 1, 2, 4

d. 1, 2, 3, 4

NOTES

2. The most unlikely method of transmission of infection in a healthcare setting would be:

   a. Airborne

   b. Vehicle

   c. Vector

   d. Contact

3. After an incident in which human milk from one mother was mistakenly fed to another mother's infant, the infection preventionist (IP) is tasked with leading a team to determine why the event occurred and how it can be prevented from happening again in the future. This type of analysis is known as:

   a. Root cause analysis (RCA)

   b. Gap analysis

   c. Strengths-weaknesses-opportunities-threats (SWOT) analysis

   d. Failure mode effect analysis (FMEA)

4. Which one of the following best describes the difference between a common point source outbreak and a propagated outbreak?

   a. Case fatality rates in common source outbreaks are higher

   b. Person-to-person transmission is a feature of common source outbreaks

   c. The attack rate in propagated outbreaks is higher

   d. All cases in a common point source outbreak occur within one incubation period of the exposure

5. Which of the following aid in the diagnosis of pseudomembranous colitis (PMC)?

   1) Colonoscopic biopsy of lesions

   2) Raised antibody levels in blood to *Clostridium difficile* toxin

   3) Positive blood culture for *Clostridium difficile*

   4) Stool assays for *Clostridium difficile*

      a. 1, 2

      b. 2, 3

      c. 3, 4

      d. 1, 4

NOTES

6. A patient is admitted with fever, nausea and vomiting, sensitivity to light, and stiff neck. Symptom onset has been progressing slowly over several weeks. The Gram stain of the cerebrospinal fluid (CSF) is India ink positive, and there is low glucose and predominant lymphocytes. What type of precautions is required for this patient?

   a. Standard plus Droplet Precautions

   b. Standard Precautions

   c. Standard plus Airborne Precautions

   d. Standard plus Contact Precautions

7. How can streptococci be differentiated from staphylococci under the microscope following the Gram stain procedure?

   a. Staphylococci are Gram positive cocci, while streptococci are Gram positive bacilli

   b. Staphylococci are Gram negative bacilli, while streptococci are Gram negative cocci

   c. Staphylococci are Gram positive, while streptococci are Gram negative

   d. Staphylococci are Gram positive and grow in grape-like clusters, while streptococci which are also Gram positive, grow in chains

8. Frequency histograms and polygons are most useful for variables of what level of measurement?

   1) Interval scale

   2) Ratio scale

   3) Nominal scale

   4) Ordinal scale

      a. 1, 2

      b. 1, 3

      c. 2, 3

      d. 3, 4

NOTES

9. Which of the following is the correct order for disinfecting endoscopes?

a. High-level disinfection, rinse the scope with sterile water, flush the channels with 70 to 90 percent alcohol, dry using forced air

b. Rinse the scope using sterile water, high-level disinfection, flush the channels with 70 to 90 percent alcohol, dry using forced air

c. Flush the channels with 70 to 90 percent alcohol, rinse the scope using sterile water, high-level disinfection, dry using forced air

d. Dry using forced air, high-level disinfection, flush the channels with 70 to 90 percent alcohol, rinse the scope using sterile water

10. The lead IP is invited to participate in an employee health process improvement project. The goal of the project is to improve influenza vaccination rates among employees. A multidisciplinary team is formed with representation from front-line employees. After conducting a root cause analysis (RCA), the team develops a proposal for improvement to present to the facility leadership team. Which of the following elements should be included as part of the proposal to most clearly communicate to the leadership team the factors contributing to the facilities' current vaccination rate among employees?

a. A timeline for implementing improvement activities

b. A Pareto chart

c. A fishbone diagram with an explanation

d. A strategic plan

NOTES

11. An IP wants to make external comparisons of the data collected relating to catheter-associated urinary tract infections (CAUTI) in the Intensive Care Unit (ICU). Which of the formulas below will allow the IP to accurately benchmark against nationally available data?

a. The number of ICU patients with urinary catheters in a given month divided by the number of urinary tract infections identified in the same month times 1,000

b. The number of ICU urinary tract infections identified in a given month divided by the number of urinary catheter days in the same month times 1,000

c. The number of urinary catheters used in the ICU in a given month divided by the number of urinary tract infections identified in the same month times 1,000

d. The number of urinary tract infections identified in a given month divided by the total number of patient days in the ICU in the same month times 1,000

12. A 16-year-old male is brought to the ER with a fever, and a wound on his left leg that is draining purulent material. He complains of swelling and pain. He is a quarterback on the high school football team and has several turf burns on both legs. Past medical history is insignificant. The culture grows gram-positive organisms in clusters. What is the most likely differential diagnosis?

a. Parasitic infection

b. Atypical mycobacterium infection

c. Methicillin resistant *Staphylococcus aureus*

d. *Streptococcus pyogenes*

13. The IP has worked with the Preoperative Services manager to plan and implement practices to help decrease the bioburden of microorganisms on patients' skin prior to planned surgeries. Which of the following might be included in their plan?

1) Active surveillance culturing for epidemiologically significant organisms

2) Preoperative showering using antimicrobial soap

3) Preoperative antibiotics given prior to the "cut time"

4) Treatment of remote site infections prior to surgery

a. 1, 2, 3

b. 1, 2, 4

c. 2, 3, 4

d. 1, 3, 4

NOTES

14. Which of the following employee infections would require that the healthcare worker be restricted from patient contact?

a. Sinus infection being treated by antibiotic

b. Small, painful vesicular lesion on the fingertip

c. Shingles, which has been treated with an antiviral for past 4 days

d. Dry, crusted lesion on right arm with no new drainage

15. You are participating in a team to select and evaluate novel environmental disinfectant products. When preparing a presentation to the team on the advantages of ultra violet (UV) irradiation, it is important to include information on:

1) Patients may remain in the room with the device operating

2) Decontamination can be achieved in 2.5 hours

3) HVAC system does not need to be disabled

4) Ability to achieve reductions in vegetative bacteria

a. 1, 4

b. 2, 4

c. 3, 4

d. 1, 3

16. Which part of a published research study contains a brief summary of the entire research process with interpretation of data, conclusions from the data, limitations of the study and recommendations for further research?

a. Introduction

b. Methods

c. Results

d. Discussion

17. An IP conducts an audit of the kitchen at an acute care facility. Which of the following would be a concern?

a. Food servers wearing a plain wedding band

b. Vegetables stored below raw meat in the refrigerator

c. Nonabsorbent cutting boards

d. Food stored 6 inches above floor

NOTES

18. As the sample size increases, what tends to happen to the 95 percent confidence interval?

a. The margin of error increases

b. They become more precise

c. They become wider

d. They become less precise

19. Which of the following is *not* an Occupational Safety and Health Administration (OSHA) requirement for healthcare linens?

a. Employers must launder all workers' personal protective garments or uniforms that are contaminated with blood or other potentially infectious materials (OPIM)

b. Contaminated textiles should be bagged or otherwise contained at their point of use

c. In the laundry facility, positive pressure should be maintained in the area where contaminated textiles are received

d. Wet contaminated laundry must be placed in leakproof and color-coded or labeled containers at the location where it was used

20. The microbiology lab calls the IP with a CSF Gram stain result. From an infection prevention and control standpoint, the most concerning result would be:

a. Gram-negative rods

b. Gram-positive cocci in pairs

c. Acid-fast bacilli

d. Gram-negative diplococci

21. The reservoir of microbes of pathogens present in potable water and its delivery network include:

1) *Staphlococci*

2) *Pseudomonas* spp.

3) Nontuberculous *Mycobacteria*

4) Arthrobacter spp.

a. 1, 2

b. 2, 3

c. 1, 4

d. 2, 4

NOTES

22. Which of the following is conducted to reduce construction hazard risk?

a. Mitigation

b. Preparedness

c. Response

d. Recovery

23. A patient is admitted with watery diarrhea and abdominal cramps. The food history interview reveals that the patient consumed raw oysters recently. Which of the following organisms is the most likely cause?

a. *Yersinia*

b. *Clostridium difficile*

c. *Vibrio*

d. *Campylobacter*

24. A patient with a history of a cough greater than 3 weeks, night sweats, weight loss and a chest x-ray "suspicious for tuberculosis (TB)" is scheduled for a bronchoscopy. The procedure should be performed in which setting?

a. The Operating Room under positive pressure

b. Radiology

c. An airborne infection isolation room with negative airflow

d. Procedure room in Endoscopy

25. A patient tells his nurse that he thinks his apartment is infested with bed bugs. Upon examination, the nurse finds bites on the patient's legs. The nurse contacts you for direction. Your response to the nurse is:

a. Assess the hospital room for mosquitoes

b. Place the patient's belongings is a plastic bag and tie securely

c. Request that the belongings be incinerated

d. This might be a rash related to a new antimicrobial that the patient is taking

NOTES

26. A p value expressed as $p < 0.01$ indicates:

a. The possibility of these results occurring by chance alone is very small, so therefore, the result is not significant

b. The possibility of these results occurring by chance alone is less than 1 in 100 and, therefore, significant enough to prove causality

c. The null hypothesis should be rejected and the alternative hypothesis should be accepted

d. The null hypothesis should be accepted

27. Which of the following must be documented when using soaking solutions for cleaning instruments?

1) Monitoring the temperature of the solution

2) Monitoring the room temperature

3) Monitoring the humidity of the room

4) The time the instruments soaked

a. 1, 2

b. 2, 4

c. 3, 4

d. 1, 4

28. The Director of Infection Prevention and Control and her infection prevention staff have decided to develop a clinical practice guideline to decrease the rate of CLABSIs in their facility. The goal is to reduce variation in practice and improve clinical outcomes. Of the choices below, what is important to remember when developing this guideline?

a. The guideline should be no more than two pages in length to ensure compliance

b. The guideline should categorize and compare data against a unit of measurement

c. The guideline should identify, summarize, and evaluate the highest-quality evidence and most current data in the literature

d. The guideline should identify how process specifications change over time

NOTES

29. The air exchanges in the decontamination area of Sterile Processing should be negative with a minimum of how many air exchanges per hour?

a. Six

b. Eight

c. Nine

d. Ten

30. A hospital has admitted an immunocompetent patient with localized herpes zoster. During unit rounds, the IP notes a sign on the door that says "No pregnant women." How should the IP best respond to this?

a. Leave the sign on the door because the patient poses a high risk of disease transmission to pregnant women

b. Remove the sign from the door but ask the charge nurse to not assign the patient to any pregnant HCP and to prevent pregnant visitors from entering the room

c. Remove the sign from the door and place the patient on both Contact and Airborne Precautions

d. Remove the sign from the door and ensure that all lesions are completely covered; Standard Precautions are sufficient to prevent the spread of the virus

31. Which of the following is *not* a component of the Needlestick Safety and Prevention Act?

a. Provide safety-engineered sharps devices and needleless systems to employees to reduce the risk of occupational exposure to bloodborne diseases

b. When selecting safety-engineered products, solicit input from employees who provide direct patient care and have a high risk of injuries from contaminated sharps

c. Maintain a sharps injury log to record injuries from contaminated sharps

d. Require the Hepatitis A vaccine for all employees who are at risk for occupational exposure

NOTES

32. Using Improved Hydrogen Peroxide offers many advantages. Those advantages are:

1) Rapid action
2) Low toxicity
3) Effective against spores
4) Low cost

a. 1, 2

b. 2, 3

c. 2, 4

d. 1, 4

33. Scabies is transmitted through:

a. Sharing combs and brushes

b. Handling books or magazines after a person infested with scabies

c. Direct contact with infested skin

d. Scabies mites crawling from person to person

34. Between cases in the operating room, the floors must cleaned and disinfected as follows:

a. Floors are only cleaned at the end of the day unless organic debris is present

b. The entire floor must be flooded and cleaned between each case

c. Spot clean the floor only if visible blood/body fluids

d. It is only necessary to clean a 3 to 4 foot perimeter around the table, unless a wider contamination area is identified

NOTES

35. A patient with a confirmed diagnosis of varicella (chickenpox) is seen in a busy ED. The staff at the registration desk immediately placed a mask on the patient until he could be moved to a negative airflow room in the ED, where he then removed his mask. A pregnant environmental services (EVS) employee, who is nonimmune to varicella, enters the room before an isolation sign is posted. She spends 6 minutes in the room with the patient, who is no longer wearing a mask. Which of the following is the most appropriate postexposure response?

a. Give the EVS employee VZIG and place off work from day 10 through day 28

b. Administer the varicella vaccine immediately and place employee off work from day 10 through day 21

c. Have the employee wear a mask from day 10 through day 21 after the exposure and watch for signs and symptoms of disease

d. Give the EVS employee the vaccine and VZIG and keep off work from day 10 through day 28 after the exposure

36. Training on the use of PPE for environmental service employees must include:

1) When to wear PPE

2) The limitations of each type of PPE

3) Maintenance of PPE

4) The cost of PPE

a. 1, 2, 3

b. 2, 3, 4

c. 1, 3, 4

d. 1, 2, 4

37. Bed bugs can survive without feeding for:

a. 48 hours

b. 24 days

c. 6 month

d. 1 year

NOTES

38. A culture of a patient's dialysis access site grew Gram-positive cocci. One of the factors contributing to this type of infection is:

a. Contamination of the water used in dialysis

b. Skin colonization with *S. aureus* at the access site

c. Contamination of the antiseptic used to prep the access site

d. Seeding of the access site by remote sites of infection

39. During outbreaks, the CDC recommends that high-touch surfaces in patient rooms be cleaned and disinfected:

a. At least three times a day

b. Hourly

c. At least twice a day

d. Only when soiled

40. A patient has been admitted to a healthcare facility with *Neisseria meningitidis* and placed on Droplet Precautions. When can the patient be removed from Droplet Precautions?

a. After three consecutive CSF cultures are negative for *N. meningitidis*

b. After the signs and symptoms of meningitis have resolved

c. 24 hours after initiation of effective therapy

d. The patient should remain on Droplet Precautions for the duration of the hospital stay

41. Which would be the most objective method to determine the need for education about hand washing for a group of employees on a unit?

a. Observational studies

b. Personal interviews

c. Focus group discussions

d. Test development

42. The IP is selecting a process measure in order to monitor and evaluate quality of care. An example of a process measure is:

a. SSI after a hip replacement

b. Conjunctivitis

c. Hepatitis B immunity rates

d. Tuberculin skin test (TST) conversions

NOTES

43. IPs should have a thorough understanding of the following when choosing a cleaning product:

1) Differences among types and uses of disinfectants
2) Manufacturing companies that produce and sell disinfectants
3) Definitions of the terms cleaning, sanitization, disinfection and sanitizer
4) Manufacturer's recommendations for use, including dilution and contact time

a. 1, 2, 3

b. 2, 3, 4

c. 1, 3, 4

d. 1, 2, 4

44. The Surgical Scheduling Department called the IP stating that a patient scheduled for surgery in on December 24 will need to reschedule his procedure due to an exposure to scarlet fever on December 3. He has no signs or symptoms. How should the IP respond?

a. The incubation period for scarlet fever is usually 1 to 7 days; he is outside the incubation period and will be able to have his surgery on the scheduled date

b. The procedure should be rescheduled

c. Request an order from the surgeon for antibiotics to treat the possible exposure

d. Place the patient in Isolation Precautions upon admission

45. Which of the following helps to prevent the aerosolization of spores during dusting?

1) A damp paper towel
2) A chemically treated cloth or dust mop
3) A microfiber cloth or dust mop
4) A dry cotton wash cloth

a. 1, 2

b. 2, 3

c. 1, 4

d. 2, 4

NOTES

46. A physician would like to use a new screening test for methicillin-resistant *Staphylococcus aureus* (MRSA), which is highly prevalent in the hospital population. The screening test has a sensitivity of 98 percent and a specificity of 58 percent. Which of the following conclusions is most accurate about this screening test?

1) The test will be very effective in correctly identifying people who have MRSA
2) The test will be very effective in correctly identifying people who do not have MRSA
3) The test will yield very few false-negative results
4) The test will yield very few false-positive results

a. 1, 3

b. 1, 4

c. 2, 3

d. 2, 4

47. The risk of infection or adverse reactions in the Dialysis Unit can be reduced by which of the following interventions?

1) Test patients and staff for MRSA colonization and treat as needed
2) Adhere to aseptic technique during all dialysis procedures
3) Have patient cleanse the access site with soap and water daily and prior to dialysis
4) Have patients take a prophylactic antibiotic prior to dialysis

a. 1, 3

b. 2, 3

c. 1, 2

d. 1, 3

NOTES

48. An IP is interested in evaluating whether her educational program on utilizing PPE has led to applied changes in practice. What is the best method of determining this?

a. Use a pretest and posttest evaluation to see how knowledge of PPE use has changed after the educational program

b. Use formative evaluation of the program so she can make necessary changes before it is implemented

c. Use exit questionnaires to find out whether participants intend to implement their new knowledge in a practice situation

d. Ask the supervisor to collect data on direct observation of practice

49. An IP is carrying out a case-control study to find out whether patients of Surgeon A had a higher likelihood of SSI than the patients of Surgeon B. The data collected show that Surgeon A operated on 300 patients and Surgeon B operated on 350 patients. Of Surgeon A's patients, 25 developed an SSI. Of Surgeon B's patients, 50 developed an SSI. Which of the following 2 × 2 tables correctly presents this data?

a.

	With Outcome	Without Outcome
Exposed	25	275
Unexposed	50	300

b.

	With Outcome	Without Outcome
Exposed	300	25
Unexposed	350	50

c.

	With Outcome	Without Outcome
Exposed	25	300
Unexposed	50	350

d.

	With Outcome	Without Outcome
Exposed	50	350
Unexposed	25	300

NOTES

50. A patient who was recently vaccinated against smallpox has been admitted to a healthcare facility for a condition unrelated to the immunization. The charge nurse would like to know what type of precautions this patient needs.

a. Standard Precautions

b. Contact Precautions

c. Droplet Precautions

d. Contact and Airborne Precautions

51. The organization that would most likely survey a U.S.-based hospital's blood bank for compliance would be:

a. Occupational Safety and Health Administration (OSHA)

b. Food and Drug Administration (FDA)

c. Environmental Protection Agency (EPA)

d. Centers for Disease Control and Prevention (CDC)

52. *C. difficile* spores can survive in the environment for:

a. 24 months

b. 3 months

c. 5 months

d. 12 months

53. Which of the following describes aerobic bacteria?

a. Do not require oxygen to grow and are harmed by its presence

b. Require oxygen to grow and survive

c. Can grow with or without oxygen

d. Do not require oxygen for growth but tolerate the presence of it

54. A 70-year-old patient is admitted with symptoms of rapid neurological degeneration. The physician orders the following diagnostic tests: 14 - 3 - 3 spinal fluid assay, an electroencephalogram (EEG), and magnetic resonance imaging (MRI). These tests, if positive, may indicate a possible diagnosis of:

a. A brain tumor

b. Viral encephalopathy

c. Multiple sclerosis

d. Creutzfeldt-Jakob disease

NOTES

55. A paramedic has been exposed to a patient's blood. The patient is Hepatitis B e Antigen (HBeAg) positive and the paramedic is Anti-HBc and Anti-HBs positive. What is the risk of the paramedic acquiring Hepatitis B infection from the source patient?

- **a.** There is no risk of infection for the paramedic because he was previously infected and is now immune
- **b.** There is no risk of infection for the paramedic because the patient is not infected
- **c.** There is no risk of infection for the paramedic because he is immune due to vaccination
- **d.** There is a high risk of infection for the paramedic

56. What column lists the numerator for each category?

High-risk category	Total number ofpatients screened	Total number of patients in category	Rate of screening compliance
Preoperative patients for high-risk surgery	191	194	98.5%
Transfers into ICU	262	268	97.8%
Transfers from other facilities	90	186	48.4%
Total Screening Compliance	543	648	83.8%

- **a.** Total number of patients screened
- **b.** Total number of patients in category
- **c.** High-risk category
- **d.** Rate of screening compliance

57. Subjects are said to be randomly assigned when:

- **a.** They are assigned to experimental and control groups from a sample representative of the larger experimental group
- **b.** They have an equal chance of being assigned to either the experimental or the control group
- **c.** They are assigned to experimental and control groups so that the groups differ on a critical variable
- **d.** Both the researcher and the subject are blinded as to know whether the subject is in the control group or the experimental group

NOTES

58. Privacy curtains are high-touch items that should be changed and cleaned:

1) On a routine schedule and when soiled
2) During construction
3) According to manufacturer's instructions
4) After a patient on Contact Isolation is discharged or transferred

a. 1, 2
b. 2, 3
c. 3, 4
d. 1, 4

59. Examples of high-level disinfectants are:

1) Glutaraldehyde
2) Hydrogen peroxide
3) Enzymatics
4) 70 percent ethyl alcohol

a. 1, 3
b. 1, 2
c. 2, 3
d. 1, 4

60. A patient with MRSA infection has been admitted and is in need of physical therapy. The physical therapist would like the patient to ambulate in the hall. The IP should recommend:

a. The patient should not ambulate in the hall
b. The patient may ambulate but only outside of the hospital
c. The patient may ambulate in the hallway if attendants wear appropriate PPE
d. The patient may ambulate in the hallway if he washes his hands and wears a clean gown

61. The IP is a member of an interdisciplinary team that has been given administrative oversight for its planning, activity scheduling, and expenditures under $500. This type of team is best described as:

a. Cross-functional
b. Virtual
c. Autonomous
d. Self-managed

NOTES

62. Commercial third-party reprocessors are regulated by which government agency?

a. Centers for Disease Control and Prevention (CDC)

b. Environmental Protection Agency (EPA)

c. Center for Medicaid/Medicare Services (CMS)

d. Food and Drug Administration (FDA)

63. An orthopedic surgeon is requesting that all "dirty" cases be scheduled for the end of the day. The IP's response is to:

a. Ask the Director of Surgical Services to comply with his request

b. Explain to the surgeon that operating rooms are cleaned after each case and that there is no benefit to scheduling procedures at the end of the day

c. Provide the surgeon with the cleaning policy and ignore his request

d. Request a meeting with the Environmental Services director to discuss

64. A patient is suspected of having bacterial meningitis. A CSF sample was taken and had the following results: opening pressure was normal, glucose concentration was normal, lymphocytes were the predominant inflammatory cell, white blood cell (WBC) count was 88 per cubic mm, protein was normal, and the Gram and AFB stains were negative. Given these results, which of the following organisms could be the cause of the meningitis?

a. Herpes simplex virus

b. *Haemophilus influenzae*

c. *Mycobacterium avium*

d. *Streptococcus pneumonia*

65. During an inservice for new employees, the IP describes how Hepatitis B and human immunodeficiency virus (HIV) are transmitted. A major difference in the epidemiology of the two diseases is:

a. Presence of the causative agent in body fluids

b. The ability of the diseases to be transmitted during sexual intercourse

c. The risk of transmission through needlestick exposures

d. The potential for airborne transmission

NOTES

66. Which of the following are attributes of a culture of safety in a healthcare organization?

1) All HCP accept responsibility for safety
2) The organization prioritizes safety over financial and operational goals
3) Only personnel in leadership positions may report safety issues
4) The organization prioritizes identifying and reprimanding individuals who are responsible for accidents

a. 1, 2
b. 2, 3
c. 3, 4
d. 1, 4

67. Last year, a hospital identified 21 CLABSIs. Which type of chart would be most useful to provide feedback regarding the effectiveness of CLABSI reduction strategies?

a. Control chart
b. Pie chart
c. Run chart
d. Display of normal distribution and standard deviation

68. Which of the following are allowed in an ICU or other unit with immunocompromised patients?

a. Latex-free balloons
b. Flowers in a vase
c. Fresh fruit
d. Fish tank

69. Which of the following educational tools is most effective to bridge the learning gap between theory and actual practice?

a. Case study
b. Lecture
c. Computer-based training
d. Game

NOTES

70. The incidence of VRE in the Burn Unit last quarter was 3.0, and the incidence of VRE in the Bone Marrow Transplant Unit last quarter was 1.0. What was the relative risk (RR) of new cases of VRE in the Burn Unit compared to the Bone Marrow Transplant Unit?

a. RR = 3.0

b. RR = 0.33

c. RR = 4.0

d. RR = 2.0

71. There has been a major bioterrorism event in the area, as is evidenced by a large number of patients being admitted to local healthcare facilities with fever >101.1° F and respiratory symptoms that are progressing rapidly. Health officials are currently unaware of the causative organism. What type of Isolation Precautions are warranted in this situation?

a. Standard Precautions

b. Droplet Precautions

c. Airborne Precautions

d. Contact and Airborne Precautions

72. The IP has identified an increased incidence of catheter-related bloodstream infections in the NICU. The IP is preparing her report for presentation to the Infection Prevention Committee. Among the following actions listed, which should be included in the IP's report as the next step?

a. Changing the type of catheter used

b. Using a multidisciplinary approach to determine corrective actions

c. Revising the NICU admission policy

d. Revising the NICU staffing plan

NOTES

73. You have been invited to tour a commercial third-party reprocessor that your organization is considering using to reprocess some equipment. As the IP, you should request to observe which of the following?

1) Observe the cleaning and decontamination process
2) Observe hand hygiene
3) Sterilizing load preparation process
4) New employee orientation

a. 1, 2
b. 2, 4
c. 2, 3
d. 1, 3

74. An example of a molecular testing methodology is:

a. Gram stain
b. Culture
c. Polymerase chain reaction (PCR)
d. Point-of-care testing

75. There is a bioterrorism event in a city. Patients are presenting to the Emergency Room with blurred vision, descending symmetrical flaccid paralysis, and respiratory failure. The most likely bioterrorism disease is:

a. Botulism
b. Pneumonic plague
c. Viral hemorrhagic fever
d. Smallpox

76. A healthcare facility requires TB screening for all employees at time of hire using two-step tuberculin skin test (TST) with purified protein derivative (PPD). A newly hired employee has provided documentation of one negative TST from 6 months prior. Which of the following actions should the IP recommend?

a. No additional TSTs are needed
b. Place one additional TST and screen for symptoms
c. Place two TSTs 1 week apart
d. Obtain a chest X-ray on the employee

NOTES

77. Which of the following is an example of a continuous data set?

1) Body temperature measurements: 98.6°F, 97.4°F, 99.8°F, 99.9°F
2) Gender: male, male, female, male
3) Blood type: O+, A-, A+, AB+
4) Body weight: 189, 144, 261, 113

a. 1, 2

b. 2, 3

c. 2, 4

d. 1, 4

78. Which of the following refers to the ability to evaluate, compare, analyze, critique, and synthesize information?

a. Inductive thinking

b. Critical thinking

c. Transductive thinking

d. Deductive thinking

79. The greatest concern in an emergency situation involving a patient with nontraditional body piercing is:

a. Bleeding from areas of high vascularity

b. Hematogeneous spread of bacteria to other sites

c. Not being familiar with the opening mechanism of the jewelry to be able to remove it

d. Causing distress to the patient

80. A patient in your facility has an infection with *Cryptosporidium parvum*. Which disinfectant would you recommend for use on potentially contaminated patient equipment?

a. Ethyl alcohol

b. Six percent hypochlorite

c. Ortho-phthalaldehyde

d. Six percent hydrogen peroxide

NOTES

81. The Infection Control Risk Assessment (ICRA) should include all of the following elements related to building design features *except*:

a. Sewage systems to allow adequate sanitation of waste

b. Location of special ventilation and filtration of heating, ventilation, air conditioning (HVAC) serving areas, such as ED waiting and intake areas

c. Water systems to limit Legionella spp. and other waterborne opportunistic pathogens

d. Air handling and ventilation for surgical services and airborne infection isolation (AII)

82. An infection prevention consultant is reviewing projected expenses for the next 2 years. Although all of the following are necessary to support the consultancy, which is considered a capital expense?

a. An increase in office rent over 2 years

b. Personal liability insurance

c. Building utilities in which the office is located

d. Expanded computer hardware and software

83. Which of the following recommendations related to disinfection and sterilization in healthcare facilities is a CDC category 1A recommendation?

1) "Before use on each patient, sterilize critical medical and surgical devices and instruments that enter normally sterile tissue or the vascular system or through which a sterile body fluid flows"

2) "Meticulously clean patient-care items with water and detergent, or with water and enzymatic cleaners before high-level disinfection or sterilization procedures."

3) "In hospitals, perform most cleaning, disinfection, and sterilization of patient-care devices in a central processing department in order to more easily control quality."

4) "Perform low-level disinfection for noncritical patient-care surfaces (e.g., bedrails, over-the-bed table) and equipment (e.g., blood pressure cuff) that touch intact skin"

a. 1

b. 1, 3

c. 1, 2, 4

d. 1, 2, 3, 4

NOTES

84. The IP is consulted prior to the construction of a new unit in her hospital. The design that is most concerning to her is:

a. All rooms (AIIR) that have negative air pressure

b. Protective environment rooms that have positive air pressure

c. Dual-purpose rooms that can alternate between negative and positive air pressure

d. All rooms with neutral air pressure

85. Which of the following clinical uses would *not* be indicated for Gram stain results?

a. Early identification of antibiotic resistance

b. Initial direction for empiric antibiotic treatment

c. Quality of the specimen

d. Need for Isolation Precautions

86. What species of the streptococci can be transferred to an infant during delivery?

a. Streptococcus pyogeses

b. Xanthomonas

c. Streptococcus agalactiae

d. Enterococcus faecalis

87. An IP recommends that chlorhexidine gluconate (CHG) be used to prepare a site for the insertion of a peripherally inserted central catheter (PICC) because it:

1) Requires only 30 seconds to dry

2) Can be used for all ages

3) Is not associated with allergic reactions

4) Can be easily rinsed after the line is inserted

a. 3, 4

b. 1, 3

c. 2, 3

d. 1, 4

NOTES

88. The laboratory runs a PCR test for MRSA. Both the positive and the negative controls amplify MRSA DNA. What can the IP conclude about this test?

- **a.** It is accurate because the positive control amplified MRSA DNA
- **b.** It is accurate because the negative control amplified MRSA DNA
- **c.** It is inaccurate because the positive control amplified MRSA DNA
- **d.** It is inaccurate because the negative control amplified MRSA DNA

89. Immunoglobulins are available for which of the following?

1) Tetanus
2) Rubella
3) Pertussis
4) Varicella-zoster

- **a.** 1, 2, 3
- **b.** 2, 3, 4
- **c.** 1, 3, 4
- **d.** 1, 2, 4

90. The Director of Infection Prevention and Control has been asked to lead a team in the development of an antimicrobial stewardship program at an organization. Core members should include:

1) Pharmacist
2) Risk manager
3) Respiratory therapist
4) Infectious disease physician

- **a.** 1, 2
- **b.** 1, 4
- **c.** 3, 4
- **d.** 2, 3

NOTES

91. The critical care classes have 48 new students. There are eight males. The ratio of females to males is:

a. 1:5

b. 5:1

c. 6:1

d. 1:6

92. A patient with a positive HBsAg must be dialyzed. Which of the following are the best measures to prevent transmission of disease?

1) Perform treatment in a separate room or area

2) Use a dedicated machine and equipment

3) Perform the treatment at the end of the day

4) Schedule the treatment on a separate day with other positive HBsAg patients

a. 1, 2

b. 2, 4

c. 3, 4

d. 1, 3

93. Which of the following tasks would require wearing sterile gloves?

a. Central line dressing change

b. Routine dressing change without debridement

c. Wound cleaning

d. Intramuscular (IM) injection

94. In a case-control study of the association between exposure to long-term nursing care and the outcome of VRE colonization, the authors report an odds ratio of 2.3. How should this odds ratio be interpreted?

a. The study is flawed because a relative risk (RR) should have been calculated

b. The risk of being placed in long-term nursing care is 2.3 times higher for people with VRE than without VRE

c. VRE cases have 2.3 times the odds of having had exposure to long-term nursing care than non-VRE cases

d. There is no association between VRE colonization and exposure to long-term nursing care

NOTES

95. A used endoscope was placed in a carrying case before being cleaned and reprocessed. Which of the following actions should be taken?

a. The endoscope should be cleaned and reprocessed and placed back in the carrying case

b. The carrying case should be retained and only utilized for endoscopes that have not yet been cleaned or reprocessed

c. The carrying case should be discarded

d. The carrying case should be retained and only used for endoscopes that have been wrapped after cleaning and disinfection

96. Based on current CDC guidelines, which of the following modes of transmission is most responsible for contamination of a central venous catheter?

a. Airborne

b. Direct contact

c. Indirect contact

d. Droplet spread

97. The IP has identified poor compliance with hand hygiene practices in one of the critical care units. She has discussed her observations with the management of the unit and together they have identified a solution to improve practices. To ensure staff's adherence to the solution, in which of the activities below should the IP engage before implementing the solution?

a. Perform a survey of fellow IPs to discuss the strategies they have found to be effective and that have sustained acceptable compliance

b. Form a focus group of unit staff to discuss her observations, the ideas to improve compliance, and the proposed solution

c. Develop a strategy with management to penalize any unit staff observed to be noncompliant

d. Each month post the names of staff members she observes to be noncompliant with hand hygiene practices

NOTES

98. Which of the following patients would have the lowest risk of SSI?

a. A 53-year-old male with insulin-dependent diabetes and coronary artery disease undergoing elective aortofemoral bypass

b. A 38-year-old female with mild but controlled hypertension undergoing a laparoscopic cholecystectomy

c. A 42-year-old, well-conditioned male undergoing elective groin hernia repair

d. A 62-year-old female on chronic renal hemodialysis undergoing emergency laparotomy for perforated diverticulitis

99. What organism is most often associated with urinary tract infections?

a. *Enterococcus* sp.

b. *Candida* sp.

c. *Klebsiella pneumoniae* or *K. oxytoca*

d. *Escherichia coli*

100. Which of the following has a low risk of transmission from sexual contact?

a. Hepatitis B

b. Hepatitis C

c. HIV

d. Syphilis

101. Of the following sharp object injury examples, which would have the highest risk of transmission of bloodborne pathogens (assuming that all patient-related risk factors are identical for each example)?

a. A nurse is stuck with an intravenous (IV) catheter stylet after withdrawing the stylet from the catheter

b. A medical resident is stuck with a suture needle that had been used to suture a head wound

c. A nurse is stuck with the needle from a syringe that had been used to give an intramuscular injection

d. A surgeon sustains a superficial skin injury from a used disposable scalpel

NOTES

102. Which letter labels the areas under the curve that represents special cause variance in healthcare-associated CLABSI?

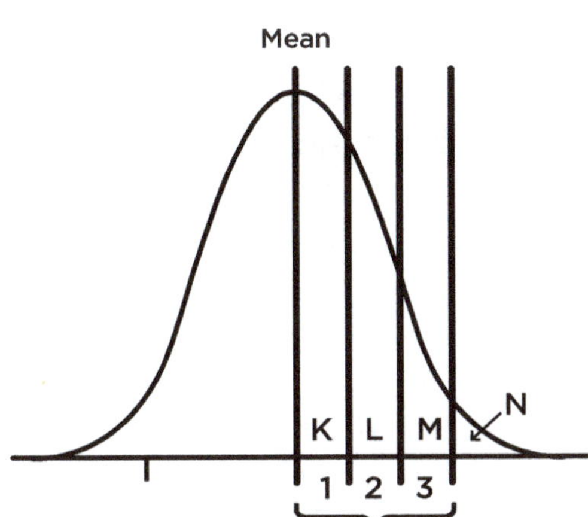

a. K

b. L

c. M

d. N

103. There is a suspected case of measles in the ED of a facility, and the patient has been admitted. A nasopharyngeal swab was taken, placed in viral transport media, and sent to the lab where it was frozen at -20°C for 12 hours and then thawed and placed in culture. The culture results are negative for measles virus. Which of the following should the IP request for this patient?

1) A new sample should be collected and placed in a -20°C environment immediately

2) A new sample should be collected and placed in culture immediately

3) The patient should be placed in an airborne infection isolation room

4) The patient should be placed in a standard room without isolation precautions

a. 1

b. 4

c. 2, 3

d. 1, 2, 3

NOTES

104. Measures of central tendency are:

a. Ratios and rates

b. Proportions and standard deviation

c. Mean and median

d. Percentiles and measures of dispersion

105. ICRA elements related to building site areas affected by construction include all of the following *except*:

a. Impact of potential outages or emergencies and protection of patients during planned or unplanned outages, movement of debris, traffic flow, cleanup, and testing and certification

b. The number of containment cubes owned by the facility

c. Impact of disrupting essential service to patients and employees

d. Determination of specific hazards and the protection levels needed for each

106. The Infection Prevention Manager has been directed to design a new system for housewide surveillance of CLABSI in a 300-bed urban community teaching hospital. Which of the following tools would be most appropriate to help ensure that all aspects of this large-scale project are addressed?

a. A detailed contingency plan

b. A summary of the scope of work

c. A quality management plan

d. A work breakdown structure

107. Which of the following would be appropriate for a graph displaying *C. difficile* infections?

a. X axis labeled with the months of the year

b. X axis labeled with the number of cases each month

c. Y axis labeled with the months of the year

d. Y axis labeled with the days of the month of April

108. When transporting used instruments from the operating room to the decontamination area, they must be transported in:

a. An open bin

b. Large plastic bags

c. Puncture-proof, sealable containers labeled as biohazardous

d. A bin draped with a sheet

109. The IP is notified of a positive *Legionella* test in an individual who has resided in the healthcare facility for 2 months. Which of the following are potential sources of *Legionella* that should be investigated?

1) Cooling towers

2) IV solutions

3) Air conditioners

4) Ice machines

a. 1, 4

b. 1, 3

c. 3, 4

d. 2, 4

110. OSHA requires the use of engineering controls to prevent transmission of bloodborne pathogens in the healthcare setting. Which of the following is an example of an engineering control?

a. Requiring Hepatitis B vaccination for all HCP with occupational exposure

b. Providing eye protection for all personnel who have potential for exposure to bloodborne pathogens

c. Implementing the use of Universal Precautions

d. Purchasing self-sheathing syringes

NOTES

NOTES

111. The IP is teaching a group of ICU nurses about the risk factors for healthcare-associated infection (HAI) during patient care. Which of the following are factors that may influence the infectious risk?

1) Type of patient care activity
2) Mode of transmission of an infectious agent
3) Patient's host defenses
4) Patient's past surgical history

- **a.** 1, 2, 3
- **b.** 2, 3, 4
- **c.** 1, 3, 4
- **d.** 1, 2, 4

112. Which of the following laboratory methods is utilized for viral testing?

- **a.** Gram staining, to quickly confirm presence of infection
- **b.** Broth dilution, to determine antimicrobial resistance via minimal inhibitory concentration (MIC)
- **c.** Antibody assay, to detect viral antibodies in the serum
- **d.** Antibody assay, to detect viral antibodies in clinical specimen

113. Seventy-five patients were admitted to the Medical-Surgical ICU. Forty were on the surgical service and 35 were on the medical service. Fifteen patients developed a HAI with MRSA. Nine of the patients with MRSA infection were on the surgical service. There were 230 patient days in the ICU for the surgical patients in January, and 325 patient days for medical patients. What was the MRSA attack rate for patients on the medical service?

- **a.** 8 percent
- **b.** 2 percent
- **c.** 17 percent
- **d.** 15 percent

NOTES

114. A dialysis patient has recently tested positive for HBsAg. Previous tests have been negative. The manager is concerned that the patient may have been exposed during a treatment. Which of the following is the most likely explanation of the patient's positive test result?

a. The patient is resolving an acute Hepatitis B infection

b. The patient received a dose of Hepatitis B vaccine in the last 21 days

c. The result is inaccurate

d. The patient is immune due to natural infection

115. A patient is admitted with fever, rash, headache, abdominal pain, vomiting, and muscle pain. The IP is aware that Rocky Mountain spotted fever is endemic in the area. The patient reports a recent camping trip with exposure to ticks. Which of the laboratory tests listed below should be ordered to detect and differentiate the appropriate antibodies in the serum?

a. Blood culture

b. Weil-Felix agglutination

c. Sedimentation rate

d. Cold agglutinin

116. Breaches in patient safety are being studied to determine the cause and effect of human error. Human factors engineering is a tool that:

a. Studies processes to achieve "failure-free" operation over time to reduce defects and improve system safety

b. Studies people at work, then designs tasks and the working environment so that people can be safe, effective, and productive

c. Studies human characteristics and is concerned with design of tools, machines, and systems that take into account human capabilities

d. Studies the elements involved with human-machine interface to improve working conditions

NOTES

117. Immunizations recommended for all HCP include:

1) Human papillomavirus vaccine (HPV)
2) Shingles (herpes zoster) vaccine
3) Influenza vaccine
4) Tetanus, diphtheria, and pertussis (Tdap) vaccine

- **a.** 1, 4
- **b.** 2, 3
- **c.** 3, 4
- **d.** 2, 4

118. Which classroom setup best promotes interaction between learners and teachers?

- **a.** Stadium or auditorium style with clear sight lines and good acoustics
- **b.** Rectangular conference tables that promote a more formal space for learning
- **c.** Classroom style with straight rows of desks that also provide writing surfaces
- **d.** A horseshoe shape that also provides writing surfaces

119. An IP is reviewing the below data from a cohort study that examined the relationship between VRE colonization and long-term care. What was the incidence density of VRE colonization in this study?

Participant	Person-time observed	Colonized with VRE?
1	6 months	Yes
2	1 Year	Yes
3	3 months	No
4	1.5 years	Yes
5	9 months	No

- **a.** Three cases/4 person-years
- **b.** Five cases/4 person-years
- **c.** Three cases/3 person-years
- **d.** Two cases/1 person-year

NOTES

120. The Joint Commission National Patient Safety Goal (NPSG) 7 focuses on the prevention of infections. The IP has been asked to help identify what education should be provided to the patients regarding prevention of SSI, CLABSI, CAUTI, and management of multidrug-resistant organisms (MDROs). What recommendation is applicable to all of these issues and would apply to all patients receiving care in the hospital?

- **a.** Cough containment to reduce transmission of airborne pathogens
- **b.** Importance of hand hygiene and asking caregivers if they have washed their hands
- **c.** Mode of transmission of microorganisms from one area of the body to another
- **d.** Symptoms associated with infection and the need to report them to healthcare providers

121. The viral load in a patient with HIV:

- **a.** Increases during the antiretroviral phase, decreases during asymptomatic HIV infection, then increases as the patient progresses to acquired immune deficiency syndrome (AIDS)
- **b.** Remains low during the antiretroviral phase, increases during asymptomatic HIV infection, then decreases as the patient progresses to AIDS
- **c.** Remains low during the antiretroviral phase, increases during asymptomatic HIV infection, then increases as the patient progresses to AIDS
- **d.** Increases during the antiretroviral phase, decreases during the asymptomatic HIV infection, and continues to decrease as the patient progresses to AIDS

122. What type of surveillance is the monitoring of bloodstream infection rates?

- **a.** Outcome surveillance
- **b.** Mandatory reporting
- **c.** Process surveillance
- **d.** Combined surveillance

NOTES

123. A patient in the Neurosurgical ICU develops a fever. Cultures are ordered and collected. The physician decides to start an antibiotic while waiting for the culture results because the patient is critically ill. This type of antibiotic usage is called:

a. Empiric

b. Prophylactic

c. Therapeutic

d. Pathogen-directed

124. The IP has completed a series of education programs and summarized both the mean and standard deviation for four groups of participants. Which set of scores indicates the most consistent level of performance among the attendees?

a. Group 1: Mean 88 SD 6.4

b. Group 2: Mean 87 SD 3.5

c. Group 3: Mean 90 SD 15.8

d. Group 4: Mean 92 SD 20.3

125. The Infection Prevention Director is revising roles within the infection prevention team to better utilize individual skills and increase the effectiveness of the infection prevention and control program. By exploring ways to add responsibilities, to use additional skills and abilities, and to include more recognition, the director is accomplishing:

a. Job enrichment

b. Job enlargement

c. Job intensification

d. Job rotation

126. There is a shortage of influenza vaccine, and the IP has been asked to help prioritize the administration of the vaccine among HCP in the facility. Which of the following employee groups would be among the highest priority for immunization?

a. The admissions clerk in the ED

b. The Lung Transplant Coordinator

c. A nurse in labor and delivery

d. The CEO of the hospital

NOTES

127. An outbreak of norovirus in a LTCF would most likely have an epidemic curve (epi curve) that:

a. Indicated a common source of infection

b. Indicated a propagated source of infection

c. Indicated a point source of infection

d. Indicated a common vehicle of infection

128. What healthcare-associated viral outbreaks are most frequently reported among infants and children?

a. Hepatitis A

b. Coxsackie A

c. *Staphylococcus aureus*

d. RSV

129. Which of the following is *not* confirmatory of an active measles infection?

a. Positive measles immunoglobulin M (IgM)

b. Fourfold increase in measles immunoglobulin G (IgG)

c. Positive measles PCR from a skin biopsy

d. Rash in a patient nonimmune to measles

130. Which of the following statements is *true* regarding the evaluation of an educational program?

a. The evaluation should only be done at the end of the program

b. Evaluation measurements must be consistent with the objectives of the program

c. The evaluation always includes one-on-one interviews to assess the ability of the individual learner to perform

d. The evaluation should not be used to monitor the behavior change—this is the role of the presenter

131. Which of the following studies is experimental rather than observational?

a. Cohort

b. Clinical trial

c. Case-control

d. Cross-sectional

NOTES

132. Another name for "flash sterilization" is:

a. Immediate-use

b. High-level disinfection

c. Low-level disinfection

d. Ethylene oxide (ETO) sterilization

133. Because of the potential for rapid spread, one confirmed case of this disease is considered an urgent public health situation, and the IP should immediately report suspected and confirmed cases to the health department:

a. Chickenpox

b. Influenza

c. Measles

d. Legionnaires' disease

134. Maximal barrier precautions for central line insertion include:

1) Sterile surgical gown and gloves

2) Closing the door to the room

3) Nonsterile gown and gloves

4) Mask, cap, sterile drape (head to toe)

a. 1, 4

b. 2, 3

c. 1, 3

d. 2, 4

135. The new IP for a LTCF assesses adherence to the facility's hand hygiene policies. In reporting her findings, she includes one of the following:

a. The number of hand hygiene episodes performed by personnel divided by the volume of soap used in the facility

b. The number of hand hygiene episodes performed by personnel divided by the number of patient days times 1,000

c. The number of hand hygiene episodes performed by personnel divided by the volume of alcohol-based hand rub

d. The number of hand hygiene episodes performed by personnel divided by the number of hand hygiene opportunities by ward or service

ANSWERS AND RATIONALES

NOTES

1. **(B) 2, 4**

Rationale: An antibiogram provides the percentage of samples for a given organism that were sensitive to certain antibiotics and can be unit-specific or reflect hospital-wide isolates. There should be at least 30 diagnostic isolates included in an antibiogram, with only the first isolate from each patient included. The greater the number of isolates, the more accurate the sensitivity results for the given organism. Therefore the antibiogram might not accurately reflect all resistant microbes isolated in the facility.

Reference: *APIC Text*, 4th edition, Chapter 26 - Antimicrobials and Resistance

CBIC Core Competency: Identification of Infectious Disease Processes

2. **(C) Vector**

Rationale: Vectors, such as insects, may transmit infectious organisms in the healthcare setting; however, this method of transmission is of less importance in most industrialized nations. External vector-borne transmission is the mechanical transfer of microorganisms by a vector, such as a fly on food. Internal vector-borne transmission involves transfer of infectious material directly from the vector into the new host, such as occurs in mosquitoes and malaria, fleas and plague, and louse-borne typhus. The vector may simply harbor the infectious organism, with no biological interaction taking place, or the agent may actually undergo changes within the vector (e.g., malaria parasites require that part of their life cycle take place within a mosquito).

Reference: *APIC Text*, 4th edition, Chapter 10 - General Principles of Epidemiology

CBIC Core Competency: Identification of Infectious Disease Processes

3. **(A) Root cause analysis (RCA)**

Rationale: RCA, gap analysis, SWOT analysis, and FMEA are tools that can be used to improve quality. The RCA process takes a retrospective look at adverse outcomes and determines what happened, why it happened, and what an organization can do to prevent the situation from recurring. Gap analysis is a tool that is used to take an organization from a current state to a future state where organizational objectives are met. A SWOT analysis is a process where the organization or group assesses their own positive and negative points, outlines opportunities for improvement and growth, and lists any threats that might impede those opportunities. A FMEA can be used to identify potential system failures or errors before they occur.

Reference: *APIC Text*, 4th edition, Chapter 16 - Quality Concepts

CBIC Core Competency: Management and Communication

NOTES

4. **(D) All cases in a common point source outbreak occur within one incubation period of the exposure**

Rationale: A common source epidemic is characterized by a rapid spread with cases presenting at the same stage of the disease, indicating the single source of the pathogen. Propagated outbreaks are outbreaks in which the disease propagates in one or more initial cases and then spreads to others, a relatively slow method of spread.

Reference: *APIC Text*, 4th edition, Chapter 12 - Outbreak Investigations

CBIC Core Competency: Surveillance and Epidemiologic Investigation

5. **(D) 1, 4**

Rationale: Pseudomembranous colitis (PMC) is an acute colitis characterized by the formation of an adherent inflammatory membrane (pseudomembrane) overlying sites of mucosal injury. *Clostridium difficile* infection is responsible for the majority of cases of PMC and for as many as 20 percent of cases of antibiotic-induced diarrhea without colitis. The method of choice fore establishing the diagnosis is done by stool assays for *C. difficile* toxins or by colonoscopy.

Reference: *APIC Text*, 4th edition, Chapter 72 - *Clostridium difficile* Infections and Colitis

CBIC Core Competency: Identification of Infectious Disease Processes

6. **(B) Standard Precautions**

Rationale: Cryptococcosis is the most common fungal infection of the central nervous system. Cryptococcal meningitis is caused by the fungus *Cryptococcus neoformans*. This fungus is found in soil around the world. Cryptococcosis is believed to be acquired by inhalation of the fungus from the environment. Unlike bacterial meningitis, this form of meningitis comes on more slowly, over a few days to a few weeks. India ink will stain the polysaccharide capsule of *C. neoformans*, and *C. neoformans* meningitis is characterized by low glucose in the CSF and predominant lymphocytes. These results allow fungal meningitis to be distinguished from (1) bacterial meningitis, which is characterized by fairly normal glucose levels and predominant neutrophils; (2) viral meningitis, which is stain negative with normal glucose; and (3) mycobacterial meningitis, which is AFB-stain positive. Meningitis with C. neoformans is not communicable so only Standard Precautions are needed in this case.

Reference: *APIC Text*, 4th edition, Chapter 74 - Central Nervous System Infections

CBIC Core Competency: Preventing/Controlling the Transmission of Infectious Agents

NOTES

7. **(D) Staphylococci are Gram positive and grow in grape-like clusters, while streptococci, which are also Gram positive, grow in chains**

Rationale: Both staphylococci and streptococci have round, spherical cell shapes, but the arrangement of cells is different due to a different binary fission. Streptococci form a chain of round cells, because their division occurs in one linear direction, while staphylococci divide in various directions forming grape-like clusters. Both are facultatively anaerobic gram-positive bacteria.

Reference: *APIC Text*, 4th edition, Chapter 9 - Streptococci

CBIC Core Competency: Identification of Infectious Disease Processes

8. **(A) 1, 2**

Rationale: A histogram is a graphic of a frequency distribution in which one bar is used for each time interval, and there is no space between the intervals (see Figure PE3-1). It is used to portray the (grouped) frequency distribution of a variable at the interval or ratio level of measurement.

A frequency polygon (see Figure PE3-2) is similar to a line graph, but each coordinate point is represented by a point displayed on the graph with straight lines connecting them. A frequency polygon will provide the same data information as a histogram.

Figure PE3-1. Histogram

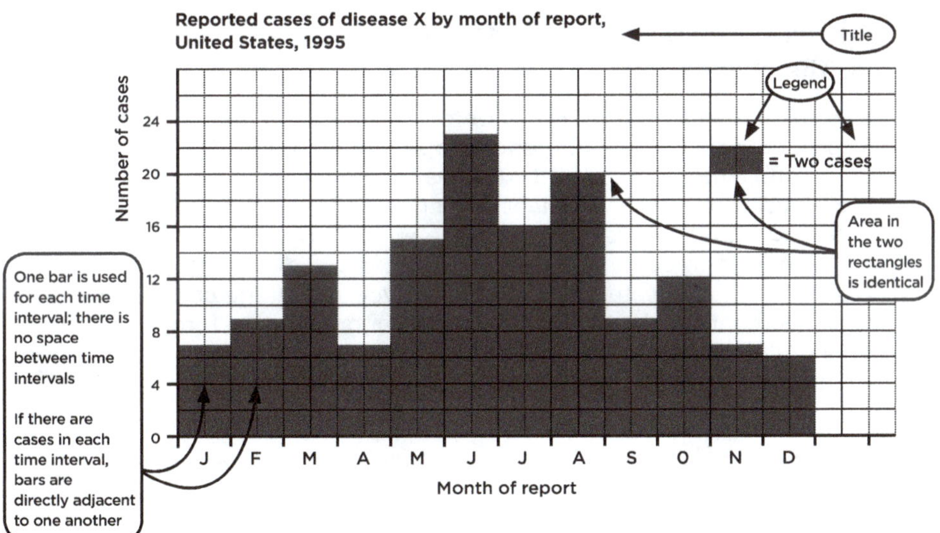

Source: Tweeten SM. General Principles of Epidemiology. In: Grota P, ed. *APIC Text of Infection Control and Epidemiology*, 4th edition. Washington, DC: Association for Professionals in Infection Control and Epidemiology, 2014.

NOTES

Figure PE3-2. Frequency polygon

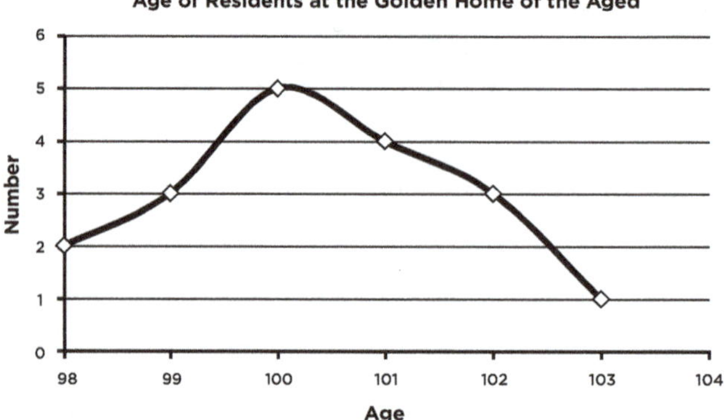

Source: Potts A. Use of Statistics in Infection Prevention. In: Grota P, ed. *APIC Text of Infection Control and Epidemiology*, 4th edition. Washington, DC: Association for Professionals in Infection Control and Epidemiology, 2014.

References: *APIC Text*, 4th edition, Chapter 13 - Use of Statistics in Infection Prevention; *APIC Text*, 4th edition, Chapter 10 - General Principles of Epidemiology

CBIC Core Competency: Surveillance and Epidemiologic Investigation

9. **(A) High-level disinfection, rinse the scope with sterile water, flush the channels with 70 to 90 percent alcohol, dry using forced air**

Rationale: Cleaning is essential before manual or automated disinfection. Thoroughly clean the entire endoscope immediately after use, then completely immerse the endoscope and endoscope components in the high-level disinfectant/sterilant and ensure that all channels are perfused. After high-level disinfection, rinse the endoscope and flush the channels with sterile, filtered, or tap water to remove the disinfectant/sterilant. Discard the rinse water after each use/cycle. Flush the channels with 70 to 90 percent ethyl or isopropyl alcohol and dry using forced-air. The final drying steps greatly reduce the possibility of recontamination of the endoscope by waterborne microorganisms.

Reference: *APIC Text*, 4th edition, Chapter 55 - Endoscopy

CBIC Core Competency: Cleaning, Sterilization, Disinfection, Asepsis

NOTES

10. **(C) A fishbone diagram with an explanation**

Rationale: The RCA process takes a retrospective look at adverse outcomes and determines what happened, why it happened, and what an organization can do to prevent the situation from recurring in the future. The product of the RCA is an action plan that identifies the strategies that the organization intends to implement to improve safety. A thorough RCA demonstrates credibility of the recommended process to the facility leadership team. When used during the RCA process, a fishbone diagram (also called an Ishikawa diagram) will help identify and visually display both the elements involved in the improvement project and the areas of responsibility and accountability (see Figure PE3-3). Used in conjunction with the RCA, the fishbone diagram with an accompanying explanation present a clear picture of the both improvement project and rationale behind it.

Figure PE3-3. Fishbone (Ishikawa) Diagram

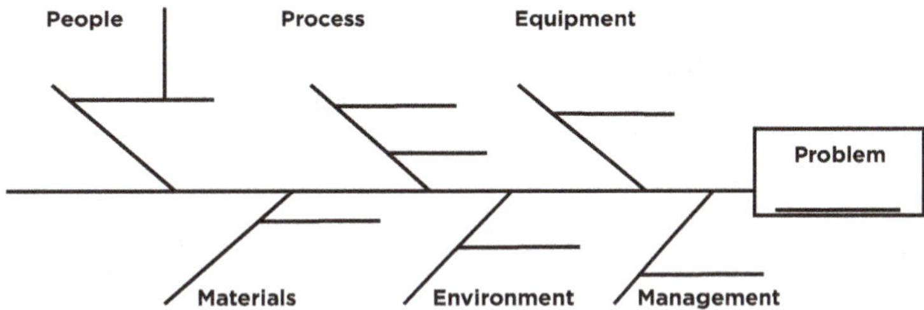

Source: Monsees E. Quality Concepts. In: Grota P, ed. *APIC Text of Infection Control and Epidemiology*, 4th edition. Washington, DC: Association for Professionals in Infection Control and Epidemiology, 2014.

Reference: *APIC Text*, 4th edition, Chapter 16 - Quality Concepts

CBIC Core Competency: Management and Communication

11. **(B) The number of ICU urinary tract infections identified in a given month divided by the number of urinary catheter days in the same month times 1,000**

Rationale: Data should be expressed as rates or ratios that are calculated using the same methodology as a nationally validated surveillance system. This allows an organization to compare its rates with another organization or a recognized benchmark. The NHSN indicator for CAUTI measures the development of a urinary tract infection associated with the risk of an indwelling urinary catheter in a defined population. The CAUTI rate is calculated as (# CAUTIs identified ÷ # indwelling catheter days) × 1,000.

Reference: *APIC Text*, 4th edition, Chapter 11 - Surveillance

CBIC Core Competency: Surveillance and Epidemiologic Investigation

NOTES

12. **(C) Methicillin resistant *Staphylococcus aureus***

Rationale: Athletes can contract CA-MRSA by close skin to skin contact, sharing athletic equipment, sharing towels, razors, or other personal items with someone who has an active infection or who is a carrier. Athletes may get abrasions from artificial turf; these abrasions may serve as an entry point for CA-MRSA. In the community, most MRSA infections are skin infections that may appear as pustules or boils which often are red, swollen, painful, or have pus or other drainage. They often first look like spider bites or bumps that are red, swollen, and painful. These skin infections commonly occur at sites of visible skin trauma, such as cuts and abrasions, and areas of the body covered by hair.

Reference: *APIC Text*, 4th edition, Chapter 93 - Staphylococci

CBIC Core Competency: Identification of Infectious Disease Processes

13. **(B) 1, 2, 4**

Rationale: Prevention strategies to reduce SSIs include:

- Administer antimicrobial prophylaxis in accordance with evidence-based standards and guidelines (within 1 hour prior to incision, 2 hours for vancomycin and fluoroquinolones).
- Identify and treat remote infections before elective operation.

Preoperative antibiotics are not given to reduce the microorganism bioburden prior to surgery. The following are examples of activities that may reduce the bioload of microorganisms on patients' skin:

- Washing from clean to less-clean areas using clean washcloths to prevent cross contamination
- Preoperative showering using antimicrobial soap
- Washing with antimicrobial soaps, such as chlorhexidine gluconate, to reduce carriage of resistant organisms, such as MRSA
- Active surveillance culturing for epidemiologically significant organisms based on the facility's epidemiology
- Encouraging or assisting patients in maintaining good oral hygiene and caring for the mouth to reduce the risk of mucositis in immunosuppressed persons
- Encouraging good genital-area cleansing
- Good hand hygiene practices using soap and water or alcohol-based hand rubs, as appropriate
- Treatment of remote site infections prior to surgery
- Additional personal risk-reduction strategies, include smoking cessation or weight loss if possible and appropriate

Reference: *APIC Text*, 4th edition, Chapter 21 - Risk Factors Facilitating Transmission of Infectious Agents

CBIC Core Competency: Preventing/Controlling the Transmission of Infectious Agents

NOTES

14. (B) Small, painful vesicular lesion on the fingertip

Rationale: Herpetic whitlow is a skin infection of the fingers, most commonly found on the tips of the thumb and index finger. Herpetic whitlow is caused by the herpes simplex virus. Herpetic whitlow is common among HCP who come into contact with the virus regularly and in children who have the virus and suck their fingers or thumb. Recommendations from the Advisory Committee on Immunization Practices (ACIP) include restricting HCP with herpetic whitlow from patient contact and contact with the patient's environment until the lesions have healed.

References: *APIC Text*, 4th edition, Chapter 80 - Herpes Virus; *APIC Text*, 4th edition, Chapter 100 - Occupational Health

CBIC Core Competency: Employee/Occupational Health

15. (C) 3, 4

Rationale: UV irradiation has been used for the control of pathogenic microorganisms in a variety of applications, such as control of Legionellosis, as well as disinfection of air, surfaces, and instruments. UV irradiation is effective substantially reducing levels of vegetative bacteria. All patients and staff must be removed from the room prior to decontamination. Rooms can be rapidly decontaminated of vegetative bacteria in 15 to 20 minutes. All patients and staff must be removed from the room prior to decontamination

Reference: *APIC Text*, 4th edition, Chapter 31 - Cleaning, Sterilization, Disinfection

CBIC Core Competency: Environment of Care

16. (D) Discussion

Rationale: The discussion section of a research study reviews, interprets, and evaluates the results of the study. This section usually lists the hypothesis or hypotheses and reports whether the results supported or contradicted the hypothesis. Similarities and differences between the current findings and findings of previous research are reviewed. Limitations of the current study are discussed and suggestions are made on improving the research design. The discussion section usually ends with recommendations for future research.

References: *APIC Text*, 4th edition, Chapter 20 - Research Study Design; *APIC Text*, 4th edition, Chapter 19 - Qualitative Research Methods

CBIC Core Competency: Education and Research

17. (B) Vegetables stored below raw meat in the refrigerator

Rationale: Improper storage or environmental sanitation may introduce contamination or allow low microbial load to proliferate if not kept at appropriate temperatures. Food storage must be done in a systematic manner to ensure that all food safety requirements are met. Food must be protected from cross-contamination by separating raw animal foods during storage, preparation, holding, and display from raw ready-to-eat food, including fruits and vegetables, as well as cooked ready-to-eat foods per the FDA Food Code 3-302.11.

Reference: *APIC Text,* 4th edition, Chapter 109 - Nutrition Services

CBIC Core Competency: Preventing/Controlling the Transmission of Infectious Agents

NOTES

18. **(B) They become more precise**

Rationale: Larger sample sizes generate narrower and more precise confidence intervals. There is an inverse square root relationship between confidence intervals and sample sizes. To cut the margin of error in half, the sample size needs to be quadrupled, approximately.

Reference: *APIC Text*, 4th edition, Chapter 13 - Use of Statistics in Infection Prevention

CBIC Core Competency: Surveillance and Epidemiologic Investigation

19. **(C) In the laundry facility, positive pressure should be maintained in the area where contaminated textiles are received**

Rationale: Laundry facilities must maintain negative pressure in the area where contaminated textiles are received compared with the clean areas of the facility.

Reference: *APIC Text*, 4th edition, Chapter 111 - Laundry, Patient Linens, Textiles, and Uniforms

CBIC Core Competency: Preventing/Controlling the Transmission of Infectious Agents

20. **(D) Gram-negative diplococci**

Rationale: Growth of oxidase-positive colonies and Gram-negative diplococci with the right clinical context provides a presumptive identification of *N. meningitidis.*

Reference: *APIC Text*, 4th edition, Chapter 87 - *Neisseria meningitidis*

CBIC Core Competency: Identification of Infectious Disease Processes

21. **(B) 2, 3**

Rationale: Disruption of water utility systems during construction or renovation can disturb the biofilm present in water delivery pipes and pose a threat to patients. Microbes present in potable water and its delivery network include gram-negative bacteria, e.g., Legionellae and Pseudomonas spp, nontuberculous Mycobacteria, protozoa, and fungi.

Reference: *APIC Text*, 4th edition, Chapter 117 - Construction and Renovation

CBIC Core Competency: Environment of Care

NOTES

22. (A) Mitigation

Rationale: An ICRA is a multidisciplinary, organizational, documented process that after considering the facility's patient population and program:

- Focuses on reduction of risk from infection,
- Acts through phases of facility planning, design, construction, renovation, facility maintenance, and
- Coordinates and weighs knowledge about infection, infectious agents, and care environment, permitting the organization to anticipate potential impact.

The ICRA elements are divided into three areas: processes for design, construction, and mitigation. Mitigation recommendations should address the following:

- Patient placement and relocation.
- Standards for barriers and other protective measures required to protect adjacent areas and susceptible patients from airborne contaminants.
- Temporary provisions or phasing for construction or modification of heating, ventilation, air conditioning, and water supply systems.
- Protection from demolition.
- Measures taken to train hospital staff, visitors and construction personnel.

Reference: *APIC Text*, 4th edition, Chapter 117 - Construction and Renovation

CBIC Core Competency: Environment of Care

23. (C) *Vibrio*

Rationale: *Vibrio* gastroenteritis is caused by eating undercooked or raw seafood, such as fish and shellfish.

Reference: *APIC Text,* 4th edition, Chapter 83 - Foodborne Illnesses

CBIC Core Competency: Identification of Infectious Disease Processes

24. (C) An airborne infection isolation room with negative airflow

Rationale: When TB is suspected, a bronchoscopy should be performed only if medically necessary. The procedure should only be performed in a room that meets the ventilation requirements for an AIIR (negative directional airflow, a minimum of 12 air exchanges per hour, and direct exhaust to the outside more than 25 feet from an air intake or discharge through a high-efficiency particulate air [HEPA] filtration system).

Reference: *APIC Text*, 4th edition, Chapter 95 - Tuberculosis and Other Mycobacteria

CBIC Core Competency: Identification of Infectious Disease Processes

25. (B) Place the patient's belongings in a plastic bag and tie securely

Rationale: If bed bugs are suspected, the patient must be examined and his or her personal belongings should be placed in plastic bags that are tied securely closed or in other sealed containers. Environmental clutter should be removed and the area vacuumed, preferably using a HEPA-filtered vacuum.

Reference: *APIC Text*, 4th edition, Chapter 107 - Environmental Services

CBIC Core Competency: Environment of Care

NOTES

26. (C) The null hypothesis should be rejected and the alternative hypothesis should be accepted

Rationale: A common use of statistics is hypothesis testing. The hypothesis is a statement of expected results. Hypothesis testing uses the distribution of a known area in the normal curve. It estimates the likelihood (probability) that a result did not occur by chance. First, a research or alternate hypothesis is formulated. The hypothesis states the expectation to be tested (e.g., Doctor A has a higher SSI rate than Doctor B). Then a statement that is opposite to the research or alternate hypothesis is developed (e.g., Doctor A has a lower infection rate than Doctor B). The latter is called the null hypothesis (H_0). The H_0 is always stated to be rejected. The research or alternate hypothesis (H_a) is the desired result. Only two outcomes are possible with hypothesis testing.

The level of significance is the probability value arbitrarily chosen by the researcher as the desired level of probability at which one may feel secure in rejecting the null hypothesis. This probability of rejecting a null hypothesis when it is true is the level of significance or α level. Most researchers use 0.05(5 percent) or 0.01(1 percent) values for α to minimize the chances of incorrectly rejecting the null hypothesis. This specified level states a sufficiently small likelihood that the given observation could occur by chance variation alone (e.g., 0.05 or a 1-in-20 chance). The *p* value is commonly compared to α, the specified significance level of the test. If $\alpha = 0.01$, then a *p* value less than 0.01 would cause one to reject the null hypothesis, whereas a *p* value greater than 0.01 would cause one to fail to reject the null hypotheses.

A *p* value expressed as $p<0.01$ indicates that we should reject the null hypothesis because there is sufficient evidence to support that sampling variation or chance is an unlikely explanation for difference between the null hypothesis and sample values. This does not prove that the null hypothesis is true.

Reference: *APIC Text*, 4th edition, Chapter 13 - Use of Statistics in Infection Prevention

CBIC Core Competency: Surveillance and Epidemiologic Investigation

27. (D) 1, 4

Rationale: The temperature of the soaking solution should be monitored and documented to ensure that the temperature of the cleaning solution meets the requirement of the cleaning solution's written IFU. The time the instruments are soaked should also be recorded.

Reference: *APIC Text*, 4th edition, Chapter 106 - Sterile Processing

CBIC Core Competency: Cleaning, Disinfection, Sterilization, Asepsis

28. (C) The guideline should identify, summarize, and evaluate the highest-quality evidence and most current data in the literature

Rationale: Clinical practice guidelines are evidenced-based standards, such as algorithms and consensus statements, that address reducing variation in practice and improving clinical outcomes.

Reference: *APIC Text*, 4th edition, Chapter 16 - Quality Concepts

CBIC Core Competency: Preventing/Controlling the Transmission of Infectious Agents

NOTES

29. **D Ten**

Rationale: The ventilation of the decontamination area should be negative air pressure (pulls air into the work area) with 10 air exchanges/hour and all air exhausted to the outside atmosphere.

Reference: *APIC Text*, 4th edition, Chapter 106 - Sterile Processing

CBIC Core Competency: Environment of Care

30. **D Remove the sign from the door and ensure that all lesions are completely covered; Standard Precautions are sufficient to prevent the spread of the virus**

Rationale: According to CDC recommendations, following Standard Precautions and completely covering lesions are sufficient to prevent transmission of localized zoster to susceptible visitors and personnel. If a woman has a history of varicella-zoster infection or vaccination, her antibodies will protect her fetus from infection, so there is no risk for her to enter the room or care for the patient. Infection with zoster virus during pregnancy can be harmful to the fetus; however, all HCP should be immune to zoster through history of illness or through immunization upon employment. If unvaccinated or susceptible HCP at risk for severe disease and for whom vaccination is contraindicated (e.g., pregnant HCP) are exposed, the CDC recommends that those personnel receive VZIG after exposure.

References: *APIC Text*, 4th edition, Chapter 80 - Herpes Virus;
APIC Text, 4th edition, Chapter 103 - Immunization of Healthcare Personnel

CBIC Core Competency: Preventing/Controlling the Transmission of Infectious Agents

31. **D Require the Hepatitis A vaccine for all employees who are at risk for occupational exposure**

Rationale: Hepatitis A is spread person to person; occupational exposure generally does not increase HCP risk for Hepatitis A virus (HAV) infection. To be compliant with the Needlestick Safety and Prevention Act, healthcare facilities should:

- Provide safety-engineered sharps devices and needleless systems to employees to reduce the risk of occupational exposure to bloodborne diseases.
- Solicit input from employees responsible for direct patient care who are potentially exposed to injuries from contaminated sharps in the identification, evaluation, and selection of effective safety-engineered products and work practice controls.
- Document the solicitation of input in the exposure control plan.
- Maintain a sharps injury log to record injuries from contaminated sharps. The injury log must contain the type and brand of product involved in the incident, the work area where the incident occurred, and an explanation of how the incident occurred.

Reference: *APIC Text*, 4th edition, Chapter 7 - Product Evaluation

CBIC Core Competency: Employee/Occupational Health

NOTES

32. Ⓐ 1, 2

Rationale: A major advantage of improved hydrogen peroxide is its rapid action, high effectiveness, and low toxicity. A disadvantage is it is more expensive than a quaternary ammonium compound in ready-to-use containers. Improved hydrogen peroxide is considered safe for humans and equipment, and benign for the environment. In fact, improved hydrogen peroxide has the lowest EPA toxicity category based on its oral, inhalation, and dermal toxicity, which means that it is practically nontoxic and is not an irritant.

Reference: *APIC Text*, 4th edition, Chapter 31 - Cleaning, Disinfection and Sterilization

CBIC Core Competency: Cleaning, Sterilization, Disinfection, Asepsis

33. Ⓒ Direct contact with infested skin

Rationale: Transfer of parasites commonly occurs through prolonged direct contact with infested skin and also during sexual contact. Transfer from undergarments and bedclothes occurs only if these have been contaminated by infested persons immediately beforehand. People with crusted scabies syndrome are highly contagious because of the large number of mites present in the exfoliating scales.

References: Scabies. In: Heymann D. *Control of Communicable Diseases Manual*, 19th edition. Washington, DC: American Public Health Association, 2008; *APIC Text*, 4th edition, Chapter 99 - Parasites

CBIC Core Competency: Identification of Infectious Disease Processes

34. Ⓓ It is only necessary to clean a 3 to 4 foot perimeter around the table, unless a wider contamination area is identified

Rationale: Floors in the operating room must be cleaned and disinfected after each case. Reusable string or microfiber mops may be used in between cases and should be changed after each use. If a cotton mop and bucket system is used, a clean mop head and fresh disinfectant must be used for each case. It is only necessary to clean a 3 to 4 foot perimeter around the operative table after each case unless a wider perimeter of contamination is identified.

Reference: *APIC Text*, 4th edition, Chapter 107 - Environmental Services

CBIC Core Competency: Cleaning, Sterilization, Disinfection, Asepsis

NOTES

35. Ⓐ **Give the EVS employee VZIG and place off work from day 10 through day 28**

Rationale: According to the recommended immunization practices by the U.S. Public Health Service's ACIP, varicella vaccine should not be administered to pregnant women because the possible effects on fetal development are unknown. The EVS employee should receive the VZIG, and she should be excluded from duty for 28 days (see Table PE3-1).

Table PE3-1. Summary of Suggested Work Restrictions for Healthcare Personnel Exposed to or Infected with Infectious Diseases of Importance in Healthcare Settings, in the Absence of State and Local Regulations (Modified from ACIP Recommendations)

Disease/Problem	Work Restriction	Duration	Category
Varicella			
Active	Exclude from duty	Until all lesions dry and crust	IA
Postexposure (susceptible personnel)	Exclude from duty	From tenth day after first exposure through 21st day (28th day if VZIG given) after last exposure	IA
Zoster Localized, in healthy person	Cover lesions; restrict from care of high-risk patient†	Until all lesions dry and crust	II
Generalized or localized in immunosupressed person	Restrict from patient contact	Until all lesions dry and crust	IB
Postexposure (Susceptible personnel)	Restrict from patient contact	From 10th day after 1st exposure through 21st day (28th day if VZIG given) after last exposure or, if varicella occurs, until all lesions dry and crust	IA

†Those susceptible to varicella and who are at increased risk of complications of varicella, such as neonates and immunocompromised persons of any age.

Source: Bolyard EA, Tablan OC, Williams WW, et al. Guideline for infection control in healthcare personnel, 1998. *Am J Infect Control* 1998 June;26(3): 289-354.

References: *APIC Text*, 4th edition, Chapter 100 - Occupational Health; Advisory Committee on Immunization Practices (ACIP). *ACIP Recommendations*. ACIP website. 2014. Available at: http://www.cdc.gov/vaccines/acip/recs/index.html

CBIC Core Competency: Employee/Occupational Health

NOTES

36. (A) 1, 2, 3

Rationale: The PPE training program must include the following:

1. When PPE is worn
2. What PPE to wear
3. How to don, remove, adjust, and wear each type of PPE
4. Limitations of each type of PPE
5. Care, maintenance, useful life, and storage or disposal of PPE
6. Written certification indicating that the employee has received and understood the training

Reference: *APIC Text*, 4th edition, Chapter 107 - Environmental Services

CBIC Core Competency: Environment of Care

37. (D) 1 year

Rationale: Immature bed bugs may live for several months without feeding, while adults may survive as long as one year without a meal. Under normal conditions, adult bed bugs will live for about ten to eleven months.

Reference: *APIC Text*, 4th edition, Chapter 107 - Environmental Services

CBIC Core Competency: Environment of Care

38. (B) Skin colonization with *S. aureus* at the access site

Rationale: Skin colonization with *S. aureus* at the access site has been significantly associated with *S. aureus* access site infections. Persistence of *S. aureus* after skin preparation has been shown to be significantly higher in patients with poor hygiene. The importance of personal hygiene and its possible relation to access site infections should be emphasized to patients. All patients should wash their access site with soap and water daily and before hemodialysis. Patients should also be instructed to ensure that all staff accessing the access site are preparing the skin appropriately prior to cannulation and wearing a mask for all access connections.

Reference: *APIC Text*, 4th edition, Chapter 39 - Dialysis

CBIC Core Competency: Preventing/Controlling the Transmission of Infectious Agents

39. (A) Three times a day

Rationale: During outbreaks, the environment, especially high-touch surfaces, is heavily contaminated with microorganisms. High-touch surfaces include commodes, toilets, toilet handles, faucets, bathroom rails, bedrails, telephones, computers, and food preparation areas. The CDC recommends that these surfaces be cleaned and disinfected at least three times a day and that low-touch surfaces be cleaned at least twice a day.

Reference: *APIC Text*, 4th edition, Chapter 107 - Environmental Services

CBIC Core Competency: Environment of Care

NOTES

40. C 24 hours after initiation of effective therapy

Rationale: The patient must remain on Isolation Precautions for 24 hours after appropriate antimicrobial therapy has been initiated.

Reference: *APIC Text*, 4th edition, Chapter 29 - Isolation Precautions (Transmission-Based Precautions)

CBIC Core Competency: Preventing/Controlling the Transmission of Infectious Agents

41. A Observational studies

Rationale: Methods that can be used to determine educational needs of the learner population include the following:

- Learner self-assessment: The learner develops a self-achievement model and compares the current situation to the standard.
- Focus group discussion: Learning needs are assessed in small groups with members assisting each other to clarify needs.
- Interest-finder surveys: These are data-gathering tools, such as checklists or questionnaires.
- Test development: Tests can be used as diagnostic tools to identify areas of learning deficiencies.
- Personal interviews: The educator consults with random or selected individuals to determine learning needs.
- Job analysis and performance reviews: These methods provide specific, precise information about work and performance.
- Observational studies: Direct observation of personnel working can be performed by quality management analysts or IPs (e.g., hand-washing study in critical care units).
- Review of internal reports: Incident reports, occupational injury and illness reports, and performance improvement studies can be reviewed to determine specific learning needs of healthcare providers

Reference: *APIC Text*, 4th edition, Chapter 3 - Education and Training

CBIC Core Competency: Education and Research

42. C Hepatitis B immunity rates

Rationale: Process measures are commonly used to evaluate compliance with desired care or support practices or to monitor variation in these practices. They may also be used when the outcome to be measured is rare or difficult to measure (e.g., infections after endoscopy) or when there is difficulty acquiring the data (e.g., contacting the discharged and relocated patient after surgery). Process measures are also helpful in evaluating the effectiveness of an educational effort as a measure of behavior (e.g., compliance with aseptic technique for dressing change) or performance of basic infection prevention procedures, such as hand hygiene. Hepatitis B immunity rates are an example of a process indicator. The other answers are examples of outcome indicators.

Reference: *APIC Text*, 4th edition, Chapter 11 - Surveillance

CBIC Core Competency: Surveillance and Epidemiologic Investigation

NOTES

43. **(C) 1, 3, 4**

Rationale: Environmental services managers, IPs, and other individuals responsible for selecting, purchasing, and/or educating others on the use of cleaning products should have a thorough understanding of the differences and uses of these chemicals. Specifically, these individuals should know:

- Definitions of the terms cleaning, sanitization, disinfection, and sterilization
- Definitions of soap, antiseptic, disinfectant, sterilant, and sanitizer
- Differences among the types and uses of antiseptics
- Differences among the types and uses of disinfectants, including sporicidal disinfectants
- Differences among a disinfectant, a disinfectant-detergent, and a cleaning agent containing no antimicrobial properties
- Manufacturer's specification for use, including dilution and contact time
- Difference between products registered with the EPA and the FDA

Reference: *APIC Text*, 4th edition, Chapter 107 - Environmental Services

CBIC Core Competency: Cleaning, Disinfection, Sterilization, Asepsis

44. **(A) The incubation period for scarlet fever is usually 1 to 7 days; he is outside the incubation period and will be able to have his surgery on the scheduled date**

Rationale: Group A *Streptococcus* (GAS) is one of the most frequent and important pathogens in humans. Spread of GAS occurs by direct person-to-person contact. Symptoms of scarlet fever typically appear 3 days after exposure to another person with the illness, though this incubation period can be anywhere from 1 to 7 days. When scarlet fever occurs, it is usually the result of pharyngeal infection, but it can occur in the setting of GAS skin infection or sepsis. It is characterized by a diffuse red rash that typically appears on the second day of illness, lends a sandpaper texture to the skin, and fades over the course of a week. It is followed by desquamation of the skin. The patient is outside the incubation period and will be able to have his surgery on the scheduled date. He should also be instructed to call back if he develops a fever or other signs/symptoms of an illness prior to the surgery date.

Reference: Streptococcal Diseases. In: Heymann D. *Control of Communicable Diseases Manual*, 19th edition. Washington, DC: American Public Health Association, 2008.

CBIC Core Competency: Identification of Infectious Disease Processes

45. **(B) 2, 3**

Rationale: Dust contains fungal spores. To capture dust without aerosolizing spores, dusting should be performed using a cloth or dust mop that is chemically treated or made of microfiber. Dusters should never be shaken.

Reference: *APIC Text*, 4th edition, Chapter 107 - Environmental Services

CBIC Core Competency: Environment of Care

NOTES

46. (A) 1, 3

Rationale: A high sensitivity means that most people who actually have the disease will have a positive test result; this also means that few people who have the disease will have a negative test result, so the number of false negatives will be low.

Reference: *APIC Text*, 4th edition, Chapter 11 - Surveillance

CBIC Core Competency: Surveillance and Epidemiologic Investigation

47. (B) 2, 3

Rationale: Most common types of dialysis-associated infections include access site infection, bacteremia, and peritonitis. The risk of infection or adverse reactions in the dialysis unit can be reduced by strict adherence to aseptic technique during all dialysis procedures. Skin colonization with *S. aureus* at the access site has been significantly associated with *S. aureus* access site infections. Persistence of *S. aureus* after skin preparation has been shown to be significantly higher in patients with poor hygiene. Therefore, the importance of personal hygiene and its possible relation to access site infections should be emphasized. It is recommended that all patients be taught to wash their access site with soap and water daily and before hemodialysis.

Reference: *APIC Text*, 4th edition, Chapter 39 - Dialysis

CBIC Core Competency: Preventing/Controlling the Transmission of Infectious Agents

48. (D) Ask the supervisor to collect data on direct observation of practice

Rationale: Educators may use evaluation at different points within the program development process. Formative evaluation is conducted during the planning of the educational session to provide immediate feedback and to allow appropriate changes to be made. Data collected by pretest and posttest before and after an intervention are used to measure change in individual or group understanding of the content but will not provide information on application of knowledge in a practice setting. Exit questionnaires are used to gather information about the overall success of the program to ask for feedback on all aspects of the course, including objectives, the presenter, the quality of teaching aids, and the learning environment.

Direct observation of practice would provide the best method to assess whether employees are applying the learning objectives on the job.

Reference: *APIC Text*, 4th edition, Chapter 3 - Education and Training

CBIC Core Competency: Education and Research

NOTES

49. 

	With Outcome	Without Outcome
Exposed	25	275
Unexposed	50	300

Rationale: A 2 × 2 or contingency table categorizes study subjects on disease and exposure status. Study subjects are classified as:

A = number of people with both the disease and exposure

B = number of people with the exposure but not the disease

C = number of people with the disease but not the exposure

D = number of people with neither the disease nor the exposure

The layout is as follows:

	DISEASE YES	DISEASE NO
EXPOSURE YES	A	B
EXPOSURE NO	C	D

In this example, exposed persons are those who were operated on by Surgeon A, and unexposed persons are those who were operated on by Surgeon B. The outcome of interest (disease) is the number of SSIs. Surgeon A had 300 exposed patients, 25 of whom had the outcome of interest and 275 of whom did not have the outcome of interest. Surgeon B had 350 patients (who were unexposed to Surgeon A), 50 of whom had the outcome of interest and 300 of whom did not have the outcome of interest.

Reference: *APIC Text*, 4th edition, Chapter 13 - Use of Statistics in Infection Prevention

CBIC Core Competency: Surveillance and Epidemiologic Investigation

50. (A) Standard Precautions

Rationale: Vaccinia virus is the poxvirus that is used to vaccinate against smallpox. The vaccine is a live vaccine that is administered using a bifurcated needle; a positive vaccine reaction results in a pustule at the vaccine site that lasts for approximately 30 days. Live virus can be transmitted through direct contact with the pustule or the scab that grows over it, but in a healthy person the pustule is limited to the vaccine site and is not widespread. The pustule should be covered with a bandage to prevent the patient from self-inoculating other sites of his own body. HCP should use Standard Precautions in this case, including wearing gloves to change the vaccine site dressing. Conditions directly related to immunization including eczema vaccinatum and generalized vaccinia warrant Contact Precautions until the immunization site has dried out and the scab has separated from the skin.

References: *APIC Text*, 4th edition, Chapter 103 - Immunization of Healthcare Personnel; *APIC Text*, 4th edition, Chapter 120 - Infectious Disease Disasters: Bioterrorism, Emerging Infections, and Pandemics

CBIC Core Competency: Preventing/Controlling the Transmission of Infectious Agents

NOTES

51. (B) **Food and Drug Administration (FDA)**

Rationale: The FDA is responsible for the safety of the nation's blood supply. The FDA has specific standards for collection, testing, and distribution of blood, as well as disposal of contaminated or untested blood. These standards apply to all facilities that have blood-banking operations.

Reference: *APIC Text*, 4th edition, Chapter 4 - Accrediting and Regulatory Agencies

CBIC Core Competency: Management and Communication

52. (C) **5 months**

Rationale: CDI has emerged as a major pathogen of healthcare-associated infections. Multiple outbreaks caused by strains with high mortality rates have been reported. The organism produces spores in feces. Surfaces contaminated with feces become a potential reservoir of spores, which can survive in the environment for 5 months.

Reference: *APIC Text*, 4th edition, Chapter 107 - Environmental Services

CBIC Core Competency: Environment of Care

53. (B) **Require oxygen to grow and survive**

Rationale: Oxygen is a universal component of cells. Prokaryotes display a wide range of responses to oxygen. Aerobic bacteria require oxygen to grow and survive.

Reference: Bacteria. In: Brooks K. *Ready Reference for Microbes*, 3rd edition. Washington, DC: Association for Professionals in Infection Control and Epidemiology, 2012.

CBIC Core Competency: Identification of Infectious Disease Processes

NOTES

54. (D) Creutzfeldt-Jakob disease

Rationale: Classic Creutzfeldt-Jakob disease (CJD) is a human prion disease. It is a neurodegenerative disorder with characteristic clinical and diagnostic features. This disease is rapidly progressive and always fatal. Infection with this disease leads to death usually within 1 year of onset of illness. A probable diagnosis of CJD is made using the following algorithm:

Probable:

i. Rapidly progressive dementia; and at least two out of the following four clinical features:
ii. Myoclonus
iii. Visual or cerebellar signs
iv. Pyramidal/extrapyramidal signs
v. Akinetic mutism

AND a positive result on at least one of the following laboratory tests:

i. A typical EEG (periodic sharp wave complexes) during an illness of any duration; and/or
ii. A positive 14-3-3 CSF assay in patients with a disease duration of less than 2 years
iii. Magnetic resonance imaging high-signal abnormalities in caudate nucleus and/or putamen on diffusion-weighted imaging (DWI) or fluid-attenuated inversion recovery (FLAIR)

AND without routine investigations indicating an alternative diagnosis.

Confirmation of the diagnosis is by brain biopsy or pathological analysis of the mortem brain.

Reference: *APIC Text*, 4th edition, Chapter 73 - Creutzfeldt-Jakob Disease and Other Prion Diseases

CBIC Core Competency: Preventing/Controlling the Transmission of Infectious Agents

55. (A) There is no risk of infection for the paramedic because he was previously infected and is now immune

Rationale: The patient is infected and can transmit Hepatitis B, but the paramedic has been previously infected and is now immune to Hepatitis B. Antibody to the Hepatitis B core antigen is made in response to actual infection with the virus and antibody to the HBsAg is made after the virus is cleared from the patient. Anti-HBs prevent the person from becoming re-infected.

Reference: *APIC Text*, 4th edition, Chapter 101 - Occupational Exposure to Bloodborne Pathogens

CBIC Core Competency: Employee/Occupational Health

NOTES

56. (A) Total number of patients screened

Rationale: The numerator is the actual number of patients screened.

Basic Formula for All Types of Rates

- Rate = x/y × k

Where:

- x = The numerator, which equals the number of times the event (e.g., infections) has occurred during a specified time interval.
- y = The denominator, which equals a population (e.g., number of patients at risk) from which those experiencing the event were derived during the same time interval.
- k = A constant used to transform the result of division into a uniform quantity so that it can be compared with other, similar quantities. A whole number (fractions are inconvenient) such as 100, 1,000, 10,000, or 100,000 is usually used (selection of k is usually made so that the smallest rate calculated has at least one digit to the left of the decimal point) or is determined by accepted practice (the magnitude of numerator compared with denominator).

Reference: *APIC Text*, 4th edition, Chapter 13 - Use of Statistics in Infection Prevention

CBIC Core Competency: Surveillance and Epidemiologic Investigation

57. (B) They have an equal chance of being assigned to either the experimental or the control group

Rationale: Random assignment is a procedure used in experimental studies to create multiple study groups that include subjects with similar characteristics so that the groups are equivalent at the beginning of the study. Participants are assigned to an experimental treatment or program at random so that each individual has an equal chance of being assigned to either group.

Reference: *APIC Text*, 4th edition, Chapter 20 - Research Study Design

CBIC Core Competency: Education and Research

58. (D) 1, 4

Rationale: Privacy curtains are considered high-touch items and are to be changed and cleaned on a routine schedule and whenever soiled. It is also recommended that they be changed after a patient on Contact Isolation is either transferred or discharged.

Reference: *APIC Text*, 4th edition, Chapter 107 - Environmental Services

CBIC Core Competency: Preventing/Controlling the Transmission of Infectious Agents

59. (B) 1, 2

Rationale: Semi-critical items minimally require high-level disinfection using chemical disinfectants. Glutaraldehyde, hydrogen peroxide, orthophthaladehyde, improved hydrogen peroxide, peracetic acid with hydrogen peroxide, and chlorine-based products are approved by the U.S. Food and Drug Administration and are dependable high-level disinfectants provided the factors influencing germicidal procedures are met.

Reference: *APIC Text*, 4th edition, Chapter 32 - Reprocessing Single Use Devices

CBIC Core Competency: Cleaning, Sterilization, Disinfection, Asepsis

NOTES

60. (D) The patient may ambulate in the hallway if he washes his hands and wears a clean gown

Rationale: Transmission of MDROs such as MRSA is an issue of great concern for all types of healthcare facilities. Barrier protection should be used to contain wound drainage, urine, feces, and other excretions or secretions whenever possible to allow for patient independence and participation in therapeutic sessions. If the patient has an acute contagious disease or illness, or if excretions or secretions cannot be contained, appropriate Isolation Precautions (Transmission-based Precautions) should be used. If the patient on Transmission-based Precautions needs to leave the room for any reason, it is important that:

- Appropriate barriers are worn or used by the patient (i.e., masks, dressings that contain drainage)
- All team members, including the patient and family/significant other(s), are aware of the precautions needed
- Patients are informed of ways they can help in preventing the transmission of MDRO to others (i.e., hand washing with soap and water or alcohol-based hand rub before leaving the room and clean clothing)

Reference: *APIC Text*, 4th edition, Chapter 66 - Rehabilitation Services

CBIC Core Competency: Preventing/Controlling the Transmission of Infectious Agents

61. (D) Self-managed

Rationale: Self-managed teams, also called self-directed teams, are small autonomous groups of employees who determine, plan, and manage their daily activities with little or no supervision. Self-managed teams offer cost savings and increased productivity.

Reference: *APIC Text*, 4th edition, Chapter 1 - Infection Prevention and Control Programs

CBIC Core Competency: Management and Communication

62. (D) Food and Drug Administration (FDA)

Rationale: When considering reprocessing SUDs, hospitals are faced with the decision whether to contract with a third-party reprocessor or formulate an in-house plan. No matter the approach, the process must comply with the FDA regulations.

Reference: *APIC Text*, 4th edition, Chapter 32 - Reprocessing Single Use Devices

CBIC Core Competency: Cleaning, Sterilization, Disinfection, Asepsis

NOTES

63. (B) Explain to the surgeon that operating rooms are cleaned after each case and that there is no benefit to scheduling procedures at the end of the day

Rationale: There are three distinct cleaning times for operating rooms: before the first case of the day, between cases, and at the end of the day. Before the first case of the day, horizontal surfaces in the operating room should be damp-dusted with a clean lint-free cloth or a wipe dampened with a disinfectant. After each case, EVS, nursing, and anesthesia personnel decontaminate horizontal surfaces, equipment, examination tables, anesthesia machines, medication carts, and other items used during a procedure. Personnel should pay particular attention to high-touch surfaces, taking care not to overlook machine controls, the tops of linen hampers, waste containers, computers, and phones. Cleaning of equipment should be delegated to personnel specifically trained to perform each task. Clean, lint-free cloths or disposable wipes should be used for each case. Cleaning cloths or wipes should be changed frequently and after contact with blood and body fluids. The cleaning process should progress from high to low and from clean to dirty. Items that are reprocessed, sharps, and biohazardous and nonbiohazardous waste must be placed in their respective containers and transported to their respective holding areas.

Floors in the operating rooms must be cleaned and disinfected after each case. It is only necessary to clean a 3- to 4-foot perimeter around the operative table after each case unless wider perimeter of contamination is identified. At the conclusion of the operating schedule, blood spills and splatters not wiped up during the case must be cleaned and all items in the operating room decontaminated. Personnel should pay meticulous attention to high-touch surfaces. AORN recommends that floors be cleaned with a wet-vacuum and an EPA-registered disinfectant after the completion of scheduled cases. Ventilation grilles, shelves, and cabinets in the operating rooms should be cleaned routinely and when soiled. If not removed, dust and particles collecting in these areas can become airborne and be a source of contamination or infection. Scrub sinks, work rooms, utility rooms, and corridors should also be thoroughly cleaned and disinfected regularly when operating room traffic is low, not in use, and/or whenever visibly contaminated.

Reference: *APIC Text*, 4th edition, Chapter 107 - Environmental Services

CBIC Core Competency: Cleaning, Sterilization, Disinfection, Asepsis

NOTES

64. Ⓐ **Herpes simplex virus**

Rationale: The lumbar puncture (LP) is widely recognized as a necessary part of the early diagnostic evaluation of patients with suspected meningitis because the sensitivity of clinical symptoms, including the classic triad of fever, neck stiffness, and altered mental status exam, is low. CSF appearance, opening pressure (taken during this collection by using a simple column manometer; can be used for both for diagnosis and therapeutically), cellularity, biochemical evaluation, and Gram stain provide critically important diagnostic information as well as guidance for therapy. The preliminary CSF findings can provide keys to the diagnosis quickly and guide treatment for the patient and potential need for infection prevention precautions/isolation and prophylaxis for close contacts. The results of this CSF analysis and culture would rule out bacterial and fungal causes of meningitis, but a viral cause is possible. See Table PE3-2.

Table PE3-2. Typical Results of Preliminary Cerebrospinal Fluid Examination in Acute/Subacute Meningitis

Causative Organism	Opening Pressure	Glucose (Ratio of CSF to Serum Glucose)	Predominant Inflammatory Cell	WBC Counts	Total Protein	Staining
Bacteria	Elevated	Normal to decreased	Neutrophils (early or partially treated may have lymphocyte predominance)	≥1,000/mm^3	Elevated (mild to very)	Gram[a] stain may show GPC or GNC
Virus	Usually normal	Usually normal	Lymphocytes	<100per mm^3	Normal to elevated	Gram stain, negative
Fungi	Variable	Low	Lymphocytes	Variable	Elevated	India ink, positive
Tuber-culosis	Variable	Low (can be extremely depressed levels)	Lymphocytes	Variable	Elevated	AFB stain, positive

Source: Ostrowsky B. Central Nervous System Infection. In: Grota P, ed. *APIC Text of Infection Control and Epidemiology*, 4th edition. Washington, DC: Association for Professionals in Infection Control and Epidemiology, 2014.

[a] Positive in 60 to 80 percent of untreated bacterial meningitis/40 to 60 percent of partially treated cases. AFB, acid-fast bacillus (e.g., Mycobacterial species); GNC, Gram-negative coccus; GNR, Gram-negative rods (bacillus); GPC, Gram-positive coccus.

References: *APIC Text*, 4th edition, Chapter 74 - Central Nervous System Infection; *APIC Text*, 4th edition, Chapter 94 - Streptococci

CBIC Core Competency: Identification of Infectious Disease Processes

NOTES

65. (C) The risk of transmission through needlestick exposures

Rationale: Infection with HBV is a well-recognized occupational risk for HCP. The risk of HBV infection is primarily related to the degree of contact with blood in the work place and also the HBeAg status of the source person. The risk of developing clinical hepatitis if the blood was positive for both HBsAg and HBeAg has been estimated at 22 to 31 percent. In contrast, the average risk of HIV transmission after a percutaneous exposure to HIV-infected blood has been estimated to be approximately 0.3 percent.

Reference: *APIC Text*, 4th edition, Chapter 101 - Occupational Exposure to Bloodborne Pathogens

CBIC Core Competency: Employee/Occupational Health

66. (A) 1, 2

Rationale: The NPSF outlines five attributes of a safety culture that all healthcare organizations should strive to operationalize through implementation of string safety management systems:

- All workers (including front-line staff, physicians, and administrators) accept responsibility for the safety of themselves, their coworkers, patients, and visitors
- Safety has priority over financial and operational goals
- The organization encourages and rewards the identification, communication, and resolution of safety issues
- There are provisions for organizational learning from accidents
- The organization allocates appropriate resources, structure, and accountability to maintain effective safety systems

Reference: *APIC Text*, 4th edition, Chapter 18 - Patient Safety

CBIC Core Competency: Management and Communication

67. (C) Run chart

Rationale: Two common methods used to measure and plot variation in the process of care include run charts and control charts. A run chart is the simplest of charts. It is a single line plotting observed data over time. A run chart can help identify upward and downward trends, and it can show a general picture of a process.

A control chart also plots a single line of data over time. However, control charts include upper and lower control limit lines with a centerline. Control charts are more sensitive at detecting abnormalities than run charts but require at least 25 data points for reliability and validity. Run charts require at least 20 data points. With such a small number of observations in our data set, the run chart would be the most appropriate choice.

Reference: *APIC Text*, 4th edition, Chapter 14 - Process Control Charts

CBIC Core Competency: Surveillance and Epidemiologic Investigation

NOTES

68. (A) Latex-free balloons

Rationale: Infectious diseases cause significant morbidity and mortality in immunocompromised patients. Water is a reservoir for pathogenic microorganisms and can be a source for HAIs. As organizations recognize the importance of care delivery sites as therapeutic environments, they may consider installation of features such as fish tanks, decorative water fountains, water walls, or other water features. In balancing the risk of adding a potential reservoir of waterborne opportunistic pathogens, the CDC *Guidelines for Environmental Infection Control in Health-Care Facilities* recommend facilities avoid placing them in patient care areas. It is well established that both potted plants and fresh flowers carry microbial flora that are pathogenic for the immunocompromised host. Fresh fruits and vegetables also carry several species of Gram-negative rods as part of their natural flora. Latex-free balloons are a safe choice in healthcare facilities.

References: *APIC Text*, 4th edition, Chapter 23 - The Immunocompromised Host; Sehulster LM, Chinn RYW, Arduino MJ, et al. *Guidelines for environmental infection control in health-care facilities. Recommendations from CDC and the Healthcare Infection Control Practices Advisory Committee (HICPAC).* Chicago: American Society for Healthcare Engineering/American Hospital Association, 2004.

CBIC Core Competency: Preventing/Controlling the Transmission of Infectious Agents

69. (A) Case study

Rationale: Case studies can be used as a training method to help bridge the learning gap between theory and actual practice. The method builds on a variety of learner skills: analytical, critical, and interactive. Learners explore multiple solutions and enhance creativity and problem-solving approaches often using a discussion-based format.

Reference: *APIC Text*, 4th edition, Chapter 3 - Education and Training

CBIC Core Competency: Education and Research

70. (A) RR = 3.0

Rationale: RR is the incidence in the exposed group divided by the incidence in the unexposed group. This case is simply comparing the incidence in two units. Because the question asks for the relative risk in the Burn Unit as compared to the Bone Marrow Transplant Unit, the Burn Unit should be considered to be the exposed group. The RR is the incidence in the Burn Unit divided by the incidence in the Bone Marrow Transplant Unit, which is 3.0/1.0. This is equal to 3.0. Thus patients in the burn unit had 3 times higher risk of newly acquired VRE than patients in the bone marrow transplant unit.

Reference: *APIC Text*, 4th edition, Chapter 13 - Use of Statistics in Infection Prevention

CBIC Core Competency: Surveillance and Epidemiologic Investigation

NOTES

71. (C) Airborne Precautions

Rationale: During the beginning of an infectious disease disaster when the agent may not have been identified or when there is not enough evidence regarding the disease transmission route, IPs need to base infection prevention decisions on syndromes and symptomatology. This is referred to as syndrome-based isolation/control measures. General guidelines include implementing Airborne Precautions if the patient is severely ill with rapidly progressing respiratory symptoms and an airborne spread disease is suspected (i.e., severe acute respiratory syndrome or avian influenza).

Reference: *APIC Text*, 4th edition, Chapter 120 - Infectious Disease Disasters: Bioterrorism, Emerging Infections, and Pandemics

CBIC Core Competency: Preventing/Controlling the Transmission of Infectious Agents

72. (B) Using a multidisciplinary approach to determine corrective actions

Rationale: Answers A, C, and D may be actions recommended following thorough review and discussion of the surveillance data, but they are not the next steps to take without first seeking input on the appropriate corrective actions from the appropriate stakeholders.

Reference: *APIC Text*, 4th edition, Chapter 11 - Surveillance

CBIC Core Competency: Management and Communication

73. (D) 1, 3

Rationale: Healthcare facilities considering contracting with a commercial third-party reprocessor have the responsibility of knowing that reprocessing an SUD presents no greater risk to their patients' health and safety. An on-site visit should be scheduled, with the opportunity to meet with personnel involved in the process, and a review of the company's policies. The visit should include an opportunity to observe the cleaning and decontamination, inspection and testing, and sterilization load preparation processes, as well as reviewing quality control records.

Reference: *APIC Text*, 4th edition, Chapter 32 - Reprocessing Single Use Devices

CBIC Core Competency: Cleaning, Sterilization, Disinfection, Asepsis

74. (C) Polymerase chain reaction (PCR)

Rationale: Molecular testing methodologies have greatly enhanced the speed, specificity, and sensitivity of tests for clinically significant microbes. Examples of molecular testing methods are PCR, pulse field gel electrophoresis, Western blot assay, enzyme linked immunoassays, and molecular genotypic assays.

Reference: Cultures and Gram Stains. In: Kulich P, Taylor D, eds. *Infection Preventionists' Guide to the Lab*. Washington, DC: Association for Professionals in Infection Control and Epidemiology, 2012.

CBIC Core Competency: Identification of Infectious Disease Processes

NOTES

75. **(A) Botulism**

Rationale: Botulism is a public health emergency. Botulism is a neuroparalytic illness caused by a toxin made by the bacterium *C. botulinum*. Symptoms of botulism include blurred vision, diplopia, dysarthria, dysphagia, symmetrical descending flaccid paralysis and respiratory failure. Prompt diagnosis and early treatment of botulism are essential to minimize the number of affected persons and the severity of illness.

Reference: *APIC Text*, 4th edition, Chapter 120 - Infectious Disease Disasters: Bioterrorism, Emerging Infections, and Pandemics

CBIC Core Competency: Preventing/Controlling the Transmission of Infectious Agents

76. **(B) Place one additional TST and screen for symptoms**

Rationale: HCP with documentation of a previous negative TST within the prior 12 months should have a second TST placed and be screened for signs and symptoms of TB. The TST should be read in 48 to 72 hours. If negative, the employee is cleared for work. If the TST is positive, a chest x-ray should be performed.

References: *APIC Text*, 4th edition, Chapter 95 - Tuberculosis and Other Mycobacteria; Centers for Disease Control and Prevention. Guidelines for Preventing the Transmission of Mycobacterium tuberculosis in Health-Care Settings, 2005. *MMWR* 2005;54(RR-17):

CBIC Core Competency: Employee/Occupational Health

77. **(D) 1, 4**

Rationale: Continuous data contain information that can be measured on a continuum or scale and can have numeric values between the minimum and maximum value (a continuum) (e.g., age; serum cholesterol level; temperature, such as 98.6°F, 98.7°F, and 98.8°F; infection rates); continuous data require the process of measuring, rather than counting, and may contain whole numbers, decimals, or percentages. Conversely, discrete data contain whole numbers and are mutually exclusive (e.g., infected or not infected, male or female, blood type).

Reference: *APIC Text*, 4th edition, Chapter 13 - Use of Statistics in Infection Prevention

CBIC Core Competency: Surveillance and Epidemiologic Investigation

78. **(B) Critical thinking**

Rationale: Critical thinking is the identification and evaluation of evidence to guide decision-making. The list of core critical thinking skills includes observation, interpretation, analysis, inference, evaluation, explanation, and metacognition. Critical thinking is imperative when evaluating and interpreting research studies.

Reference: *APIC Text*, 4th edition, Chapter 2 - Competency and Certification of the Infection Preventionist

CBIC Core Competency: Education and Research

NOTES

79. **C Not being familiar with the opening mechanism of the jewelry to be able to remove it**

Rationale: It is becoming more common for HCP to provide care for patients with body jewelry, and it is sometimes unclear whether removal of the jewelry is necessary. Removal of these items is sometimes required for radiological purposes and removal is not usually difficult if the patient is able to assist with the opening mechanism. In an emergency situation, attempts at removal may cause unnecessary trauma to the site. Many HCP are unaware of the procedures for removing body piercing. In a survey of 28 accident and emergency doctors, only six were able to accurately describe the opening mechanisms of all three commonly used types of jewelry.

Reference: *APIC Text*, 4th edition, Chapter 123 - Body Piercing, Tattoos, and Electrolysis

CBIC Core Competency: Preventing/Controlling the Transmission of Infectious Agents

80. **D Six percent hydrogen peroxide**

Rationale: *Cryptosporidium parvum* are protozoa that are resistant to many disinfectants, including chlorine. The only disinfectant with known effectiveness against *C. parvum* at working concentrations is hydrogen peroxide.

Reference: CDC Guideline for Disinfection and Sterilization in Healthcare Facilities, 2008, Page 23

CBIC Core Competency: Cleaning, Sterilization, Disinfection, Asepsis

81. **A Sewage systems to allow adequate sanitation of waste**

Rationale: Planning for new construction or major renovation requires early collaboration among IPs, epidemiologists, architects, engineers, and other stakeholders to ensure that design of specific structures facilitates desired infection prevention program practices. An essential first step in the planning process is ICRA, followed by interventions, monitoring, and continuous assessment and improvement at a broad, organizational program level and during operational projects.

ICRA elements related to building design features include the following:

- Numbers, location, and types of AII and protective environment (PE) rooms
- Location of special ventilation and filtration of HVAC serving such areas as emergency department waiting and intake areas
- Air handling and ventilation needs in surgical services, AII and PE rooms, laboratories, local exhaust systems for hazardous agents/chemicals, and other areas with special needs
- Water systems to limit *Legionella* spp. and other waterborne opportunistic pathogens
- Finishes and surfaces

Reference: *APIC Text*, 4th edition, Chapter 116 - Construction and Renovation

CBIC Core Competency: Environment of Care

NOTES

82. D Expanded computer hardware and software

Rationale: Capital expenses or expenditures are business expenses for fixed assets such as buildings or equipment. Operating expenses such as rent, utilities, and insurance are not considered capital expenses.

Reference: *APIC Text*, 4th edition, Chapter 1 - Infection Prevention and Control Programs

CBIC Core Competency: Management and Communication

83. A 1

Rationale: The CDC has established a system for cataloging recommendations based on the amount of data available to support the recommendation. Category 1A recommendations are strongly supported by epidemiologic, clinical, or experimental data from well-designed studies. Sterilization of medical instruments that will come into contact with sterile tissue or the vascular system is a Category 1A recommendation.

Reference: CDC Guideline for Disinfection and Sterilization in Healthcare Facilities, 2008, Page 83-84

CBIC Core Competency: Cleaning, Sterilization, Disinfection, Asepsis

84. C Dual-purpose rooms that can alternate between negative and positive air pressure

Rationale: Isolation rooms can serve two purposes. The first is to provide appropriate isolation for patients infected with pathogens that are transmitted by the airborne route (e.g., *M. tuberculosis*, varicella-zoster virus, rubeola [measles] virus). The major goal in this situation is to prevent transmission of pathogens from an infected patient to other patients, staff, or visitors. This is generally achieved by maintaining AIIRs. The second purpose is to provide a PE for severely immunosuppressed patients. AIIRs have negative air pressure, and PE rooms have positive air pressure with respect to adjacent areas. Correct direction of airflow and properly balanced air pressure in AIIR or PE areas are essential elements to consider during construction and renovation. The Facility Guidelines Institute's (FGI) Guidelines do not support "reversible" airflow rooms based on complexity of pressure relationships, concerns for serious patient and HCP outcomes if errors are made, and labor intensity needed for preventive maintenance.

Reference: *APIC Text*, 4th edition, Chapter 116 - Construction and Renovation

CBIC Core Competency: Environment of Care

85. A Early identification of antibiotic resistance

Rationale: Gram staining of a specimen may help to determine the quality of a specimen, initial direction for therapy (empiric antibiotics), or the need for Isolation Precautions (e.g., Gram-negative diplococci in CSF, suggesting meningococci). It does not identify antibiotic resistance.

Reference: *APIC Text*, 4th edition, Chapter 24 - Microbiology Basics

CBIC Core Competency: Identification of Infectious Disease Processes

NOTES

86. (C) ***Streptococcus agalactiae***

Rationale: Asymptomatic carriage of *Streptococcus agalactiae* or group B *Streptococcus* (group B strep) in gastrointestinal and genital tracts is common. Intrapartum transmission via ascending spread from vagina occurs. Neurologic sequelae include sight or hearing loss and cerebral palsy. Death occurs in 5 percent of infants.

Reference: *APIC Text*, 4th edition, Chapter 9 - Streptococci

CBIC Core Competency: Identification of Infectious Disease Processes

87. (B) **1, 3**

Rationale: CHG products are increasingly used because of their effectiveness, 30-second dry time, and low incidence of allergic reactions. CHG products do not need to be removed or rinsed from the skin following venipuncture. CHG is not approved for use with infants younger than 2 months of age.

References: *APIC Text*, 4th edition, Chapter 24 - Microbiology Basics; Blood Cultures. In: Kulich P, Taylor D, eds. *Infection Preventionists' Guide to the Lab*. Washington, DC: Association for Professionals in Infection Control and Epidemiology, 2012.

CBIC Core Competency: Cleaning, Sterilization, Disinfection, Asepsis

88. (D) **It is inaccurate because the negative control amplified MRSA DNA**

Rationale: PCR is an automated technique used to detect a target sequence of DNA that is unique to an organism. Positive and negative PCR controls are designed to monitor assay performance. The positive control is intended to monitor for substantial reagent failure. The negative control is used to detect reagent or environmental contamination by either MRSA DNA or MRSA amplicons. The negative control should not produce any amplification signal. Amplification of MRSA DNA in this control indicates that there was contamination of the samples with MRSA DNA, so the test results are not accurate.

Reference: *APIC Text*, 4th edition, Chapter 25 - Laboratory Testing and Diagnostics

CBIC Core Competency: Identification of Infectious Disease Processes

89. (D) **1, 2, 4**

Rationale: Immunoglobulins are special concentrated antibody preparations that provide immediate short-term protection against disease for individuals who are at high risk of experiencing severe disease or of developing serious complications from the disease. Human normal immunoglobulin preparations for Hepatitis A, measles, polio, and rubella, and specific immunoglobulin preparations for Hepatitis B, rabies, and varicella-zoster for intramuscular use, are available.

References: *APIC Text*, 4th edition, Chapter 100 - Occupational Health; Centers for Disease Control and Prevention (CDC). *Vaccines and Immunizations*. CDC website. 2010. Available at: http://www.cdc.gov/vaccines/

CBIC Core Competency: Employee/Occupational Health

NOTES

90. (B) **1, 4**

Rationale: Multidisciplinary groups, including pharmacists, should establish a system for monitoring resistance and antibiotic usage, establish practice guidelines and other polices to control the use of antibiotics, respond to data from the monitoring system, and measure outcomes to evaluate the effectiveness of policies. Ideally, core members of an antimicrobial stewardship team include an infectious diseases physician, a clinical pharmacist with infectious diseases training, a clinical microbiologist, an information system specialist, an IP, and a hospital epidemiologist.

Reference: *APIC Text*, 4th edition, Chapter 110 - Pharmacy Services

CBIC Core Competency: Management and Communication

91. (B) **5:1**

Rationale: A ratio is a relationship between two numbers of the same kind expressed as "a to b" or a:b. It provides a comparison of two quantities. The ratio of females to males is **40:8 or 5:1**.

Reference: *APIC Text*, 4th edition, Chapter 13 - Use of Statistics in Infection Prevention

CBIC Core Competency: Surveillance and Epidemiologic Investigation

92. (A) **1, 2**

Rationale: The CDC recommends separating HBsAg patients by room or area and using a separate, dedicated machine and equipment to reduce the risk of transmission of HBV in the dialysis setting. Patients who are known to be positive for HBsAg should be excluded from reprocessing programs because of the risk of transmission to susceptible reuse personnel. The incidence of HBsAg has been found to be higher in dialysis units that do not follow recommendations.

Reference: *APIC Text*, 4th edition, Chapter 39 - Dialysis; Centers for Disease Control and Prevention (CDC). Recommendations for Preventing Transmission of Infections Among Chronic Hemodialysis Patients. *MMWR* 2001 April 27;50(RR05):1-43.

CBIC Core Competency: Preventing/Controlling the Transmission of Infectious Agents

NOTES

93. Ⓐ **Central line dressing change**

Rationale: Sterile supplies and sterile technique should be used for central line dressing changes (see Table PE-2).

Table PE3-2. Examples of Suggested Techniques by Procedure

Procedure/ Intervention	Hand Hygiene Indicated	Type of Glove to Be Used*	Supplies Indicated	Instrumentation
Wound cleaning	Yes	Clean exam gloves	Normal saline or prepared sterile wound cleanser; sterile supplies such as 4×4 or cotton applicators	Irrigation performed with sterile device while maintaining clean technique
Routine dressing changes without debridement	Yes	Clean exam gloves	Sterile supplies using clean technique	Sterile supplies using clean technique
Dressing change with mechanical, chemical, or enzymatic ebridement	Yes	Clean exam gloves	Sterile supplies using clean technique	Sterile supplies using clean technique
Dressing change with sharp, conservative bedside debridement	Yes	Sterile gloves	Sterile supplies and sterile technique due to the potential for entering new, unaffected tissues	Sterile supplies and sterile technique
Central line dressing change	Yes	Sterile gloves for removing old dressing and new sterile gloves for dressing change procedure	Sterile dressing change kit and sterile technique; surgical mask should be worn	Sterile supplies and sterile technique
Tracheal suctioning where the tracheal suction catheter is not within a closed sheath	Yes	Sterile gloves when suctioning	Sterile suction catheter	Sterile supplies using clean technique
Tracheostomy care or suctioning with a suction catheter within a closed sheath	Yes	Clean exam gloves	Sterile supplies using clean technique	Sterile supplies using clean technique

Reference: *APIC Text*, 4th edition, Chapter 30 - Aseptic Technique

CBIC Core Competency: Preventing/Controlling the Transmission of Infectious Agents

NOTES

94. **C VRE cases have 2.3 times the odds of having had exposure to long-term nursing care than non-VRE cases**

Rationale: A case-control study groups participants by their disease status (in this example, VRE-colonized cases or VRE-noncolonized controls) and looks retrospectively to determine whether they had an exposure of interest. The odds ratio that is calculated from a case-control study is the odds of the cases having had the exposure divided by the odds of the controls having had the exposure. Although this is often interpreted the same way as an RR, a case-control study does not give information about risk because incidence rates are not calculated in this study design. The odds ratio is not the risk of developing the disease given the exposure, but rather the ratio of the odds of having had the exposure given the disease status.

Reference: *APIC Text*, 4th edition, Chapter 13 - Use of Statistics in Infection Prevention

CBIC Core Competency: Education and Research

95. **C The carrying case should be discarded**

Rationale: Of all medical instruments, endoscopes have the highest association with healthcare outbreaks. Endoscope carrying cases should not be used to store clean or dirty endoscopes within a healthcare facility. If an unprocessed endoscope is placed in a carrying case then the case should be discarded because of the potential for a clean endoscope to become contaminated through contact with the case.

Reference: CDC Guideline for Disinfection and Sterilization in Healthcare Facilities, 2008 Page: 17, 88

CBIC Core Competency: Cleaning, Sterilization, Disinfection, Asepsis

96. **B Direct contact**

Rationale: According to the CDC *Guidelines for the Prevention of Intravascular Catheter-Related Infections*, there are four recognized routes for contamination of catheters: (1) migration of skin organisms at the insertion site into the cutaneous catheter tract and along the surface of the catheter with colonization of the catheter tip; this is the most common route of infection for short-term catheters; (2) direct contamination of the catheter or catheter hub by contact with hands or contaminated fluids or devices; (3) less commonly, catheters might become hematogenously seeded from another focus of infection; and (4) rarely, infusate contamination might lead to catheter-related bloodstream infections.

Reference: *APIC Text*, 4th edition, Chapter 34 - Intravascular Device Infections

CBIC Core Competency: Preventing/Controlling the Transmission of Infectious Agents

NOTES

97. **(B) Form a focus group of unit staff to discuss her observations, the ideas to improve compliance, and the proposed solution**

Rationale: Focus groups provide an opportunity for investigators to explore the beliefs of participants and provide an avenue for perceptions and concerns to be identified and addressed. Focus groups are a qualitative research method that can be used in quality improvement initiatives. For example, focus groups are used to obtain reactions to proposed changes or proposed solutions to problems, to describe perspectives that may differ from the researcher's, to describe relationships within groups (e.g., coping strategies), to assess programs and outcomes of services, and to confirm hypotheses.

Reference: *APIC Text*, 4th edition, Chapter 19 - Qualitative Research Methods

CBIC Core Competency: Management and Communication

98. **(C) A 42-year-old, well-conditioned male undergoing elective groin hernia repair**

Rationale: Elective procedures carry a lower risk for postoperative infection than urgent ones. It is important to consider these factors when making decisions regarding surgical outcomes and quality improvement assessments. A surgical risk index is a score used to predict a surgical patient's risk of acquiring a surgical site infection. The risk index score, ranging from 0 to 3, is the sum of the number of risk factors present among the following:

- Surgical site wound classification of contaminated or dirty (class III or IV)
- American Society of Anesthesiology (ASA) score as rated by an anesthesiologist before operation of ≥ 3
- Prolonged procedure time, where the threshold in minutes (i.e., the cut point) is above the 75th percentile of the duration of surgery for the specific procedure being performed as determined by the NHSN database

The higher the score by this index, the greater is the risk for subsequent SSI.

Reference: *APIC Text*, 4th edition, Chapter 37 - Surgical Site Infection

CBIC Core Competency: Surveillance and Epidemiologic Investigation

99. **(D) *Escherichia coli***

Rationale: In the United States, urinary tract infections account for about 4 million ambulatory care visits each year, representing about 1 percent of all outpatient visits. Gram-negative bacilli and enterococci are the primary enteric bacteria that can grow in human urine. The presence of bacteria in urine almost always precedes intestinal colonization by the infecting bacteria. *E. coli* is the predominant aerobic Gram-negative organism of normal bowel flora, and thus is the most common organism isolated from urinary tract infections.

Reference: *APIC Text*, 4th edition, Chapter 33 - Urinary Tract Infection

CBIC Core Competency: Identification of Infectious Disease Processes

NOTES

100. (B) Hepatitis C

Rationale: HCV is inefficiently transmitted by sexual intercourse (prevalence ranging from 1.3 percent in North America to 27 percent in Asia in long-term partners), though homosexual men, persons with multiple sexual partners and HIV patients have higher rates of seroprevalence for HCV than monogamous heterosexuals. The average risk for vertical transmission is 6 percent overall and 17percent in mothers with HIV, which appears to be related to viral titer. No difference in transmission is noted whether the child is breast- or bottle-fed.

Reference: *APIC Text*, 4th edition, Chapter 97 - Viral Hepatitis

CBIC Core Competency: Preventing/Controlling the Transmission of Infectious Agents

101. (A) A nurse is stuck with an intravenous (IV) catheter stylet after withdrawing the stylet from the catheter

Rationale: IV catheter stylets are involved in only about 3 percent of sharp object injuries, but they have the highest risk of transmission of bloodborne pathogens because they are hollow-bore needles that can be filled with blood. This results in greater exposure to bloodborne pathogens.

References: *APIC Text*, 4th edition, Chapter 105 - Minimizing Exposure to Blood and Body Fluids; Centers for Disease Control and Prevention (CDC). Updated U.S. Public Health Service guidelines for the management of occupational exposure to HBV, HCV, and HIV and recommendations for postexposure prophylaxis. *MMWR* 2001 June 29;50(RR11):1–42.

CBIC Core Competency: Employee/Occupational Health

102. (D) N

Rationale: Special cause variation is variation that lies more than 3 standard deviations outside the mean of the sample distribution. Common cause variation represents variation within 3 standard deviations of the mean and includes 99.73 percent of all probably events, so special cause variation represents the remaining 0.27 percent of all events.

Reference: *APIC Text*, 4th edition, Chapter 14 - Process Control Charts

CBIC Core Competency: Surveillance and Epidemiologic Investigation

103. (C) 2, 3

Rationale: Measles, or Rubeola, virus is a temperature labile virus that should be transported on ice to the lab as soon as possible after collection and placed in culture immediately or frozen at -70°C until being placed in culture. Measles virus samples should not be kept at room temperature or frozen at -20°C because these temperatures will lower the infectivity of the virus in the sample and this could produce a false negative result. The patient must be placed in an airborne infection isolation room because there is a clinical suspicion of measles and the initial negative test was not performed properly.

References: *APIC Text*, 4th edition, Chapter 86 - Measles, Mumps, Rubella, Varicella; CDC Website - Measles (http://www.cdc.gov/measles/index.html

CBIC Core Competency: Identification of Infectious Disease Processes

NOTES

104. (C) Mean and median

Rationale: Measures of central tendency describe the values around the middle of a set of data. Two measures of central tendency used in healthcare surveillance are the arithmetic mean and median. The mean is the mathematical average of the values in a set of data. The median is the middle value in a ranked set of data.

Reference: *APIC Text*, 4th edition, Chapter 11 - Surveillance

CBIC Core Competency: Surveillance and Epidemiologic Investigation

105. (B) The number of containment cubes owned by the facility

Rationale: An ICRA must guide a strategic, proactive design to mitigate environmental sources of microbes, to prevent infectious hazards through architectural design (e.g., hand washing and hand hygiene stations, isolation rooms; materials selection for surfaces and furnishings) and to provide control measures that mitigate potential contamination during actual construction or renovation (e.g., dust barriers, pressure differentials, protection of air handlers).

ICRA elements related to building site areas affected by construction include the following:

- Impact of disrupting essential services to patients and employees
- Determination of the specific hazards and protection levels for each
- Location of patients based on susceptibility to infection and definition of risks to each
- Impact of potential outages or emergencies and protection of patients during planned or unplanned outages, movement of debris, traffic flow, cleanup, and testing and certification
- Assessment of external and internal construction activities
- Location of known hazards

Reference: *APIC Text*, 4th edition, Chapter 116 - Construction and Renovation

CBIC Core Competency: Environment of Care

106. (D) A work breakdown structure

Rationale: A work breakdown structure (WBS), is the decomposition of a project into smaller components. Elements of the plan may be a product, data, service, or any combination thereof. A WBS also provides the necessary framework for detailed cost estimating and control along with providing guidance for schedule development and control.

Reference: *APIC Text*, 4th edition, Chapter 5 - Infection Prevention and Behavioral Interventions

CBIC Core Competency: Management and Communication

NOTES

107. Ⓐ **X axis labeled with the months of the year**

Rationale: Graphs are a method of showing quantitative data using a system of coordinates. A well-constructed graph consists of two sets of lines that intersect at right angles. Each axis (line) has a scale measurement and a label. Time (year, month, quarter, day, etc.) is usually represented on the horizontal (x) axis. The vertical (y) axis usually reflects the frequency of occurrence of an event (e.g., the number of cases of disease) or the proportion (e.g., percent, cases per 1,000 patient days) with the event. Each graph should be simple and self-explanatory.

Reference: *APIC Text*, 4th edition, Chapter 10 - General Principles of Epidemiology

CBIC Core Competency: Surveillance and Epidemiologic Investigation

108. Ⓒ **Puncture-proof, sealable containers labeled as biohazardous**

Rationale: Contaminated items should be placed in puncture-proof, sealable containers and visibly labeled biohazardous. The selection of the container will depend on the size, presence of sharps, configuration, and volume/numbers of medical devices or instruments being transported.

Reference: *APIC Text*, 4th edition, Chapter 106 - Sterile Processing

CBIC Core Competency: Preventing/Controlling the Transmission of Infectious Agents

109. Ⓐ **1, 4**

Rationale: *L. pneumophila* is a common cause of both community-acquired and healthcare-associated pneumonia. Clinical manifestations are nonspecific, but high fever, diarrhea, and hypernatremia are common. Infection has been linked to drinking water distribution systems of acute care and extended care facilities. When a patient receives a diagnosis of healthcare-associated Legionnaires' disease, culturing of the water sites to which the patient was exposed is indicated. Distal sites include water faucets, ice machines, water used in respiratory tract devices, and water sources to which the patient is exposed. Air conditioners have not been implicated in Legionnaires' disease. IV solutions are not known to be sources of *Legionella* infections.

Reference: Other Microbiology Contributions. In: Kulich P, Taylor D, eds. *The Infection Preventionist's Guide to the Lab*. Washington, DC: Association for Professionals in Infection Control and Epidemiology, 2012.

CBIC Core Competency: Environment of Care

110. Ⓓ **Purchasing self-sheathing syringes**

Rationale: Engineering controls prevent transmission of bloodborne pathogens. These controls use technology to reduce and remove the potential for contact with sharp objects that may be contaminated with blood and body fluids. Examples of engineering controls include safety needles, retractable scalpels, and sharps containers. Engineering controls are only valuable if they are used correctly. Education about correct use of the technology is a key factor in reducing exposure to bloodborne pathogens.

References: Occupational Safety and Health Administration. *OSHA Fact Sheet: OSHA's Bloodborne Pathogens Standard*. OSHA website. 2011. Available at: https://www.osha.gov/OshDoc/data_BloodborneFacts/bbfact01.pdf; *APIC Text*, 4th edition, Chapter 105 - Minimizing Exposure to Blood and Body Fluids

CBIC Core Competency: Employee/Occupational Health

NOTES

111. A 1, 2, 3

Rationale: The risk of HAI during patient care is related to the mode of transmission of the infectious agent, the type of patient care activity or procedure being performed, and the individual's underlying host defenses. The duration of exposure, inoculum, and pathogenicity of the infectious agent also significantly influences the infection risk.

Reference: *APIC Text*, 4th edition, Chapter 21 - Risk Factors Facilitating Transmission of Infectious Agents

CBIC Core Competency: Preventing/Controlling Transmission of Infectious Agents

112. C Antibody assay to detect viral antibodies in the serum

Rationale: There are three major methods to diagnose viral infections: direct detection in the clinical specimen, specific antibody assay to detect viral antibodies in the serum, and viral culture. Gram staining and broth dilution are used for bacterial pathogens. Antibody assays are performed on serum.

Reference: *APIC Text*, 4th edition, Chapter 24 - Microbiology Basics

CBIC Core Competency: Identification of Infectious Disease Processes

113. C 17 percent

Rationale: An attack rate is a special form of incidence rate. It is not truly a rate, but a proportion. It is the proportion of persons at risk who become infected over an entire period of exposure or a measure of the risk or probability of becoming a case. It is usually expressed as a percentage and is used almost exclusively for epidemics or outbreaks of disease where a specific population is exposed to a disease for a limited period of time. The attack rate equals the number of new cases of disease (for a specified time period) divided by the population at risk for the same time period multiplied by 100. Attack rate is the same as incidence rate, except that attack rates are always expressed as cases per 100 populations or as a percentage.

The MRSA attack rate for this scenario is $6 \div 35 \times 100 = 17$ percent

Reference: *APIC Text*, 4th edition, Chapter 13 - Use of Statistics in Infection Prevention

CBIC Core Competency: Surveillance and Epidemiologic Investigation

114. B The patient received a dose of Hepatitis B vaccine in the last 21 days

Rationale: HBsAg is a protein on the surface of HBV; it can be detected in high levels in serum during acute or chronic HBV infection. Care should be taken when testing for HBsAg because recent administration of Hepatitis B vaccine may result in positive HBsAg results for 7 to 30 days following vaccination.

References: *APIC Text*, 4th edition, Chapter 97 - Viral Hepatitis; *APIC Text*, 4th edition, Chapter 39 - Dialysis

CBIC Core Competency: Preventing/Controlling the Transmission of Infectious Agents

NOTES

115. (B) Weil-Felix agglutination

Rationale: Rocky Mountain spotted fever (RMSF) is a tickborne disease caused by the bacterium *Rickettsia rickettsii*. This organism is a cause of potentially fatal human illness in North and South America and is transmitted to humans by the bite of infected tick species. Weil-Felix agglutination is a test performed to differentiate rickettsial antibodies in the serum. This test can be useful in diagnosing RMSF.

Reference: *APIC Text*, 4th edition, Chapter 25 - Laboratory Testing and Diagnostics

CBIC Core Competency: Identification of Infectious Disease Processes

116. (C) Studies human characteristics and is concerned with design of tools, machines, and systems that take into account human capabilities

Rationale: Human factors engineering (HFE) involves research in human psychological, social, physical, and biological characteristics and is concerned with design of tools, machines, and systems that take into account human capabilities, limitations, and characteristics. The goal is to create designs that are safe, comfortable, and effective for humans to use.

Reference: *APIC Text*, 4th edition, Chapter 18 - Patient Safety

CBIC Core Competency: Management and Communication

117. (C) 3, 4

Rationale: The ACIP recommends that all HCP regardless of their age receive a single dose of Tdap if they have not been previously vaccinated. ACIP also recommends that all HCP receive seasonal influenza vaccine annually.

References: Shefer A, Atkinson W, Friedman C, et al. Immunization of Health-Care Personnel: Recommendations of the Advisory Committee on Immunization Practices (ACIP). *MMWR* 2011 Nov 25; 60(RR07):1-45.; Centers for Disease Control and Prevention. Influenza Vaccination Coverage Among Health-Care Personnel — United States, 2012–13 Influenza Season. *MMWR* 2013 Sept 27;68(38):781-786.

CBIC Core Competency: Employee/Occupational Health

118. (D) A horseshoe shape that also provides writing surfaces

Rationale: A horseshoe shape allows face to face participant contact while allowing the educator and equipment to be easily positioned for visibility. Whatever classroom setup is used, efforts should be made to encourage interaction via chair placement or grouping of participants.

Reference: *APIC Text*, 4th edition, Chapter 3 - Education and Training

CBIC Core Competency: Education and Research

NOTES

119. (A) Three cases/4 person-years

Rationale: Incidence density is the total number of new cases over the period of time that each participant was observed during the study period. In this table there are three new cases of VRE over the study period, so the numerator for the incidence density calculation is 3. Participants were observed for a total of four person-years (add up the number of months of observation of all study participants) so the denominator is 4 person-years.

Reference: *APIC Text*, 4th edition, Chapter 13 - Use of Statistics in Infection Prevention

CBIC Core Competency: Surveillance and Epidemiologic Investigation

120. (B) Importance of hand hygiene and asking care givers if they have washed their hands

Rationale: The Joint Commission's National Patient Safety Goal 7 emphasizes the importance of patient education concerning key topics such as SSI prevention, prevention of central line-associated infections, and the management of resistant organisms. All patients should be taught the concepts of hand hygiene, including when to use soap and water or alcohol-based hand rubs. Patients should also be taught to ask their care givers if they have washed their hands prior contact with the patient.

Reference: *APIC Text*, 4th edition, Chapter 18 - Patient Safety

CBIC Core Competency: Management and Communication

121. (A) Increases during the antiretroviral phase, decreases during asymptomatic HIV infection, then increases as the patient progresses to acquired immune deficiency syndrome (AIDS)

Rationale: During the acute retroviral syndrome there is a high level of HIV viremia with plasma HIV RNA titers of 105 copies per mL. Therefore, when a patient presents with signs and symptoms compatible with acute retroviral syndrome, the laboratory diagnosis is based on the determination of HIV RNA titers or viral load, not determination of HIV serology.

Reference: *APIC Text*, 4th edition, Chapter 81 - HIV/AIDS

CBIC Core Competency: Preventing/Controlling the Transmission of Infectious Agents

122. (A) Outcome surveillance

Rationale: Surveillance programs should measure outcomes of healthcare, processes of healthcare, and selected events of importance to the healthcare organization. Examples of outcome indicators that may be monitored include HAIs (e.g., bloodstream, urinary tract, pneumonia, surgical site, conjunctivitis, upper respiratory tract, or local intravenous site); infection or colonization with a specific organism (e.g., *C. difficile*, MRSA, VRE, or other MDRO, RSV, or rotavirus); decubitus ulcers; phlebitis related to peripheral intravascular therapy; pyrogenic reaction or vascular access infection in hemodialysis patients; resident or patient falls; influenza or TST conversions in patients, residents, or HCP; and sharps injuries and blood/body fluid exposures in HCP.

Reference: *APIC Text*, 4th edition, Chapter 11 - Surveillance

CBIC Core Competency: Surveillance and Epidemiologic Investigation

NOTES

123. (A) Empiric

Rationale: When no definitive information about a causative pathogen is available (though Gram stain can be highly suggestive), therapy is said to be empirical. Typically, hospitalized patients are sufficiently ill to warrant treatment before culture and sensitivity results are available, and therapy while the results of cultures are pending may represent most empirical therapy. Especially in hospitalized patients, appropriate cultures, usually including more than one blood culture, should be collected before the initiation of therapy. The site of infection determined clinically (e.g., lung, urinary tract) and host factors (e.g., HIV, organ transplant patient) give an indication of likely pathogens and should shape the decision regarding empirical therapy. Empirical therapy, compared with pathogen-directed therapy, is broader in spectrum due to uncertainty about the causative agent.

Reference: *APIC Text*, 4th edition, Chapter 26 - Antimicrobials and Resistance

CBIC Core Competency: Identification of Infectious Disease Processes

124. (B) Group 2: Mean 87 SD 3.5

Rationale: Standard deviation is a measure of dispersion of the raw scores that reflects the variability in values around the mean. It employs the squared deviations from the mean (variance), which therefore gives added emphasis to larger deviations. The standard deviation indicates how small the variability is (i.e., the spread) among observations. If the variability is small, all the values are close to the mean. If it is large, the values are not close to the mean. Group 2 has the smallest standard deviation, indicating less variability and thus greater consistency among the scores.

Reference: *APIC Text*, 4th edition, Chapter 13 - Use of Statistics in Infection Prevention

CBIC Core Competency: Education and Research

125. (A) Job enrichment

Rationale: Job enrichment is defined as a way to motivate employees by giving them more responsibilities and variety in their work. The concept was developed by American psychologist Frederick Herzberg in the 1950s. According to Herzberg, a well-enriched job should contain a range of tasks and challenges of varying difficulties, meaningful tasks, and feedback, encouragement, and communication. Allowing employees more control over their work can stimulate their desire to succeed.

Reference: *APIC Text*, 4th edition, Chapter 5 - Infection Prevention and Behavioral Interventions

CBIC Core Competency: Management and Communication

126. (B) The Lung Transplant Coordinator

Rationale: Of all HCP listed, this employee would get priority because they work postoperatively with immunocompromised patients who are at high risk for influenza infection. Any HCP who work with high-risk patients should be vaccinated against influenza.

Reference: *APIC Text*, 4th edition, Chapter 103 - Immunization of Healthcare Personnel

CBIC Core Competency: Employee/Occupational Health

NOTES

127. (B) Indicated a propagated source of infection

Rationale: An epidemic curve gives a graphical display of the numbers of incident cases in an outbreak or epidemic, plotted over time. The form of the resulting distribution of cases can be used to propose hypotheses on the nature of the disease and its mode of transmission.

A propagated source means that infections are transmitted from person to person in such a way that cases identified cannot be attributed to agent(s) transmitted from a single source. Propagated (continuing) source cases occur over a longer period than in common source transmission. Explosive epidemics resulting from person-to-person transmission may occur (e.g., chickenpox). If secondary and tertiary cases occur, intervals between peaks usually approximate average incubation period.

Reference: *APIC Text*, 4th edition, Chapter 12 - Outbreak Investigations

CBIC Core Competency: Surveillance and Epidemiologic Investigation

128. (D) RSV

Rationale: RSV is one of the most important causes of respiratory tract infection in infants and the elderly worldwide. It is transmitted by direct and indirect contact. RSV is a major preventable HAI with frequent outbreaks that can lead to high mortality rates in healthcare facilities. Proper infection prevention measures, including hand hygiene, Standard and Contact Precautions, cohorting, and rapid diagnostic techniques are critical in controlling the spread of RSV in healthcare facilities.

Reference: *APIC Text*, 4th edition, Chapter 41 - Neonates

CBIC Core Competency: Surveillance and Epidemiologic Investigation

129. (D) Rash in a patient nonimmune to measles

Rationale: A specific diagnosis of measles usually can be made on the basis of clinical presentation alone because of the characteristic prodrome (cough, coryza, and conjunctivitis with or without Koplik spots) and febrile exanthem.

Detection of measles virus or antigens in clinical specimens or tissue can establish a recent infection with the measles virus. Viral isolation is possible from respiratory secretions, blood, urine, and, in special circumstances, skin biopsy. Serologic testing may be used to confirm the clinical diagnosis of measles or to assess immunity. The presence of measles IgM antibody by enzyme immunoassay (EIA) confirms a diagnosis of recent measles. Measles-specific IgM antibodies may not be present until 72 hours after the onset of the rash, however. Seroconversion or a fourfold increase in measles IgG antibody titer by EIA, hemagglutination inhibition (HAI), or neutralizing antibodies can also be used to confirm a recent measles infection.

Reference: *APIC Text*, 4th edition, Chapter 86 - Measles, Mumps, Rubella

CBIC Core Competency: Identification of Infectious Disease Processes

NOTES

130. (B) Evaluation measurements must be consistent with the objectives of the program

Rationale: The educator may use evaluation at different points within the program development process using a variety of methods. Whatever evaluation methodology is used, evaluation measurements must be consistent with the objectives established for the educational program. Data must be gathered, tabulated, and analyzed to assess impact and make recommendations for curriculum revision before the next presentation.

Reference: *APIC Text*, 4th edition, Chapter 3 - Education and Training

CBIC Core Competency: Education and Research

131. (B) Clinical trial

Rationale: Experimental studies are prospective studies designed to compare outcomes in individuals who are assigned to an experimental (intervention) or control (placebo or standard care) group. The intervention may be a procedure, drug, or other treatment, and the comparison group usually receives a placebo, the previously accepted treatment, or, if appropriate, no treatment. The two major types of experimental studies are randomized clinical and community trials.

Reference: *APIC Text*, 4th edition, Chapter 20 - Research Study Design

CBIC Core Competency: Education and Research

132. (A) Immediate-use

Rationale: Flash sterilization (flashing), a form of point-of-use processing, occurs immediately before use and close to the patent care area, where it will be used.

Reference: *APIC Text*, 4th edition, Chapter 106 - Sterile Processing

CBIC Core Competency: Cleaning, Sterilization, Disinfection, Asepsis

133. (C) Measles

Rationale: Measles (rubeola, 7-day measles) is a distinct clinical syndrome with characteristic prodrome respiratory tract symptoms (cough, coryza, and conjunctivitis), followed by a febrile exanthem and a recovery period that includes a persistent cough for many weeks. Measles occurs throughout the world. It is one of the most highly contagious infectious diseases in humans.

Reference: *APIC Text*, 4th edition, Chapter 86 - Measles, Mumps, Rubella

CBIC Core Competency: Surveillance and Epidemiologic Investigation

134. (A) 1, 4

Rationale: Use maximal sterile barrier precautions, including the use of a cap, mask, sterile gown, sterile gloves, and a sterile full body drape for the insertion of central venous catheters, peripherally inserted central venous catheters, or guidewire exchanges.

Reference: *APIC Text*, 4th edition, Chapter 34 - Intravascular Device Infectious

CBIC Core Competency: Preventing/Controlling the Transmission of Infectious Agents

NOTES

135. (D) The number of hand hygiene episodes performed by personnel divided by the number of hand hygiene opportunities by ward or service

Rationale: The CDC guideline and The Joint Commission require that HCP adherence to recommended hand hygiene policies be monitored and that HCP be provided with information about their performance. Acceptable methods for measuring hand hygiene adherence include:

- Periodically conduct an observational study to determine the rate of adherence (number of hand hygiene episodes performed/number of hand hygiene opportunities) by ward or service. In addition to monitoring the rate of adherence, facilities may also assess the quality of hand hygiene adherence (time spent per hand hygiene episode, whether soap was used, etc.)
- Monitor the volume of specific hand hygiene products (e.g., soap, hand rub, hand lotion) used per 1,000 patient days
- Monitor adherence to artificial fingernail policies

Reference: Boyce JM, Pittet D. Guideline for hand hygiene in health-care settings. *Morbid Mortal Weekly Rev*. 2002 October 25; 51(RR1):1-44. Available at: http://www.cdc.gov/mmwr/PDF/rr/rr5116.pdf.

CBIC Core Competency: Surveillance and Epidemiologic Investigation

PRACTICE EXAM 3 ASSESSMENT

Category	Total Questions	Number Correct	Percent Correct
Identification of Infectious Disease Processes	22		
Surveillance and Epidemiologic Investigation	24		
Preventing/Controlling the Transmission of Infectious Agents	25		
Employee/Occupational Health	11		
Management and Communication	13		
Education and Research	11		
Environment of Care	14		
Cleaning, Sterilization, Disinfection, Asepsis	15		
Total	135		

The purpose of this assessment is to help the user evaluate his or her strengths and weaknesses by content area, in order to identify topics that may need further study. This practice exam employs similar, but not identical methodology that CBIC uses to score their computer-based tests, and it should not be used as a predictor of actual performance on the CBIC exam.

LIST OF ABBREVIATIONS

AAMI	Association for the Advancement of Medical Instrumentation
AC	Acute care
ACH	Air changes per hour
AER	Automated endoscope reprocessor
AFB	Acid-fast bacillus (bacilli)
AIA	American Institute of Architects
AIDS	Acquired immunodeficiency syndrome
AII	Airborne infection isolation
ANC	Absolute neutrophil count
ANSI	American National Standards Institute
APACHE II	Acute Physiology and Chronic Health Evaluation II
APIC	Association for Professionals in Infection Control and Epidemiology, Inc.
ASA	American Society of Anesthesiologists
ASHRAE	American Society of Heating, Refrigerating, and Air-Conditioning Engineers
ASP	Antimicrobial stewardship program
AST	Antimicrobial susceptibility testing
BAL	Bronchoalveolar lavage
BSI	Bloodstream infection
BUN	Blood urea nitrogen
CABG	Coronary artery bypass graft surgery
CABSI	Catheter-associated bloodstream infection

C. difficile	*Clostridium difficile*
CAP	Community-acquired pneumonia
CAUTI	Catheter-associated urinary tract infection
CBC	Complete blood count
CBIC	Certifition Board of Infection Control and Epidemiology, Inc.
CBT	Computer based test
CDC	Centers for Disease Control and Prevention
CEO	Chief Executive Officer
CFR	Code of Federal Regulations
CFU	Colony-forming unit
CHF	Congestive heart failure
CHG	Chlorhexidine gluconate
CI	Confidence Interval
CJD	Creutzfeldt-Jakob disease
CL	Central line
CLABSI	Central line-associated bloodstream infection
CLIP	Central-line insertion practices
CMS	Centers for Medicare & Medicaid Services
CMV	Cytomegalovirus
CNS	Coagulase-negative *Staphylococcus*
CO	Community onset
COPD	Chronic obstructive pulmonary disease
CRBSI	Catheter-related bloodstream infection
CRE	Carbapenem-resistant Enterobacteriaceae
CSF	Cerebrospinal fluid
CVC	Central venous catheter
CXR	Chest X-ray

DEA	Drug Enforcement Administration
DFA	Direct fluorescence assay
DHHS	U.S. Department of Health and Human Services
DIP	Deep incisional infection at the primary surgical site
DIS	Deep incisional infection at the secondary surgical site
DOT	U.S. Department of Transportation
DU	Device utilization
EC	Environment of care
ELISA	Enzyme-linked immunosorbent assay
EPA	U.S. Environmental Protection Agency
ESBL	Extended-spectrum beta-lactamases
FDA	U.S. Food and Drug Administration
FMEA	Failure mode effect analysis
FTE	Full-time equivalent
GBS	Group B *Streptococcus*
HA	Healthcare-associated infection
HBV	Hepatitis B virus
HCW	Healthcare worker
HCP	Healthcare personnel
HCV	Hepatitis C virus
HEPA	High-efficiency particulate air
HH	Hand hygiene
HICPAC	Healthcare Infection Control Practices Advisory Committee
HIV	Human immunodeficiency virus
HF	Human factors
HFE	Human factors engineering
HPV	Human papilloma virus

HSV	Herpes simplex virus
HVAC	Heating, ventilation, air conditioning
IC	Infection control
ICD	International Classification of Diseases
ICRA	Infection control risk assessment
ICU	Intensive Care Unit
IDSA	Infectious Diseases Society of America
Ig	Immunoglobulin
IHI	Institute for Healthcare Improvement
IP	Infection preventionist
IT	Information technology
KPC	*Klebsiella pneumoniae* carbapenemase
LCBI	Laboratory-confirmed bloodstream infection
LTAC	Long-term acute care
LTC(F)	Long-term care (facility)
MDR-GNB	Multidrug-resistant Gram-negative bacilli
MDRO	Multidrug-resistant organism
MERS	Middle East respiratory syndrome
MIC	Minimal inhibitory concentration
MRSA	Methicillin-resistant *Staphylococcus aureus*
MSSA	Methicillin-sensitive *Staphylococcus aureus*
MTB	Mycobacterium tuberculosis
NHSN	National Healthcare Safety Network
NICU	Neonatal Intensive Care Unit
NIOSH	National Institute for Occupational Safety
NPSG	National Safety Patient Goals
NQF	National Quality Forum

NTM	Nontuberculous mycobacteria
ONS	Oncology Nursing Society
OR	Odds ratio (statistical term)
OR	Operating Room
OS	Organ/space infection
OSHA	Occupational Safety and Health Administration
PAD	Peripheral Artery Disease
PCR	Polymerase chain reaction
PDS	Post-discharge surveillance
PE	Protective environment
PFGE	Pulsed-field gel electrophoresis
PICC	Peripherally inserted central catheter
POA	Present on admission
PPE	Personal protective equipment
QC	Quality control
RCA	Root cause analysis
ROI	Return on investment
RR	Risk ratio
RSV	Respiratory syncytial virus
SARS	Severe acquired respiratory syndrome
SENIC	Study on the Efficacy of Nosocomial Infection Control
SCIP	Surgical Care Improvement Project
SDV	Single-dose vial
SHEA	Society for Healthcare Epidemiology of America
SIP	Superficial incisional infection
SIR	Standardized infection ratio
SIS	Superficial incisional infection at the secondary surgical site

SOP	Standard operating procedure
SSI	Surgical site infection
SWOT	Strength-weaknesses-opportunities-threats
TB	Tuberculosis
TJC	The Joint Commission
TST	Tuberculin skin test
UA	Urinalysis
UC	Umbilical catheter
UCABSI	Umbilical catheter–associated bloodstream infection
USDA	U.S. Department of Agriculture
USP	United States Pharmacopeia
UTI	Urinary tract infection
UV	Ultraviolet
UVGI	Ultraviolet germicidal irradiation
VAE	Ventilator-associated event
VAP	Ventilator-associated pneumonia
VISA	Vancomycin intermediate-resistant *Staphylococcus aureus*
VHF	Viral hemorrhagic fever
VRE	Vancomycin-resistant enterococci
VRSA	Vancomycin-resistant *Staphylococcus aureus*
VSM	Value stream mapping
VZV	Varicella-zoster virus
WBC	White blood cells
WHO	World Health Organization
WNV	West Nile virus